NFL DRAFT
2016 PREVIEW

NOLAN NAWROCKI

ACTA SPORTS

NFL Draft 2016 Preview
by Nolan Nawrocki

Research: Matt Feminis
Design and typesetting: Bob Peters

Photo credits: Ohio State Athletics; Joshua McCoy/Ole Miss Athletics; Jeremy Esbrandt; Eric Evans/Oregon Athletics; North Dakota State Athletics; UAA Communications.

Published by ACTA Sports, a division of ACTA Publications,
4484 N. Clark Street, Chicago, IL 60640, (800) 397-2282, www.actasports.com

ISBN: 978-0-87946-568-1

Library of Congress Catalog number: 2016933739

Printed in the U.S.A. by McNaughton and Gunn

CONTENTS

Carson Wentz

Almost every player in this book was an exceptional college football player or athlete and stands among the best in the country. NFL standards are the most stringent in the world, and it requires immense grit to rigorously compete against the world's most nuanced pros. All players graded were measured against these most demanding measures.

Included with many player profiles is a "Scout's Take," actual feedback reflecting unique and consensus opinions from NFL evaluators, stemming anywhere from veteran area scouts blanketing a region of the country to the savvy GMs going over the top of it when they can fit it into their busy schedules. Much of the information was gathered through the course of the fall, up until the day of publishing this book, and reflects hundreds of conversations aimed at pinpointing the measurables, critical traits, football instincts, work ethic, toughness, competitiveness, leadership, intelligence, temperament, character, scheme fit and league value of the nation's top talent.

Some information and grades might have changed by the time the book is being read, as more workouts, interviews and private workouts take place following the early March press date and verified measurements and character research is ascertained.

Much gratitude is owed to everyone who helped contribute to the production of the book in some way, from college coaches and sports information directors to all the NFL executives, scouts and coaches with whom I have had the pleasure to talk football.

A special thank-you belongs to Greg Pierce and the ACTA Sports team for their guidance, Ron Pollack for his draft acumen, Bob Peters for his creativity and Matt Feminis for his diligence and attention to detail. Not to be forgotten is the late Joel Buchsbaum and the PFW family that helped found independent draft analysis. I am most grateful for the patience and strength of my inspiration, Christie and the A-team.

— *Nolan Nawrocki*

DRAFT OUTLOOK

As the NFL Draft heads to Chicago for its second consecutive year, the strength of its talent once again will be found in the blue-collar, gritty trenches. Mississippi OT **Laremy Tunsil**, Notre Dame OT **Ronnie Stanley**, Ohio State DE **Joey Bosa** and Oregon DL **DeForest Buckner** all figure to become foundational franchise pieces in a draft that will be remembered for the quality of its big men.

Tunsil and Stanley are near prototype left tackles, with the feet to protect the blind side for a decade in the pros. Bosa is the draft's most disruptive edge rusher. Buckner is one of the most stout and has similar havoc-wreaking potential. Two big, athletic cornerbacks — Florida State's **Jalen Ramsey** and Florida's **Vernon Hargreaves** — also could become immediate impact contributors defensively, as could UCLA LB **Myles Jack**, the best cover linebacker, entering an overwhelmingly pass-first league.

The defensive line crop is the draft's strongest positional group and could include as many as six defensive linemen in the first round, beginning with the disruptive Bosa and Buckner. Mississippi DT **Robert Nkemdiche** and Alabama DT **A'Shawn Robinson** both have immediate impact potential and unique athletic talent for big men. Other defensive tackles who could factor readily in the pros include Alabama's physical **Jarran Reed**, Penn State's stout **Austin Johnson**, Louisville's penetrating **Sheldon Rankins** and Louisiana Tech's versatile **Vernon Butler**. Pass rushers with impact potential include Oklahoma State sack artist **Emmanuel Ogbah**, Eastern Kentucky's explosive **Noah Spence** and Clemson's powerful **Kevin Dodd** and **Shaq Lawson**.

Beyond Tunsil and Stanley, the building blocks of future NFL protection units include Michigan State's **Jack Conklin**, Ohio State's **Taylor Decker**, Indiana's **Jason Spriggs** and Texas A&M's **Germain Ifedi**. The tenacity and desire of Conklin and Decker are their signature traits. Spriggs profiles as the group's best athlete. Ifedi is the most stout and the top right tackle of the group. Kansas State's **Cody Whitehair**, though he lined up at left tackle in college, projects as the top zone-blocking guard in this draft's class. Teams seeking power will be more enticed by Stanford's **Josh Garnett**. The top center in a crop featuring solid depth at the position is Alabama's **Ryan Kelly**.

The always-anticipated QB crop features three passers that could be expected to carry their franchises in the near future. North Dakota State's **Carson Wentz** possesses the most upside. He has the size, arm talent, intelligence and athletic skill to become a terrific pro. However, with only two years at the helm of a FCS program, he will face a big jump in competition in the NFL. California's **Jared Goff** is the most NFL-ready of the group. Memphis' **Paxton Lynch** possesses the most explosive skill set as a runner and passer.

Ohio State's **Ezekial Elliott** stands as the most complete, all-around back to enter the draft the last decade, and is the only surefire first-round talent. Alabama's **Derrick Henry** is the draft's best inside runner. UCLA's **Paul Perkins** is the draft's most elusive runner. Louisiana Tech's **Kenneth Dixon** is one of the best natural catchers. Notre Dame's **C.J. Prosise** might have as much upside as any. Northwestern's **Dan Vitale** is the draft's most well-rounded fullback.

Coming off two of the draft's richest receiving classes, top-end talent is down this year. Mississippi's **Laquan Treadwell** headlines as the draft's most talented pass catcher and will overcome his lack of stopwatch speed because he plays fast. Others that could make immediate impacts include Notre Dame's blazer **Will Fuller**, Baylor's explosive **Corey Coleman**, Oklahoma's ultra-competitive **Sterling Shepard** and TCU's sure-handed **Josh Doctson**.

The TE crop, for the third-year running, remains void of depth, and could push up the value of TE talent. Arkansas' **Hunter Henry** is the draft's most sure-handed catcher. Stanford's **Austin Hooper** is the most well-

Laremy Tunsil

Joey Bosa

Ronnie Stanley

DeForest Buckner

rounded. Ohio State's **Nick Vannett** is the best blocker of the group.

Durability is a key theme in this year's linebacker crop, with two of the best — Notre Dame's **Jaylon Smith** and UCLA's **Myles Jack** — both coming off injuries. The severity of Smith's injury, suffered in the season-ending Fiesta Bowl, could have a notable impact on his draft standing. That leaves Jack, who is on his way to being fully recovered from an early-season injury, as the most coveted linebacker in the draft. On the inside, Alabama's **Reggie Ragland** is the draft's most physical and complete "Mike" linebacker. Georgia'a **Leonard Floyd** and Boise State's **Kamalei Correa** are the two most talented rush linebackers. Ohio State's **Darron Lee** is the draft's fastest cover linebacker.

The top-graded defensive player in the draft is Ramsey, a big, fast, physical playmaking cornerback who has proven capable of locking down receivers with his physicality. Hargreaves is the most pure cover man in the draft. Others that could contribute readily in the pros include Clemson's speedy **Mackensie Alexander** and Oklahoma's aggressive **Zach Sanchez**.

The safety class is without a true first-round talent. Ohio State's instinctive **Von Bell**, West Virginia's hammer **Karl Joseph**, Florida's hard-hitting **Keanu Neal** and Boise State's productive **Darian Thompson** all have plug-and-play potential.

For the first time in five years, the draft could potentially see a placekicker selected in the 100 picks. Florida State junior **Roberto Aguayo** has been automatic and could warrant interest as early as the third round.

QUARTERBACKS

QUARTERBACKS

EDITOR'S NOTE:

e — Measurement is estimated.

#00 — Player's jersey number.

GRADE — Player's grade reflects consensus league value where player should expect to be drafted.

On all positions, 40-yard-dash times are taken from the Combine when available and are curved to account for conditions (turf, wind, track shoes).

QB **VERNON ADAMS**, #3 (Sr-5)

OREGON ▶ GRADE: 5.02

Ht: 5-107/8 | Wt: 200 | 40: 4.81 | Arm: 301/4 | Hand: 91/8

History: Has a son, Vernon II. Grew up in Pasadena, Calif. and attended a private high school, where he amassed 6,500 all-purpose yards and 68 touchdowns his last two seasons. Was too short to draw major scholarship offers and could not afford preferred walk-on opportunities. Played his first three seasons at FCS Eastern Washington, where he redshirted in 2011. In Week Three of the '12 season, overtook Kyle Padron and didn't look back — completed 131-of-215 pass attempts (60.9 percent) for 1,961 yards with 20 touchdowns and eight interceptions in 12 starts. Also rushed 65 times for 342 yards (5.3-yard average) and one touchdown. Started all 15 games in '13, passing 319-486-4,994-55-15 (65.6) and rushing 132-605-4 (4.6). Was the Big Sky Offensive Player of the Year for the second straight season in '14 despite missing four games because of a broken right foot suffered against Idaho State. In 10 starts, produced 251-380-3,483-35-8 (66.1) passing and 100-285-6 (2.8) rushing. Was a finalist for the Walter Payton Award (FCS outstanding player) as a sophomore and junior, and departed EWU as the Big Sky record holder with 110 touchdown passes. Went to Oregon as a graduate transfer, but did not qualify academically until mid-August (also was barred from working out at EWU). Made 10 starts for the Ducks in '15 — produced 168-259-2,643-26-6 (64.9) through the air and 83-147-2 (1.8) on the ground. Led the nation in yards per attempt (10.2) and pass efficiency (179). In the season opener against EWU, sustained a head injury and broke his right (throwing) index finger — played hurt the following week, but struggled and sat out three of the next four contests. Was also forced out of the Alamo Bowl against TCU because of a head injury. Finished career 35-9 as a starter. Was MVP of the East-West Shrine Game. Has sickle cell trait disease.

Strengths: Has explosive arm talent with the ability to change pace on the ball and deliver it deep. Surprising downfield touch and accuracy given lack of height — is able to find throwing lanes with his feet. Good escapability in the pocket to create. Connected with June Jones at the Shrine Game and proved to be an eager student of the game and quick study. Good football IQ.

Weaknesses: Below-average height for the QB position with small hands and a low release point, often using a sidearm delivery. Mechanics break down under duress and tends to throw off his back foot. Worked heavily out of the shotgun and footwork could require some refinement. Underdeveloped weight-room strength could invite injury. Sickle cell trait could affect stamina at higher elevations.

Future: Diminutive, instinctive, athletic playmaker. Has the poise and presence to earn a job as a backup in the pros most ideally in a zone-read offense. Experienced, four-year starter proved after transferring to Oregon that he could translate his production against top competition in the Pac-12 and at the East-West Shrine game. Lack of size and durability concerns could force him to take the long road again.

Draft projection: Priority free agent.

Scout's take: "(Adams) would be perfect for the CFL. That's his best fit. I think he's best off honing his skills there for a few years than even trying to make an NFL roster. I'd be surprised if he is drafted."

QB **BRANDON ALLEN**, #10 (Sr-5)
ARKANSAS ▶ GRADE: 5.14
Ht: 6-13/8 | Wt: 217 | 40: 4.82 | Arm: 311/4 | Hand: 87/8

History: Father, Bobby, is Arkansas' director of high school and NFL relations. Fayetteville native was honored as the top high school player in the state. Redshirted in 2011. Made five appearances in '12, drawing one start as an injury replacement for Travis Wilson, and completed 21-of-49 pass attempts (42.9 percent) for 186 yards with one touchdown and three interceptions. Started all 11 games played in '13 and passed 128-258-1,552-13-10 (49.6). Sprained his right (throwing) shoulder in Week Three — did not play against Rutgers, and was

hampered the rest of the season. His truck was egged following Mississippi State loss in 2013 and set afire and totaled in one of three car fires investigated as arson in the early morning hours in summer of 2014. Started all 26 games the next two seasons — totaled 190-339-2,285-20-5 (56.0) in '14; and 244-370-3,440-30-8 (65.9) in '15. Two-time team captain graduated with a degree in recreation and sport management. Went 18-20 as a starter. Holds the school record with 64 career touchdown passes. Played for three head coaches and four offensive coordinators. Has 15 career fumbles.

Strengths: Has a smooth, quick delivery with a clean, over-the-top release. Good wrist snap. Sells play-action fakes. Well-respected leader with good preparation habits. Football is very important to him and he takes the game seriously. Made considerable strides in his final season and grew more comfortable as the season progressed in Dan Enos' offense that was tailored to his strengths as a decisive, short-to-intermediate passer. Clutch competitor — scored on all five overtime possessions and converted 3-of-3 two-point conversions in two overtime wins vs. Auburn and Mississippi. Good short-to-intermediate accuracy. Tough enough to stand in the pocket and deliver the ball in the face of pressure — pops back up after taking some big hits. Has enough escapability to roll out and effectively create plays on play-action bootlegs outside the pocket. Has weathered a lot of adversity and endured some extreme criticism. Mentally tough and determined.

Weaknesses: Extremely small, sub-9-inch hands that fall in the reject category by NFL standards for some NFL teams. Below-average height and arm strength. Velocity and placement wanes throwing off his back foot. Could improve ball placement — forces his receivers to break to catch and adjust to off-target throws. Needs to develop his field vision and learn how to look off his primary target and manipulate defensive backs with his eyes. Was not asked to cycle through many pro-style, progression reads in a streamlined passing game.

Future: Smart, savvy, rhythm timing passer most ideally suited for a play-action, rollout passing game such as those favored by the Redskins, Seahawks and Broncos. Will require several years of seasoning, yet possesses the mental toughness, delivery quickness and enough arm talent and agility to be groomed for a No. 2 job. Shows some similarities to Redskins 2012 fourth-round pick Kirk Cousins.

Draft projection: Fifth- to sixth-round pick.

Coach's take: "He's the definition of perse-

QUARTERBACKS

verance, for sure, because some of the stuff got personal. Sometimes with these hometown kids, they have it twice as bad because everybody knows them and everybody's always asking about them. I know it was very rough on Brandon, probably more than any of us could imagine." – *Arkansas head coach Brett Bielema*

QB-RB **TREVONE BOYKIN**, #2 (Sr-5)

TCU ▶GRADE: 4.92

Ht: 6-0 | Wt: 212 | 40: 4.72 | Arm: 31 5/8 | Hand: 9 3/8

History: First name is pronounced "TRUH-von." Dallas native. Tore ligaments in his right foot during his junior season in high school. Redshirted in 2011. Played 12 games in '12, starting the final eight — was thrust into action following Casey Pachall's suspension — and completed 167-of-292 pass attempts (57.2 percent) for 2,054 yards with 15 touchdowns and 10 interceptions. Also rushed 127 times for 417 yards (3.3-yard average) and three touchdowns. In '13, saw time at quarterback, running back and receiver, becoming the first player in TCU history and the only player in the nation to record a 100-yard rushing game, 100-yard receiving game and 200-yard passing game. Started 7-of-12 games (season opener against LSU at WR, other six at QB in place of the injured Pachall) and totaled 105-176-1,198-7-7 (59.7) passing and 105-313-7 (3.0) rushing. Added 26 receptions for 204 yards (7.8-yard average) and zero touchdowns. Pachall returned to start the final four games, and the Horned Frogs subsequently installed a new "Air Raid" system, even signing Texas A&M graduate transfer Matt Joeckel for the '14 season. Boykin missed spring practice (left wrist surgery), but won the training camp competition and didn't relinquish the job — was the Big 12 Offensive Player of the Year, as well as a finalist for the Heisman Trophy, Davey O'Brien Award, Walter Camp Player of the Year Award and Manning Award after setting school single-season records for passing yards, touchdown passes, total touchdowns and total offense (4,608 yards). On the season, started all 13 games and piled up 301-492-3,901-33-10 (61.2) passing and 152-707-8 (4.7) rushing. In '15, started all 11 games played and tossed 167-292-2,054-15-10 (57.2) and ran 123-612-9 (5.0). Hurt his right ankle against Kansas and did not play against Oklahoma. College career came to a premature end two days prior to the Alamo Bowl when Boykin was arrested and suspended for his involvement in a bar fight — was charged with assault of a public servant, a third-degree felony, as well as misdemeanor public intoxication and resisting arrest. Reportedly Boykin went out after curfew, was heckled and engaged in a fight, during which he struck a police officer. Finished senior season with 17 TD passes, no interceptions and eight rushing touchdowns in the red zone. Two-time team captain graduated with a general studies degree. Won 27 games as a starter. Owns TCU records for career passing yards (10,728), passing touchdowns (86), total touchdowns (114) and total offense (12,777 yards), among others. Has 19 career fumbles. Did not perform the 3-cone drill at the Combine because of a right ankle injury.

Strengths: Outstanding athlete — makes deft moves outside the pocket to avoid the rush and make defenders miss (see juke past five defenders late in third quarter vs. West Virginia in 2015). Nifty footed to escape the rush and create with his feet. Has a live arm to uncork it and throw with velocity. Excellent career production, with his arm and feet.

Weaknesses: Marginal height that creates field vision issues inside the pocket. Poor overall size by NFL QB standards, with very small hands that have led to ball security issues. Often threw to wide-open receivers and was not required to make complex reads. Is too quick to pull the ball down and flee the pocket at the flash of coverage, seldom stepping up into the pocket and continuing to scan the field. Marginal pocket awareness. Needs to improve ball placement and touch — tends to put too much zip on the ball. Still learning what it means to lead on and off the field — finished his college career on a sour note suspended for his final game. Has been injury-prone in high school and college.

Future: Terrific college football player, yet an undersized, athletic developmental project for the NFL game being projected to running back by some teams. Best chance to contribute could come as a situational, red-zone quarterback capable of hurting a team with his feet. Could benefit honing his passing instincts and pocket presence in the CFL.

Draft projection: Priority free agent.

Scout's take: "I actually saw him as a receiver. He is (Niners 2013 seventh-round pick) B.J. Daniels or (Cowboys 2002 undrafted free agent) Woodrow Dantzler."

QB **JACOBY BRISSETT**, #12 (Sr-5)

NORTH CAROLINA STATE ▶GRADE: 5.32

Ht: 6-3 3/4 | Wt: 231 | 40: 4.93 | Arm: 32 1/4 | Hand: 9 3/4

History: Last name is pronounced "briss-ETT." Also played basketball as a prep in Florida, where he won a state championship.

QUARTERBACKS

Began his college career at Florida. Originally bristled at a grayshirt offer from then-head coach Urban Meyer in 2010, but Charlie Weis, who was hired as offensive coordinator by incoming coach Will Muschamp, took a liking to Brissett late in the recruiting process. Signed with the Gators (along with Jeff Driskel) and saw action in five games (two starts) as a true freshman in 2011 — completed 18-of-39 pass attempts (46.2 percent) for 206 yards with two touchdowns and four interceptions. Backed up Driskel in '12, seeing action in three games (one start) and tossing 23-35-249-1-0 (65.7). Seeking playing time, transferred to NC State and sat out the '13 season per NCAA rules (earned Scout Team Player of the Year). Started all 26 games the next two seasons — totaled 221-370-2,606-23-5 (59.7) in '14; and 237-395-2,662-20-6 (60.0) in '15. Was team MVP both his years in Raleigh. Had arthroscopic surgery on his left knee (meniscus) after his junior season. Rushed 283 times in his career for 902 yards (3.2-yard average) and 12 touchdowns. Went 16-13 as a starter. Graduated. Team captain

Strengths: Good athlete. Has a well-distributed build with fine musculature and good corresponding strength in the pocket and on the run. Can brush off the rush, eat ground with long strides and extend plays with his feet. Has power in his body to fall forward. Played in a balanced offense and worked from underneath center and out of the gun. Clean over-the-top delivery. Great touch — can change pace on the ball and spin it hard when needed. Good arm strength to make all the throws. Accurate on the move. Good football-playing temperament. Takes the game seriously with good football and personal character. Solid work habits in the weight room and on the practice field. Very durable throughout his career and will play through pain.

Weaknesses: Inconsistent mechanics — tends to throw off his back foot, off-balance and with his feet not set, diminishing his accuracy. Has some wind-up in his delivery and does not have dynamic arm talent to fire it off rapidly. Deep ball placement and timing were consistently off. Sill developing his pocket awareness and field vision after having run a lot of zone reads. Will lock on receivers and telegraph some throws, leaving production on the field. Was not asked to make many full-field, professional-style, NFL reads and will require some time acclimating to NFL defenses.

Future: Very good-sized, spread, touch passer who operated with a marginal supporting cast and was often asked to roll out and create on the move. Has the physical tools to develop into a fine pro with several years of seasoning. Emerged as a leader and has the determination, focus and strength of character to become an NFL starter in time.

Draft projection: Third- to fourth-round pick.

Scout's take: "I'm not sure he can sit back in the pocket and get the job done. He's going to need time. I put him in the fourth (round)."

QB JAKE COKER, #14 (Sr-5)

ALABAMA ▶ GRADE: 5.09

Ht: 6-5 1/2 | Wt: 236 | 40: 5.19 | Arm: 32 | Hand: 9 1/2

History: Three-star prospect who also excelled on the hardwood as an Alabama prep. Began his college career at Florida State, where he redshirted in 2011. Was third-string in '12 when he completed 3-of-5 pass attempts (60.0 percent) for 45 yards with one touchdown and zero interceptions. Dealt with a broken right foot during '13 spring practice. Backed up Jameis Winston in the fall, appearing in seven games and tossing 18-36-250-0-1 (50.0) before tearing his left meniscus in November. Graduated early and transferred to Alabama. Did not beat out Blake Sims in '14, and had 38-59-403-4-0 (64.4) in seven appearances as the backup. Had minor foot surgery during '15 fall camp before guiding the Crimson Tide to the national championship — passed 263-393-3,110-21-8 (66.9) in 15 games (14 starts). Head coach Nick Saban explained the decision to start Cooper Bateman against Ole Miss by saying, "We had some things in the game plan early that the quarterback was going to pull the ball on and do some things, so we thought that Cooper's speed would be a change of pace for them. We thought that it could be a little bit of an element of surprise. We knew we were going to play Jake in the game. Jake knew he was going to play in the game." Team captain has a master's degree.

Strengths: Exceptional size. Made considerable strides down the stretch as a senior and played with more confidence. Delivers the ball well under pressure and can drop the fade in a bucket (see sideline fade under duress in national championship game). Takes care of the football and distributes it well. Tough, hard-nosed runner. Has a hard-working approach and brings his lunchpail with him every morning ready to grind. Intelligent and competitive.

Weaknesses: Marginal athlete — very heavy-footed with limited pocket mobility. Average arm talent with a long delivery —labors to deliver the ball under duress, cannot

QUARTERBACKS

hasten his delivery and ball tends to die when his feet are not set. Could stand to improve timing and anticipation. Needs to learn how to slide and avoid landing awkwardly on the move. Only a one-year starter. Not a natural, take-charge leader. Has been injury-prone.

Future: A big, stationary pocket passer, Coker emerged after being benched in the SEC opener, nearly leading the team back to a come-from-behind victory out of the bullpen vs Mississippi, and leading the Tide to a national championship as a functional caretaker. Has enough tools for a team to consider molding as a No. 3 quarterback or practice-squad candidate.

Draft projection: Priority free agent.

QB CONNOR COOK, #18 (Sr-5)

MICHIGAN STATE ▶ GRADE: 5.57
Ht: 6-4 | Wt: 217 | 40: 4.79 | Arm: 33 | Hand: 9 3/4

History: Prepped in Ohio. Redshirted in 2011. Backed up Andrew Maxwell in '12, completing 9-of-17 pass attempts (52.9 percent) for 94 yards with one touchdown and one interception. Started all 14 games in '13 and passed 223-380-2,755-22-6 (58.7). Earned MVP honors in the Spartans' Rose Bowl victory over Stanford. Started all 13 games in '14 and completed 212-365-3,214-24-8 (58.1). Won the Johnny Unitas Golden Arm Award in '15 after producing 229-408-3,131-24-7 (56.1). Injured his right (throwing) shoulder against Maryland and did not play against Ohio State, pushing through the injury wearing a shoulder harness in starts against Penn State, Iowa and Alabama. Had 176 career rushes for 209 yards (1.2-yard average) and three touchdowns. Also became the first two-time Big Ten Championship game MVP in victory over Iowa. Ended his career as the winningest quarterback in MSU history — went 34-5, including 23-2 in conference play. Also owns school records for passing yards (9,194), touchdown passes (71) and total offense (9,403 yards). Graduated with a degree in media and information.

Strengths: Looks the part with a powerful arm to make every throw and drive the ball downfield. Sets quickly and throws on balance. Efficient release quickness. Very careful with the ball and makes sound decisions within the framework of the offense. Feels pressure well and climbs the pocket keeping his eyes downfield. Plays with poise and is battle-tested to handle pressure situations — has led six career fourth-quarter comebacks and responds well to a challenge, playing his best in critical, game-defining situations. Has

shown he can work through progressions in a pro-style offense and distribute the ball to secondary targets. Very competitive, experienced, three-year starter with a .872 career winning percentage. Excellent career production. Physically tough and will battle through injuries. Is accustomed to braving the cold elements.

Weaknesses: Just average escapability to buy a second chance, create plays with his feet and throw on the move. Struggles to find throwing lanes, leading to nine batted balls as a senior, among the most in the nation. Has a bad habit of short-arming and pushing the ball, not following through, negating short-to-intermediate accuracy. Low elbow also forces balls to sail. Ball location and placement is consistently out of sync with receivers, forcing them to slow to catch and adjust mightily to the ball. Suspect football character for the QB position. Has not yet figured out what it truly means to prepare like a pro and will need to be better prepared to make pre-snap reads, read coverages, anticipate pressure and make sight adjustments. Lacks self-awareness and did not squelch concerns. Carries a swagger that can grate on some teammates and rub support staff the wrong way. Does not have a strong on-field presence. Was shut out vs. Alabama and unable to escape pressure or make quick decisions vs. an NFL-caliber front when his primary target was taken away. Generated a Combine-low 45 m.p.h ball velocity and was the only QB not to crack the 50 mark.

Future: Physically has all the quarterbacking tools to start in the NFL, though still has a lot to learn about leadership and could be relegated to a lifelong backup role similar to Lions 2007 second-round pick Drew Stanton. A Bruce Arians- or Todd Haley-type of quarterback with the size, toughness, durability and sense of calm in the pocket to take shots down the field and create chunk yardage. Clutch factor as a game-day competitor could override concerns about his makeup, though he must mature to ever become great.

Draft projection: Second- to third-round pick.

Scout's take: "Sometimes when you have a group of blue-collar guys, they want to humble the Hollywood quarterback and not make him a captain. I can remember when the same thing happened to Boomer Esiason at Maryland. It didn't stop him from being drafted in the second round and having a long NFL career. ...I'm honestly more worried about (Cook's) accuracy. He's proven he can make money throws. He's just not consistently accurate. He has never been a 60-percent passer in any season. ...The other question you need to ask — how much did he do to win? That is a well-coached, talented team. Did he win games, or did he just not lose them? When (our area scout) read his character report, the scary part is that it sounded just like the *Draft Day* quarterback (Bo Callahan)."

QB BRANDON DOUGHTY, #12 (Sr-6)

WESTERN KENTUCKY ▶ GRADE: 5.13

Ht: 6-2 3/4 | Wt: 213 | 40: 5.16 | Arm: 32 | Hand: 9 1/8

History: Last name is pronounced "DOW-tee." Married on March 6, 2016. Prepped in Florida. Redshirted in 2010. Appeared in just two games in '11 — completed 13-of-22 pass attempts (59.1 percent) for 106 yards with zero touchdowns and one interception, though he suffered a season-ending torn right ACL injury against Indiana State (his first career start). Saw very limited action in '12, managing 1-1-7-0-0 (33.3) in two appearances. Missed a chunk of the season after tearing his right meniscus (granted medical hardship waiver). Started all 12 games in '13 and completed 246-374-2,857-14-14 (65.8). Was the Conference USA MVP and Sammy Baugh Trophy winner in '14 after piling up 375-552-4,830-49-10 (67.9) in 13 starts. Led the country in passing yards, passing touchdowns and points responsible for per game (24.2). Was the C-USA MVP for the second straight year in '15 after leading the country in completion percentage, passing yards and passing touchdowns — aired it out 388-540-5,055-48-9 (71.9) in 14 starts. Also caught a seven-yard touchdown pass. His 97 touchdown passes the last two years is an FBS record. Rewrote the WKU passing record book while posting a 29-11 career mark. Three-time captain graduated with a sport management degree. Will turn 25 during rookie season.

Strengths: Efficient release with good delivery quickness and short-to-intermediate accuracy. Sound decision-maker and caretaker — produced a 5:1 TD-to-INT ratio the last two seasons. Football smart and understands how to dissect coverages. Delivers the ball in the face of pressure. Film junkie with a passion for the game. Good timing, rhythm and anticipation. Three-year starter with solid career production and 68.6-percent career completion percentage.

Weaknesses: Lacks the arm talent and velocity to drive the ball into tight windows. Marginal downfield accuracy. Heavy-footed with limited escapability and scrambling skill. Could do a better job of feeling pressure. Did not regularly match up against top competition and was overmatched and out of sync against LSU. Overaged.

Future: Light-framed, modest-armed, high-percentage touch passer with inflated production from operating a quick-strike, dink-and-dunk passing game. Has the maturity, football intelligence and reliability desired in a spot backup, though lacks the physical tools to win games if pressed into a regular starting role. Ideally suited for a No. 3 QB role, Doughty will be best in a rhythm-timing passing game.

Draft projection: Late draftable pick.

QB JEFF DRISKEL, #6 (Sr-5)

LOUISIANA TECH ▶ GRADE: 5.18

Ht: 6-4 | Wt: 234 | 40: 4.49 | Arm: 33 | Hand: 9 3/4

History: Was the Maxwell Football Club National Player of the Year and Gatorade Player of the Year in Florida. Elite recruit who was the consensus No. 1 pro-style passing prospect in the country. Began his college career at Florida. As a true freshman in 2011, completed 16-of-34 pass attempts (47.1 percent) for 148 yards with zero touchdowns and two interceptions. Sprained his left ankle against Alabama and did not play against LSU. Hurt his left (non-throwing) shoulder (scapula contusion) during '12 fall camp, but started all 12 games played and completed 156-of-245 pass attempts (63.7 percent) for 1,646 yards with 12 touchdowns and five interceptions. Sprained his right ankle against Louisiana-Monroe and sat out against Jacksonville State. Missed the beginning of '13 fall camp (appendectomy). Managed 42-61-477-2-3 (68.9) in three starts, though he sprained his left knee against Miami then suffered a season-ending broken right fibula injury against Tennessee. Played nine games in '14, starting the first six, and tossed 114-212-1,140-9-10 (53.8) before he was benched in favor of Treon Harris. Joined the Conference USA Ragin' Cajuns as a graduate transfer. Started all 13 games in '15 and passed 281-450-4,033-27-8 (62.4). Team captain. Compiled a 24-10 record as a starter.

Strengths: Outstanding size — looks the part. Moves well for his size and will drop his shoulder to move the chains. Good weight-room strength. Adequate arm talent and nice touch to place the deep fade. Good straight-line speed to dash for the sticks — produced the fastest 40 time of any quarterback at the Combine. Diligent worker. Very intelligent and well-spoken.

Weaknesses: Struggles in the pocket to avoid pressure and make good decisions under duress. Tight-shouldered. Accuracy and ball placement could improve — forces his receivers to work hard for the ball and is consistently off the mark the further he is asked to throw. Tends to birddog his primary target and needs to learn how to disguise his eyes to manipulate coverage and lessen the number of batted balls at the line of scrimmage. Played in a streamlined offense at Louisiana Tech involving a lot of one-look, confidence-building throws and did not make NFL-style, progression reads. The game too often becomes too big for him — lacks poise and toughness in the pocket and is not a confident, triggerman. Has been prone to injury.

Future: A smart, well-built, athletic quarterback with similar traits as Browns 2007 first-round pick Brady Quinn. Driskel has the physical talent and intelligence to intrigue NFL teams. Yet, he has struggled to live up to his press clippings since exiting high school and lacks the passing instincts, decision-making skills and ice in his veins required to function in the NFL. Is smart and athletic enough to make a living as an NFL backup, though he could struggle to carry a team if pressed into a starter role.

Draft projection: Fifth- to sixth-round pick.

Scout's take: "I did not like him. He doesn't have any arm strength — none. Sometimes his ball is not tight. I don't think he can drive the ball downfield at all. I've heard some (scouts) getting enamored by him because he's good-looking on the hoof and has some athletic ability. But, man, the pocket needs to be clean for him to operate. I'm not even sure I gave him a draftable grade. I think he's a pretender. I'd be surprised if he goes before the sixth (round)."

QB JARED GOFF, #16 (Jr-3)

CALIFORNIA ▶ GRADE: 6.24
Ht: 6-4 | Wt: 215 | 40: 4.79 | Arm: 32 3/4 | Hand: 9

History: Father, Jerry, played 90 MLB games with the Expos, Pirates and Astros over six seasons (1990, 1992-96). Jared is a California native. Enrolled early in the spring of '13 and started all 37 games of his career — completed 320-of-531 pass attempts (60.3 percent) for 3,508 yards with 18 touchdowns and 10 interceptions in 2013 (12 games); 316-509-3,973-35-7 (62.1) in '14 (12 games); and 341-529-4,719-43-13 (64.5) in '15 (13 games). Separated his right (throwing) shoulder against Baylor in '13 and had surgery after the season. Also had his ankle rolled in the fourth quarter against Texas in '15. Also had 12 career punts for a 38.6-yard average with six inside the 20-yard line. In three years as a starter, went 14-23 while claiming nearly 30 school records, including passing yards

(12,200) and touchdown passes (96). Has 24 career fumbles. Two-year captain.

Strengths: Very good height and pocket vision. Clean, advanced footwork. Good arm talent and release quickness. Sharp decision-maker. Plays with urgency, recognizes mismatches and knows when and where to go with the ball. Is quick to identify coverage and trigger — fast processing speed. Fine eye manipulation to move safeties and open some windows. Steps up in the pocket against pressure and is more efficient rushing than he appears. Good lateral agility to slide and spin out of the pocket to avoid the first wave of pressure and buy a second chance. Sells play-action and pump fakes and lures defenders to bite. Good wrist snap. Can fire BB's and change pace on the ball when needed and deliver the ball with timing and touch, throwing receivers open on timing routes (slants, posts, outs). Good situational awareness. Can hasten his delivery when needed and manipulate his arm and throwing platform. Smart, articulate and even-keeled demeanor. Interviewed well at the Combine. Comes from a very supportive family with a strong support network.

Weaknesses: Has a slight frame with a body that does not look like it has seen the weight room and very small hands. Could struggle to grip the ball in the rain and cold conditions. Goes down easy when hit, lacking pocket stature. Has taken very few snaps from underneath center operating an offense with a lot of simple 1-2 reads. Has a low release point that leads to batted balls. Deep-ball timing and trajectory needs refinement. When pressured, leads receivers into traffic and exposes them to big hits (see Utah). Can continue improving timing and anticipation — too often places the ball on the back hip. Is not a take-charge, vocal leader and does not have a strong, on-field presence or inspiring sideline demeanor. Had a .378 career winning percentage in college (after entering a rebuilding program following Jeff Tedford's departure). Has not often had to deal with cold elements in sunny California or had to knife the ball through heavy winds. Could better protect the ball in the pocket and cut down on fumbles.

Future: A lean-framed, nifty-footed pocket passer. Played with a competitive urgency and excelled in an up-tempo, no-huddle offense and a streamlined, concept-based passing game that preyed on opponent mismatches. Proved he could walk into the starting lineup in college and learn on the job. Showed improvement every season and possesses the footwork, delivery quickness and toughness to develop into a high-quality, rhythm-match-up NFL passer.

Draft projection: Top-15 pick.

Scout's take: "Goff doesn't feel pressure at all. He telegraphs his throws. He was sacked five times against Washington. Then throw on the Utah game — he has five picks, four in the first half. They weren't all his fault. He didn't have much around him. I think he is a solid quarterback. I don't think he is Aaron Rodgers. You're going to have to surround him with weapons. He has an arm and can drop the ball in a window. I watched him warming up on the field before the game, and he can spin it pretty good. He is accurate. He can throw the deep ball."

QB EVERETT GOLSON, #6 (Sr-5)

FLORIDA STATE ▶ GRADE: 5.01

Ht: 5-11 1/8 | Wt: 197 | 40: 4.70e | Arm: 31 | Hand: 9 1/2

History: Was a four-year varsity starter as a prep in South Carolina, where he won three state titles, threw for 11,634 yards and 151 touchdowns (sixth all-time in high school football history) and was an all-state basketball player. Missed eight games during his senior season because of a high left ankle sprain and torn ligaments in his right (throwing) hand. Verbally committed to North Carolina, but flipped to Notre Dame when the NCAA began investigating UNC for misconduct. Redshirted in 2011. Wore jersey No. 5 for the Fighting Irish. Started 11-of-12 games played in '12 and completed 187-of-318 pass attempts (58.8 percent) for 2,405 yards with 12 touchdowns and six interceptions. Also rushed 94 times for 298 yards (3.2-yard average) and six touchdowns. Sustained a concussion against USC and sat out against BYU. Was suspended for the '13 season after he was caught cheating on a test. While ineligible, moved to California and trained with George Whitfield. Was reinstated in December, and started 12-of-13 games in '14 — passed 256-427-3,445-29-14 (60.0) and rushed 114-283-8 (2.5), though he was benched in the regular season finale against USC and did not start the Music City Bowl against LSU. Sprained his right shoulder against Northwestern. After graduating with a business degree, transferred to Florida State, as the Seminoles had a quarterback opening following the departure of Jameis Winston. With the Seminoles in '15, Golson started 8-of-9 games played and tossed 147-219-1,778-11-3 (67.1). Sustained a concussion against Georgia Tech and did not play against Syracuse. Was cleared for action the follow-

ing week against Clemson, but did not play. Got the start against North Carolina State, but was pulled in that contest, did not start the next week against Chattanooga and did not play in the regular season finale against Florida. Also missed the Peach Bowl against Houston after leaving the team for personal reasons reported to be a death in the family. Concluded his career with a 25-6 mark as a starter.

Strengths: Throws with balance and has a smooth stroke and an efficient release. Can drive the ball. Sets quickly and has very good agility to buy some time and create plays with his feet. Good football intelligence. Highly competitive. Takes pride in his job and works at his craft — identifies with the game, and it is very important to him.

Weaknesses: Marginal height and poor overall size by NFL QB standards. Has a low release point that leads to many batted balls. Operated heavily out of the gun during his career. Does not make NFL, progression-style reads. Tends to vacate the pocket prematurely. Limited field vision — misses open receivers and leaves too much production on the field. Downfield accuracy is off. Streaky performer — has gone through some high-turnover stretches when confidence wanes. Has a loner personality not ideal for a leadership position and has had a tendency to tail off at the end of seasons. Does not deal well with adversity in game situations and can be rattled, leading to bad decisions. Not a natural, vocal leader.

Future: Short, athletic thrower finished his FSU career on a sour note, being replaced by Sean Maguire in the starting lineup following injury. However, has some redeemable traits to warrant a look in the CFL.

Draft projection: Priority free agent.

Scout's take: "(Golson) is accurate, and he can move around. He kind of reminds me of (Buccaneers 2000 seventh-round pick) Joey Hamilton. He is a good quarterback. He is just small. If you are carrying three QB's, he has a chance to be your 3."

QB CHRISTIAN HACKENBERG, #14 (Jr-3)

PENN STATE ▶ GRADE: 5.37

Ht: 6-4 3/8 | Wt: 223 | 40: 4.82 | Arm: 32 | Hand: 9

History: Spent three years at Fork Union Military Academy (Va.), where he won a state championship, played baseball and basketball and was a five-star prospect. Was recruited to Penn State by then-head coach Bill O'Brien. Made an immediate impact in '13 when he was honored as the Big Ten Freshman of the Year after completing 231-of-392 pass at-

QUARTERBACKS

tempts (58.9 percent) for 2,955 yards with 20 touchdowns and 10 interceptions in 12 starts. Was knocked out of the Ohio State contest with a right (throwing) shoulder injury. In '14, started all 13 games and passed 270-484-2,977-12-15 (55.8). Named MVP of the Pinstripe Bowl. Started all 13 games in '15 and completed 192-359-2,525-16-6 (53.5). Also caught a 14-yard touchdown. Injured his right shoulder in the Nittany Lions' bowl game against Georgia. Had a 21-17 career record and rewrote the school passing record book in just three seasons. Two-year captain will be a 21-year-old rookie. Was sacked a QB-unfriendly 104 times in three seasons. Was ruled a medical exclusion from the bench-press test because of a right shoulder injury.

Strengths: Well-built with a solid frame and gunslinger toughness. Has a rifle arm and square jaw that looks like he came straight out of a Western movie. Looks the part and has a commanding presence. Experienced playing in a pro-style offense. Can drive the ball effortlessly off his back foot. Good football intelligence to recognize coverage and make checks at the line of scrimmage. Has enough foot quickness to climb the pocket and avoid the first wave of pressure. Physically tough and regularly took a beating in the pocket behind a marginal offensive line. Good practice habits and weight-room work ethic. Fiery competitor driven to succeed. The game is very important to him, and he takes it seriously. Loyal, resilient and battle-tested to overcoming adversity. Takes charge in the huddle and can inspire with sharp word choice to rally a group. Has directed six comeback wins in the fourth quarter or overtime during his career and has come through in the clutch.

Weaknesses: Has very small hands. Below-average escapability and scrambling skill. Struggles when the pocket collapses — footwork breaks down and gets jumpy under duress. Needs a clean pocket to operate and lacks the play-making ability to improvise. Takes too many needless sacks and must learn to get rid of the ball more quickly. Has a funky grip and does not consistently rip a tight spiral. Needs to learn to throw with more touch and anticipation. Does not have a lot of athletic upside. Limited scrambling ability. Made too many game-changing, negative plays (see two pick-sixes vs. Michigan State and fourth-quarter interception vs. Northwestern). Is a 56-percent career passer with a completion percentage that dipped each season — was not a decisive triggerman. Prone to emotional sideline outbursts and bad on-field body lan-

guage and could learn to channel his frustration more effectively.

Future: Big, smart, passionate, pro-style dropback pocket passer regressed since freshman season when he was operating with a stronger supporting cast featuring Pro Bowl NFL WR Allen Robinson and the direction of head coach Bill O'Brien. Is most ideally suited for a confidence-building, half-field, high-low-read passing game with a lot of high-percentage throws, such as those run by the Texans, Chiefs and Patriots. Suffered through operating an offense that lacked an identity following O'Brien's departure. Could contribute readily in the pros re-uniting with O'Brien in Houston where he already is well-versed in the offensive language and schematic design and could benefit tremendously from entering a less toxic environment than the sanction-riddled program in which he endured that sent a lot of talent out the door, most notably his coach.

Draft projection: Third- to fourth-round pick.

Scout's take: "I would take the backup in Tampa (Buccaneers 2013 third-round pick Mike Glennon) over Hackenberg. ... Listen, I know (Hackenberg) is big and strong and played well against Illinois for two years. I put him in the fourth round. The blame will be that he had no (offensive) line and no receivers, but he was still a deer in headlights most of the time. (Penn State head coach) James Franklin will probably take some hits in the draft room (during the interview process)."

QB KEVIN HOGAN, #8 (Sr-5)
STANFORD ▶ GRADE: 5.27
Ht: 6-3 1/4 | Wt: 218 | 40: 4.74 | Arm: 32 3/8 | Hand: 10 1/4

History: Also played basketball as a prep in Washington D.C., where he was named Player of the Year as a senior. Has four relatives who played Division I football. Redshirted in 2011. Played 10 games in '12 — overtook Josh Nunes to start the final five games and complete 109-of-152 pass attempts (71.7 percent) for 1,096 yards with nine touchdowns and three interceptions. Transitioned from offensive coordinator Pep Hamilton to Mike Bloomgren. Started all 41 games the next three seasons — totaled 180-295-2,635-20-10 (61.0) in '13 (14 games); 232-352-2,792-19-8 (65.9) in '14 (13 games); and 206-304-2,867-27-8 (67.8) in '15 (14 games). Sprained his left ankle against USC. Lost his father to cancer in December '14. Posted a 36-10 career record. Three-year captain graduated with a degree in science, technology and society.

Strengths: Good size. Experienced, three-

QUARTERBACKS

and-a-half-year starter. Well-versed in a pro-style offense — has an advanced understanding of setting protections and making pre-snap reads. Enough arm strength. Good rhythm and timing. Very accurate short-to-intermediate. Tough, football smart and competitive. Led Stanford to three Pac-10 titles and three Rose Bowls. Well-respected team leader who exudes quiet leadership. Very business-like in his approach. Extremely competitive and craves hard coaching. Willed the Cardinal to some victories (see Washington State and Oregon) and was respected by coaches and teammates for his mental toughness. Elevates the performance of those around him.

Weaknesses: Has an unorthodox release, with a low release point that leads to batted balls. Struggles to change up his arm slots and manipulate his arm and throwing platform. Really has to wind up to generate velocity on the ball. Struggles to escape the pocket and create with his feet. Streaky performer. Sprays the ball under pressure and often panics in the pocket. Overanalyzes and outthinks the game, staring down receivers and forcing the ball into coverage. Marginal pocket presence — takes unnecessary sacks. Loses velocity on his ball on the move and struggles to connect deep.

Future: Efficient, high-percentage pocket passer finally showed some signs of settling down and developing pocket poise late in his senior season, yet his overall mechanics and poise will require refinement to earn a place in the NFL. An accomplished, type-A introvert most ideally suited to hold a clipboard in a supporting role. Will require time in the pros for the game to slow down for him and would be best in a rhythm-timing passing game.

Draft projection: Fourth- to fifth-round pick.

Scout's take: "He has some arm talent, but makes too many bone-headed decisions. They have tried to replace him a couple times. He's a backup at best to me. You can't put the game on his shoulders to win. I'd put him in the same category as a Matt Schaub. He's a mid-round-type of talent. You know what you're getting."

QB CARDALE JONES, #12 (Jr-4)

OHIO STATE ▶ GRADE: 5.29
Ht: 6-5 | Wt: 253 | 40: 4.79 | Arm: 33¾ | Hand: 9¾

History: Has a daughter named Chloe. Nicknamed "12-gauge." Prepped at Cleveland Glenville, where he played for Ted Ginn Sr. Was a non-qualifier and spent 2011 at Fork Union Military Academy (Va.). Redshirted in 2012. In October, tweeted, "Why should we have to go to class if we came here to play FOOTBALL, we ain't come to play SCHOOL classes are POINTLESS." Was "suspended" for the Nebraska contest. Was third string in '13 — completed 1-of-2 pass attempts (50.0 percent) for three yards with zero touchdowns and zero interceptions in three appearances. Rushed 17 times for 128 yards (7.5-yarrd average) and one touchdown. Played an unlikely starring role for the national champion Buckeyes in '14, as he was called upon to start the final three games after Braxton Miller and J.T. Barrett were lost to injury. In 10 games, tossed 56-92-860-7-2 (60.9) and rushed 72-296-1 (4.1). Played 10 games in '15 — started eight of the first nine — and passed 110-176-1,460-8-5 (62.5) and rushed 64-193-2 (3.0). Was benched in favor of Barrett at the end of the season. Experienced migraines the week leading up to the season opener. Went 11-0 as a starter. Was ruled a medical exlusion from the bench-press test because of a left shoulder injury and did not finish his Combine workout after pulling his right hamstring on his second run.

Strengths: Exceptional size and arm talent with the ability to uncork it deep with ease and power it into tight coverage. Difficult to corral and bring down in the pocket and not easily sacked. Stands tall in the pocket and can deliver after taking a hit. Recorded a 36-inch vertical jump at the Combine, tied for best among quarterbacks. Led the Buckeyes to a national championship after being thrust into the lineup out of the bullpen and rose to the occasion on the biggest of stages. Flawless starting record.

Weaknesses: Does not take much pace off the ball and deliver it with touch, tending to fire from close range. Takes too long to get rid of it and consistently throws behind receivers — ball placement and location could improve. Footwork is not clean, negating accuracy, and will require refinement. Throws off his back foot and arms the ball more than needed. Too streaky. Marginal situational awareness — needs to be more keen of the sticks on third down. Tends to lock onto his receivers and does not avoid pressure very well in the pocket. Immature and easily drawn to all the trappings of the game. Has only started the equivalent of a one season and lacks game experience handling live bullets and all the complexities of defensive pressure packages.

Future: Physically has all the tools desired in a front-line starter, yet is still more of a hard thrower than refined passer and must learn to

QUARTERBACKS

15

better gauge his arm talent. Lacks the desired experience, nuance and maturity to contribute readily. Is several years away from earning a top job, if he proves he can stay focused, committed and avoid the trappings of success.

Draft projection: Fourth- to fifth-round pick.

Scout's take: "(Cardale) has a live arm, size and he can run. It's just not natural for him, and he kind of went off the cliff after winning the national championship. He can't stay focused. ... He's not ready yet. He had his three games of fame and could not get through it. Now, it's like he can't hit the broad side of a barn. He could be a boom-or-bust guy."

QB CODY KESSLER, #6 (Sr-5)

USC ▶ GRADE: 5.19

Ht: 6-11/4 | Wt: 220 | 40: 4.91 | Arm: 325/8 | Hand: 10

History: Decorated California prep — USA-Today All-American, state's Gatorade Player of the Year and Bakersfield Area POY in football and basketball (averaged nearly 30 points and 11 rebounds per game). Missed a handful of football games his junior season because of a left ankle sprain. Redshirted in 2011. Was third string in '12 when he completed 2-of-2 pass attempts (100.0 percent) for nine yards with zero touchdowns and zero interceptions in two appearances. Took ownership of the job as a sophomore in '13 — started all 14 games and passed 236-361-654-2,968-20-7 (65.4). In '14, set USC single-season records for completions, completion percentage, passing efficiency (167.1) and interception rate (1.11) and tied the records for touchdown passes, 300-yard games (seven) and total touchdowns (41) — started all 13 games and produced 315-452-3,826-39-5 (69.7). Also punted seven times for a 33.0-yard average. Started all 14 games in '15 and completed 298-446-3,536-29-7 (66.8). Also had seven career rushing touchdowns. Two-time USC Trojan Way Leadership Award honoree, two-time finalist for the Unitas Golden Arm Award and a finalist for the Senior CLASS Award. Two-year captain graduated with a sociology degree. Finished his USC career as the school's most accurate (67.5 completion percentage) and judicious (1.51 interception rate) passer. Also ranks third in touchdown passes (88) and fourth in passing yardage (10,339). Posted a 27-14 career record. Sacked 38 times as a senior. Played for four different head coaches in five years.

Strengths: Has a short, compact delivery. Sets his feet quickly and delivers the ball with deft touch. Very good accuracy and ball placement. Smart, tough and durable. Good intan-

gibles and practice habits. The game is very important to him and he takes preparation seriously. Good football intelligence. Outstanding career production in a pro-style offense, with nearly a 5:1 TD-INT ratio reflective of solid decision-making and caretaking of the ball. Decisive trigger — knows when and where to go with the ball and wisely when to check down or throw it away. Effective pooch punter.

Weaknesses: Undersized with below-average height by NFL standards. Needs time to operate in the pocket and takes needless sacks under duress, struggling to hasten his delivery time and release the ball quickly. Pocket anxiety affects mechanics when initial read is taken away. Marginal reactive quickness — pressure often reaches him before he can react and struggles manipulating his arm and throwing platform on the move. Does not trust his arm — likes to wait for downfield receivers to come wide open before uncorking. Could struggle driving the ball into tight windows. Accuracy diminishes the further he is asked to throw.

Future: Fifth- to sixth-round pick.

Draft projection: Modest-sized, game-managing precision passer with quality backup potential in the pros. Is most ideally suited for a rhythm-timing passing game where he can pierce soft underneath coverage. Will require a strong supporting cast around him to function.

Scout's take: "(Kessler) can be a solid backup because he is smart. His arm is probably average to above-average. What you like about him most — he is accurate. You know what you are getting."

QB PAXTON LYNCH, #12 (Jr-4)

MEMPHIS ▶ GRADE: 6.12

Ht: 6-65/8 | Wt: 244 | 40: 4.8 | Arm: 341/4 | Hand: 101/4

History: Late bloomer who played in a wing-T offense at Trinity Christian Academy (Fla.), and didn't draw scholarships until he showcased himself in a post-season all-star game his senior year (missed the first half of the season because of a bruised kneecap). Had late interest from Florida, specifically Charlie Weis before the offensive coordinator left for Kansas. However, the Gators opted for Skyler Mornhinweg, whose father, Marty, is the Baltimore Ravens quarterbacks coach and a friend of Brent Pease, who replaced Weis as the Gators' OC. Redshirted in 2012. Became the No. 1 in '13 when he started all 12 games and completed 203-of-349 pass attempts (58.2 percent) for 2,056 yards with nine touchdowns and 10 interceptions. In '14, led the Tigers to their first conference championship in 43 years by producing 259-413-3,031-22-9 (62.7) in 13 starts. In '15, posted the best season in school history and was a finalist for the Unitas and Manning Awards — aired it out 296-444-3,778-28-4 (66.7) in 13 starts. Registered 16-37-106-0-1 passing against Auburn in a 31-10 Birmingham Bowl loss after head coach Justin Fuente departed for Virginia Tech. Had 288 career rushes for 687 yards (2.4-yard average) and 17 touchdowns. Two-time team MVP was part of the Tigers' 23-man leadership council. Went 22-16 as a starter.

Strengths: Outstanding height and movement skill for as long as he is. Extremely athletic. Very good escapability in the pocket to create plays with his feet and buy time to deliver the ball. Superb field vision to locate secondary receivers. Gets rid of the ball quickly and can hasten his delivery. Sound decision-maker with good pocket stature. Outstanding arm strength — can hum the ball with velocity, fit it into tight spaces in stride and throw with touch. Generated the highest ball velocity (59 m.p.h.) of any passer at the Combine. Accurate and efficient throwing on the move, and is ideally suited to run sprintout passes and bootlegs. Athletic zone read runner with good foot turnover for his long strides. Flashes playmaking ability as a runner and on bootlegs. Good scrambling ability. Recorded a 36-inch vertical jump, tied for best among quarterbacks at the Combine, and is more explosive reaching the corner on zone-read runs than his 40 time might suggest. Has added 30 pounds to his frame since entering the program as a 215-pound freshman and has been commended by the coaching staff for his attention to detail and practice habits polishing his game. Understands how to engage teammates and is respected as a grounded, team leader. Rallied team to come-from-behind victory over Mississippi and has shown he can steer an offense.

Weaknesses: Nearly too tall for the QB position, with a gangly frame and long limbs that add some time to his throwing motion. Has some windup in his delivery. Struggled to take pace off the ball at the Combine and only threw heat. Throws the ball too flat and could could stand to improve his touch and trajectory. Relies too much on his arm and does not consistently step into throws or spin a tight spiral. A lot of production results from short lateral tosses and bubble screens. Operated heavily out of the pistol formation and footwork will require adjustment working from underneath center. Not a physically strong runner and goes down easy on contact. Occasionally will bolt from the pocket prematurely instead of letting routes develop. Did not regularly match up against top competition in the American Athletic Conference.

Future: A cross between 49ers QB Colin Kaepernick and Broncos QB Brock Osweiler, both second-round picks, Lynch will require some time to acclimate to the NFL game. Yet, the self-made passer possesses the size, agility and upside to emerge as the gem of this year's QB class, especially if he lands with a team employing a play-action, rollout, bootleg offense such as those preferred by Broncos head coach Gary Kubiak or Chiefs head coach Andy Reid. Played with a cast of five former walk-on receivers and consistently elevated the performance of the group, showing improvement every season. Has the physical talent to earn an NFL starting job and contribute fairly readily in a vertical passing attack. Is the most intriguing movement passer in the draft.

Draft projection: Mid-to-late first-round pick.

Scout's take: "Anyone that downgrades Lynch for the Auburn game (when Memphis was outscored 21-0 in the second half) has not done their homework. It was totally dysfunctional preparation and game-planning after the head coach left. I don't like making excuses for anyone, but he was set up to fail in the bowl game. There was no structure, and it was obvious watching it."

QB DAK PRESCOTT, #15 (Sr-5)

MISSISSIPPI STATE ▶ GRADE: 5.39
Ht: 6-2¼ | Wt: 226 | 40: 4.78 | Arm: 32¼ | Hand: 10

History: Full name is Rayne Dakota Prescott. Suffered a torn MCL late in his senior season, but played hurt — unable to run — in the district championship game (on the road) and threw for 380 yards and four touchdowns to secure Haughton High's first undefeated regular season. Redshirted in 2011. Dak's mother, Peggy, was diagnosed with cancer during the summer of '12. In the fall, Prescott backed up Tyler Russell, completing 18-of-29 pass attempts (62.1 percent) for 194 yards with four touchdowns and zero interceptions Was also used as a short-yardage runner, as he carried 32 times for 118 yards (3.7-yard average) and four scores. Was bothered by turf toe, which kept him out of the Troy contest. Had surgery in February '13 to repair a ligament in his big toe. On the season, split reps with Russell — started 7-of-11 games played, completing 156-267-1,940-10-7 (58.4). Also caught a pair of touchdowns. Was the Bulldogs' leading rusher with 134-829-13 (6.2) despite sitting out the Alabama and Arkansas

QUARTERBACKS

contests because of nerve trauma in his left (non-throwing) shoulder. Suffered the injury against Texas A&M, days after his mother's funeral. Capped the season with an MVP performance against Rice in the Liberty Bowl. In '14, was a finalist for the Maxwell, Davey O'Brien, Johnny Unitas and Manning Awards — started all 13 games and amassed 244-396-3,449-27-11 (61.6) through the air and 210-986-14 (4.7) on the ground. Had a walking boot on his right foot after the Kentucky game (precautionary). In March '15, was the victim of an assault while on spring break in Panama City, Fla. — Prescott's assailants threatened to shoot him, hit Prescott in the face with a bottle and stomped on his head, leaving him bloodied and disoriented. Prescott declined to press charges. Was a finalist for the Manning and Unitas Awards again in '15 after totaling 316-477-3,793-29-5 (66.2) passing and leading the Bulldogs with 160-588-10 (3.7) rushing in 13 starts. Was MVP of the Belk Bowl against North Carolina State. Played only three series against Troy (illness). Senior CLASS Award winner — chosen by coaches, media and fans, presented to the most outstanding senior with notable achievements in areas of excellence, classroom, community, character and competition. Team captain has an undergraduate (educational psychology) and master's degree (workforce leadership). Owns 38 MSU records, including 15 career and 15 single-season marks. Finished 23-10 as a career starter. Capped his college career by being named the Senior Bowl's Most Outstanding Player. On March 12 (around 12:45 a.m.), was pulled over for speeding and charged with DUI (blood-alcohol results not available at time of publication). Had nine fumbles in 2015.

Strengths: Physically strong and powerful running through tacklers on designed runs and zone-read options. Very effective goal-line runner capable of creasing defenses in short-yardage situations. Athletic and agile to sidestep free rushers in the pocket. Can laser the ball into tight windows and deliver the ball with pressure at his feet. Snaps the ball with velocity. Outstanding competitor — wants the ball in his hands in the clutch. Unselfish team player. Well-respected team leader. Lives at the football facility and does a lot of extras in preparation. Vocal, leads by example and has superb intangibles. Outstanding career production.

Weaknesses: Has some wind-up in his delivery and holds the ball too long, waiting for receivers to uncover. Is still growing as a decision-maker in a simplified, spread offense that did not require many pro-style progres-

sion reads. Footwork is not clean and often is not set when he throws. Operated heavily out of the gun and footwork will require refinement dropping back from underneath center. Developing pocket awareness — sees pocket ghosts, often pulling the ball down and fleeing the pocket quickly if his primary read is taken away. Statistics are heavily inflated from a lot of simple, one-look, lateral tosses where receivers create after the catch. Needs to improve ball security, holding the ball carelessly like a loaf of bread at times. Consistently overshoots the deep ball and makes receivers work hard for the ball. Inconsistent footwork negates accuracy at every level. Has been dinged up a lot throughout his career.

Future: Athletic, productive thrower with the run skills to be molded in an offense designed to take advantage of his feet with a lot of streamlined, half-field, high-low concepts, such as the Panthers, Seahawks and Chiefs. Has the competitiveness and intangibles to continue molding and eventually emerge as a productive No. 2 with continued seasoning.

Draft projection: Fourth- to fifth-round pick.

Scout's take: "He's smart. He's a leader with great want-to. His mechanics are not always great, but he is pretty accurate. He can get himself out of trouble with his feet. Going into the school, I didn't think he was any better as a passer than Tim Tebow. But this kid can throw the ball. He is not a starter. He is a developmental player with some upside. There is some value there. If you have a quarterback that is long in the tooth, (Prescott) could make some sense. I honestly didn't like Osweiler when the Broncos drafted him pretty early (in the second round). He sat behind Peyton and learned. The same way, (Prescott) needs to have some time to learn. I wouldn't draft him to be a starter. He is a backup with upside."

QB JAKE RUDOCK, #15 (Sr-5)

MICHIGAN ▶ GRADE: 4.92

Ht: 6-2 3/4 | Wt: 199 | 40: 4.95e | Arm: 32 1/8 | Hand: 9 3/4

History: St. Thomas Aquinas (Fla.) product who won a state and national title in 2010 — capping his two-year run with a 70:8 touchdown-to-interception ratio and several school' records. Also played baseball. Spent four years at Iowa. Redshirted in '11 and did not play in '12 while backing up James Vandenberg. In '13, started all 13 games and completed 204-of-346 pass attempts (59.0 percent) for 2,383 yards with 18 touchdowns and 13 interceptions. Sprained his left knee against Wisconsin and sprained his right knee against Nebraska. Started all 12 games played in '14, completing 213-345-2,436-16-5 (61.7). Did not play against Purdue (hip). With interdepartmental studies-multidisciplinary sciences degree in hand, joined the Wolverines as a graduate transfer. In '15, started all 13 games and tossed 249-389-3,017-20-9 (64.0). Suffered a ribs/torso injury against Minnesota then sprained the AC joint in his left (non-throwing) shoulder against Ohio State. Had 192 career rushes for 560 yards (2.9-yard average) and 12 touchdowns. Went 16-9 as a starter.

Strengths: Scrappy, tough competitor. Fine poise in the pocket. Solid decision-maker. Fairly accurate short-to-intermediate passer. Nice touch. Has a professional attitude and blue-collar work ethic. Very intelligent and articulate. Showed gradual improvement and carried the team at times, capping his career with a Citrus Bowl MVP-winning performance picking apart a talented Florida secondary.

Weaknesses: Has a very slight frame prone to injury and does not look the part. Limited arm strength to make all the throws and drive the deep ball. Ball velocity and accuracy are negated mightily on the move. Lacks ideal agility to sidestep the rush and avoid NFL pressure. Does not easily find open throwing windows, resulting in 10 batted balls. Struggled vs. zone blitz concepts against Utah (in first game at Michigan after not participating in spring ball).

Future: Dependable game-manager with the work habits and intelligence for a team employing a rhythm-timing offense such as the Patriots, Texans, Redskins or Saints to warrant inviting to a camp.

Draft projection: Priority free agent.

Scout's take: "He doesn't have a great arm, but he is accurate. He has come a long way. He made some tight throws in the Indiana game. You have to keep in mind though — (Jim) Harbaugh makes quarterbacks look more talented than they are."

QB JOEL STAVE, #2 (Sr-5)

WISCONSIN   ▶ GRADE: 5.02

Ht: 6-5 1/2 | Wt: 236 | 40: 4.77 | Arm: 33 1/4 | Hand: 10 3/4

History: Last name is pronounced "STAH-vee." Wisconsin native also competed in basketball and track and field in high school. Redshirted in 2011. Took over in Week Four in '12 — started 6-of-8 games played and completed 70-of-119 pass attempts (58.8 percent) for 1,104 with six touchdowns and three interceptions. Suffered a broken left collarbone against Michigan State, knocking him out for four games. Started all 13 games in '13 and completed 208-336-2,494-22-13 (61.9). Sprained

the AC joint in his right (throwing) shoulder in the Capital One Bowl against Auburn, but effects of the injury lingered into the '14 season, as observers speculated Stave might have been experiencing the "yips." After not appearing in the first four games, Stave said, "I'm not hurt. Structurally, everything's good in my shoulder...Right now, my arm is just not working the way I'd like it to, I guess. I don't know what it is." Got back on the field and tossed 110-206-1,350-9-10 (53.4) in 10 games (nine starts). In '15, started all 13 games and passed 225-370-2,687-11-11 (60.8). Sustained a head injury against Illinois. Finished with a 31-10 career mark and most wins in school history. Has a civil engineering degree.

Strengths: Excellent length and hand size, the biggest of any quarterback at the Combine. Can spin the ball with good velocity when his feet are set. Classic, over-the-top delivery. Well-versed in a pro-style, play-action offense and is comfortable working underneath center. Extremely intelligent. Solid personal and football character. Accountable.

Weaknesses: Average passing instincts — needs to speed up his clock and show better awareness in the pocket. Struggles to translate superb book smarts to the field, overthinking the game. Sporadic accuracy — makes his receivers work hard for the ball. Tends to birddog his primary target. Easily rattled by pressure. Marginal decision-maker — can be gun-shy and late to pull the trigger waiting for receivers to uncover and then force throws into traffic. Accuracy diminishes beyond 15 yards, consistently overthrowing targets. Mental toughness requires deeper evaluation.

Future: Big, inconsistent pocket passer with ample arm talent to warrant consideration as a developmental project. Will require patience molding and has a chance to develop into a backup.

Draft projection: Priority free agent.

QB NATE SUDFELD, #7 (Sr-4)

INDIANA   ▶ GRADE: 5.24

Ht: 6-6 1/8 | Wt: 234 | 40: 5.10e | Arm: 34 1/4 | Hand: 9 7/8

History: Brother, Zach, is a tight end for the Jets. Nate also played basketball as a California prep. Graduated high school early in December, intending to enroll at Arizona to participate in spring practice until Mike Stoops was fired. Followed ex-Arizona offensive coordinator Seth Littrell to Indiana. As a true freshman in 2012, completed 51-of-82 pass attempts (62.2 percent) for 632 yards with seven touchdowns and one intercep-

QUARTERBACKS

tion. Started 8-of-12 games in '13, completing 194-322-2,523-21-9 (60.2). In '14, managed 101-167-1,151-6-3 (60.5) in six starts before undergoing season-ending surgery to repair a torn labrum in his left (non-throwing) shoulder. Was the Big Ten's leading passer in '15 when he started all 12 games he played and produced 247-412-3,573-27-7 (60.0). Sprained an ankle against Ohio State and sat out against Penn State. Also had eight career rushing touchdowns. Owns IU records for passing yards (7,879) and touchdowns (61).

Strengths: Exceptional size. Very good arm strength to fire the ball with velocity and drive the deep out. Is capable of throwing effortlessly downfield off-balance and from his back foot. Can throw with touch and place the deep ball in stride. Very good field vision. Knows when and where to go with the ball and snaps it off quickly. Takes few sacks. Good caretaker — places the ball out of reach of defenders and makes sharp back-shoulder throws. Fine anticipation. Puts air underneath the deep ball for his receivers to run under. Outstanding production. Studies opponents' schemes and tendencies and prepares like a pro. Has NFL pedigree.

Weaknesses: Long strider lacks foot speed to elude the rush. Operates heavily out of the shotgun and locks his legs too often. Inconsistent delivery and mechanics — arms the ball too much with limited hip rotation, negating his footwork. Needs to learn to set his feet more consistently and throw with balance. Accuracy declines on the move. Does not make a lot of progression reads. Not a confident, natural take-charge leader and does not have a commanding huddle presence.

Future: A strong-armed, pocket-passing spot thrower operating an up-tempo, pass-first, no-huddle, spread offense that featured a lot of quick-hitting screens. Played with an average supporting cast that dropped a lot of well-placed balls and would be at his best with a dynamic WR group of run-after-the-catch receivers and strong outlet tight end option to survive in an NFL saddle. Is not fond of the spotlight and may always be best in a backup capacity, yet has the pocket stature, arm talent, intelligence and touch to eventually become a respectable NFL starter if he can refine his footwork.

Draft projection: Fourth- to fifth-round pick.

Scout's take: "He is really mechanical. It does not look like it comes natural for him. He has a good arm – not a cannon. ... He's a game manager. To me, he's a dime-a-dozen quarterback."

QB CARSON WENTZ, #11 (Sr-5)

NORTH DAKOTA STATE　　　▶ GRADE: 6.35

Ht: 6-5¼ | Wt: 237 | 40: 4.71 | Arm: 33¼ | Hand: 10

History: High school valedictorian and three-sport standout — was North Dakota's 3A Player of the Year in addition to playing baseball and basketball. Did not play quarterback his junior season while dealing with arm and shoulder pain from baseball, as well as a broken right thumb that sidelined him for two games. Sustained two concussions during his senior season. Was a preferred walk-on at NDSU. Redshirted in 2011. Backed up Brock Jensen for two seasons. Appeared in eight games in '12, completing 12-of-16 pass attempts (75.0 percent) for 144 yards with two touchdowns and zero interceptions. Had surgery to repair his left meniscus prior to the '13 season when he had 22-30-209-1-0 (73.3) in 11 games. Took the reins in '14 by starting all 16 games and producing 228-358-3,111-25-10 (63.7). Also had a 16-yard touchdown reception. In '15, tossed 114-179-1,459-16-2 (63.7) in seven starts. Sustained a high ankle sprain in the season opener against Montana then broke his right wrist against South Dakota — missed eight games before returning for the FCS championship against Jacksonville State (was the game's Most Outstanding Player despite three months between starts). Had 207 career rushes for 949 yards (4.6-yard average) and 11 touchdowns. Went 20-3 as a starter for the Bison, winning two national titles. Two-year captain maintained a 4.0 GPA in health education and physical education with a minor in psychology.

Strengths: Exceptional size, with prototype dimensions for an NFL quarterback. Played in a pro-style offense and is comfortable working from underneath center and making NFL-style, whole-field, progression reads. Has a clean, compact, over-the-top delivery and can hasten it when needed. Is tough with good pocket stature and stays poised under pressure and continues to scan the field. Moves around the pocket and can maneuver to avoid the rush and extend plays with his feet — surprisingly nifty for as big as he is. Knows how to take pace off the ball and delivers a very catchable ball. Can rally a huddle in high-pressure situations, commanding a comeback victory against Northern Iowa on a big stage in a quarterfinal playoff game. Acclimated very well to Senior Bowl competition, showing the game was not too big for him, and ripped the ball with velocity at Combine workouts. Outstanding football and personal character — well respected within the program, highly motivated

QUARTERBACKS

and driven to succeed. Extremely intelligent — is a very quick study capable of handling complex playbooks and weekly adjustments. Very competitive, yet selfless team player. Displays a very relaxed, even-keeled, on-field playing temperament and has a commanding presence. Showed well against better competition at the Senior Bowl.

Weaknesses: Has a tendency to stare down targets and could improve his eyes and learn how to manipulate safeties, looking off receivers. Footwork could use more refinement and enhance his accuracy. Deep ball tends to drift and hang in the air. Is a bit underdeveloped in the weight room and strength levels could be improved to enhance durability, having been dinged up with a lot of minor injuries throughout his career. Did not regularly match up against top competition in the Missouri Valley Football Conference. Only a two-year starter with 23 career starts and will require more polish. Has suffered multiple concussions during his career and medical history requires closer scrutiny.

Future: Prototype-sized, smart, light-footed small-school passer with the mobility, arm talent, rare intelligence and work habits for a team to entrust with their future. Is loaded with upside and his best football is ahead of him. Is not yet ready for prime time and ideally will have some time to be groomed behind an established veteran, yet could be thrust into action before he is ready and has proven in post-season activities that he has the wings to learn how to fly on the job. Has the physical tools to suggest he can become a franchise-caliber quarterback.

Draft projection: Top-10 pick.

Scout's take: "The North Dakota State quarterback overall probably has the most upside in this class. He has taken snaps under center. He is athletic. He does not have a cannon, but he can throw the deep ball. He still needs some development time like all of them. He looked good at the Senior Bowl, though he was facing a lot of vanilla looks. What concerns me, when he got hurt during the season — the backup freshman came in and scored about the same amount of points and moved the offense and took the team all the way to the championship game against the best competition. That's a strong program that won a lot of championships without him quarterbacking."

QB JOSH WOODRUM, #6 (Sr-5)

LIBERTY ▶ GRADE: 5.24

Ht: 6-2 7/8 | Wt: 231 | 40: 4.78 | Arm: 31 7/8 | Hand: 9 1/4

History: Prepped in Virginia. Chose FCS Liberty over FBS offers. Redshirted in 2011.

Played all 11 games in '12, taking over the No. 1 job in Week Three — completed 183-of-267 pass attempts (68.5 percent) for 1,966 yards with 11 touchdowns and nine interceptions in nine starts. Started all 12 games in '13, completing 198-308-2,581-19-7 (64.3). Started all 11 games played in '14, passing 210-339-2,947-19-10 (61.9). Did not play against Charleston Southern or Coastal Carolina because of a leg infection in his right knee. Became Liberty's all-time leading passer in '15 under head coach Turner Gill by producing 242-390-2,772-12-4 (62.1) in 11 starts. Guided the Flames to a 28-16 career record as a starter. Three-year captain graduated with exercise science degree. Liberty career leader in passing yards (10,266).

Strengths: Outstanding size with a sturdy frame and good pocket stature. Experienced, four-year starter. Physically tough to withstand contact and will deliver the ball in the face of barreling pressure (see West Virginia, including TD strike). Sufficient arm strength. Throws a catchable ball. Quick enough to dash for the sticks and move around the pocket to avoid the rush. Flashes some scrambling skill. Recorded a 6.74-second 3-cone drill time at the Combine, best among quarterbacks, and has the feet to escape pressure. Very intelligent. Confident and competitive. Organizes off-season training and serves as a pseudo-coach.

Weaknesses: Small hands. Timing and anticipation is consistently off despite making a lot of quick, short throws involving predetermined reads. Needs to do a better job of setting his feet quickly. Average football smarts. Was not asked to make a lot of NFL progression-style reads and is still learning to trigger decisively on secondary reads. Forces the ball too often. Operates mostly from the shotgun and footwork will require refinement. Did not face NFL-style, quick-closing windows against Big South competition.

Future: Well-built, shotgun touch passer opened some eyes with a solid showing at the NFLPA all-star game. Has the size, toughness and arm talent to earn a backup job as a vertical, chunk passer. Could require a few years of seasoning to adapt to NFL speed and complexities.

Draft projection: Fifth- to sixth-round pick.

Scout's take: "(Woodrum) showed good accuracy and arm strength during the week at the NFLPA (all-star) game. He was clearly the best quarterback there. He was the only passer in the game that showed any type of possibility."

QUARTERBACKS

RUNNING BACKS

Nawrocki's TOP 10

1. **EZEKIEL ELLIOTT**
2. **Derrick Henry**
3. **C.J. Prosise**
4. **Kenneth Dixon**
5. **Devontae Booker**
6. **Jordan Howard**
7. **Paul Perkins**
8. **Kenyan Drake**
9. **Alex Collins**
10. **Josh Ferguson**

RB PEYTON BARBER, #25 (Soph-3)

AUBURN ▶ GRADE: 5.03

Ht: 5-10 | Wt: 228 | 40: 4.62 | Arm: 30 1/4 | Hand: 9 3/8

History: Was diagnosed with dyslexia as a freshman, a learning disorder shared by his father and common to those with Attention Deficit Hyperactivity Disorder (ADHD), which he also has. Second cousin of Marion Barber III, who was a seven-year NFL running back with the Cowboys and Bears (2005-11). Peyton prepped in Georgia. Redshirted in 2013. Sustained a high right ankle sprain during the Tigers' '13 spring game. In the fall, appeared in six games and carried 10 times for 54 yards (5.4-yard average) and zero touchdowns. In '15, began the season third on the depth chart, but injuries enabled him to start 9-of-13 games and rush 238-1,017-13 (4.3), while adding 11 receptions for 112 yards (10.2-yard average) and zero touchdowns. Ran for career-high 28-147-5 vs. San Jose State. Had three career fumbles in 260 career touches. Said at the Combine that he declared for the draft to support his mother who is living with his sister.

Strengths: Powerfully built, strong inside runner capable of creasing the line of scrimmage. Good short-yardage and goalline back — dips his shoulder, barrels through contact and fearlessly elevates and leaps over piles in congestion. Almost always falls forward. Functional hands-catcher.

Weaknesses: Only a one-year producer and was never a full-time starter. Short stepper with limited creativity and elusiveness. Does not possess home-run speed. Much of his production was blocked for him and does not set up blocks. Struggles to protect his legs and gets cut down like a tree.

Future: A strong inside runner, Barber can functionally contribute in pass protection and has adequate hands, yet he will need to translate his toughness to special teams to earn a roster spot.

Draft projection: Priority free agent.

RB DEVONTAE BOOKER, #23 (Sr-4)

UTAH ▶ GRADE: 5.47

Ht: 5-10 3/4 | Wt: 219 | 40: 4.55e | Arm: 31 5/8 | Hand: 8 5/8

History: Has a son named Deashon. From California, where he piled up 7,000 yards and 108 touchdowns during his high school career. Attempted to sign with Washington State then Fresno State, but failed to qualify academically, and spent two years at American River College (Calif.). In 2011, carried 100 times for 793 yards (7.9-yard average) and 12 touchdowns and had 10 receptions for 143 yards (14.3-yard average) and one touchdown (10 games). In '12, totaled 194-1,472-15 (7.6) rushing and 9-58-2 (6.4) receiving (11 games). Added 18 kickoff returns for 450 yards (25-yard average), including two scores. Was academically ineligible in '13 after reportedly trying to forge his transcript. Played all 13 games for the Utes in '14, starting the final nine after being slowed by a turf toe injury on his left foot in early September, and recorded 292-1,512-10 (5.2) rushing, 43-306-2 (7.1) receiving and 3-57 (19.0) returning kicks. In '15, posted 268-1,261-11 (4.7) on the ground and 37-318-0 (8.6) receiving in 10 stars before suffering a season-ending torn left meniscus injury. Also threw a 25-yard touchdown pass vs Oregon. Team captain graduated with a sociology degree. Had 16 fumbles in 644 touches for the Utes. Was a medical exlusion at the Combine as a result of knee injury.

Strengths: Has a smooth, gliding run style and runs with balance in his feet. Superb vision — quick and decisive in the hole and can cut on a dime, possessing an array of jump cuts to avoid tacklers and maneuver through congestion. Creative enough to make some magic in the open field — spins out of contact and accelerates. Wiggles and darts through traffic, capable of making speed cuts without gearing down. Good body lean and competitiveness, running with urgency. Great career production, with good strength after contact. Does not go down easy. Good functional, football-playing speed. Solid football IQ. Willing blocker — surprisingly efficient pass protector for his size. Southpaw passer lends to unanticipated halfback tosses. Has return experience.

Weaknesses: Has very small hands. Average bulk strength and power for an inside runner and is not ideally built to withstand the rigors of a full workload. Not an explosive, big-play threat. Recorded a 32 1/2-inch vertical jump, indicating average athletic ability. Doesn't always switch hands with the ball, flagging it at times through traffic and leaving it susceptible to big hits. Can do a better job of carrying high and tight.

Future: A quick, competitive complementary back who runs bigger than his size, Booker has enough size and the quick feet, vision and creativity to factor readily and become a key cog in an NFL offense.

Draft projection: Third-round pick.

Scout's take: "He might get knocked down once the medical comes back, coming off that knee injury. How it checks out at the April re-checks will be important for him."

RB TRA CARSON, #5 (Sr-5)

TEXAS A&M ▶ GRADE: 5.07

Ht: 5-11¼ | Wt: 227 | 40: 4.70e | Arm: 31½ | Hand: 9¼

History: Texas native who broke LaMichael James' school single-season record as a senior with 2,202 yards and 24 touchdowns. Began his college career at Oregon, where he carried 45 times for 254 yards (5.6-yard average) and one touchdown in 10 games. Transferred to Texas A&M in order to be closer to home (sat out '12 season per NCAA rules). With the Aggies in '13, rushed 62-329-7 (5.3) with three catches for 38 yards (12.7-yard average) and zero touchdowns. Suffered a neck injury against UTEP and did not play against Mississippi State. Led the team in rushing with 124-581-5 (4.7) while adding 9-78-0 (8.7) receiving in 12 games (four starts). Did not play against Lamar (toe). Sat out '15 spring practice because of a broken foot. In the fall, was team MVP after starting all 13 games — toted 242-1,165-7 (4.8) and caught 29-183-1 (6.3). Graduated with a parks and recreation degree. Has four career fumbles in 516 touches. Did not perform any running at the Combine following right toe surgery.

Strengths: Outstanding size. Has a low center of gravity or good leg churn to shred arm tackles and produce some chunk runs. Maintains a good base picking up the blitz and is a strong blocker capable of withstanding a charge. Exceptional hands — is a 95-percent catcher. Strong personal and football character. Has special teams experience and the toughness to contribute in all phases.

Weaknesses: Does not run with the power expected of a 230-plus pound back, running tall for his size. Takes choppy steps and only shows one gear — too tight-ankled and stiff-hipped to shake many tacklers in the open field or elude at the second level. Takes a lot of direct hits that will invite lower-body injuries in the pros and has been slowed by foot injuries. Marginal long speed — can be tracked to the perimeter. Only a one-year, full-time starter.

Future: Short, compact, bowling ball, downhill runner. Takes what is blocked for him and is not a punishing runner, though he could secure a role as a no. 3 back because of his well-rounded skill set and ability to factor more effectively as a blocker and receiver than he does as an inside runner.

Draft projection: Priority free agent.

RUNNING BACKS

RB ALEX COLLINS, #3 (Jr-3)

ARKANSAS   ▶ GRADE: 5.31

Ht: 5-10 | Wt: 217 | 40: 4.59 | Arm: 30 1/4 | Hand: 9 1/4

History: Highly recruited out of Florida, where he also ran track and played lacrosse. Missed three games his senior season because of an ankle injury. Mother wanted him to stay close to home and would not sign initial letter of intent, forcing his father to submit it. Made an immediate impact as a true freshman in 2013 by carrying 190 times for 1,026 yards (5.4-yard average) and four touchdowns in 12 games. Added 11 receptions for 63 yards (5.7-yard average) and zero touchdowns. Served a one-week suspension in February '14 related to his social media behavior. On the season, toted 204-1,100-12 (5.4) and caught 3-9-0 (3.0). Started all 13 games in '15, producing 271-1,577-20 (5.8) on the ground and 13-95-0 (7.3) receiving. Was named the MVP of the Liberty Bowl following a 23-185-3 performance vs. Kansas State. Had six career kickoff returns for 187 yards (31.2-yard average). Third player in Southeastern Conference history with three straight 1,000-yard seasons. Has 16 fumbles in 696 career touches. Did not perform shuttles at the Combine because of a migraine headache.

Strengths: Presses the line, with his feet churning like pistons. Good eyes and anticipation — feels holes developing, reads his blocks and sifts through traffic. Good forward lean to fall for additional yardage. Can navigate through trash and pick and slide. Functional pass protector. Consistently productive. Very solid picking up the blitz and squaring up to help in pass protection (see Alabama). Did not drop a ball thrown his way in 2015.

Weaknesses: Has a relatively thin lower body and does not generate power through his legs — is not a pile-driver or true bellcow. Pitter patters in the hole and dances more than necessary. Was seldom a factor as a receiver. Lacks home-run speed and does not have a distinct wow factor or elite trait. Was shut down against Alabama. Fumbling issues have plagued his career and must learn to better protect the football. Was used very lightly as a receiver. Recorded a 28 1/2-inch vertical jump at the Combine, the lowest among backs.

Future: Good-sized, finesse, pick-and-slide runner in a similar mold as Bears 2005 first-round pick Cedric Benson, who produced like a fourth-rounder in the pros and struggled to live up to expectations in large part because of fumbling issues and the lack of any defining elite trait. Has the size, feet and run skill to contribute readily if he can stay focused and learn to correct his fumbling flaw.

Draft projection: Third- to fourth-round pick.

Scout's take: "He is a between-the-tackles (runner). Those guys are coming back in vogue in the league. It's hard to find guys that can get yardage off-tackle. He needs more strength, but he is tough, has upside and you have to draft him earlier than you would like because he has feet."

RB MARSHAUN COPRICH, #25 (Sr-4)

ILLINOIS STATE   ▶ GRADE: 4.87

Ht: 5-8 | Wt: 207 | 40: 4.46 | Arm: 29 5/8 | Hand: 9

History: Married. Prepped in California, and was lightly recruited because of his location (edge of Mojave Desert) and test scores. As a true freshman in 2012, had 15 rushes for 70 yards (4.7-yard average) and zero touchdowns, while returning 11 kickoffs for 256 yards (23.3-yard average) in 13 games. Started 8-of-11 games in '13, producing 221-885-9 (4.0) rushing and 6-99 (16.5) returning kickoffs. Broke out in '14 when he led the Redbirds to the FCS national championship game and set school single-season records for rushing yards, rushing touchdowns, rushing yards per game (151.6), points scored (162) and total touchdowns (27) — started all 15 games and piled up 370-2,274-27 (6.1) rushing, while catching 15 balls for 54 yards (3.6-yard average) and zero touchdowns. Was arrested in April '15 for selling nine grams of marijuana to a police informant — was suspended for a month, lost his team captaincy and placed on first offender probation, meaning the conviction will be stricken from his record if he successfully completes two years on probation. On the season, totaled 321-1,967-23 (6.1) on the ground and 18-179-1 (9.9) out of the backfield. Two-time Missouri Valley Conference Player of the Year owns ISU career records for rushing yards (5,196), all-purpose yards (5,429) and touchdowns (60). Had 11 career fumbles in 978 touches.

Strengths: Good eyes and anticipation to see the cutback and instinctively find open running lanes. Runs hard with a low center of gravity. Terrific balance to sift through ankle tackles at the second and third levels. Fairly creative in the open field with a knack for darting through openings. Carried a full workload. Outstanding career production.

Weaknesses: Marginal inside runner with limited tackle-breaking ability and run strength — goes down easy on contact. Gets overpowered as a blocker. Did not regularly match up vs. top competition in the Missouri

Valley Conference and much of his production was blocked for him with wide running lanes that allowed him to produce long gains untouched. Recorded the slowest 60-yard shuttle time (12.09 seconds) of any back at the Combine. Was shut down against Iowa, South Dakota State and Richmond. Off-field transgression will require closer scrutiny.

Future: A compactly built, FCS workhorse who will need space to operate in the pros and could be best operating in a zone-based ground game. Will be challenged to produce against better competition.

Draft projection: Priority free agent.

RB KENNETH DIXON, #28 (Sr-4)

LOUISIANA TECH ▶ GRADE: 5.52
Ht: 5-10 1/8 | Wt: 215 | 40: 4.62 | Arm: 31 | Hand: 9

History: Has a daughter. Also played basketball as a prep in Arkansas, where he was named "Mr. Football" after winning a state championship and setting the state's single-season record with 3,153 yards and 39 touchdowns. Made an immediate impact in 2012 — was first-team All-Western Athletic Conference after breaking Marshall Faulk's NCAA freshman record for touchdowns (28). Carried 200 times for 1,194 yards (6.0-yard average) and 27 touchdowns while adding 10 receptions for 35 yards (3.5-yard average) and one touchdown in 12 games (five starts). In '13, started 8-of-10 games played and had 151-917-4 (6.1) rushing and 14-85-1 (6.1) receiving. Sprained his left MCL against Lamar and was limited the following week against Tulane, then missed the final two contests because of a high ankle sprain. Started 13-of-14 games in '14 and posted 253-1,299-22 (5.1) on the ground with 30-385-6 (12.8) out of the backfield. Did not start in the Conference USA championship game against Marshall after reportedly suffering a minor injury during pregame warmups. Was the Ragin' Cajuns' leading rusher for the fourth consecutive season in '15 — ran 197-1,070-19 (5.4) and caught 34-467-7 13.7). Missed two October contests and did not start a third while nursing an ankle injury. Claimed school records with 4,480 rushing yards and 72 rushing touchdowns, and his 87 total scores ranks second in NCAA history. Team captain. Had 13 career fumbles in 889 touches.

Strengths: Very good eyes to navigate through traffic and turn 2-yard losses into 8-yard gains. Runs with urgency, will drop his shoulder and drive through contact with good leg drive (see Kansas State). Has a strong stiff-arm and will deliver punishment before stepping out

of bounds. Good balance, short-area burst and acceleration — makes sharp speed cuts. Elusive in space and can shake defenders out of their shoes (see FIU and Humanitarian Bowl). Very solid after-contact production. Effective operating out of the slot, with excellent hands and concentration in a crowd — was a red-zone weapon. Has a nose for the end zone. Competitive, willing blocker effective cutting blitzers. Unselfish, team player. Has a pleaser personality. Outstanding all-around work ethic. Has a 37 1/2-inch vertical jump.

Weaknesses: Has thin legs that could be more susceptible to injury when factoring his aggressive running temperament. Lacks elite, top-end speed to pull away in the open field and could be tracked down from behind. Was not challenged heavily in Conference USA. Needs to do a much better job of securing the football.

Future: A tough, highly competitive, four-year producer with a unique blend of hands, elusiveness and physicality to factor in all phases of an offense. More quick than fast, Dixon could be best utilized as a top-tier receiving back and change-of-pace threat. One of the best receiving backs in the draft, Dixon has soft hands to contribute immediately as a complementary third-down back and is tough enough to carry a heavy workload if needed.

Draft projection: Third- to fourth-round pick.

Coach's take: "I talk more about the intangibles and the character he brings to the program when you look at the passion he plays with, the leadership he brings, almost the youthful innocence with the way he plays the game because he plays it with such a hard passion." (The News Star) – *Louisiana Tech head coach Skip Holtz*

RB/WR [F]/KR KENYAN DRAKE, #17 (Sr-4)

ALABAMA ▶ GRADE: 5.38
Ht: 6-0 5/8 | Wt: 210 | 40: 4.37 | Arm: 31 | Hand: 9

History: Was Gatorade Player of the Year in Georgia, where he also won a state championship in the 100 meters. As a true freshman in 2012, carried 42 times for 281 yards (6.7-yard average) and five touchdowns. Was suspended against Western Carolina for a violation of team rules — "It wasn't anything that was real significant or bad, but it happened once before," said head coach Nick Saban said. "He was told if he did it again that he wouldn't dress for the game." Was suspended for the '13 season opener against Virginia Tech before running 92-694-8 (7.5) and catching 12-135-1 (11.3) in 11 games (one start). Ball security issues cost him playing time late in the season, as he was benched after fumbles against Mississippi

RUNNING BACKS

State and Auburn and did not see action in the Sugar Bowl against Oklahoma. In July '14, was arrested and charged with misdemeanor obstructing governmental operations — disobeyed police orders not to cross into a crime scene, where his vehicle was parked. Served a brief suspension before being reinstated for the season — managed 22-112-4 (5.1) rushing and 5-159-2 (31.8) receiving in five games (one start) before suffering a season-ending broken right ankle injury against Ole Miss. Was behind Heisman Trophy winner Derrick Henry in '15, but contributed 77-408-1 (5.3) rushing and 29-276-1 (9.5) receiving in 13 games (four starts) for the national champs. Added 19 kickoff returns for 505 yards (26.6), including a 95-yard score against Clemson in the national title game. Broke his right arm against Mississippi State and did not play against Charleston Southern or Auburn (received just nine carries the final three contests). Graduated. Has seven career fumbles on 299 touches. Did not perform the 60-yard shuttle at the Combine after straining his left calf.

Strengths: Fast and explosive — can stick his foot in the dirt and accelerate to top speed in a heartbeat. Tied for the fastest 40-time (4.31) of any back at the Combine. Has home-run, finishing speed to take the perimeter, turn the corner and create game-breaking big plays in the return game (see clutch, 95-yard, game-changing kickoff return in national championship game vs. Clemson). Very reliable 90/10 catcher. Sudden route runner with slot experience, working with receivers in the spring and summer. Excels as a gunner on special teams. Broad-jumped 10-foot, 10 inches at the Combine, showing rare lower-body explosion. Booksmart and personable.

Weaknesses: Has small hands and a narrow, high-cut build with a thin lower body that is not suitable to inside running. Tends to bounce outside and miss open holes. Must learn to carry the ball high and tight and secure it with five points of pressure. Lacks bulk strength to anchor against oncoming blitzers. Only bench-pressed 10 reps at the Combine, lowest among running backs. Was never a full-time starter and lack of discipline was a consistent theme early in his career, with repeated suspensions and off-field distractions. Durability has been an issue with multiple broken bones.

Future: Lean, long-striding, big-play crease runner and explosive return man with the short-area suddenness and finishing speed to flip the field. Can make an immediate impact in the return game and as a gunner on special teams and factor as a perimeter runner if he learns to correct his fumbling flaw.

Draft projection: Fourth- to fifth-round pick.

Scout's take: "If you factor his value on special teams, maybe he pushes up to the third (round) where we have him stacked right now, but as a pure running back, I struggle seeing him as more than a fifth-rounder."

RB EZEKIEL ELLIOTT, #15 (Jr-3)

OHIO STATE ▶ GRADE: 6.54

Ht: 5-11 3/4 | Wt: 225 | 40: 4.48 | Arm: 31 1/4 | Hand: 10 1/4

History: Decorated Missouri athlete. Was a U.S. Army All-American, St. Louis offensive player of the year and three-time state runner-up at Burroughs High, where he was coached by former NFL QB Gus Frerotte. Racked up nearly 5,300 yards rushing and receiving and 90 touchdowns his final two seasons. Was also an exceptional track athlete — captured state titles in the 100 meters, 200 meters, 110-meter high hurdles and 300-meter hurdles. As a true freshman in 2013, carried 30 times for 262 yards (8.7-yard average) and two touchdowns while snagging three receptions for 23 yards (7.7-yard average) and one touchdown in 11 games played. Broke his left wrist during '14 fall camp, had surgery and carried the ball in his right hand during his breakout sophomore season for the national champion Buckeyes —started 14-of-15 games, amassing 273-1,878-18 (6.9) rushing and 28-220-0 (7.9) receiving. Named Championship game MVP after rushing 36-246-4 against Alabama. Ceded the start against Illinois to Curtis Samuel, who was rewarded for his "extremely high level" practice performance. Had his left wrist surgically repaired again in February '15, sitting out spring practice. Was the Big Ten Offensive Player of the Year in the fall — started all 13 games and toted 289-1,821-23 (6.3) with 27-206-0 (7.6) receiving. Also returned two punts for 13 yards (6.5-yard average). Spent two days in the hospital leading up to the Michigan State contest because of a leg infection and 103-degree fever. Openly criticized the coaching staff's playcalling following the team's only loss to Michigan State after not receiving enough carries. Passed Eddie George for second place on OSU's all-time rushing list. Produced at least 100 yards in 22 of his 39 career games. Has four career fumbles in 653 touches. Opted not to perform shuttles at the Combine and wrist injury prevented him from benchpressing.

Strengths: Excellent balance and vision. Hits the hole hard, runs through arm tackles

RUNNING BACKS

and fearlessly attacks the A gaps. Very good competitive playing speed and is capable of breaking big runs and taking the perimeter. Runs with urgency downhill, yet with enough patience to follow his blocks and be his own blocker. Excellent effort as a blocker and will continually seek defenders to pick off — exceptional finisher with a tenacious finishing style (see blocking vs. Michigan State). Good ball security. Highly driven and motivated. Reliable hands. Physically and mentally tough and battles through injuries. Has risen to the occasion on the biggest of stages. Very durable, playing through wrist and ankle (taped) injuries during championship sophomore season.

Weaknesses: Lacks elite, breakaway speed to consistently pull away and can be tracked down from behind. Will need to learn how to protect his body better and preserve himself in the pros. Seldom used on routes beyond flares and is not a nuanced receiver or natural hands-catcher, as confirmed in drills at the Combine, where he let the ball into the frame of his body and fought it. Must learn to better manage his emotions following defeat. Wrist injury history could require closer medical scrutiny.

Future: A tough, extremely competitive, every-down back capable of factoring as an inside runner, outside receiver and most uniquely in pass protection. The most complete, all-around back to enter the draft in the last decade, Elliott is an immediate impact performer capable of elevating the performance of a team and unselfishly contributing as much without the ball as he does with it. Strong, decisive bellcow back with a special blend of eyes, instincts and balance to blast the best defenses.

Draft projection: Top-15 pick.

Scout's take: "He is a very smart football player. He can come off the field and tell the coaches how to roll protections and make corrections to man-blocking assignments. He tells them how to pick up the blitz. That is what separates him from the rest. There are not many backs in the league smart enough to do that. For him to be able to diagnose the way he does in college is rare."

RB/WR[F]/KR **TYLER ERVIN**, #7 (Sr-5)
SAN JOSE STATE   ▶ GRADE: 5.17

Ht: 5-9⅞ | Wt: 192 | 40: 4.41 | Arm: 29¾ | Hand: 9⅛

History: Played running back, defensive back and kick returner as a California prep. Played all 12 games as a true freshman in 2011 and carried 29 times for 107 yards (3.7-

yard average) and one touchdown and caught three balls for 17 yards (5.7-yard average) and zero touchdowns. Also was the Spartans' primary kickoff returner — had 28 returns for 672 yards (24.0-yard average), including one score. In '12, rushed 45-205-1 (4.5), caught 10-126-1 (12.6) and returned kickoffs 22-599-2 (27.2). Fractured his right collarbone against Texas State and missed four November contests. Ervin's 2013 season ended after two carries, as he suffered a season-ending fractured right ankle injury. Played all 12 games in '14, starting the final eight, and totaled 158-888-4 (5.6) rushing and 29-306-1 (10.6) receiving. Also returned kickoffs 26-506-0 (19.5) and punts 7-81-1 (11.6). Healthy in '13, started all 13 games and ranked second nationally in all-purpose yardage (2,637) — set SJSU single-season records for rushing yards and all-purpose yards by producing 294-1,601-13 (5.4) on the ground, 45-334-2 (7.4) out of the backfield, 25-597-0 (23.9) on kickoffs and 7-105-1 (15.0) on punts. Had 371 touches on the season. Finished his career as the Spartans' career leader for all-purpose yards (6,146), kickoff return yards (2,734) and return touchdowns (five). Team captain graduated with a communications degree. Has five fumbles in 730 career touches. Did not perform shuttles at the Combine because of a right calf injury.

Strengths: Explosive first-step — presses the line with squared shoulders and runs bigger than his size. Patient inside runner — follows his blocks. Good agility to dart through traffic and find lanes. Showed he could carry a full workload despite his lack of size (see 27-161-1 vs Auburn and 42-300-3 vs. Fresno). Very reliable 90/10 catcher. Recorded a 39-inch vertical jump at the Combine. Versatile — has some experience at cornerback and as a cover man on special teams.

Weaknesses: Thinly built, high-cut and lacks run strength to push the pile. Runs upright and leaves his body vulnerable to some hard hits. Does not have the bulk strength to withstand the rigors of running between the tackles. Gets re-routed and outmuscled easily in the slot (see Auburn). Has broken multiple bones, and long-term durability could become an issue. Underpowered blocker.

Future: An explosive space player most ideally utilized on screens, counters and perimeter runs for a creative offense such as the Steelers or Chiefs. Could also contribute situationally as a one-cut, zone runner and has the versatility to factor readily returning kicks and punts and mismatching linebackers in the

RUNNING BACKS

slot.

Draft projection: Late draftable pick.

Scout's take: "He looked (extremely) tiny to me when I went through the school. I thought he was a free agent. … There was a buzz on him during the all-star games because he is so fast. Someone will draft him."

RB/KR **JOSH FERGUSON**, #6 (Sr-5)

ILLINOIS ▶ GRADE: 5.26

Ht: 5-9½ | Wt: 198 | 40: 4.47 | Arm: 30 | Hand: 9

History: Illinois native starred at prep powerhouse Joliet Catholic Academy. As a true freshman in 2011, recorded 14 carries for 52 yards (3.7-yard average) and zero touchdowns and two receptions for 14 yards (7.0-yard average) and zero touchdowns before suffering a season-ending torn left hamstring injury (granted medical hardship). Returned to start 6-of-10 games played in '12, toting 75-312-0 (4.2) and catching 29-251-0 (8.7). Also returned 19 kickoffs for 344 yards (18.1-yard average) and threw a 22-yard touchdown pass. Did not play against Charleston Southern (concussion) or Ohio State (hip pointer). Set U of I's single-season record for receiving yards by a running back in '13 — started 8-of-12 games and recorded 141-779-7 (5.5) rushing and 50-535-4 (10.7) receiving. Also returned two kickoffs for 37 yards (18.5-yard average). Started 9-of-13 games in '14 and had 146-735-8 (5.0) on the ground and 50-427-2 (8.5) out of the backfield. Was the Illini's Most Outstanding Player in '15 after amassing 129-708-3 (5.5) rushing and 37-280-2 (7.6) receiving. In the process, passed Pierre Thomas for second on U of I's career all-purpose yardage list (4,474). Injured his right shoulder against Nebraska and missed three games. Team captain graduated with a kinesiology degree. Has 11 career fumbles in 694 touches. Did not perform shuttles at the Combine after pulling his right hamstring during his first positional drill.

Strengths: Nifty-footed with superb balance and lateral agility to shake tacklers in the hole, spin out of trouble and make defenders miss. Deft body control and burst to pull a rabbit out of a hat and create some magic in the open field. Very good eyes and spatial awareness to cut back against the grain and follow his blocks. Strong pound-for-pound. Natural hands — can pluck it with one hand and make difficult grabs look easy. Very productive career catcher (168 career catches). Intelligent and football smart.

Weaknesses: Modest size with a maxed-out frame. Pitter patters too much and loses yardage at times trying to be overly creative. Limited tackle-breaking power and finishing strength. Lacks savvy as a route runner — gears down and signals routes. Struggles escaping man coverage from the slot. Lacks the bulk to be effective blocking. Does not play through injuries and taps out for soft-tissue injuries. Has some diva qualities. Ball security needs to improve — leaves the ball exposed on contact too often, leading to fumbles.

Future: Dynamic athlete with the balance, body control and agility to create with the ball in his hands when his mind is right. Flashes playmaking ability, though highlight-reel runs must strongly outnumber lost fumbles before he earns the trust of NFL coaches.

Draft projection: Fourth- to fifth-round pick.

Scout's take: "Talent-wise, he looks like a future star. My concern is longevity. You wonder if he has been saving himself for the NFL with some of the phantom injuries that have kept him out. The National Football League is for full-grown men. I'm not sure he is tough enough to play in this league."

FB/H-Back **GLENN GRONKOWSKI**, #48 (Jr-4)

KANSAS STATE ▶ GRADE: 5.16

Ht: 6-2⅛ | Wt: 239 | 40: 4.72 | Arm: 30¾ | Hand: 9½

History: Nicknamed "Goose." Brother, Rob, is an All-Pro tight end for the Patriots and brothers Chris and Dan had cups of coffee in the NFL. Glenn prepped in western New York, where he played receiver and safety — caught 125 balls for 2,076 yards (16.6-yard average) and 23 touchdowns during his high school career. Was lightly recruited before signing with KSU to play for offensive coordinator Dana Dimel, who coached Glenn's brothers Rob and Chris at Arizona. Grayshirted in 2011 then redshirted in '12. Transitioned to fullback for the Wildcats, and played all 39 games the next three seasons — made four starts in '13; three starts in '14; and 13 starts in '15. Totaled 16 career rushes for 51 yards (3.2-yard average) and one touchdown and 15 career receptions for 369 yards (24.6-yard average) and five touchdowns. Also tossed a four-yard touchdown pass. Graduated cum laude with a degree in marketing and management.

Strengths: Versatile and aligns all over the field — H-back, fullback, tight end and slot receiver. Fast enough to threaten the seam. Efficient cut blocker. Functional positional/sustain blocker to seal linebackers on the move. Flashes some savvy as a route runner. Has NFL pedigree. Takes a business-like approach to the game.

Weaknesses: Very short arms with an underdeveloped frame. Marginal run strength and run-after-the-catch creativity. Not an aggressive isolation lead-blocker or true hammer — takes a tentative approach and has marginal peripheral lead-blocking vision. Limited hip snap and explosive power to strike linebackers. Only bench-pressed 225 pounds 17 times at the Combine and needs to get functionally stronger. Has 60/40 hands and needs to become more confident catching cleanly.

Future: A finesse, athletic fullback who must prove capable of making a mark on special teams to secure a roster spot.

Draft projection: Late draftable pick.

RB DERRICK HENRY, #2 (Jr-3)

ALABAMA ▶ GRADE: 5.92

Ht: 6-2 5/8 | Wt: 247 | 40: 4.54 | Arm: 33 | Hand: 8 3/4

History: Born to teenage parents and raised primarily by his grandparents. Prepped in Florida, where he garnered consensus All-American honors and multiple national player of the year awards after breaking the national rushing record with 12,124 career yards. Joined Alabama in 2013 as an early enrollee, but suffered a broken fibula during a spring scrimmage. As a true freshman, carried 35 times for 382 yards (10.9-yard average) and three touchdowns in 12 games played. Added one reception for 61 yards (61.0-yard average) and one touchdown in the Sugar Bowl against Oklahoma. In '14, rushed 172-990-11 (5.8) and caught 5-133-2 (26.6) in 14 games (two starts). In '15, won the Heisman Trophy, Doak Walker and Maxwell Awards and was named Walter Camp Player of the Year and Southeastern Conference Offensive Player of the Year. Broke the SEC single-season rushing and rushing touchdowns records and led the nation in attempts (fifth-highest total in NCAA history), yards and rushing touchdowns — piled up 395-2,219-28 (5.6) and snagged 11-91-0 (8.3) in 15 starts for the national champion Crimson Tide. Joined Herschel Walker and Bo Jackson as the only backs in SEC history to post four 200-yard games in a season. Team captain. Has five career fumbles in 619 touches.

Strengths: Rare size with exceptional speed for as big as he is — can open up his stride in space and eat ground. Intimidating punisher with good inside running power. Gets better with a lather and wears down defenses in the second half. Ideal four-minute back capable of grinding out the clock. Has long arms and a wide catching radius. Exceptional production against Southeastern Conference competition. Eye-popping Combine workout results — produced a 37-inch vertical jump and 10-foot, 10-inch broad jump while clocking in the low 4.5's in the 40-yard dash at nearly 250 pounds.

Weaknesses: Galloping long-strider. Very high cut and leggy. Almost too tall for the RB position — linear, upright running style and overall body stiffness will leave his lower body very susceptible to big hits in the pros. Runs a bit narrow-based — is not sudden off spots, gears down to cut and lacks lateral agility. Lacks home-run, finishing speed. Developing pass protector and receiver that was seldom used in the passing game. Bodies the ball too much and is not a natural hands catcher. Absorbed a lot of contact averaging 30-plus carries as a junior. Ran behind a much more dominant O-line in college than he might experience in the pros.

Future: A straight-line, downhill, power runner with the sheer force to crease defenses between the tackles, Henry is a physical specimen that looks like he was born to rush the passer more than carry the rock. Has a similar running style to St. Louis Rams 2004 first-round pick (24th overall) Steven Jackson and would be an ideal fit for an offense premised on power, such as the Panthers or Cowboys. Will make his mark creating tough yardage. Limited contributions as a receiver and blocker could lessen his value. Unorthodox dimensions and huge body surface area could be more likely to create durability issues.

Draft projection: Top-50 pick.

Scout's take: "The wildcard of the draft is Henry. Scouts are all over the boat with him. Some graded him in the first round in our building. Some have him in the fourth. You can contradict yourself from one play to the next writing him up — he is one of the most consistently inconsistent players I have written. I have never seen a body like his before — it's the oddest I have ever seen. From afar, he looks almost like an alien, with long arms like a defensive end, a six-pack (stomach) like a receiver and the longest tibia-to-fibia I have ever seen. I've never even seen it that long on basketball players. He almost looks elastic with how long his knee is to the ground. You get up close and he's shredded with big biceps, a tapered waist, a v-back and a six-pack. It's crazy. You're going to think I'm nuts, but I would like to work him out as a defensive end."

RUNNING BACKS

FB QUAYVON HICKS, #48 (Sr-4)

GEORGIA ▶ GRADE: 4.97

Ht: 6-07/8 | Wt: 239 | 40: 4.72 | Arm: 311/4 | Hand: 95/8

History: Georgia native also wrestled and competed in track and field, in addition to playing fullback, tight end, defensive line and linebacker. As a true freshman in 2012, saw limited action — primarily on special teams — without recording any stats in 12 games. Did not play against Florida (concussion). Was recognized as the Bulldogs' most improved offensive player in '13 when he started 6-of-13 games — rushed 10 times for 72 yards (7.2-yard average) and one touchdown and caught five balls for 67 yards (13.4-yard average) and zero touchdowns. Started 6-of-13 games in '14, recording 9-85-2 (9.4) rushing and 4-31-0 (7.8) receiving. Also returned three kickoffs for 26 yards (8.7-yard average). In '15, logged 4-9-0 (2.2) on the ground and 3-34-0 (11.3) out of the backfield in 12 games (three starts). Did not play in the Bulldogs' bowl game against Penn State (knee) and also was medically excluded from participating at the Combine because of it.

Strengths: Outstanding size with a thick, well-distributed frame and well-developed muscularity. Functional lead blocker. Excellent weight-room strength. Tough and competitive. Capable short-yardage/goalline plunger. Flashed enough run skills and physicality to be cross-trained as a tailback and also saw time as an H-Back and tight end.

Weaknesses: Very tightly wound with limited body control and agility. Struggles to unlock his hips and gauge his power. Marginal functional football-playing speed. Not a natural knee bender. Lacks awareness and is late to locate blocking targets. Stiff route runner. Limited run vision and skill.

Future: A robotic, straight-line, throwback fullback with special teams' experience. Will need to carve out a role on special teams to stick on a roster.

Draft projection: Priority free agent.

RB JORDAN HOWARD, #8 (Jr-3)

INDIANA ▶ GRADE: 5.45

Ht: 5-117/8 | Wt: 230 | 40: 4.65e | Arm: 321/4 | Hand: 9

History: Wore No. 7 at UAB. Jordan's father, Reginald, died of pulmonary fibrosis when Jordan was 12 (also lost two grandparents in same six-month timespan). Prepped in Alabama. Endured a hip injury between his junior and senior years which limited his exposure to recruiters. Began his college career at Alabama-Birmingham (wore jersey No. 7). As a true freshman in 2013, started 5-of-11 games and carried 145 times for 881 yards (6.1-yard average) and two touchdowns and had four receptions for 83 yards (20.8-yard average) and one touchdown. Dressed in the season opener against Troy, but did not see action. Missed '14 spring practice with a shoulder injury. Played all 12 games, starting the final 11, and toted 306-1,587-13 (5.2) and snagged 9-72-1 (8.0). Did not start the season opener against Troy then was forced out of the Alabama A&M contest with an eye injury. The UAB football program was shut down, enabling Howard to transfer with immediate eligibility. Struck an instant connection with IU running backs coach Deland McCullough, who offered the chance to replace Tevin Coleman (Falcons '15 third-rounder). With the Hoosiers in '15, produced 196-1,213-9 (6.2) on the ground with 11-106-1 (9.6) out of the backfield. Sprained his left ankle against Ohio State, causing him to miss October contests against Penn State and Rutgers then suffered a knee injury against Maryland and sat out the final two games against Purdue and Duke. Has six career fumbles in 672 touches. Opted not to run at the Combine.

Strengths: Outstanding size with a thick trunk. Runs behind his pads, can deliver bruising hits and keep churning his legs. Runs with good forward lean to barrel through arm tackles. Good run vision. So strong in the lower body that it takes a full defense to bring him down (see Michigan). Effective inside runner — good feet in tight quarters. Finishes runs. Very productive and piled up yardage against stout defenses (35-238-2 vs. Michigan) despite regularly seeing stacked boxes.

Weaknesses: A bit of a short-stepper with tightness in his hips — gears to cut, does not open up his stride in the open field and gets caught from behind. Cannot string moves together and shows little gear change. Leaves his lower body susceptible to a lot of square hits and long-term durability needs to be a consideration. Seldom used as a receiver and did not appear natural catching at the Combine. Could stand to learn more nuances of pass protection and blitz pickup. Shut down against Ohio State. Only bench-pressed 225 pounds 16 times at the Combine.

Future: A big, strong, competitive chunk runner with bruising power to produce tough yardage between the tackles and wear down defenses. Lack of elusiveness on the second level could invite durability issues.

Draft projection: Third- to fourth-round pick.

Scout's take: "He is a second-round pick to me. He is an NFL back. When did Leveon Bell go, in the second (round)? That is what this kid is. He's thick with strong hips and (the) feet to get in and out of traffic. He has some build-up speed once he gets running. He is a load."

FB ANDY JANOVICH, #35 (Sr-4)

NEBRASKA ▶ GRADE: 5.12
Ht: 6-1 | Wt: 238 | 40: 4.78 | Arm: 31 5/8 | Hand: 9 3/4

History: Running back-linebacker who also won a pair of state wrestling championships — went a combined 99-0 in the 189-pound and 220-pound weight classes — as a Nebraska prep. Joined the Huskers as a preferred walk-on, but played as a true freshman in 2012 — logged three carries for six yards (2.0-yard average) and zero interceptions and two catches for 13 yards (6.5-yard average) and zero interceptions in 11 games (two starts). Earned a scholarship prior to the '13 season when he played all 13 games without recording any stats. Played all 13 games in '14, drawing starts in the final two, and caught 1-16-1 (16.0). In '15, started 6-of-13 games and produced 42-265-3 (6.3) rushing and 2-58-0 (29.0) receiving. Also contributed 13 tackles and a blocked punt on special teams. Had five career kickoff returns for 69 yards (13.8-yard average).

Strengths: Excellent special teams temperament — attacks blockers fearlessly and beelines to the ball. Assignment sound. Has a good feel for angles and leverage. Adequate vision and functional straight-line power as a runner and lead blocker. Keeps legs churning through contact and is effective in short-yardage and goalline situations. Bench-pressed 225 pounds 30 times at the Combine and is extremely strong pound for pound. Caught the ball well at the Combine. Unselfish, team player.

Weaknesses: Not naturally big-boned. Tightly wound. Runs upright. Builds to speed. Lacks bulk and base strength — is not a blow-up isolation blocker or sledgehammer short-yardage back. Seldom used as a receiver with five career catches.

Future: Self-made, try-hard overachiever who makes the most of each opportunity. Has the making of a core special-teams standout and situational West Coast fullback, capable of contributing as a short-yardage runner and positional move blocker. Is the type of player who will be difficult to cut.

Draft projection: Priority free agent.

RB/FB DEVON JOHNSON, #47 (Sr-4)

MARSHALL ▶ GRADE: 5.07
Ht: 6-0 1/2 | Wt: 238 | 40: 4.75e | Arm: 31 1/4 | Hand: 9 1/4

History: Prepped in Virginia. Prior to his junior season in high school, Devon lost his father to a heart attack. During the season, dislocated his thumb and sustained a high ankle sprain. Running back-linebacker was the state's Group AA Offensive Player of the Year. Played tight end as a true freshman in 2012, recording three receptions for 21 yards (7.0-yard average) and one touchdown in 11 games. Also tallied 11 special teams tackles and one forced fumble. In '13, snagged 12-218-2 (18.2) and carried five times for 13 yards (2.6-yard average) and three touchdowns. Added 13 special teams tackles. Moved to running back in '14 and was the team's leading rusher — started all 12 games played and produced 206 carries for 1,767 yards (8.6-yard average) and 17 touchdowns while catching 6-121-2 (20.2). Strained his left knee against Florida Atlantic and did not play against Southern Miss, then suffered a torn left labrum against Western Kentucky which limited him the final three contests. Had surgery after the season and was limited during '15 spring practice. In the fall, started 6-of-7 games played and managed 94-593-5 (6.3) rushing and 6-63-1 (10.5 receiving). Missed six games and parts of others because of back and ankle injuries. Had five fumbles in 332 touches. Was a medical exclusion at the Combine for a left upper extremity injury.

Strengths: Very good lower-body strength and run balance — does not go down easy and carries piles with him. Short-yardage plower — can outmuscle defenders as an inside runner, with very good leg churn. Plays with aggression. Terrific game-day competitor. Outstanding weight-room work habits. Runs through defensive backs if he clears the first wave. Very dependable catcher. Strong pass protector with good anchor strength — steps up to fill holes and takes on linebackers with authority.

Weaknesses: Has small hands and is not a natural catcher. Runs upright with limited knee extension to open up his stride. Marginal functional speed and lateral agility to hit the perimeter cleanly. Not sudden off spots. Only knows one speed. Limited eyes and anticipation to see holes uncovering and leaves production on the field. Needs to do a better job of securing the football in traffic, carrying it away from his body.

Future: Big, strong, broad-shouldered, lumbering, dinosaur runner who made his junior season his best after converting from tight end, yet profiles as a fullback in the pros. Has overcome a lot of adversity to get where he is and identifies with the game. Passion for the game could allow him to stick on a roster

RUNNING BACKS

in a limited role.

Draft projection: Priority free agent.

RB DANIEL LASCO, #2 (Sr-5)

CALIFORNIA ▶ GRADE: 5.14

Ht: 6-0¼ | Wt: 209 | 40: 4.44 | Arm: 32 | Hand: 9⅛

History: California native. Redshirted in 2011 and was named Co-Scout Team Player of the Year. Earned Most Valuable Special Teams Player in '12 — carried just six times for 109 yards (18.2-yard average) and one touchdown, but notched 12 tackles and two forced fumbles on special teams. Sat out '13 spring practice because of a shoulder injury. In the fall, ran 67-317-2 (4.7) and caught 11 balls for 78 yards (7.1-yard average) and zero touchdowns in eight games (one start). Did not play against Portland State (left hamstring strain), then missed the Oregon State, Washington and Colorado contests (sprained right AC joint). Was the Bears' MVP in '14 after producing 210-1,115-12 (5.3) on the ground with 33-356-2 (10.8) out of the backfield in 12 games (11 starts). Was part of a running back committee in '15, contributing 65-331-3 (5.1) rushing and 4-24-0 (6.0) receiving. Missed September games against Texas and Washington (strained right hip muscle), as well as November contests against Stanford and Arizona State (ankle). Had five career kickoff returns for 65 yards (15.0-yard average). Two-year captain graduated with a sociology degree. Had nine career fumbles in 401 touches.

Strengths: Explosive athlete, as confirmed with exceptional workout results. Produced a Combine-best 41 1/2-inch vertical jump (tied with Jalen Ramsey) and 11-foot, 3-inch broad jump, the best of any back at the Combine the last decade. Quick and agile with the short-area burst and acceleration to turn the corner. Nifty in space to sidestep defenders and step out of and spin away from some tackles. Good finishing speed once he hits the clear. Bench-pressed 225 pounds 23 times — very strong for his size. Proven special-teams performer early in college career. Soft hands. Willing in pass protection.

Weaknesses: Takes choppy steps and runs small. Lacks finishing strength and goes down easy on initial contact — is not a strong tackle-breaker. Marginal YAC production. Takes too many direct hits given his upright running style, and long-term durability is concerning. Only one year of standout production. Dances too much inside, misses holes and runs with indecision. Average eyes and run instincts —

likes to bounce outside. Needs to carry the ball more securely.

Future: An upright, one-cut, zone runner coming from a Cal program that consistently has churned out some fine unheralded rushing talent (Justin Forsett, CJ Anderson) the last decade on top of game changers such as Marshawn Lynch and Shane Vereen. Lasco is most ideally suited for a special-teams role in the pros, though he has the hands and burst to contribute more heavily in a receiving role. Will require some time to acclimate to the NFL and must prove he can stay healthy and secure the ball to earn a roster spot.

Draft projection: Priority free agent.

RB CURTIS "TRE" MADDEN, #23 (Sr-5)

USC ▶ GRADE: 4.91

Ht: 6-0¼ | Wt: 223 | 40: 4.55e | Arm: 29¾ | Hand: 9⅜

History: Grandfather, Lawrence McCutcheon, was a 10-year NFL running back (1872-81) and an All-Pro with the Rams; and uncle, Daylon McCutcheon, was a seven-year NFL cornerback with the Browns (1999-2005). Tre was born in Texas before moving to California when he was seven. Garnered USA Today and U.S. Army All-American honors as a linebacker (was also used as a "Wildcat" quarterback). Missed four games his senior season because of a foot injury then separated his shoulder in the final game of the season. As a true freshman in 2011, served as a backup linebacker and recorded 15 tackles, one for loss and zero sacks in 12 games (one start). Switched to running back in '12, but tore his left ACL during spring practice. Played 11 games in '13, starting the first six, and carried 138 times for 703 yards (5.1-yard average) and three touchdowns with 15 receptions for 201 yards (13.4-yard average) and four touchdowns. Strained his left hamstring against Arizona and did not play against Notre Dame or California. Also sat out the Las Vegas Bowl against Fresno State because of an ankle injury. Did not play in '14 because of a sesamoid fracture of his right toe (turf toe). Played 10 games in '15, starting the first six, and logged 85-452-5 (5.3) on the ground and 17-133-1 (7.8) out of the backfield. Missed four second-half contests and was limited in others because of a knee bone bruise. Won team awards for commitment and weightlifting. Graduated with a communications degree and was working on a second in sociology. Was medically excluded from running at the Combine because of left knee injury.

Strengths: Rare-sized back — has a solid frame with good muscularity throughout his body and looks the part. Runs hard through contact, makes subtle cutbacks and stay on his feet through traffic. Good balance to lower his shoulder and fall forward in short-yardage situations. Very competitive and business-like in his approach. Football smart. Has NFL pedigree. Linebacker experience as a freshman will help translate to special teams.

Weaknesses: Straight-linish with an upright running style and limited creativity that translates to frequent injuries. Takes time to get rolling and tends to build to speed — makes few tacklers miss in the box or the open field. Durability is a serious concern, keeping him from ever being a full-time starter.

Future: A big, finesse weaver who has been snake-bitten by injuries throughout his career and must shake his china doll reputation in his first NFL training camp to have a chance of sticking in the pros. Has intriguing size, vision and power to factor readily when healthy, though odds are more in favor of becoming waived injured than emerging as a late-round gem. Durability will define his pro career. Special teams will have to be his ticket.

Draft projection: Fifth- to sixth-round pick.

Scout's take: "The guy I wish was healthy more is No. 23 because I think he is talented. He is big, pretty strong and deceptively fast, but he has been hurt all year and all his career. He's a middle-round talent who will go later because of the longevity concerns. He should get drafted."

RB / KR KEITH MARSHALL, #4 (Jr-4)
GEORGIA ▶ GRADE: 5.22
Ht: 5-113/8 | Wt: 219 | 40: 4.33 | Arm: 315/8 | Hand: 93/8

History: Father, Warren, was James Madison's all-time leading rusher before being drafted by the Broncos in the sixth round of the 1987 draft. Keith was highly recruited out of North Carolina, where he was the state's Gatorade Player of the Year and a 100-meter state champion. As a true freshman in 2012, carried 117 times for 759 yards (6.5-yard average) and eight touchdowns with 11 receptions for 91 yards (8.3-yard average) and one touchdown in 14 games (one start). In '13, managed 56-246-1 (4.4) rushing and 8-111-1 (13.9) receiving in five games (one start) before suffering a torn right ACL injury. In '14, ran 12-24-0 (2.0) in three games before right knee and ankle injuries ended his season. Rehabbed for the better part of two years. Shared the backfield with Sony Michel and Nick Chubb in '15 when he ran 68-350-3 (5.1). Sat out against Auburn and

Georgia Southern because of an ankle injury. Graduated with a finance degree. Entered the draft despite potentially having another year of eligibility. Fumbled twice in 278 career touches, both as a freshman. Injured his right hamstring during positional drills and did not perform shuttles at the Combine.

Strengths: Extremely explosive in a straight-line and shows the speed to go the distance. Combine workout warrior — blazed the fastest 40-yard time of any player at the event and bench-pressed 225 pounds 25 times. Has a lot of tread left on his tires from playing in an overcrowded backfield.

Weaknesses: Lacks the lateral agility and niftiness to step off the track and avoid collisions, contributing to a host of injuries throughout his career that have limited his playing time. China doll. Runs small and narrow-based. Marginal career production. Recorded a 30 1/2-inch vertical jump, second lowest among backs at the Combine. Has never been a full-time starter.

Future: A stiff-hipped, straight-line runner who burst onto the scene as a freshman and flashed big-play potential before taking a backseat to a stable of the most talented backs in the country featuring 2015 NFL Offensive Rookie of the Year Todd Gurley, Nick Chubb and Sony Michel. Could turn out to be a surprise producer in the pros similar to Bills 2015 fifth-rounder Karlos Williams if healthy.

Draft projection: Priority free agent.

Scout's take: "He is a backup. He's a straight-line runner. What's he had, 15 carries in his career? I'd like to see a greater body of work."

RB PAUL PERKINS II, #24 (Jr-4)
UCLA ▶ GRADE: 5.42
Ht: 5-103/8 | Wt: 208 | 40: 4.53 | Arm: 315/8 | Hand: 9

History: Father, Bruce, played four games as a fullback for the Buccaneers and Colts (1990-91); uncle Don, was a Pro Bowl running back/fullback for Cowboys (1961-68); and younger brother, Bryce, is a quarterback at Arizona State. Paul prepped in Arizona, where he was part of two state champion track teams. Redshirted in 2012. Played all 13 games in each of the next three seasons. In '13, carried 134 times for 573 yards (4.3-yard average) and six touchdowns and had 24 receptions for 296 yards (12.3-yard average) and zero touchdowns (four starts). In '14, was the first Bruin to lead the Pac-12 in rushing since DeShaun Foster in '01 — totaled 251-1,575-9 (6.3) on the ground and 26-201-2 (7.7) out of the backfield (11 starts). Started all 13 games in '15 and recorded 237-1,343-14 (5.7) rushing and 30-242-1 (8.1) receiving. Exited the California contest after hurting his left knee. Needed just three seasons to become UCLA's all-time receptions leader for running backs (80). Team captain. Pulled up with a left hamstring injury while running the 40-yard dash at the Combine. Has five career fumbles on 702 touches. Pulled his left hamstring running his first 40-yard dash at the Combine and did not perform shuttles or positional drills.

Strengths: Outstanding vision, balance and anticipation to navigate through traffic — cuts back against the grain and consistently finds open running lanes (see signature, ankle-breaking runs vs. Stanford and Kansas State where makes four tacklers miss). Understands angles and how to set up blocks, create in the open field and follow his blocks. Elusive in the open field, with outstanding lateral quickness to make the first tackler miss. Can string some moves together and leave tacklers grasping for air. Very good second-level angles. Good competitive playing speed. Runs hard in short-yardage situations and has a nose for the goal line. Adequate hands.

Weaknesses: Has a thin build not suited to be a bellcow and lacks the mass, power and run strength to push the pile inside and keep his shoulders squared through the line. Does not possess elite top-end speed and is not an explosive gamechanger capable of breaking long runs each carry. Recorded a 32-inch vertical jump, indicating average athletic ability and lower-body explosion. Lacks ideal bulk to withstand a charge in pass protection. Measured only 4 percent body fat at the Combine, too lean by NFL RB standards, and could use some more armor on his frame to help absorb contact.

Future: A very productive, competitive and highly creative slasher capable of spinning tacklers in circles and putting on a show in the open field, Perkins will fit most ideally as a complementary change-of-pace back. Could require a few years to adapt to the physicality of the NFL and become an every-down performer, yet has the traits to factor immediately and evolve into a full-time role.

Draft projection: Third- to fourth-round pick.

Scout's take: "I think he is a good no. 2 back. He is not a power back. He needs a little space to operate, but he is creative and he can juke. He's kind of a poor man's Tiki Barber, with his vision and ability to weave. The third (round) is the highest (Perkins) will go. I put him a little lower down."

RB/WR [F] **C.J. PROSISE,** #20 (Jr-4)

NOTRE DAME ▶ GRADE: 5.58

Ht: 6-01/2 | Wt: 220 | 40: 4.47 | Arm: 321/8 | Hand: 81/2

History: Played receiver, safety and kick returner as a prep in Virginia, where he also excelled in track and field. Had nine kick return scores in two years. Redshirted in 2012. Played slot receiver in '13 when he recorded seven receptions for 72 yards (10.3-yard average) and zero touchdowns in 13 games (three starts). Also tallied four special teams tackles. Started 6-of-13 games at slot receiver in '14 and caught 10-126-1 (12.6) while collecting a team-high 11 special teams tackles, earning ND's Special Teams Player of the Year honors. Moved to running back in '15 — missed approximately 10 days of fall camp (hip flexor), but started 9-of-11 games played and carried 156 times for 1,032 yards (6.6-yard average) and 11 touchdowns with 26-308-1 (11.8) receiving. Tarean Folston started the season opener versus Texas, but tore his ACL, opening the door for Prosise's breakout. Was concussed against Pittsburgh and sat out against Wake Forest, then sustained a high left ankle sprain against Boston College which sidelined him against Stanford and rendered him a non-factor against Ohio State in the Fiesta Bowl (played one snap before pulling himself out). Has five career fumbles on 229 touches. Did not bench press at the Combine because of an injury and opted out of the shuttles.

Strengths: Good size with a sleek frame. Good foot energy —makes sharp jump cuts. Great burst to hit the corner, with distinguishable gear change to stick his foot in the dirt and go in space. Accelerates to top speed quickly once he sees it and can pull away from tacklers. Excellent hands — catches the ball naturally in stride, tracks it well over his shoulder and knows when to use his body to shield defenders. Functional pass protector with good mass to hold up.

Weaknesses: Has very small hands. Only has one year of experience in the backfield and eyes and instincts are still developing. Is still learning how to block and feeling his way as an inside runner. Does not run with power and slows through contact, leaving him susceptible to some big hits that will be more dangerous to withstand in the pros. Durability was an issue during his one year in college at running back. Can get wide-eyed and overwhelmed in congestion and must learn to better protect the ball. Lacks nuance and polish and could require some time to assimilate an NFL playbook.

Future: An intriguing, energetic, dual threat

with starter-caliber physical traits, Prosise has undeniable talent, yet is still learning how to play the position. Displayed flashes of brilliance and has a lot of upside if he can continue to develop.

Draft projection: Second- to third-round pick.

Scout's take: "I've heard the comparisons to (49ers 1991 second-round pick) Ricky Watters. I see some flashes of it, but I was left wanting to see so much more. The kid is gifted — no question. But's he's not instant oatmeal. I don't know how natural it is to him. He's going to need some time."

RB **WENDELL SMALLWOOD**, #4 (Jr-3)

WEST VIRGINIA ▶ GRADE: 5.20
Ht: 5-10½ | Wt: 208 | 40: 4.44 | Arm: 30½ | Hand: 9¼

History: Prepped in Delaware. As a true freshman in 2013, carried 39 times for 221 yards (5.7-yard average) and one touchdown, had 11 receptions for 132 yards (12.0-yard average) and zero touchdowns and returned 30 kickoffs for 541 yards (18.0-yard average) in 12 games (one start). Was arrested in July 2014 and charged with witness intimidation in a murder case after trying to get a witness to recant statements implicating a friend of his charged with first-degree murder, but all charges were dropped after his friend pleaded guilty. Started 9-of-13 games in '14 and recorded 148-722-2 (4.9) rushing and 31-326-0 (10.5) receiving. Was the Mountaineers' Offensive Player of the Year in '15 after starting 12-of-13 games and producing 238-1,519-9 (6.4) on the ground and 26-160-0 (6.2) out of the backfield. Sprained his left ankle against Oklahoma in Week Four and was nagged by the injury the rest of the way — missed significant practice time and did not start against Oklahoma State. Had eight career fumbles on 524 touches.

Strengths: Runs with urgency and is quick to and through the hole. Presses the line and makes sharp cuts on zone runs. Fine body control to change directions, with an effective spin move. Recorded the fastest 3-cone drill time (6.83 seconds) and 60-yard shuttle (11.14) of any back at the Combine. Has good hands and concentration to track the ball over his shoulder and make one-handed snags, as he did at the Combine on the wheel route. Surprisingly willing to face up defenders and help in pass protection — alert and aware.

Weaknesses: Much of his production was blocked for him and too often goes down on initial contact. Stiff-hipped with limited power. Is not a strong pile-driver or tackle-breaker. Lacks top-end, breakaway speed and creativity in the open field. Rigid route runner.

Future: Hard-charging, shifty back hits the hole quickly and showed a flair for some big plays. Runs bigger than his size and proved he could bang between the tackles, yet will be most optimal operating in space as a change-of-pace runner in the pros.

Draft projection: Fifth- to sixth-round pick.

Scout's take: "He ran well (at the Combine) and catches the ball well. He has good feet. He's not big, but he has the feet to get out of trouble. He is a rotational back. Someone might take a chance in the fourth (round)."

RB **KELVIN TAYLOR**, #21 (Jr-3)

FLORIDA ▶ GRADE: 5.24
Ht: 5-10¼ | Wt: 207 | 40: 4.61 | Arm: 29¼ | Hand: 8¼

History: Son of Fred Taylor, who starred for the Gators and played 13 years in the NFL for the Jaguars and Patriots (1998-2010). Kelvin, who played varsity football as an eighth grader, is the state of Florida's all-time leading rusher with 12,121 yards and 191 touchdowns. Had surgery to repair a torn right meniscus in June 2010. As a true freshman in 2013, carried 11 times for 508 yards (4.6-yard average) and four touchdowns with five receptions for 37 yards (7.4-yard average) and zero touchdowns in nine games (four starts). In '14, was No. 2 on the depth chart behind Redskins '15 third-rounder Matt Jones — played all 12 games, starting two, and rushed 116-565-6 (4.9) and snagged 2-8-0 (4.0). Was featured in '15 when he started 11-of-14 games, toting 259-1,035-13 (4.0) with 17-150-0 (8.8) receiving. Never fumbled in 510 career carries. Opted not to perform shuttles at the Combine.

Strengths: Good vision and feel for running lanes — anticipates where lanes will develop and is decisive hitting the hole. Good leg churn and forward body lean to push through contact. Can make himself skinny and shimmy through small spaces. Runs with confidence and carries a swagger. Exceptional ball security. Has NFL bloodlines.

Weaknesses: Short stepper with limited long speed and playmaking ability. Lacks explosiveness to create in the open field. Often goes down on first contact between the tackles. Struggled with pass protection and must become more assignment-sound. Has a 32-inch vertical jump. Had the shortest arms of any player at the Combine and extremely small hands, the smallest of any back; and struggled catching the ball cleanly at the event, dropping too many.

Future: A better football player than tester, Taylor is an urgent, competitive hard-charging back who runs with determination and can pick up tough yardage. Superb ball security, confidence and pedigree will earn the confidence of coaches quickly. However, he lacks the speed, power and pass-blocking ability to readily become an NFL starter. Could get a team through a game or two if called upon, but has not proven he could handle full-time duty as a starter. Ideal situational short-yardage and goalline back. Must prove he could contribute on special teams.

Draft projection: Fourth- to fifth-round pick.

RB **SHAD THORNTON**, #10 (Sr-4)

NORTH CAROLINA STATE   ▶ GRADE: 4.84

Ht: 5-11 5/8 | Wt: 217 | 40: 4.71 | Arm: 30 | Hand: 9 3/4

History: Prepped in Georgia. As a true freshman in 2012, carried 154 times for 694 yards (4.5-yard average) and three touchdowns with 30 receptions for 274 yards (9.1-yard average) and one touchdown in 10 games (four starts). Wasn't called upon until Week Four when NC State's top three backs were hurt or suspended. In June '13, was arrested and charged with misdemeanor assault for allegedly grabbing his girlfriend's arm and pushing her against a wall at NC State's library — received deferred prosecution, underwent counseling, served a one-game suspension and did not receive any carries in Week Two. On the season, played 11 games — started final nine — and produced 165-768-4 (4.7) rushing and 16-97-0 (6.1) receiving. In December, was the subject of a sexual battery investigation — was not charged for that, but was cited for marijuana possession (and again in March). Played all 13 games in '14, and was the Wolfpack's leading rusher despite starting just two games — totaled 164-907-9 (5.5) on the ground and 15-133-1 (8.9) out of the backfield. In '15, logged 30-203-3 (6.8) in three games (one start) before he was kicked off the team — was driving a scooter that struck and injured a pedestrian. Was charged with failure to stop and render aid, failure to provide information, driving on the sidewalk and operating an unregistered vehicle. Thornton already had pending charges of operating a moped without a helmet and exceeding a safe speed in a previous incident. Has seven career fumbles in 576 touches.

Strengths: Competitive inside runner — presses the line, attacks holes and runs with a sense of urgency. Almost always falls forward. Has a good feel for finding creases and enough patience to let plays develop and follow his blocks. Tough, willing blocker. Identifies with

the game and has a passion for it.

Weaknesses: Not a dynamic or creative back. Tends to run upright and create a big target. Stiff route runner. Pedestrian long speed. Trouble has followed him too much throughout his career and has not been able to get out of his own way. Immature and will require a lot of maintenance.

Future: A good-sized, instinctive runner who runs with a chip on his shoulder and has enough talent to warrant an opportunity in a camp. However, has been taken off draft boards for lack of maturity, and history of off-field transgressions could limit his opportunities.

Draft projection: Priority free agent.

FB **SOMA VAINUKU**, #31 (Sr-5)

USC   ▶ GRADE: 5.10

Ht: 5-11 1/2 | Wt: 246 | 40: 4.64 | Arm: 32 | Hand: 9 1/2

History: Cousin of Bengals linebacker (and USC All-American) Rey Maualuga. High school fullback-linebacker who rushed for 2,200 yards and 38 touchdowns as a senior in California. Was a non-qualifier and did not play in 2010. Redshirted in '11. Played all 13 games in '12, drawing four starts, and logged seven carries for 26 yards (3.7-yard average) and zero touchdowns with eight receptions for 50 yards (6.2-yard average) and zero touchdowns. Had surgery in the spring of '13 to repair his left PCL and meniscus. In the fall, played all 14 games in '13, starting three, and recorded 8-78-1 (9.8) rushing and 9-74-1 (8.2) receiving. Also blocked three punts. Played 10 games in '14, starting two, and logged 7-40-1 (5.7) on the ground. Injured his left hamstring against Arizona and missed three games. Appeared in all 14 games in '15, carrying 2-4-1 (2.0). Vainuku, who tallied 38 career tackles, was recognized as USC's Special Teams Player of the Year twice. Graduated with a sociology degree. Injured his left groin during positional drills at the Combine and did not perform shuttles.

Strengths: Outstanding size and can run with some power. Good finisher who stays after blocks through the whistle. Stood out most as a blocker early in his career, riding some defenders into the sideline. Effective cut blocker capable of eliminating linebackers on the move. Aggressive tackler in special teams coverage. Lays out and will sacrifice his body to block punts.

Weaknesses: Offensive play time diminished the last few years and contributions could be very limited outside special teams in the pros. Very limited production as a runner and receiver. Runs upright. Overruns the ball on special teams coverage and plays a bit recklessly and out of control. Weight has fluctuated throughout his career. Could stand to play with more discipline.

Future: A fearless blocker and stalwart special teams player who set the tone for his Trojans' career when he dented his facemask blowing up a blocker and forced a fumble on his first play covering a kick as a redshirt freshman. Earned a reputation as one of the premier special teams performers in the country and has the special teams temperament to make a living as a four-phase, core special teamer if he learns to be more disciplined.

Draft projection: Sixth- to seventh-round pick.

FB DAN VITALE, #40 (Sr-4)

NORTHWESTERN ▶ GRADE: 5.19

Ht: 6-0 7/8 | Wt: 239 | 40: 4.61 | Arm: 31 3/4 | Hand: 9 3/4

History: Last name is pronounced "vy-TAL-ee." High school running back who also ran track at Illinois' Wheaton-Warrenville South. Suffered a broken right elbow and broken right collarbone in high school. Made an immediate impact as a true freshman in 2012 — took ownership of the "Superback" position (hybrid tight end/fullback) by starting 10-of-13 games and catching 28 balls for 288 yards (10.3-yard average) and two touchdowns. Started all 37 games the next three seasons — totaled 34-382-3 (11.2) in '13 (12 games); 18-221-2 (12.3) in '14 (12 games); and 33-355-4 (10.8) in '15 (13 games). Had six career rushes for 29 yards (4.8-yard average) and zero touchdowns. Team captain. On track to graduate with an economics degree.

Strengths: Experienced, four-year starter. Versatile and lines up all over the field at fullback, wing, in the slot and as an in-line tight end. Football smart. Very good hands. Protects the ball in traffic. Outstanding weight-room strength. Very willing, competitive blocker who understands angles and leverage. Good balance. Has a 38 1/2-inch vertical jump. Recorded the fastest 20-yard shuttle time (4.12 seconds) of any back at the Combine, and tied for the most bench-press reps (30). Terrific personal and football character. Unselfish, team player. Has been very durable and played through injuries.

Weaknesses: Feet tend to stop on contact and does not generate a lot of power through his lower body. Limited creativity and make-you-miss in the open field. Is a bit straight-linish and gathers to cut. Body-catches too much instead of catching the ball outside his frame, leading to drops. Could stand to learn how to sharpen his routes and come out of his breaks more cleanly. Has a lot of room for improvement as a blocker.

Future: A smart, versatile, sure-handed West Coast fullback with the run and receiving skill desired to earn a starting job readily in the pros and contribute on special teams. Earned respect the minute he stepped onto campus as an immediate contributor and could make a similar impact in the pros as a jack-of-all-trades and special teams staple.

Draft projection: Late draftable pick.

Scout's take: "I like Vitale. He could play for us. He is (Northwestern's) best (senior) prospect. He's a helluva college player."

RB DeANDRE WASHINGTON, #21 (Sr-5)

TEXAS TECH ▶ GRADE: 5.14

Ht: 5-8 1/4 | Wt: 204 | 40: 4.48 | Arm: 30 | Hand: 9

History: Texas native. As a true freshman in 2011, carried 77 times for 366 yards (4.8-yard average) and three touchdowns and had 19 receptions for 109 yards (5.7-yard average) and zero touchdowns (5.7-yard average). Added seven kickoff returns for 131 yards (18.7-yard average). Suffered a torn right ACL in Week 11 against Missouri. Did not play in '12. Played 12 games in '13, drawing two starts, and had 107-450-4 (4.2) rushing and 34-269-0 (7.9) receiving. In '14, started 11-of-12 games and produced 188-1,103-2 (5.9) rushing and 30-328-2 (10.9) receiving. Did not start against TCU (five receivers). Started 12-of-13 games in '15, totaling 233-1,492-14 (6.4) on the ground and 41-385-2 (9.4) out of the backfield. Did not start against Arkansas (five receivers). Team captain graduated with an exercise and sport science degree. Has seven career fumbles in 736 touches.

Strengths: Very tough with good lower-body strength, base and balance. Runs strong and consistently falls forward. Good football temperament. Solid showing at the Senior Bowl — made continual strides during the week in pass protection and responded to one-on-one challenges in drills. Outstanding weight-room strength. Caught the ball with ease at the Combine.

Weaknesses: Has small hands. Lacks ideal size to withstand the rigors of running inside. Overly muscled and has some tightness in his body. Gathers to cut, pitter patters too much

RUNNING BACKS

in tight quarters and takes some direct hits. Average elusiveness. Gets overwhelmed in pass protection and could stand to do a better job of sustaining as a blocker on the perimeter. Ball security could improve — always carries low in his right hand.

Future: Compact, muscular, competitive back with the toughness, balance and determination to overcome his lack of size in the pros. Has make-it qualities.

Draft projection: Late draftable pick.

RUNNING BACKS

RB BRANDON WILDS, #22 (Sr-5)

SOUTH CAROLINA　　▶ GRADE: 5.18

Ht: 6-03/4 | Wt: 220 | 40: 4.54 | Arm: 32 | Hand: 101/4

History: Has a daughter. South Carolina native. As a true freshman in 2011, began the season fifth on the depth chart, but injuries forced him into action — carried 107 times for 486 yards (4.5-yard average) and caught 15 balls for 136 yards (9.1-yard average) and zero touchdowns in 13 games (five starts). Redshirted in 2012 because of a high ankle sprain. Was behind Mike Davis (49ers '15 fourth-rounder) for two years. In '13, managed 43-221-3 (5.1) rushing and 9-119-2 (13.2) receiving in seven games (two starts). Missed six games with a dislocated left elbow. Played 12 games in '14, starting four games, and carried 106-570-4 (5.4) with 18-143-1 (7.9) receiving. Sprained his shoulder against Vanderbilt and sat out against Furman because of a right knee sprain. Was the team's leading rusher in '15 — started all nine games played and rushed 123-567-3 (4.6) with 17-142-0 (8.4) receiving. Suffered bruised ribs against Georgia and missed three games. Graduated with an interdisciplinary studies degree. Has six fumbles in 439 career touches.

Strengths: Outstanding size. Good movement skill for a big back. Presses the line and can sort through traffic. Is a load to tackle — runs hard and drives his legs on contact. Good competitive playing speed. Sufficient contact balance. Adjusts well to the thrown ball and catches cleanly. Willing blocker with enough mass to hold ground in blitz pickup. Functional positional blocker on the move. Is tough and will play through pain.

Weaknesses: Runs too upright and leaves his body susceptible to square hits. Limited make-you-miss to shake tacklers in the open field. Lacks breakaway speed. Not polished as a route runner, tending to drift. Has never made it through a full season healthy, and durability has been an issue throughout his career with injuries to every part of his body.

Future: A lean-bodied, strong zone runner with enough balance and body control to contribute as a complimentary inside runner and outlet valve in the receiving game. Has neither the low pad level nor second-level elusiveness to consistently stay healthy.

Draft projection: Late draftable pick.

RB JONATHAN WILLIAMS, #32 (Sr-4)

ARKANSAS　　▶ GRADE: 5.25

Ht: 5-103/4 | Wt: 220 | 40: 4.60e | Arm: 315/8 | Hand: 10

History: Prepped in Texas. As a true freshman in 2012, carried 45 times for 231 yards (5.1-yard average) and zero touchdowns and caught eight balls for 208 yards (26.0-yard average) and two touchdowns in 11 games (two starts). Started 11-of-12 games in '13 and produced 150-900-4 (6.0) rushing and 7-72-2 (10.3) receiving. Was benched for a quarter against Mississippi State because he was late to weight training. Was the Razorbacks' leading rusher in '14 when he ran 211-1,190-12 (5.6) and caught 11-65-2 (5.9) in 13 games (11 starts). Missed the '15 season after having left foot surgery in August — had two screws inserted to help mend ligament damage. Team captain graduated with a communications degree. Has six career fumbles in 436 touches. Was medically excluded from working out at the Combine because of foot injury.

Strengths: Good contact balance to run through arm tackles, spin out of the grasp of tacklers and produce yardage after contact. Runs with a strong base and carries tacklers on his back. Tough and competitive — does not go down easy. Physical inside runner.

Weaknesses: Lacks breakaway speed and second-level elusiveness is only average — will continue to take a lot of direct hits from the knee down that will invite durability concerns. Gears down to cut. Runs few routes and has not been much of a factor in the passing game.

Future: Good-sized, urgent, north-south runner with a competitive running style that will endear him to evaluators and could allow him to become a functional, contributing chunk runner in the pros when healthy. Would fit most ideally in a zone-based ground game where he could stick his foot in the dirt and go.

Draft projection: Fourth- to fifth-round pick.

Scout's take: "I didn't see any great traits. I know he had a lot of yards when he was healthy a year ago. I just thought he was average across the board, his speed and vision. I did like his toughness and grit based on 2014."

WIDE RECEIVERS

Nawrocki's TOP 10

1. **LAQUON TREADWELL**
2. **Corey Coleman**
3. **Will Fuller**
4. **Josh Doctson**
5. **Sterling Shepard**
6. **Tyler Boyd**
7. **Michael Thomas**
8. **Paul McRoberts**
9. **Braxton Miller**
10. **Aaron Burbridge**

WR [F]-PR BRALON ADDISON, #2 (Jr-4)

OREGON ▶ GRADE: 5.27

Ht: 5-9 1/4 | Wt: 197 | 40: 4.64 | Arm: 29 1/2 | Hand: 9 1/8

History: Played quarterback as a Texas prep. Played inside and outside for the Ducks in their signature spread, no-huddle, fast-paced offense. As a true freshman in 2012, tallied 22 receptions for 243 yards (11.0-yard average) and three touchdowns in 13 appearances. Started 11-of-13 games in '13 and produced 61-890-7 (14.6). Was sidelined for the '14 season after tearing his left ACL during spring practice. Returned to start 12-of-13 games in '15, snagging 63-804-10 (12.8) to lead the team in receiving. Also threw a 39-yard touchdown pass. Had 21 career rushes for 103 yards (4.9-yard average) and two touchdowns. Returned 36 career punts for 451 yards (12.5-yard aver-age) and three scores. Returned 11 career kickoffs for 217 yards (19.7-yard average).

Strengths: Versatile — aligns at multiple spots on and off the line of scrimmage and in the backfield. Good quickness, agility and balance. Gets into his routes quickly. Adjusts well to the ball and can track it out over his shoulder. Shows some creativity after the catch. Tough, competitive and productive, with three career TD returns on punts. Has a knack for sifting through traffic as a returner.

Weaknesses: Has short arms and a small catching radius. Susceptible to jams. Limited strength to run through contact or sustain blocks. Ran simple routes that will require more polish. Produced a pedestrian 40 time at the Combine, indicative of a lack of breakaway speed. Is not a game-breaking returner. Still did not appear fully recovered

WIDE RECEIVERS

from knee injury as a junior.

Future: Decent-sized slot receiver with good athletic ability, agility and hands. Could find a role as a multi-purpose threat and return man. His greatest contribution could come as a punt returner.

Draft projection: Fourth- to fifth-round pick.

Scout's take: "Addison is more quick than fast. He'll make it as a special teams player and returner. He is going to get knocked down in the draft because of the way he ran."

WR [X] GERONIMO ALLISON, #8 (Sr-4)

ILLINOIS ▶ GRADE: 5.06

Ht: 6-3 1/8 | Wt: 196 | 40: 4.64 | Arm: 32 7/8 | Hand: 9 1/2

History: Grew up in a gang-infested area of Tampa, Fla., where he was academically ineligible for football until his senior year. Spent two years at Iowa Western. Wore jersey No. 18 in 2012 — had 26 receptions for 428 yards (16.5-yard average) and two touchdowns in 11 games. Wore jersey No. 1 in '13 — caught 69-872-8 (12.6) in '13 (11 games). Broke his left arm in early November. With the Illini in '14, started all 12 games at wide receiver and produced 41-598-5 (14.6) in Bill Cubit's spread offense. Did not play against Texas State (left leg bruise). In '15, was the team's leading receiver with 65-882-3 (13.6) in 12 games (11 starts). Reeled in 47 percent of his 134 targets. Did not start against Minnesota, as U of I opened in a "jumbo" package. Sustained a concussion against Iowa. Graduated with a communications degree. Opted not to bench press at the Combine.

Strengths: Good overall length and ball skills to pluck the ball out of the air and win 50-50 balls. Works at his craft and is accountable.

Weaknesses: Has small hands. Leggy and non-explosive with limited burst out of his breaks. Lacks functional football-playing strength to beat the jam at the line of scrimmage. Choppy route runner. Struggles creating separation vertically. Can be knocked off route. Not a strong tackle-breaker. Could take some additional time to get acclimated to NFL complexities. Thin frame has been prone to injury. Double-caught the ball too much during Shrine all-star week. Recorded the slowest 3-cone drill time (7.47 seconds) of any receiver at the Combine, indicative of a lack of burst and body control.

Future: Long-limbed, developmental receiver lacking ideal speed, strength and craftiness desired in the pros to earn a roster spot. Camp body.

Draft projection: Priority free agent.

Scout's take: "I'm not a big Allison fan. I think he is a developmental player, but I still would not draft him."

WR [F] / KR DeMARCUS AYERS, #10 (Jr-3)

HOUSTON ▶ GRADE: 5.09

Ht: 5-9 3/8 | Wt: 182 | 40: 4.67 | Arm: 31 1/4 | Hand: 9 1/4

History: Also played basketball as a prep in Texas, where he totaled 1,800 yards passing and 1,300 yards rushing with 38 touchdowns as a senior (led his team to the state final). Missed a chunk of his junior season with a broken left collarbone. Played all 13 games in 2013, starting the final three at "X" receiver, and tallied 11 receptions for 130 yards (11.8-yard average) and one touchdown. Was the American Conference Co-Special Teams Player of the Year after returning 37 kickoffs for 1,021 yards (27.6-yard average), including one score. In '14, started 8-of-13 games — five at "Z," three at "X" — and totaled 33-335-2 (10.2) receiving and 34-592-0 (17.4) on kickoff returns. Stepbrother was shot and killed on 4th of July '15. On the season, started all 14 games at the "H" receiver and racked up 98-1,222-6 (12.5). Hurt his left shoulder against Vanderbilt and dealt with pain the rest of the season. Was one of the most efficient pass catchers amongst draft-eligible receivers, as he reeled in 71.5 percent of his 137 targets. Had 27 career rushes for 151 yards (5.6-yard average) and one touchdown. Played in Travis Bush's multiple spread system until his junior season when Tom Herman and Major Applewhite brought the "smashmouth spread" to Houston. Was a medical exclusion from the bench-press test and positional drills at the Combine and did not run shuttles because of finger injury.

Strengths: Has a knack for seeing creases, following blocks and cutting back across the grain to make tacklers miss in the open field. Very dependable hands-catcher. Good concentration to make difficult one-handed grabs. Tracks the ball surprisingly well. Makes defenders miss in the open field and can string moves together.

Weaknesses: Skinny and light-framed with average play strength. Lacks breakaway speed. Struggles some beating the jam and needs to get stronger. Was a bit of an immature frontrunner early in his career and must learn to keep his emotions in check.

WIDE RECEIVERS

Future: A more quick than fast, undersized slot receiver who can offer immediate value in the return game. Shows some similarities to Broncos undrafted WR Jordan Norwood and could compete for a role as a No. 4 or 5 receiver and return man in the pros. Character concerns may force him to take the long road and prove an NFL team can depend on him. Creativity, elusiveness, sure hands and return ability could allow him to overcome shortcomings and emerge as a solid contributor.

Draft projection: Priority free agent.

Scout's take: "We put him on our back (non-draftable) board. We wouldn't draft him. Someone might for his return abilities."

WR [F,Z] TYLER BOYD, #23 (Jr-3)

PITTSBURGH ▶ GRADE: 5.72

Ht: 6-1¼ | Wt: 197 | 40: 4.58 | Arm: 32 | Hand: 9¾

History: Decorated Pennsylvania prep — won four state titles at Clairton High, where he played all over the field, garnered U.S. Army All-American honors and was a two-time Class A Player of the Year after piling up 5,755 yards and 117 touchdowns (Western Pennsylvania Interscholastic Athletic League record). Also played basketball and baseball. Was the most productive freshman receiver in the country in 2013 — lined up opposite Cowboys '14 fifth-rounder Devin Street and broke Larry Fitzgerald's first-year marks by producing 85 receptions for 1,174 yards (13.8-yard average) and seven touchdowns in 13 games (10 starts). Gave way to tight ends in non-starts. Started 12-of-13 games in '14 — despite dislocating a finger on his left hand in the season opener against Delaware — and totaled 78-1,261-8 (16.2). Lone non-start was against Syracuse when he sat out the first play from scrimmage after his 96-yard kickoff return touchdown was negated by a penalty. Was busted for DUI in June '15 — sentenced to 12 months' probation and suspended for the season opener against Youngstown State. On the season, started 11-of-12 games played and hauled in 91-926-6 (10.2). Gave way to a tight end against Miami. Had 63 career rushes for 520 yards (8.3-yard average) and one touchdown; 46 career kickoff returns for 1,124 yards (24.4-yard average); and 27 career punt returns for 238 yards (8.8-yard average) and one score. Needed just three seasons to claim Pitt records for receptions (254) and receiving yards (3,361), as well as rank second behind Tony Dorsett in all-purpose yards (5,243).

Strengths: Very strong hands. Can climb the ladder and take the ball away from defensive backs. Great body control. Good run vision after the catch and finding open lanes as a returner — knows how to set up blocks. Played in a pro-style offense and runs a full route tree. Outstanding career production. Tracks the ball well over his shoulder. Extends to snag throws outside his frame. Can make spectacular, acrobatic, in-air adjustments and sensational one-handed grabs — highlight-reel TD producer. Strong after the catch. Has kickoff and punt return experience. The game is important to him.

Weaknesses: Has a narrow frame and is not physically strong. Average burst off the line. Lacks separation speed and most of his catches are contested. Could struggle escaping physical press coverage. Is not a creative runner after the catch. Has room to improve as a blocker. Only bench-pressed 225 pounds 11 times at the Combine and produced among the five slowest 20-yard shuttles (4.40 seconds) of receivers at the event.

Future: A sure-handed, go-to receiver who made average quarterbacks look good, Boyd is a smooth, dependable West Coast target capable of becoming a very productive No. 2 receiver in the pros. Could evolve as a very efficient slot receiver, racking up consistent production to move the chains.

Draft projection: Second- to third-round pick.

Scout's take: "Boyd might be the best route runner in the draft. I wish he were a little faster. I'm still very confident he will be a productive NFL receiver. I think he starts yesterday for us."

WR [X] CHRIS BROWN, #2 (Sr-4)

NOTRE DAME ▶ GRADE: 5.03

Ht: 6-2 | Wt: 194 | 40: 4.45e | Arm: 32¼ | Hand: 9

History: Prepped in South Carolina, where he played receiver, defensive back and kick returner and was an elite track and field competitor — ranked as the No. 1 triple-jumper nationally, was the state's Gatorade performer of the year, ran 10.8 in the 100 meters and 21.6 200 meters and ran with the U.S. Junior National Track team. Suffered a broken collarbone during his senior season. Played 12 games as a true freshman in 2012 — started two at "X" (outside receiver), two at "Z" (slot receiver) — and grabbed two catches for 56 yards (4.7-yard average) and zero touchdowns. Did not see

WIDE RECEIVERS

action in the national championship game against Alabama. Played all 13 games in '13, drawing three starts at wide receiver, and collected 15-209-1 (16.1). In '14, took on a more prominent role in Brian Kelly's power-spread scheme — started 11-of-13 games at the "W" (boundary) and produced 39-548-1 (14.1). Started all 13 games at the "W" in '15 and caught 48-597-4 (12.4). On track to graduate. Was a medical exclusion from the Combine and did not work out because of injuries to both feet.

Strengths: Solid route runner — displays some savvy to set up his routes and work back to the ball. Is quick in and out of breaks. Has a good feel for finding soft spots in zones and knowing where to settle.

Weaknesses: Has a very lean frame despite adding 14 pounds in the month from the Shrine game to the Combine. Lacks strength to fend off the jam or run through contact after the catch — knocked off routes too easily. Not an elusive or strong tackle-breaker. Hears footsteps and alligator-arms some balls. Overwhelmed blocker. Suspect durability.

Future: A lean, outside-the-numbers receiver with few distinguishable traits. Inability to produce on special teams could make it difficult to hold a roster spot.

Draft projection: Priority free agent.

WR [F] AARON BURBRIDGE, #16 (Sr-4)

MICHIGAN STATE   ▶ GRADE: 5.36

Ht: 6-0 | Wt: 206 | 40: 4.49 | Arm: 31 5/8 | Hand: 8 1/4

History: Michigan native won a state championship at Harrison High. Missed 2012 fall camp after having arthroscopic knee surgery. Played 11 games, starting the final seven at the "X" receiver, and caught 29 balls for 364 yards (12.6-yard average) and two touchdowns. Played 13 games in '13, starting three at "X," and collected 22-194-0 (8.8). Did not play against Illinois (hamstring). Was a backup in '14 when he snagged 29-358-1 (12.3) in 13 games. Was the Big Ten Receiver of the Year in '15 after the leading the conference in receptions (MSU single-season record), receiving yards and receiving touchdowns — posted 85-1,258-7 (14.8) in 14 games (13 starts at "X"). Had 22 career rushes for 149 yards (6.9-yard average) and zero touchdowns. Ranks second in MSU history with 165 career receptions.

Strengths: Good competitive urgency — sells out his body to make difficult grabs and is strong with the ball in his hands. Outstanding body control to contort in the air and make in-air adjustments. Bench-pressed 225 pounds 20 times, tied for the most among all receivers at the Combine and indicative of his physical strength that leads to him overpowering the jam, posting up defensive backs in coverage and running through contact after the catch. Has deceptive speed to slip by defenders. Solid showing at the Senior Bowl. Well-versed in a pro-style offense. Has taken snaps out of the wildcat formation and has the some run skill and the toughness to be effective taking some carries.

Weaknesses: Has very small hands and some tightness in his body. Needs to become a more consistent hands-catcher. Makes some concentration drops. Has a 30 1/2-inch vertical jump, indicative of below-average leaping ability. Also posted an 11.96-second 60-yard shuttle, the slowest of any receiver and indicative of a lack of dynamic acceleration. Is not sudden with the ball in his hands and lacks top-end speed to separate down the field. Could be challenged to release cleanly and beat physical, bump coverage in the pros. Needs to do a better job of using his hands to get into his routes quickly. Only a one-year, full-time starter

Future: A solid possession receiver with the body strength, physicality and competitiveness ideally desired working the short-to-intermediate passing game from the slot. Broke out as a senior despite playing with an inaccurate quarterback and has the toughness to earn a no. 3 inside receiving role. Could require some time to acclimate to the pro game.

Draft projection: Third- to fourth-round pick.

WR [Z] DEVON CAJUSTE, #89 (Sr-5)

STANFORD   ▶ GRADE: 5.23

Ht: 6-3 3/4 | Wt: 234 | 40: 4.63 | Arm: 33 | Hand: 10 3/4

History: Also played basketball and ran track as a New York prep. Redshirted in 2011 after tearing his left ACL. Was used at "Z" and slot for the Cardinal. Saw limited action in eight games in '12, recording one catch for seven yards (7.0-yard average) and zero touchdowns. Started 7-of-13 games in '13 and caught 28-642-5 (22.9). Bruised his right knee against UCLA and sat out against Oregon. Was suspended for the '14 season opener against UC Davis. On the season, started all 11 games played at wide receiver and produced 34-557-6 (16.4). Sustained a concussion against Washington State and sat out against Arizona State. In '15, started 12-of-13 games and grabbed 27-383-3 (14.2). Did not start in the season opener against Northwestern (ankle), did not play against Washington State (illness) and suffered a strained right leg muscle against Colorado. Was targeted less than 70 times the last two seasons.

Strengths: Well-versed in a pro-style offense. Has an 80-inch wingspan with a big body and good catching radius to be a factor in the red zone. Recorded the fastest 3-cone time (6.49 seconds) of any player at the Combine, demonstrating superb agility and rare body control for a 235-pounder. Tough enough to get in the way as a blocker.

Weaknesses: Builds to speed and takes time to get started coming off the line. Limited deep speed to separate. Could do a better job of working back to the ball. Not dynamic or strong with the ball in his hands and goes down too easy. Monotone route runner. Only bench-pressed 225 pounds 12 times, indicating average strength for his size. Mediocre career production.

Future: Long-limbed, possession receiver who resisted a move to H-back at Stanford and does not play with the physicality desired at the position in the pros. Could compete for a job as a No. 5 receiver and contribute on special teams.

Draft projection: Fifth- to sixth-round pick.

Scout's take: "I gave (Cajuste) a draftable grade. He had a pretty good Combine. He's going to be best as an inside possession receiver. He's a backup at the next level. He has enough size to play on special teams."

WR [F] LEONTE CARROO, #4 (Sr-4)

RUTGERS ▶ GRADE: 5.18

Ht: 5-11 7/8 | Wt: 211 | 40: 4.49 | Arm: 31 | Hand: 9 5/8

History: Lived with another family in order to play at Don Bosco Prep (N.J.), where his teams went 48-0 and won four state championships. Also ran track. Missed time during his senior year because of hamstring and shoulder injuries. Played for four offensive coordinators in four years at Rutgers. As a true freshman in 2012, recorded just one tackle and one blocked punt in 13 appearances. Played 10 games in '13, drawing three starts before a concussion sidelined him for the final three contests — caught 28 balls for 478 yards (17.1-yard average)

and nine touchdowns. Played the "X" receiver his final two seasons in Piscataway. Started all 13 games in '14 and produced 55-1,086-10 (19.7). Sustained a head injury against Michigan then played with a hurt right hand in the bowl game against North Carolina. In '15 was voted team MVP after leading the team in receiving for the second year in a row. Started just 6-of-8 games played and totaled 39-809-10 (20.7). Was suspended the first half of the season opener against Norfolk State for a curfew violation. In September, was charged with simple assault for his role in a domestic incident in which a former Rutgers recruiting hostess — reportedly romantically linked to Carroo — engaged in a fight with Carroo's girlfriend and mother, among others. Ultimately the charge was dropped, and Carroo, who has told NFL teams he was merely intervening in the altercation, was reinstated after a two-game suspension. Sustained a high right ankle sprain against Indiana — re-aggravated the injury against Ohio State and sat out against Wisconsin and Michigan. Rolled the same ankle during Senior Bowl week and did not play in the all-star game. Owns Rutgers' career receiving touchdowns record (29). Team captain graduated with a communications degree. Did not perform shuttles and was limited in positional drills at the Combine because of right ankle injury.

Strengths: Well-built with good muscularity. Has strong hands. Very football smart and understands every WR position. Has some craftiness as a route runner — understands where to settle into zones and adjust routes to find soft spots. Get-in-the-way positional blocker. Blocked multiple punts in his career and could bring some value on special teams. Vocal leader. Tough and competitive.

Weaknesses: Has some tightness in his hips, comes off the ball too upright and struggles a bit with physical press coverage. Is not field-fast and struggles to create separation vertically. Does not consistently win jumpball situations or exert his will in the blocking game. Durability needs to be evaluated given history of concussions.

Future: Lined up on the outside as an "X" receiver in college and regularly had coverage rolled his way, yet still found ways to produce. Would fit more ideally in the slot where he would have more free releases and could work the field as a short-to-intermediate receiver and third-down chains-mover

WIDE RECEIVERS

in the pros.

Draft projection: Late draftable pick.

WR [X,F] / RS COREY COLEMAN, #1 (Jr-4)

BAYLOR   ▶ GRADE: 5.97

Ht: 5-10 5/8 | Wt: 194 | 40: 4.45e | Arm: 30 1/4 | Hand: 9

History: Father was convicted of felony cocaine distribution charges in 2014. His godfather Ray Crockett, a 14-year NFL standout defensive back, helped raise him from the time he was nine years old. Also competed in track and field as a prep in Texas, where he was an all-purpose threat on the football field. Redshirted in 2013. Started 10-of-13 games in '13 — eight outside, two inside — and recorded 35 receptions for 527 yards (15.1-yard average) and two touchdowns. Injured his hamstring during '14 fall camp and missed the first three games. On the season, started 6-of-10 games played — five outside, one inside — and tallied 64-1,119-11 (17.5). In '15, won the Biletnikoff Award after pacing the nation in touchdown receptions (school single-season record) in Baylor's relentless, up-tempo, no-huddle spread offense — reeled in 74-1,363-20 (18.4) in 12 starts at wide receiver. Sat out the bowl game against North Carolina after undergoing hernia surgery that kept him from running at the Combine. His 33 career touchdown receptions are a school record. Also had 24 career kickoff returns for 633 yards (26.3-yard average), including a 97-yard score against Iowa State his redshirt freshman year.

Strengths: Excellent speed to create separation vertically. Has explosive leaping ability with a 40 1/2-inch vertical jump and 10-foot, 9-inch broad jump and translates it to the field skying for the ball. Tracks the ball well over his shoulder. Effective creating after the catch on short bubble screens. Can spin cornerbacks in place with subtle moves (see West Virginia) and create some magic after the catch. Tough, competitive and battle-tested. Has overcome a lot of adversity to accomplish what he has in his life.

Weaknesses: Undersized with small hands and short arms — has a small catching radius. Played in a simplified scheme that did not require him to run a full route tree, and will require time to learn how to be craftier and set up defensive backs. Struggles some to avoid press coverage and can be re-routed too easily. Tends to let the ball into his frame and body-catch, leading to drops. Was not used heavily between the numbers and can

be phased by traffic — makes some concentration drops.

Future: An undersized, explosive and dynamic downfield receiving threat, Coleman has the physical traits to emerge as a legitimate, big-play weapon and return specialist. Has the athletic talent to warrant drafting in the top-15, but could slip to the second round because of the patience that will be needed for him to develop. Is the most talented in a long line of Baylor receivers (Terrance Williams, Kendall Wright, Josh Gordon) to make an impact in the pros and will be best utilized outside the numbers.

Draft projection: Top-40 pick.

Scout's take: "Coleman has all the physical tools, and I put him in the last third of the first (round), but you better give him some time. Maybe it's just because I have gotten burned on Baylor with the natural holes in their offense. There's no playbook. They have a simple route tree. They don't come off the ball. Receivers take more time than people think anyway, and he is starting with half a deck."

WR [F] / RS PHAROH COOPER, #11 (Jr-3)

SOUTH CAROLINA   ▶ GRADE: 5.23

Ht: 5-11 1/8 | Wt: 203 | 40: 4.55e | Arm: 32 1/4 | Hand: 1/8

History: Grew up in a family of Marines. Played all the skill positions, returned kicks and won a pair of state titles as a North Carolina prep. Played the "Z" (slot) position in Steve Spurrier's multiple, spread offense. As a true freshman in 2013, recorded three receptions for 54 yards (18.0-yard average) and one touchdown with 20 carries for 202 yards (10.1-yard average) and one touchdown in 11 games (one start). Also returned 16 kickoffs for 359 yards (22.4-yard average) and nine punts for 40 yards (4.4-yard average). Was the team's leading receiver in '14 when he started 12-of-13 games and produced 69-1,136-9 (16.5) receiving, 27-200-2 (7.4) rushing and 15-75 (5.0) on punts. Lone non-start was against Vanderbilt when the Gamecocks opened with just two receivers and targeted Damiere Byrd on a deep pass the first play from scrimmage. In '15, missed time during fall camp with hand and knee injuries, but started all 12 games and hauled in 66-973-8 (14.7) with 24-111-1 (4.6) on the ground and 12-55 (4.6) on punt returns. Was knocked out of the Tennessee contest with a head injury. Completed 9-of-16 career pass attempts (56.3 percent) for 118 yards with four touchdowns and zero interceptions. Team captain. Will be a 21-year-old rookie.

Strengths: Good quickness, body control and athletic ability. Has a good feel for soft spots in coverage and knows where to settle. Adjusts well to the thrown ball and can track it over his shoulder. Runs hard after the catch. Willing blocker — gets good fits. Good personal character described as "once in a lifetime" by his high school coach — aims to please and does a lot of extras. Smart and versatile — has contributed as a runner, receiver, return man and wildcat quarterback.

Weaknesses: Takes choppy steps and does not cover a lot of ground. Is not a blazer. Routes are unrefined — has not run a full route tree. Takes too many stutter steps in his routes and will have more difficulty releasing cleanly in the pros. Average elusiveness in the open field. Has some concentration drops. Recorded a 31-inch vertical jump, indicating marginal athletic ability and lower-body explosion.

Future: Smart, sure-handed receiver who could be most optimal in the slot in the pros. Has a chance to earn a role as a No. 4 or No. 5 receiver and contribute on special teams as a return man.

Draft projection: Fifth- to sixth-round pick.

Scout's take: "He's similar but not as quick or explosive as (Jaguars 2013 fourth-round pick) Ace Sanders."

WR [X] CODY CORE, #88 (Sr-4)

MISSISSIPPI ▶ GRADE: 5.08

Ht: 6-2 5/8 | Wt: 205 | 40: 4.42 | Arm: 32 | Hand: 10 3/8

History: Mississippi native. Father played football at Troy. Also lettered in baseball and track. As a true freshman in 2012, scratched one catch for four yards (4.0-yard average) and zero touchdowns with eight tackles in 13 appearances. In '13, recorded 4-91-0 (22.8) with eight tackles in 12 appearances. Sat out against Missouri (left ankle sprain). Lost his mother to a brain aneurysm in July '14. In the fall, started 10-of-13 games at slot receiver and produced 41-558-6 (13.6). Started 9-of-13 games in '15 in the slot and snagged 37-644-4 (17.4). Recorded 18 career tackles on special teams. Did not run shuttles at the Combine because of calf cramps.

Strengths: Very good length with big hands. Flashes some run-after-the-catch ability. Good football intelligence — understands all the receiver positions. Keeps working to uncover and has a knack for finding open areas in coverage. Good practice habits. Takes a serious approach to the game. Strong, competitive blocker.

Weaknesses: Lacks weight-room strength and functional strength to press off the line. Has some tightness in his hips and body and is straight-linish. Unpolished route runner. Not going to string many moves together in the open field or make defenders miss. Has a 31 1/2-inch vertical jump, indicating below-average athletic ability and lower-body explosion.

Future: Very lean, high-cut receiver with a maxed-out frame. Physical limitations could keep him from being drafted, yet has the football smarts, versatility and special teams coverage ability to earn a roster spot as a no. 4 or 5 receiver. A soft-spoken introvert who lets his play do the talking. Has the makings of a core special teams player.

Draft projection: Priority free agent.

WR [X] / KR TREVOR DAVIS, #9 (Sr-5)

CALIFORNIA ▶ GRADE: 5.12

Ht: 6-1 1/8 | Wt: 188 | 40: 4.39 | Arm: 31 | Hand: 10

History: Also competed in track and field as a California prep. Began his college career at Hawaii (wore jersey No. 89). Was slated to redshirt in 2011, but injuries forced him into action seven weeks into the season — started 6-of-7 games played (five at the "X" receiver, one at "Z"), catching 28 balls for 366 yards (13.1-yard average) and three touchdowns. Played eight games in '12, starting four at "X," and grabbed 17-235-2 (13.8). Missed two October contests because of a hamstring injury then a neck injury sidelined him the last four weeks. Decided to transfer to Cal, telling Rivals, "Hawaii just didn't fit me. . . .Going from the run and shoot to the power run. . .It was a big transition, I got the offense quickly, I just didn't think it was the best fit for my type of play." Did not play in '13 per NCAA transfer rules. In '14, played 10 games (started first two at "X") and contributed 24-399-5 (16.6) in Sonny Dykes' "Bear Raid" offense. Also returned 13 kicks for 424 yards (32.6) and two TDs. Injured his neck against UCLA and sat out two games. Started 9-of-13 games at "X" in '15 and caught 40-672-2 (16.8) and returned kicks 32-686-0 (21.4). Returned 14 career punts for 115 yards (8.2-yard average). Graduated with a sociology degree.

Strengths: Good straight-line speed to threaten the field vertically and gain some separation. Good body control to adjust to off-target throws behind him. Tested very

WIDE RECEIVERS

well at the Combine — recorded a 38 1/2-inch vertical jump showing outstanding leaping ability; and a 6.60-second 3-cone drill time, indicating outstanding agility that shows up most when he is darting through traffic with the ball in his hands. Quick, decisive and productive after the catch.

Weaknesses: Slight-framed and lacks strength coming off the line. Unpolished route runner — could do a better job of sinking his hips, setting up cornerbacks and playing the ball in the air. Is not a clean hands catcher and tends to cradle the ball to his body. Goes down easy after the catch and at times looks for a soft landing spot in the middle of the field. Average career production. Was not touched on either of his well-blocked kickoff TD returns. Has had some nagging injuries (neck), and durability must be weighed.

Future: Wiry lean, downfield receiver with the vision and traffic burst to create with the ball in his hands on bubble screens and outside the numbers. Has a chance to contend for a role as a No. 4 or No. 5 receiver and potential kickoff returner.

Draft projection: Late draftable pick.

WR [Z,F] JOSH DOCTSON, #9 (Sr-5)

TCU   ▶ GRADE: 5.89

Ht: 6-2 | Wt: 202 | 40: 4.44 | Arm: 31⅞ | Hand: 9⅞

History: Mother, Tracy, is TCU's vice chancellor of marketing and communication and also ran track in college. Also played basketball as a Texas prep. Suffered a broken right collarbone his junior season. Only received two scholarship offers out of high school and began his college career at Wyoming (wore jersey No. 89), where he started 9-of-12 games played in '11 and caught 35 balls for 393 yards (11.2-yard average) and five touchdowns. Transferred to TCU in order to be close to family, as his grandfather was diagnosed with terminal brain cancer. Walked on and redshirted in '12 per NCAA transfer rules. Was utilized as a "Z" and slot receiver by the Horned Frogs. In '13, started 6-of-12 games and recorded 36-440-4 (12.2). Broke out when the Horned Frogs adopted the "Air Raid." Started 12-of-13 games in '14 and posted 65-1,018-11 (15.7). Did not start against Kansas State (ankle). Broke his right hand during '15 spring practice. In the fall, was a Biletnikoff finalist after posting the best receiving season in school history — totaled 79-1,327-14 (16.8) in 10 starts before injuring his left wrist against Kansas and missing the final three games. Graduated with a degree in film.

Strengths: Willing to work the middle of the field. Good bend in his routes. Transitions cleanly out of his breaks and bursts out of the top of his routes. Adjusts very well to the path of the ball — runs underneath it like a centerfielder. Great ball skills and body control. Sharp route runner makes defined cuts and settles into soft spots in coverage. Deceptively fast to get on top of defensive backs. Has soft, natural hands and adjusts very well to off-target throws. Made some spectacular snags outside his frame, as he displayed again during the gauntlet drill at the Combine when he contorted his body to haul in a ball thrown well behind him. Tied for the best vertical jump (41 inches) among receivers at the event, correlating to exceptional leaping ability and in-air adjustments. Produced the third-best 20-yard shuttle (4.08 seconds) among receivers, indicative of outstanding agility. Willing blocker. Outstanding production. Highly motivated and driven to succeed. Outstanding personal and football character.

Weaknesses: Could become more nuanced beating the jam at the line of scrimmage and escaping press coverage. Does not have a great catching radius. Lacks elusiveness after the catch to shake defenders in the open field. Does not power through contact or break many tackles. Goes down easy. Is not a strong or consistent blocker — could do a better job fitting on the second level.

Future: A well-built, highly competitive, clutch receiver who consistently produces. Has the reliable hands, route savvy, body control and ball skills to make an impact in the pros. Exceptional Combine performance added to a very productive senior season. Should emerge as a safe, dependable No. 2 receiver most ideally suited for a West Coast offense.

Draft projection: Top-50 pick.

Scout's take: "I think he is a product of the system. His hands are too inconsistent. I might be nitpicking. The game I have a hard time forgetting is the Texas Tech game. (TCU) got lucky and scored a TD with 30 seconds remaining to win it. The ball was thrown to him in the end zone, and he dropped it and another receiver caught it behind him to win the game. It wasn't a great throw. He was lucky to get his hands on it, but I thought he could have extended better. He has short arms, and I think it affects his catching radius. I just don't see great speed. And I have charted too many drops. He was barely an 80-percent catcher in the four games I (viewed of) him. I was expecting to see better."

WR [F] / RB **D.J. FOSTER**, #8 (Sr-4)

ARIZONA STATE   ▶ GRADE: 5.10
Ht: 5-10 1/4 | Wt: 193 | 40: 4.54 | Arm: 30 1/2 | Hand: 9 1/4

History: Highly recruited Arizona native whose commitment to ASU represented a major recruiting coup. Running back-defensive back who won a pair of state titles, earned all-state honors on both sides of the ball and was named the state's player of the year after piling up 3,058 yards and 60 touchdowns his senior year. Lost his older sister Jennifer to a drug overdose when he was a sophomore in high school. Played in Mike Norvell's run-play-action system with zone-read concepts. As a true freshman running back in 2012, carried 102 times for 493 yards (4.8-yard average) and two touchdowns with 38 receptions for 533 yards (14.0-yard average) and four touchdowns in 13 games (one start). Started 12-of-14 games in '13, rushing 93-501-6 (5.4) and catching 63-653-4 (10.4). Was the team's leading rusher in '14 when he toted 194-1,081-9 (5.6) and caught 62-688-3 (11.1) in 13 starts. Transitioned from running back to seeing more time as a "Z" receiver in '15 — was voted team MVP after he amassed 59-584-3 (9.9) receiving and 55-280-1 (5.1) rushing in 13 starts. Had receptions on 57.9 percent of his 209 targets the last two seasons. One of just five players in NCAA history to gain 2,000 yards rushing and 2,000 yards receiving. Team captain and Dean's List student-athlete on track to graduate in the spring.

Strengths: Experienced, three-year starter. Tied for the fastest 20-yard shuttle (4.07 seconds) among receivers at the Combine, indicative of outstanding quickness and lateral agility. Can create mismatches against linebackers and is effective on wheel routes. Makes some tacklers miss and shows some creativity in space. Good competitor. Outstanding multi-purpose production. Very mature and has served as an ambassador of the program.

Weaknesses: Limited size with short arms and small, unreliable hands. Makes too many concentration drops looking upfield before he secures the ball. Not a polished route runner and is still learning the route-running trade. Lacks blazing speed. Overwhelmed blocker. Limited special teams value.

Future: A converted running back who transitioned outside as a senior and still saw action all over the field as a multi-purpose threat. A good college football player lacking ideal traits for the pro game, Foster is the type of player you root for, yet will need to make an impact on special teams to factor in the NFL. Could warrant interest as a backup change-of-pace back and slot receiver.

Draft projection: Late draftable pick.

WR [X] **WILL FULLER**, #7 (Jr-3)

NOTRE DAME   ▶ GRADE: 5.92
Ht: 6-0 1/8 | Wt: 186 | 40: 4.28 | Arm: 30 3/4 | Hand: 8 1/4

History: Philadelphia native played receiver and cornerback in high school. Played all 13 games as a true freshman in 2013, starting three at wide receiver, and recorded six receptions for 160 yards (26.7-yard average) and one touchdown. Started all 26 games at the "X" receiver in Brian Kelly's power-spread the next two seasons — totaled 76-1,094-15 (14.4) in '14; and 62-1,258-14 (20.3) in '15. Returned two punts for 10 yards in his career. Voted team MVP. Fuller's 30 career receiving touchdowns ranks second in school history behind Michael Floyd.

Strengths: Recorded the fastest 40-time (4.28 seconds) of any player at the Combine, demonstrating his rare speed to separate and take a top off a defense. Good gear change to stop and start suddenly and pop out of his breaks. Makes speed cuts at top speed and accelerates out of his breaks. Can run by defensive backs and tracks the ball well over his shoulder. Explosive in the open field when he has a clear lane. Is a threat to score every time he touches the ball and has game-breaking speed.

Weaknesses: Has a very thin build and is not built to withstand contact, making him more susceptible to injury in the pros. Not a consistent catcher or polished route runner. Slowed to catch the ball in the gauntlet drill at the Combine, showing tightness in his hips, weaving off the line and not naturally catching. Average ball skills and depth perception. Had 21 drops the last two years. Needs to become a more focused hands catcher, especially on short routes and screens. Only bench-pressed 225 pounds 10

WIDE RECEIVERS

times at the Combine and lacks functional playing strength as a perimeter blocker. Has not factored on special teams.

Future: Lean, playmaking vertical threat with rare speed. Is not yet a polished route runner or secure hands catcher and still has a lot to learn about the receiver position. Rare speed will command early interest, yet does not factor on special teams and lack of bulk, inconsistent hands and raw route running temper his draft value.

Draft projection: Top-40 pick

Coach's take: "His drops are specific. Specific to wanting to turn quick, short routes where he stops his feet into bigger plays. When he's moving his feet, he's pretty good. His concentration, he looks at the ball into his hands, so they're specific." — *Notre Dame Head Coach Brian Kelly*

WR [X] KEYARRIS GARRETT, #1 (Sr-5)

TULSA ▶ GRADE: 5.14
Ht: 6-3 3/8 | Wt: 220 | 40: 4.48 | Arm: 34 1/2 | Hand: 9

History: First name is pronounced "Key-air-is." Cousin of former Falcons WR David Mims. Has a three-year-old daughter. Won three state football championships and played basketball as a Texas prep. Appeared in six games in 2011, recording two receptions for 10 yards (5.0-yard average) and zero touchdowns. Started 11-of-14 games at split end in '12, producing 67-845-9 (12.6). In '13, had 7-68-0 (9.7) in two starts before suffering a season-ending broken left leg injury (granted medical hardship waiver). In '14, started all 10 games played at the "X" and caught 47-698-5 (14.9). Missed two games because of a left LCL sprain. In '15, led the nation in receiving yards — started all 13 games at "X" and racked up 96-1,588-8 (16.5). Had receptions on 56.5 percent of his 170 targets as a senior. Played for Philip Montgomery — an Art Briles disciple — as a senior. Sat out the East-West Shrine Game because of a foot injury. On track to graduate.

Strengths: Excellent length and uses it to create last-second separation. Good ball skills — tracks the ball very well and uses his body to create positioning and shield the ball from receivers. Tough enough to enter traffic and catch on contact coming across the field. Willing blocker with the enough size to cover up linebackers and safeties. Arms and wingspan (82 5/8 inches) measured the longest of any receiver at the

Combine, helping haul in the ball down the field and produce chunk yardage. Nation-leading production.

Weaknesses: Struggles beating press coverage. Average strength and elusiveness after the catch. Is not a burner and many of his catches are contested. Is leggy and not sudden out of his breaks, as confirmed by pedestrian 7.33-second 3-cone drill time at the Combine. Takes long strides and builds to speed. Could take some time to acclimate to NFL complexities. Non-factor on special teams.

Future: Long-limbed, outside-the-numbers, jumpball catcher. Offers a big receiving target in the red zone and projects to a No. 4 role as a possession receiver.

Draft projection: Late draftable pick.

WR [X] RASHARD HIGGINS, #82 (Jr-3)

COLORADO STATE ▶ GRADE: 5.19
Ht: 6-1 3/8 | Wt: 196 | 40: 4.59 | Arm: 32 1/4 | Hand: 9 3/4

History: Nicknamed "Hollywood." Also played basketball and ran track as a Texas prep. Made an immediate impact as the Rams' "X" receiver. Started all 14 games in 2013 and produced 68-837-6 (12.3). Started all 12 games played in '14 and racked up 96-1,750-17 (18.2). Hurt his shoulder against San Jose State, and did not play against Hawaii. As a junior, transitioned from Jim McElwain to Mike Bobo's pro-style, no-huddle offense. Missed time during '15 spring practice (hamstring) and fall camp (groin). On the season, started 11-of-12 games played and caught 66-933-8 (14.1). Did not play against Minnesota (foot sprain), dealt with a nagging hamstring in October and was ill against Air Force. In three seasons became CSU's all-time leader in receptions (238), receiving yards (3,643) and receiving touchdowns (31). Did not run shuttles at the Combine because of tight quads.

Strengths: Experienced three-year starter with outstanding production. Chews up ground with long strides. Has a sizable catching radius. Flashes some run-after-the-catch creativity. Shows natural receiving skills to track, concentrate and adjust. Can extend and pull in a throw off his body.

Weaknesses: Has a thin frame and could stand to add some more bulk to his frame. Builds to speed, coming off the ball with little suddenness and could struggle to beat the jam in the pros. Not a crisp route runner. Only recorded a 32-inch vertical jump at the Combine, indicating average leaping ability. Not aggressive or physical as a blocker. Limited special teams utility.

Future: Narrowly built, long-levered receiver whose best asset is his hands. Needs to incorporate more physicality into his overall game. Has the tools to be an effective zone-beater and red-zone target. Best season came as a sophomore.

Draft projection: Fourth- to fifth-round pick.

WR [X] / KR JOHNNY HOLTON, #3 (Sr-5)

CINCINNATI   ▶ GRADE: 4.93
Ht: 6-0 5/8 | Wt: 190 | 40: 4.53 | Arm: 32 7/8 | Hand: 9 7/8

History: Has 10 siblings. Did not play high school football — was spotted playing recreationally. Spent two years at College of Dupage (Ill.). In 2011, recorded 17 receptions for 289 yards (17.0-yard average) and seven touchdowns, while returning 12 kickoffs for 254 yards (21.2-yard average) in eight games. In '12, caught 23-548-8 (23.8) and returned kickoffs 13-352 (27.1), including a score. Redshirted in 2013 —sat out while becoming eligible academically. Was utilized as an outside receiver in the Bearcats' spread offense. In '14, contributed 29-431-5 (14.9) and returned kickoffs 35-722 (20.6). Played seven games in '15, starting the first four, and snagged 17-461-5 (27.1) with 10-220 (22.0) on kickoff returns. Did not play against Miami (lower leg) then sat out the final four contests with a right hamstring injury that also limited him from running shuttles at the Combine.

Strengths: Has a very smooth stride and covers ground quickly. Climbs the ladder to get the ball and has big-play potential. Flashes some run-after-the-catch ability — accelerates quickly, can elude tacklers in space and will run through contact.

Weaknesses: Raw positional instincts. Does not know how to sift through zones to uncover. Tends to catch with his body. Unpolished route runner. Marginal production. Only bench-pressed 225 pounds eight times at the Combine, tied for the fewest of any receiver and indicating a lack of physical strength. Inconsistent blocker — does not apply himself enough and does not finish.

Future: Linear, outside-the-numbers, vertical receiver still learning the nuances of the game after not playing high school football. Has some developmental potential and

upside. Practice-squad candidate.

Draft projection: Priority free agent.

WR [Z] CAYLEB JONES, #1 (Jr-4)

ARIZONA   ▶ GRADE: 5.14
Ht: 6-2 5/8 | Wt: 209 | 40: 4.63 | Arm: 32 3/4 | Hand: 9 1/4

History: Father, Robert, was a 10-year NFL linebacker with the Cowboys, Rams, Dolphins and Redskins (1992-2001); and uncle, Jeff Blake, was a 13-year NFL quarterback who made the Pro Bowl with the Bengals. Cayleb prepped in Texas and began his college career at UT. As a true freshman in 2012 (wore jersey No. 4), scratched two catches for 35 yards (17.5-yard average) and zero touchdowns. Was charged with second-degree felony aggravated assault in March '13 — allegedly broke the jaw of a UT tennis player who had a relationship with Jones' ex-girlfriend. Charge was ultimately reduced to a misdemeanor. Transferred to Arizona and sat out the '13 season per NCAA rules. Played outside receiver in Rich Rodriguez's spread-option attack and led the Wildcats in receiving his two years in Tucson. In '14, started 13-of-14 games and hauled in 73-1,019-9 (14.0). Also returned an onside kick 44 yards for a touchdown. Was suspended for the first quarter of the Fiesta Bowl against Boise State. Started all 13 games in '15 and totaled 55-904-5 (16.4). Also had a 25-yard completion. Left the Northern Arizona contest because of a left ankle sprain that also kept him from performing the broad jump at the Combine.

Strengths: Good body length. Can climb in the air to get the ball, separate with his body and take it out of a crowd. Solid red-zone target and overall production. Has some run strength after the catch to push through contact. Good competitor. Has NFL pedigree.

Weaknesses: Average athlete. Lacks long speed and can be tracked from behind. Only bench-pressed 225 nine times at the Combine and needs to get physically stronger and improve as a blocker. Lacks physicality for his size. Average bend and body control in his routes. Did not run a full route tree in a simplified offense. Monotone route runner. Could stand to do a better job of dropping his weight in and out of breaks and running more crisp routes. Production faded in 2015.

Future: A big, productive receiver with

WIDE RECEIVERS

developmental potential, Jones could offer the most value as a red-zone target in the pros capable of creating some mismatches with his length.

Draft projection: Late draftable pick.

Scout's take: "I didn't see any special traits. He's a big receiver with average athletic ability, quickness and speed. Guys like him are a dime a dozen to me. He could get drafted late. I wouldn't count on him making a roster."

WR [F] KENNY LAWLER, #4 (Jr-4)

CALIFORNIA   ▶ GRADE: 5.21

Ht: 6-2½ | Wt: 203 | 40: 4.62 | Arm: 33 3/8 | Hand: 10½

History: California native. Redshirted in 2012 while the NCAA investigated his eligibility. Considered transferring, but was convinced to stay when Sonny Dykes arrived. Was the Golden Bears' "Z" receiver in Dykes' "Bear Raid" system. Played 11 games in '13, starting four, and tallied 37-347-5 (9.4). Did not play against Portland State (head). Played 11 games in '14, starting five, and collected 54-701-9 (13.0). Did not play against Oregon State (ankle). Was the team's leading receiver in '15 when he played all 13 games — started the first nine — and caught 52-658-13 (12.7). Was limited by bruised buttocks the final 3-4 games. Was a medical exclusion (left shoulder) from the bench-press test at the Combine.

Strengths: Has very long arms and big hands with a fine catching radius. Good functional, football-playing speed. Adjusts well to the ball in the air and makes some difficult catches look routine. Can sink his hips in and out of breaks and get out of his breaks quickly. Snatches the ball outside his frame and tracks it well over his shoulder.

Weaknesses: Very lean frame could pose some issues beating physical press coverage. Drops some very well-placed balls (see Utah) and can be phased by traffic. Limited athlete with a 31-inch vertical jump, among the lowest of receivers at the Combine and indicative of marginal leaping ability and lower-body explosion. Marginal run strength after the catch — goes down too easily. Overmatched in crowds. Only a one-year starter. Limited special-teams value. Character could require closer scrutiny.

Future: Thin-bodied, quick-footed athlete with good enough hands, route-running and athletic ability to compete for a job as a no. 4 or 5 receiver. Inability to con-

tribute on special teams could hinder his draft value.

Draft projection: Fifth- to sixth-round pick.

Scout's take: "He has some talent, but he coasts too much on his natural ability. He needs to figure out fast that he's not on scholarship anymore. We downgraded him some for his character."

WR [X] ROGER LEWIS, #1 (Soph-3)

BOWLING GREEN   ▶ GRADE: 5.10

Ht: 6-0 3/8 | Wt: 201 | 40: 4.51 | Arm: 32 | Hand: 9 3/4

History: Also competed in basketball and track as an Ohio prep. Committed to Ohio State prior to his junior season, but was arrested days before '12 Signing Day and charged with two counts of first-degree felony rape. Lewis claimed he and the woman had a four-year, consensual sexual relationship and he never raped her. He was acquitted on one count, and the jury deadlocked on the second, resulting in a mistrial. Ultimately pleaded guilty to misdemeanor falsification of statements he made to police and was sentenced to three years' probation in exchange for dismissal of the rape charge. The alleged victim requested the case be resolved before being retried. Attended Jireh Prep in 2013. Played inside and outside for BGSU, which employed a Baylor-esque spread, no-huddle, up-tempo offense under Dino Babers. In '14, started all 14 games and produced 73-1,093-7 (15.0). Started all 14 games in '15 and racked up 85-1,544-16 (18.2). Did not run shuttles at the Combine because of a tight hamstring.

Strengths: Good athlete. Flashes big-play ability. Outstanding production — attacks the ball in the air and makes good in-air adjustments to it. Elusive enough after the catch to avoid direct contact and slip through some arm tackles. Tracks the ball well over his shoulder. Very competitive — sacrificed his body laying out to make a difficult catch at the Combine (and had to be reminded not to dive to risk injury). Adjusts well to the low ball and uses his body well to shield defenders from it. Responds well to pressure and made game-winning catch against Indiana with seconds remaining. Film junkie who has had to be kicked out of the office from studying film too long. Has a passion for the game and it shows in his approach on the field. Good football temperament.

Weaknesses: Is not a blazer and is a bit

WIDE RECEIVERS

choppy and unrefined as a route runner with some tightness in his hips. Only bench-pressed 225 pounds eight times at the Combine, tied for the fewest of any receiver and indicating a lack of physical strength. Did not regularly match up against top corner-backs in the Mid-American Conference and struggled vs. better competition (see Tennessee). Registered 13.3 body-fat percentage at the Combine, indicating a relative lack of conditioning. Character must be vetted — remains on probation.

Future: A very productive football player that has been removed from some draft boards for lingering character concerns. Emerged as a playmaker for Bowling Green upon his arrival and has the physical tools to be molded into a solid pro.

Draft projection: Priority free agent.

Scout's take: "His charges sound bad, but I'm not worried about him at all. He has matured. He knows what was almost taken away from him. He's not a bad person. He works at it. He's a good player."

WR [X]/ KR **KOLBY LISTENBEE**, #7 (Sr-4)
TCU   ▶ GRADE: 5.27
Ht: 6-0 | Wt: 197 | 40: 4.34 | Arm: 31 3/8 | Hand: 8 1/4

History: High school quarterback who excelled on the track as a Texas prep. Sustained a concussion his junior season. Made nine appearances as a true freshman in 2012, scratching one catch for 59 yards (59.0-yard average) and zero touchdowns. Made seven appearances in '13 and had 2-23-0 (11.5). Played the "Z" receiver for the Horned Frogs' "Air Raid" attack. In '14, started 12-of-13 games and produced 41-753-4 (18.4). Sustained a concussion against Iowa State. Started 10-of-11 games played in '15 and managed 30-597-5 (19.9). Injured his hip against SMU — did not play against Texas Tech or Texas and did not start against Kansas State. Had three career rushes for 30 yards (10.0-yard average) and zero touchdowns, as well as eight kickoff returns for 177 yards (22.1-yard average). Also ran track for the Horned Frogs. Graduated with a communications studies degree. Did not run shuttles at the Combine because of injuries to both groins.

Strengths: Very rare timed speed — accelerates to top speed in a heartbeat and can take the top off a defense. Explosive movement skill. Catches the ball well outside his frame and can track it over his shoulder. Capable of beating man coverage.

Weaknesses: Has extremely small hands that lead to some drops. Struggles to beat physical press coverage and routes can be altered. Straight-linish. Limited run-after-the-catch strength and elusiveness to create with the ball in his hands. Unpolished route runner with raw positional instincts — lacks a feel for coverage and drifts in his routes. Not dynamic or elusive in the open field.

Future: A lean-framed, vertical receiver with legitimate track speed that could force defenses to play honestly. Could make a living in the pros as a field-stretching, big-play weapon most ideally for a team employing an aggressive downfield passing attack such as the Cardinals, Panthers or Steelers. Limited effectiveness on special teams diminishes his value. Still must prove he is more than a track athlete playing football following injury-riddled senior season.

Draft projection: Late draftable pick.

Scout's take: "He's always hurt. That is the problem. He didn't play all year. I was excited about his speed and upside when I passed through the school. But his hands are a little shaky, he's not special as a kick returner and durability has been an issue. Add it all up and he's a late rounder at best. I could see someone taking a flier on the kid in the fifth (round) because of the way he can run."

WR [X]/ RB **RICARDO LOUIS**, #5 (Sr-4)
AUBURN   ▶ GRADE: 5.17
Ht: 6-1 3/4 | Wt: 215 | 40: 4.41 | Arm: 32 3/8 | Hand: 9 1/2

History: Miami native. As a true freshman in 2012, collected three catches for 36 yards (12.0-yard average) and zero touchdowns. Was primarily a flanker in Gus Malzahn's up-tempo, play-action, vertical scheme. Started 7-of-14 games in '13 and tallied 28-325-2 (11.6). Started 5-of-12 games played in '14 and snagged 21-261-3 (12.4). Did not play against Samford while nursing turf toe on his left foot. Started 8-of-13 games in '15 and caught 46-716-3 (15.6). Was banged up and hampered beginning in Week Three. Also had an eye injury against Kentucky. Had 68 career rushes for 578 yards (8.5-yard average) and two touchdowns. Did not run shuttles at the Combine because of a left groin injury.

Strengths: Intriguing size-speed ratio with explosion in his body. Can stretch the field. Versatile and aligns all over the field, lining up inside and outside as a receiver and out of the backfield. Good run skills — vision, balance and short-area burst. Posted an 11-foot broad jump at the Combine, the most explosive of any receiver. Also registered a 38-inch vertical jump and tied for the second-highest number of bench-press reps (18) among receivers. Caught the game-winning TD against Georgia on a tipped ball.

Weaknesses: Tight-hipped and a bit straight-linish. Runs a limited route tree. Hands are not natural — fights the ball. Struggles to escape from press coverage and can be phased by traffic. Has never been a full-time starter.

Future: Explosive athlete and raw, developing football player who capped an average all-star game showing with an explosive Combine workout that could allow him to be drafted late. Height-weight-speed prospect who was used in a multitude of roles and best fit will likely come as an outside-the-numbers vertical threat.

Draft projection: Late draftable pick.

Scout's take: "He did not play well at the NFLPA all-star game. He is just a free agent."

WR [F]/RB/KR BYRON MARSHALL, #9 (Sr-4)
OREGON ▶ GRADE: 5.12
Ht: 5-9 3/8 | Wt: 201 | 40: 4.45e | Arm: 30 1/4 | Hand: 9 1/2

History: Also ran track as a California prep — recorded a 10.61-second 100 meters. Was recruited as a running back to the Ducks' high-octane, no-huddle, up-tempo spread-option offense. As a true freshman in 2012, received the fourth-most rushes behind Kenjon Barner, Marcus Mariota and De'Anthony Thomas — rushed 87 times for 447 yards (5.1-yard average) and four touchdowns in 11 games. Was the Ducks' leading rusher in '13 when he carried 168-1,038-14 (6.2) and caught 13 balls for 155 yards (11.9-yard average) and zero touchdowns. Did not play against Oregon State (right ankle sprain). Transitioned to a slot receiver role in '14 — started 12-of-15 games and led the Ducks with 74-1,003-6 (4.9), while running 52-392-1 (7.5). In '15, managed 9-121-2 (13.4) before injuring his right ankle on a kickoff return against Utah and undergoing season-ending surgery. Had 19 career kickoff returns for 450 yards (23.7-yard average). Did not work out at the Combine because of a right ankle injury.

Strengths: Versatile — lines up all over the field and contributes as a runner, slot receiver and return man. Quick and athletic with the ability to string moves together in the open field and create some magic. Good balance and body control with a low center of gravity to absorb contact and spin off some tackles. Shifty changing direction with quick foot turnover. Tracks the ball well over his shoulder.

Weaknesses: Developing route runner still learning how to operate in the slot — needs to learn how to be more precise, set up routes and transition out of breaks more cleanly. Makes some concentration drops. Tends to let the ball into his frame.

Future: Short, compact, converted running back that fits most ideally as a slot receiver in the pros. Quick and athletic with developmental traits and return capability.

Draft projection: Late draftable pick.

Scout's take: "Some teams have him stacked as a running back. Some have him as a receiver. He can be a gadget guy and do a little bit of both, but I see him as being more of a receiver."

WR [F]/PR JALIN MARSHALL, #17 (Soph-3)
OHIO STATE ▶ GRADE: 5.34
Ht: 5-10 1/2 | Wt: 200 | 40: 4.62 | Arm: 31 1/2 | Hand: 9 5/8

History: Ohio native who played quarterback in high school and won a state long jump championship. Sustained his first concussion in high school, then another in 2013, his redshirt year. Tore his left meniscus during '14 spring practice, requiring arthroscopic surgery. Was used as the Buckeyes' hybrid H-back in the fall — played all 15 games for the national champs and contributed 38 receptions for 499 yards (13.1-yard average) and six touchdowns with 25 carries for 145 yards (5.8-yard average) and one touchdown. Also returned 24 punts for 283 yards (11.8-yard average), including one score, and two kickoffs for 56 yards (28.0-yard average). In '15, moved out wide in the Buckeyes' pro-style spread — started 11-of-12 games played and logged 36-477-5 (13.2) receiving with 28-379 (13.5) on punts. Added 2-30-0 (15.0) on the ground. Was suspended for the '15 season opener against Virginia Tech (violation team rules) and did not start in Week Two against Hawaii.

Strengths: Has a thick, compact build and looks like a running back. Athletic, sudden movement skills with good balance and lateral agility to create with the ball on designed runs, after the catch and as a returner. Effective working the middle of the field. Can make sensational, one-handed snags outside his frame (see Indiana). Recorded a 37 1/2-inch vertical jump, indicating good lower-body explosion. Good eyes and anticipation as a returner.

Weaknesses: Has some lower-body tightness and is still learning how to run routes. Stays covered too long and needs to do a better job of separating with savvy and quickness. Lacks top-end speed to pull away and can be tracked down from behind.

Future: A strong, thickly-built, well-muscled, productive slot receiver who was overshadowed in a strong receiving cast and is likely to make the most immediate impact in the pros as a punt returner. Was not targeted a lot in a weak throwing offense and was more productive as a sophomore than he was a junior.

Draft projection: Fourth- to fifth-round pick.

WR [X] MEKALE McKAY, #2 (Sr-4)

CINCINNATI ▶ GRADE: 5.03
Ht: 6-3 5/8 | Wt: 207 | 40: 4.54 | Arm: 30 5/8 | Hand: 9 1/2

History: Also an all-state basketball player as a Kentucky prep. Began his college career at Arkansas (wore jersey No. 82), where he started 10-of-12 games at "X" receiver and caught 21 balls for 317 yards (15.1-yard average) and two touchdowns. Slid down the depth chart during '13 spring practice and did not feel like the transition from Bobby Petrino's spread offense to the Hogs' more pro-style system suited him well, prompting a decision to transfer just prior to fall camp. Also wanted to be closer to his ailing grandmother (who raised him), a situation which the NCAA deemed worthy of a hardship waiver, granting immediate eligibility at Cincinnati. On the season, logged 16 catches for 485 yards (30.3-yard average) and seven touchdowns in the Bearcats' spread system. In '14, started 12-of-13 games at the "Z" and produced 44-725-8 (16.5). Part of a deep receiver corps when he played 12 games, drawing three starts, and chipped in 27-507-2 (18.8). Did not play against Miami (Fla.). Graduated with a degree in Health Education.

Strengths: Very fluid and graceful in his movement. Catches in stride and adjusts well to the thrown ball. Excellent height with good leaping ability to go up and play the ball in the air. Good feet to run underneath it and create big plays. Good redzone target with a wide catching radius to win jumpball situations.

Weaknesses: Has short arms for his frame

and is disinterested catching in traffic. Takes long strides and is not quick to pop out of breaks. Posted a 4.67-second 20-yard shuttle at the Combine, the slowest of any receiver and indicative of a lack of quickness and agility that shows in his monotone route-running. Limited burst and explosion create difficulty releasing cleanly from press coverage. Not a natural hands catcher. Does not play on special teams.

Future: A raw developmental project with some upside to grow into a no. 5 receiver. Limited burst, shaky hands and lack of special teams' contributions could hinder his roster chances.

Draft projection: Priority free agent.

WR [Z] PAUL McROBERTS, #1 (Sr-4)

SOUTHEAST MISSOURI STATE ▶ GRADE: 5.42
Ht: 6-1 3/4 | Wt: 202 | 40: 4.55e | Arm: 33 1/2 | Hand: 9 3/4

History: Father died of a heart attack when Paul was nine. Played baseball growing up then played basketball (won state championship) and competed in track and field (jumps) as a prep in St. Louis. Tore his left labrum during his junior year. As a true freshman in 2012 (wore jersey No. 85), had 11 receptions for 138 yards (12.5-yard average) and two touchdowns. Wore jersey No. 11 in '13 when he started 10-of-12 games at "X" receiver and led the Redhawks with 44-646-9 (14.7). Did not start against Tennessee State or Jacksonville State (sustained a concussion against JSU in the season finale). Joined the basketball team after the season — saw action in 13 games and averaged six points a game, though he missed the final five games (fractured rib). Changed to jersey No. 1 in '14 when he caught 44-711-9 (16.2) in seven starts at the "X." Also tossed a 28-yard pass. Missed five games with a Lisfranc fracture in his right foot. Was the leading receiver again in '15 — started all 11 games at "X" and totaled 76-940-9 (12.4) with 14 punt returns for 162 yards (11.6-yard average), including a score, and four kickoff returns for 78 yards (19.5-yard average). Two-time captain owns school's career receiving touchdowns record (29). Earned invitations to the East-West Shrine Game and Senior Bowl, and would be the first Redhawk drafted since Eugene Amano in 2004 (Titans, seventh round).

Strengths: Good length. Outstanding athletic ability and body control — is fluid and flexible for his size. Exceptional competitor — attacks the ball in the air and plays strong-handed in a crowd. Very solid showing at the Senior Bowl, making dif-

53

ficult catches look routine and competing on special teams. Plays with physicality as a blocker and does not back down from a challenge. Battles thru pain.

Weaknesses: Is not a blazer and lacks polish as a route runner. Tight press coverage presents some challenges escaping the line cleanly. Could require a little extra time to acclimate to the complexities of an NFL offense. Underdeveloped body — could benefit from more time in the weight room. Has been slowed by various injuries.

Future: Big, small-school, clutch go-to receiver who showed he could match up with better competition at the Senior Bowl. Is still relatively raw and learning how to run NFL routes, yet has tools to develop and the toughness and competitiveness to earn a job as an eventual starter.

Draft projection: Third- to fourth-round pick.

WR [F] / QB **BRAXTON MILLER**, #5 (Sr-5)

OHIO STATE ▶ GRADE: 5.38

Ht: 6-1 3/8 | Wt: 201 | 40: 4.47 | Arm: 31 3/4 | Hand: 9 1/8

History: Has a son named Landon. High school quarterback who also played basketball as an Ohio prep. Played all 12 games in 2011 — took over the starting quarterback job in Week Four and completed 85-of-157 pass attempts (54.1 percent) for 1,159 yards with 13 touchdowns and four interceptions. Also rushed 159 times for 715 yards (4.5-yard average) and seven touchdowns. Was the National Freshman of the Year, according to College Performance Awards, and took home Big Ten Freshman of the Year honors. Started all 12 games in '12, passing 148-254-2,039-15-6 (58.3) and running 227-1,271-13 (5.6). Suffered a head injury against Purdue. In '13, started all 12 games played and totaled 162-255-2,094-24-7 (63.5) through the air and 171-1,068-12 (6.2) on the ground. Sprained his left MCL against San Diego state and missed two September contests. Suffered a torn right labrum in his right (throwing) shoulder in the Orange Bowl against Clemson — had arthroscopic surgery, but reinjured the shoulder during '14 fall camp and had season-ending surgery. Was the Big Ten's Offensive Player of the Year his final two seasons at quarterback. In '15, returned as a hybrid receiver in the Buckeyes' pro-style spread — started 7-of-13 games and totaled 26 receptions for 341 yards (13.1-yard average) and three touchdowns with 42-260-1 (6.2) on the ground. Suffered a head injury

against Minnesota. Team captain graduated with a communications degree. Voted best practice performer at the Senior Bowl.

Strengths: Flashes playmaking ability with the ball in his hands (see spin move vs. Virginia Tech) and elite separation quickness. Adjusts well to off-target throws and catches without breaking stride. Tied for the fastest 60-yard shuttle (10.84 seconds) of any player at the Combine and the fastest 20-yard shuttle (4.07) of any receiver at the event, revealing excellent quickness, burst and dynamic acceleration that correlates to his on-field performance. Registered a sleek 3.3 body-fat percentage, indicative of a highly conditioned athlete with excellent stamina. Has passing experience to design specialty plays. Very competitive. Produced a 22-2 record as a quarterback and could serve as an emergency passer and zone-read package runner.

Weaknesses: Lacks polish as a route runner — needs to learn how to set up defensive backs with stems and nods and sell his routes. Only played non-QB for one season. Modest career receiving production. Relies too much on his natural talent and needs to be challenged by competitive situations. Not a self-starter. Can still learn how to adopt a more professional work ethic.

Future: A dynamic slot receiver still learning the nuances of the receiver craft, Miller possesses the quickness, burst and acceleration to develop into a game-changing playmaker with continued refinement. Is not a throwaway as a quarterback and quarterbacking career could still be resurrected situationally on gadget plays or specialty packages in the pros for a zone-read offense such as the Bills or Seahawks.

Draft projection: Second- to third-round pick.

Scout's take: "Everyone was talking Miller up at the Senior Bowl. I was watching him closely, and I thought he really struggles with his routes. He's very unorthodox and has a lot of funky moves. He's feisty and battled, and people got excited about him competing — I understand that. But there is a rawness there that I don't get as fired up about."

WR [F] / CB **MALCOLM MITCHELL**, #26 (Sr-5)

GEORGIA ▶ GRADE: 5.32

Ht: 5-11 5/8 | Wt: 198 | 40: 4.43 | Arm: 32 5/8 | Hand: 10 1/2

History: Georgia native. Made an immediate impact in 2011 — started 9-of-11 games played at split end and recorded 45 catches for 665 yards (14.8-yard average) and four touchdowns. Pulled a hamstring against Tennessee and missed three mid-season contests. Missed time during '12 spring practice (hamstring). Sat out the season opener against Buffalo (left ankle sprain). Started 9-of-13 games in '12 — three September contests at cornerback, six more at split end — and recorded 40-572-4 (14.3) receiving, while returning 16 kickoffs for 360 yards (22.5-yard average) and 11 punts for 57 yards (5.2-yard average). On defense was credited with 12 tackles, three pass breakups and zero interceptions. Had arthroscopic surgery to repair a torn right meniscus in April '13 then tore his right ACL in the season opener against Clemson. Returned for '14 spring practice, but was sidelined by a left leg injury. Had his right knee scoped a month before the '14 season. Logged 31-248-3 (8.0) in nine games (three starts). Healthy in '15, started all 13 games at split end and led Bulldogs receivers with 58-865-5 (14.9). Team captain graduated with a communications degree. Mitchell, who has written a children's book, was recognized as a member of the AFCA Good Works Team.

Strengths: Has very big hands for his size. Dependable catcher has come thru in the clutch and can be trusted on third down. Good concentration in traffic — willingly enters the middle and catches on contact. Plays the ball well in the air and makes good adjustments. Runs hard with urgency thru contact and plays bigger than his size. Assignment-sound. Smart, tough and focused. Fine route savvy, setting up defensive backs with nods and stems and breaking off his routes cleanly with little wasted motion. Recorded a 1.51-second 10-yard split at the Combine, indicative of excellent short-area burst. Effortful blocker. Plays with confidence, brings energy to the field and elevates the performance of the WR group. Outstanding all-around character. Leads vocally and by example and is a well-respected team leader. Has return experience.

Weaknesses: Has a lean frame. Struggles some escaping press coverage and is best with free releases. Lacks top-end speed to take the top off a defense. Average run strength and elusiveness after the catch. Durability requires close scrutiny.

Future: A tough, passionate, crafty slot receiver who can be trusted to move the sticks in critical situations, Mitchell gained more confidence in his knee in his second year removed from ACL surgery. Brings similar energy, toughness and attitude as

Steelers 1998 third-round pick Hines Ward. Smart and versatile enough to contribute in multiple roles, perhaps even at cornerback where he began his Georgia career, and could be most attractive to a veteran coaching staff such as the Patriots or Steelers.

Draft projection: Fourth- to fifth-round pick.

Scout's take: "Mitchell had a solid week at the Senior Bowl. In terms of route running, adjusting to the ball away from his frame and using tempo to set up defensive backs, I think he played well."

WR [X] CHRIS MOORE, #15 (Sr-5)

CINCINNATI ▶ GRADE: 5.24

Ht: 6-1 | Wt: 206 | 40: 4.49 | Arm: 33 3/8 | Hand: 9 3/8

History: Prepped in Florida, where he won a state championship and garnered Parade All-American honors. Redshirted in 2011 after breaking his left collarbone during fall camp. Played 12 games in '12 and had four catches for 113 yards (28.3-yard average) and two touchdowns. Became the Bearcats' "X" receiver in '13 when he recorded 45-645-9 (14.3) in 13 starts. Started all 13 games in '14 and caught 30-673-8 (22.4). In '15, started 9-of-12 games played and notched 40-870-7 (21.8). Did not play against Miami (Fla.) because of a lower leg injury. Had four career carries for 26 yards (6.5-yard average) and zero touchdowns, as well as 11 career kickoff returns for 226 yards (20.5-yard average).

Strengths: Has long arms. Experienced three-year starter. Very good straight-line speed to gain a step on defenders and make plays down the field — averaged 20-plus yard per catch the last two years. Urgent turning upfield after the catch. Tracks the deep ball well and will highpoint it in a crowd. Has a 37-inch vertical, indicative of great leaping ability. Beat Ohio State's Eli Apple on a deep post for a TD and produced 3-221-3 against the Buckeyes as a junior.

Weaknesses: A bit straight-linish with tightness in his body coming off the line of scrimmage that allows him to be knocked off routes. Shies from the middle and does not do a lot of dirty work inside. Loses concentration and does not make a lot of contested catches. Only bench-pressed 225 pounds 10 times at the Combine and lacks functional playing strength as a blocker. Has no special teams experience, and his stiffness and strength deficiency would not translate well to covering kicks.

Future: Raw, big-play vertical receiver

WIDE RECEIVERS

who has stepped up against better competition and consistently shown he could create big plays in the passing game.

Draft projection: Fifth- to sixth-round pick.

WR [X] **MARQUEZ NORTH**, #8 (Jr-3)

TENNESSEE ▶ GRADE: 5.07

Ht: 6-2½ | Wt: 223 | 40: 4.46 | Arm: 33⅜ | Hand: 10¼

History: Also ran track as a North Carolina prep. Took ownership of the "X" position in the Vols' power-spread offense as a true freshman in 2013 when he produced 38 receptions for 496 yards (13.1-yard average) and one touchdown in 11 starts. Sustained a high ankle sprain against Vanderbilt and did not play against Kentucky. Started all 10 games played in '14 and snagged 30-320-4 (10.7). Was in the training room all year for foot, back and shoulder pain — missed the final three games because of a torn labrum which required surgery and sidelined him for '15 spring practice. Had a minor knee sprain in August then was plagued by back pain in the fall when he started 4-of-7 games played and collected 6-59-0 (9.7). Will be a 21-year-old rookie.

Strengths: Has an NFL body, with a well-distributed frame, very long arms, big hands and outstanding timed speed. Athletic tester at the Combine who showed well in every event, including running a 4.13 20-yard shuttle and 6.90-second 3-cone drill revealing outstanding agility for his size.

Weaknesses: Marginal, declining production each season. Has been nagged by a series of injuries and has not been able to stay healthy. Is still learning how to run a full route tree.

Future: Big, strong, fast athletic specimen whose production has regressed every year since he arrived on campus and made an immediate impact as a freshman. Has the athletic talent to eventually earn a starting job in the pros if he finds a way to stay healthy and committed. Could have benefitted from another year in school.

Draft projection: Priority free agent.

Coach's take: "I give Marquez a lot of credit. He tried to fight through some nagging injuries, and he's worked really hard to get himself back. The thing I like about him right now is he's become a very good student of the game. He's always asking the question why; he's always asking for extra help; he's always asking for an extra set of eyes. 'Coach, how's this?' Now when we talk about the

maturity in conversations, the level of conversation with him has increased and not just what's his route, but the inner-workings of everything and the small details of getting open. That's what I've really liked. He's really, really committed himself to the football intelligence part of it." (TFP) — *Tennessee Head Coach Butch Jones*

WR [X] **JORDAN PAYTON**, #9 (Sr-4)

UCLA ▶ GRADE: 5.21

Ht: 6-1⅛ | Wt: 207 | 40: 4.44 | Arm: 32½ | Hand: 10⅛

History: Prepped at Oaks Christian (Calif.), where he was a U.S. Army All-American. Switched his commitment four times before signing with UCLA. As a true freshman in Noel Mazzone's spread, up-tempo offense in 2012, recorded 18 balls for 202 yards (11.2-yard average) and one touchdown in 13 games (four starts at wide receiver). Started 11-of-13 games at the "X" in '13 and caught 38-440-1 (11.6). Started all 26 games at "X" the next two seasons — totaled 67-954-7 (14.2) in '14; and 78-1,105-5 (14.2) in '15 when he led Bruins receivers for the second straight year. Owns the school record for career receptions (201). Started his own clothing line.

Strengths: Experienced three-year starter with very good production. Good size, athletic ability and body control. Deceptively fast and capable of gaining a step on defenders. Competes for the ball in the air. Solid hands. Fine field awareness to move the chains. Good coverage recognition — knows where to settle into zones. Solid positional blocker — locks on and steers defensive backs and flashes some aggression in the run game.

Weaknesses: Has some tightness in his body and does not show much burst or acceleration off the line of scrimmage. Limited creativity after the catch. Most of his catches are contested. Could do a better job of finishing blocks.

Future: A good-sized, possession receiver with enough toughness and field awareness to be effective as a zone-beating, chain-moving target. An ideal backup with some physical talent to develop, Payton is most suited to work outside the numbers as a vertical receiver.

Draft projection: Fifth- to sixth-round pick.

Scout's take: "There are grades all over the board on Payton. He's a great kid, but I thought he was a backup at best."

WIDE RECEIVERS

WR [Z] **CHARONE PEAKE**, #19 (Sr-5)

CLEMSON ▶ GRADE: 5.24

Ht: 6-2 3/8 | Wt: 209 | 40: 4.42 | Arm: 34 | Hand: 9 1/4

History: South Carolina native won a state championship, garnered USA Today and U.S. Army All-American honors and also competed in basketball and track. Played inside and outside in Clemson's up-tempo, "smashmouth spread." Was a reserve as a true freshman in 2011, collecting four receptions for 71 yards (17.8-yard average) and zero touchdowns. In '12, played all 13 games — started the first two in place of the suspended Sammy Watkins — and recorded 25-172-2 (6.9). In '13, managed 8-84-1 (10.5) in two starts before suffering a season-ending torn left ACL injury. Tore his left meniscus in July '14. In the fall, started 4-of-7 games played and logged 12-129-2 (10.8). Missed six mid-season contests (left knee scope). Healthy in '15, contributed 50-716-5 (14.3) in 15 starts. Team captain graduated with a degree in parks, recreation and tourism management.

Strengths: Excellent size-speed ratio with rare arm length to pluck the ball. Can create separation vertically and win with jumpball situations with his length. Tracks it well over his shoulder. Good field awareness. Very good run-after-the-catch strength. Very competitive blocker (see Miami) — attacks cornerbacks with aggression and is effective sealing the edges.

Weaknesses: Has very small hands for as big-framed as he is. Has some stiffness in his body with below-average agility, as reflected in 4.46-second 20-yard shuttle time. Limited run creativity after the catch — struggles to re-direct. Only a one-year producer and will require time to learn NFL complexities. Had to re-start a drill at the Combine for not following direction. Average career production. Durability has been an issue throughout his career.

Future: An excellent-sized, big-framed, competitive boundary receiver with dimensions that will excite scouts on paper and blocking physicality that will peak the interest of evaluators. However, Peake is a tight-hipped, straight-line, injury-prone athlete with small, inconsistent hands and will require some patience to acclimate to an NFL offense. Medical evaluations and team interviews could affect draft standing.

Draft projection: Fourth- to fifth-round pick.

Scout's take: "(Peake) is a height-weight-speed prospect that gets drafted late. He has small hands and little production. He is a strider, not an accelerator. The highlight of his career was in the Miami game. He smacked around (Miami CB) Artie Burns two plays in a row. The first time, Burns tries to tackle him, and Peake doesn't move. Artie was literally hanging on his arm like a little kid. The next play was an outside stretch-zone run. Peake is blocking and hits Burns so hard he just drops and the ball goes right around him for a 60-yard touchdown. (Peake) has not produced the way the staff expected, but he really took it to Miami in that game."

WR [X] **DEMARCUS ROBINSON**, #11 (Jr-3)

FLORIDA ▶ GRADE: 5.24

Ht: 6-1 3/8 | Wt: 203 | 40: 4.59 | Arm: 33 | Hand: 9 1/2

History: Nephew of Marcus Robinson, who was a nine-year NFL receiver with the Bears, Ravens and Vikings (1998-2006). Demarcus lost his father when he was just a toddler. Had a tumultuous freshman year in 2013 — had five receptions for 23 yards (4.6-yard average) and zero touchdowns in seven appearances. Was suspended three times for marijuana use (did a 45-day rehab stint). Demarcus says he has not smoked since his freshman year in Gainesville. In '14, started 11-of-12 games at the "X" and produced 53-810-7 (15.3). Started 9-of-13 at "X" and caught 48-522-2 (10.9). Was suspended for the Florida State contest for a curfew violation. Played for three different offensive coordinators and schemes, including spread and pro-style.

Strengths: Outstanding arm length. Field fast. Very good ball skills. Flashes playmaking ability. Has some creativity to make sharp cuts and elude tacklers. Catches well in a crowd. Good agility, body control and bend to sink his hips and get in and out of breaks. Has a good feel for coverage and knows how to position to get open. Very competitive. The game comes natural to him. Has NFL pedigree.

Weaknesses: Lacks top-end speed and acceleration. Does not make many tacklers miss in the open field. Tends to body-catch and trap the ball even when he is in the clear uncontested — plays small and seldom extends outside his frame and plucks the ball out of the air. Not a consistent hands catcher. Tends to drift and freelance in his routes — not precise. Inconsistent blocker. Track record demonstrates a consistent disregard for authority and the inability to follow direction. Did not listen very well dur-

WIDE RECEIVERS

ing receiving drills at the Combine, having to repeat drills from the start.

Future: A very good-sized, athletic play-maker with a rogue, undisciplined approach to the game. Has the physical talent to earn a starting job in the pros, yet will struggle to maximize his potential given his immaturity. High-risk, high-reward prospect likely to slide several rounds in the draft because of repeated off-field issues and a lack of discipline on and off the field.

Draft projection: Fifth- to sixth-round pick.

Scout's take: "(Robinson) is off our board. Talk about Mayday Moscow — he has too many red flags for us to mess around with him. He'd drive our coaches crazy."

WR [X] ALONZO RUSSELL, #9 (Sr-6)

TOLEDO　　　　　　　▶ GRADE: 4.94

Ht: 6-3 5/8 | Wt: 206 | 40: 4.48 | Arm: 33 7/8 | Hand: 9 1/2

History: Also played basketball and ran track as a Washington D.C. prep. Did not score high enough on his SAT, and attended Milford Academy (N.Y.) in 2010. Redshirted in '11 while working to become eligible academically. Took ownership of the "X" position in Toledo's spread offense in '12 by starting all 13 games and producing 56 receptions for 960 yards (17.1-yard average) and five touchdowns. Started 11-of-12 games in '13 and caught 59-728-6 (12.3). Started all 13 games in '14 and totaled 51-770-8 (15.1). In '15, started 11-of-12 games and had 36-618-8 (15.1). Sat out the first half of the Temple contest after he was ejected for targeting against Western Michigan. Graduated.

Strengths: Excellent body length. Four-year starter. Has enough speed and length to separate at the top of his routes. Tracks the ball well in the air and will climb the ladder to go get it. Has a wide catching radius. Functional, get-in-the-way blocker.

Weaknesses: Unrefined route runner with little gear change or suddenness. Comes off the line too upright. Ran a limited route tree. Does not have a good feel for zones. Declining annual production. Average athletic ability reflected in 29 1/2-inch vertical jump, the second lowest among receivers at the Combine. Also produced marginal shuttle times indicative of modest agility. Average positional instincts. Could require some additional time to acclimate to a complex NFL playbook.

Future: Very linear, narrow-shouldered, tight-waisted, long-limbed, vertical, out-side-the-numbers target. Career under-achiever lacking desirable toughness to function in the middle of the field. Could compete for a backup job as an "X" receiver.

Draft projection: Priority free agent.

WR [X] RASHAWN SCOTT, #11 (Sr-5)

MIAMI (FLA.)　　　　　▶ GRADE: 4.86

Ht: 6-0 7/8 | Wt: 199 | 40: 4.55e | Arm: 31 3/8 | Hand: 9 3/8

History: Also played basketball and ran track as a Florida prep. Appeared in six games in 2011, mainly on special teams, and caught one ball for two yards (2.0-yard average) and zero touchdowns. Missed the second half of the season because of a shoulder injury. Played nine games in '12 and contributed 35-512-3 (14.6). Was suspended the final three games of the season (violation team rules). In '13, managed just 3-38-0 (12.7) in four games. Broke his left collarbone in the season opener against Florida Atlantic, which sidelined him for six games and rendered him a virtual non-factor the rest of the season. Was suspended for the bowl game against Louisville. Suffered another clavicle fracture in '14, causing him to redshirt. In '15, returned to start 11-of-13 games at "X" in Miami's up-tempo, pro-style offense, producing 52-695-5 (13.2). Exited the Clemson game (left shoulder). Was a medical exclusion from the 40 at the Combine because of a right knee injury and did not perform shuttles because of a right calf injury.

Strengths: Willing to enter traffic and make plays across the middle and flashes some playmaking ability (see Florida State when beat Jalen Ramsey one-on-one for TD). Adjusts well to the ball. Functioned in a pro-style offense.

Weaknesses: Has been too brittle in college and will struggle to withstand the rigors of the NFL game — shoulder injuries have been recurring. Very tight-hipped. Lacks polish as a route runner. Has concentration lapses and at times gets beat up by the ball with hands like skillets.

Future: Emerged as a senior following an injury-riddled, suspension-shortened career. Could compete for a roster spot in a camp and will need to make his mark on special teams to stick.

Draft projection: Priority free agent.

Scout's take: "He is stiff with inconsistent hands. He weighed about 185 pounds when I passed through there. He's really skinny, and he has too many drops. He's a free agent."

WR [F] **HUNTER SHARP**, #3 (Sr-4)

UTAH STATE ▶ GRADE: 5.11

Ht: 5-11½ | Wt: 198 | 40: 4.58 | Arm: 31 5/8 | Hand: 9 3/8

History: Cousin, Derrick Johnson, is a Pro Bowl linebacker for the Chiefs. Sharp prepped in California. Spent two years at Antelope Valley College (Calif.). Played six games in 2012 and recorded 23 receptions for 304 yards (13.2-yard average) and three touchdowns. Missed four games because of a pulled left quad. Played nine games in '13 and logged 49-657-6 (13.4). Totaled 21 punt returns for 214 yards (10.2-yard average), including two scores, and returned five kickoffs for 48 yards (9.6-yard average) as a sophomore. Played the "X" in the Aggies' spread offense and was their leading receiver the last two seasons. Started 12-of-14 games in '14, producing 66-939-7 (14.2). Was suspended the first two games of the '15 season (violation team rules) before starting 10-of-11 games and catching 71-835-9 (11.8). Over two seasons with USU, had 14 carries for 48 yards (3.4-yard average) and zero touchdowns and 13-394-1 (30.3) on kickoff returns. Was injured during East-West Shrine Game practice. Graduated with an interdisciplinary studies degree.

Strengths: Plays with urgency. Shows some creativity with the ball in his hands and runs with fearlessness after the catch. Tough competitor. Makes good adjustments to the ball. Versatile and lines up all over the field — in the slot, split wide, out of the backfield, as a kickoff and punt returner and even as a gunner on kickoff team. Very confident playing demeanor and plays with a lot of emotion. Willing blocker. Has return experience.

Weaknesses: Average size and length. Could do a better job of attacking the ball in the air. Produced the shortest broad jump (8-feet, 10 inches) of any receiver at the Combine, indicative of a lack of lower-body explosion. Average athlete with a 32 1/2-inch vertical jump. Suspension reveals an underlying issue that he has not been able to manage.

Future: A better football player than athlete, Sharp has the toughness and competitiveness to earn a role as a contributing slot receiver and special teams player in the pros if he could learn to be more disciplined off the field — a big "if". Must prove that football is more important to him than recreational activities to earn a job in the NFL.

Draft projection: Late draftable pick.

Scout's take: "(Sharp) has some draftable traits — quickness, athleticism, hands and some production. The problem is that he has been suspended three times all for the same issue, and if the past is a predictor of the future, it's going to continue to be an issue. He's not a bad kid."

WR [F,X] **TAJAE SHARPE**, #1 (Sr-4)

MASSACHUSETTS ▶ GRADE: 5.32

Ht: 6-2 | Wt: 194 | 40: 4.52 | Arm: 32 1/4 | Hand: 8 3/8

History: First name is pronounced "TAHJ-a." Receiver-safety who won a pair of state championships at Piscataway (N.J.) Township. As a true freshman in 2012, started 8-of-11 games played and had 20 receptions for 206 yards (10.3-yard average) and zero touchdowns. A broken right hand cost him three starts then sat out the season finale against Central Michigan because of a concussion. Was UMASS' leading receiver his final three seasons. Started 11-of-12 games in '13 and produced 61-680-4 (11.1). Started all 12 games in '14 and totaled 85-1,281-7 (15.1). Was targeted more than any receiver in the country (190+) in '15 when he led the NCAA in receptions — hauled in 111-1,319-5 (11.9) in 12 starts. Team captain owns UMASS records for career receptions (277) and receiving yards (3,486). Was knocked out of the Senior Bowl with a quad injury. Doesn't turn 22 until December. Did not perform shuttles at the Combine because of left groin and hip flexor injuries.

Strengths: Experienced, four-year starter well-versed in a pro-style offense. Sharp route runner — makes defined cuts with very little wasted motion. Works through traffic and shows no hesitation catching on contact. Has enough speed to gain a half-step of separation. Adjusts well to the thrown ball. Very good hands. Competes hard. Outstanding career production. Has a pleaser personality and is very accountable.

Weaknesses: Has very small hands with a narrow bone structure. Tight in the hips. Is not a burner. Could struggle some releasing cleanly vs. physical press corners in the pros. Does not attack the ball in the air.

Future: Thinly built, productive jack-of-all-trades who was deployed in a many different ways to create mismatches in college. Has the reliable hands to develop into a solid No. 3 or 4 receiver in the pros and could be most ideal operating out of the slot.

Draft projection: Third- to fourth-round pick.

WIDE RECEIVERS

WR [F]/ PR **STERLING SHEPARD**, #3 (Sr-4)
OKLAHOMA ▶ GRADE: 5.84
Ht: 5-10¼ | Wt: 194 | 40: 4.44 | Arm: 30 3/8 | Hand: 9 3/4

History: Father, the late Derrick Shepard, was a receiver for Oklahoma before playing 36 games with the Redskins, Saints and Cowboys (1987-91) in the NFL. Sterling amassed 5,100 all-purpose yards as an Oklahoma prep. Also played basketball and was one of the best long jumpers in the state. Primarily a slot receiver in OU's up-tempo, no-huddle offense (had four offensive coordinators/co-coordinators in four years). Was the Big 12 Offensive Freshman of the Year in 2012 when he caught 45 balls for 621 yards (13.8-yard average) and three touchdowns in 13 games (four starts). Started all 12 games played in '13 and produced 51-603-7 (11.8). Sustained a concussion against Baylor and sat out against Iowa State. Started all 12 games played in '14 and grabbed 51-970-5 (19.0) in 12 starts. Also returned 11 punts for 73 yards (6.6-yard average). Did not play against Baylor while nursing a left groin strain. Healthy in '15, racked up 86-1,288-11 (15.0) with 19-148 (7.8) on punts. Had 17 career carries for 120 yards (7.1-yard average) and one touchdown. Graduated with a political science degree.

Strengths: Extremely strong pound-for-pound and can bench press nearly twice his weight, producing 20 reps at the Combine, tied for the most among all receivers and indicative of his physical strength that shows beating the jam. Also tied for the most explosive vertical jump (41 inches) among receivers at the Combine, correlating to exceptional leaping ability and lower-body explosion. Is quick and sudden with very good route savvy. Understands how to set up defensive backs and open their hips before snapping off his routes. Catches the ball very naturally and makes it look easy adjusting to it. Fearless working through traffic and wins jumpball situations. Extremely competitive and driven to succeed. Physical, pestering blocker and will finish blocks.

Weaknesses: Undersized with a small frame that could be more stressed by the rigors of the NFL. Measured the smallest wingspan (71 5/8 inches) of any receiver at the Combine and offers a small catching radius. Is not a dynamic or creative punt returner. Could struggle shaking more physical cornerbacks at the line of scrimmage.

Future: A superb football player and natural receiver who plays much bigger than his size. Will quickly earn the trust of his quarterback as a rookie and is capable of making an immediate impact as a dependable slot receiver and potential punt returner.

Draft projection: Top-50 pick.

Scout's take: "Shepard is not the biggest guy. He is just a good football player. You know exactly what you are getting. He's safe. I know he's not going to go there, but I put a late first-round grade on him. Love the person, love the player."

WR [F]/ PR **NELSON SPRUCE**, #22 (Sr-5)
COLORADO ▶ GRADE: 5.18
Ht: 6-1 1/8 | Wt: 206 | 40: 4.59 | Arm: 30 | Hand: 10

History: Receiver-defensive back prepped in California, where he also starred on the diamond. Was arrested in the spring of 2011 for marijuana possession. Redshirted that fall. Started 9-of-12 games at the "Z" in '12, catching 44 balls for 446 yards (10.1-yard average) and three touchdowns. Started all 12 games at "Z" in '13, producing 55-650-4 (11.8) while returning 10 punts for 45 yards (4.5-yard average) and two kickoffs for 63 yards (31.5-yard average), including a 46-yard return of an onside kick for a score. Moved to the "X" in '14 when he started all 12 games and hauled in 106-1,198-12 (11.3) with 12-90 (7.5) on punts. Had a Pac-12 record 19 grabs in California game. Capped his record-setting career by starting all 13 games at the "X" in '15, totaling 89-1,053-4 (11.8) with 10-61 (6.1) on punts. Completed 5-of-8 career pass attempts (62.5 percent) for 83 yards with one touchdown and zero interceptions. Two-time team MVP and two-year team captain. Was targeted nearly 300 times the last two seasons and netted completions at a clip of approximately 66 percent. Caught more balls (294) than any receiver in Pac-12 history, and owns 41 school records. Graduated with a business degree (emphasis in finance and management).

Strengths: Experienced four-year starter in a pro-style offense. Excellent career production. Has exceptional hands and concentration in a crowd. Outstanding personal and football character and was regarded as the face of the program.

Weaknesses: Lacks top-end speed, burst and acceleration — one-speed, controlled route runner who takes measured steps. Most catches are contested. Does not play fast and will struggle to beat physical press coverage in the pros. Allows the ball inside his frame too much.

Future: Very smart, productive, sure-handed, short-to-intermediate receiver

WIDE RECEIVERS

most ideally suited for the slot where he could release cleanly and help a team as a clutch, chains-moving, third-down target. Compensates for his speed deficiency with route savvy, field awareness and superb hands. Ability to return punts could allow to earn a roster spot.

Draft projection: Late draftable pick.

WR [Z] **MICHAEL THOMAS**, #3 (Jr-5)
OHIO STATE   ▶ GRADE: 5.66
Ht: 6-2 3/4 | Wt: 212 | 40: 4.56 | Arm: 32 1/8 | Hand: 10 1/2

History: Nephew of Pro Bowl receiver Keyshawn Johnson (1996 No. 1 overall), who played 11 years with the Jets, Buccaneers, Cowboys and Panthers (1996-2006). Thomas was one of the most productive receivers in California as a senior when he racked up 86 receptions for 1,656 yards (19.3-yard average) and 21 touchdowns. Attended Fork Union (Va.) Military Academy in 2011 (roomed with quarterback Cardale Jones). With the Buckeyes in 2012, saw action in 11 games (two starts) and grabbed 3-22-0 (7.3). Redshirted in '13 in order to preserve a year of eligibility. Ascended to the top of the depth chart at "X" receiver in the Buckeyes' pro-style spread. Started 14-of-15 games in '14 and produced 54-799-9 (14.8). Had sports hernia surgery in the spring of '15. On the season, was the Buckeyes' leading receiver for the second year in a row with 56-781-9 (13.9). Graduated with a sport industry degree.

Strengths: Looks the part with a big-frame, long arms and big hands. Good agility to make the first tackler miss with sharp, defined cuts. Bench-pressed 225 pounds 18 times at the Combine and has good strength and body power to push through contact and break some arm tackles. Has a wide catching radius and the size and length to factor in the red zone — beat Virginia Tech's Kendall Fuller for a TD with a double-move on a stop-and-go route and Minnesota's Brian Boddy-Calhoun on a corner fade.

Weaknesses: Lacks polish in his routes and is still learning how to sift through zones and settle. Weaved heavily in the gauntlet drill at the Combine, exposing his hip tightness. Struggles getting off the line of scrimmage cleanly against physical press corners (see Michigan State). Disinterested blocker with inconsistent effort. Has had multiple Twitter outbursts and will require some maintenance controlling his emotion.

Future: A better athlete than football player at this stage of his development, Thomas plays with a chip on his shoulder and can make a living as a solid complimentary No. 2 receiver with continued refinement and maturity.

Draft projection: Second- to third-round pick.

Scout's take: "No. 3 is big, tall and lean looking with a decent upper body. I don't think he has really good hands to snatch and pull the ball down out of a crowd. I saw him catch two or three balls and all were within his frame."

WR [Z,F,X] **LAQUON TREADWELL**, #1 (Jr-3)
MISSISSIPPI   ▶ GRADE: 6.24
Ht: 6-2 | Wt: 221 | 40: 4.60e | Arm: 33 3/8 | Hand: 9 1/2

History: Has a child. Also played basketball as a prep in south suburban Chicago, where he won a state championship in football, was a consensus All-American and No. 1 receiver recruit in the country. Was Southeastern Conference Freshman of the year in 2013 when he started 12-of-13 games at slot receiver and produced 72 catches for 608 yards (8.4-yard average) and five touchdowns. In '14, started 8-of-9 games at wide receiver — caught 48-632-5 (13.2) before breaking his left fibula and ankle against Auburn. Was a Biletnikoff finalist in '15 after leading the SEC in receiving yards and setting single-school records for receptions and receiving yards — started 11-of-13 games (gave way to two-tight end formations in non-starts) at wide receiver and hauled in 82-1,153-11 (14.0). His 82 catches came on 133 targets (61.7 percent). Was flagged seven times on the season. Needed just 34 games to claim Ole Miss' career receptions record (202). Will be a 21-year-old rookie. Opted not to run the 40 or shuttles at the Combine and went through positional drills wearing a gold cross chain wearing a backwards hat.

Strengths: Outstanding size. Physically imposing. Good spatial awareness to pick apart zones. Can drop his weight, accelerate at the top of his stems and knows how to uncover. Ultra-tough and competitive and seeks to bury defenders as a blocker, especially early in his college career. Carries a swagger and is extremely confident in his ability. Plays smart and instinctive. Attacks the ball in the air and is aggressive in the red zone. Tracks the ball well over his shoulder and wins jump-ball situations with regularity. Plays much faster than he times and has very good functional speed. Good feet to stem in his routes and uncover. Strong and patient with the ball in his hands and does not go down easy. Brandishes a fierce stiff-arm and plays with pride. Has blue-collar toughness, does not back down from anyone and carries the mentality of a defensive player on and off the field.

Weaknesses: Lacks blazing speed and most of his catches are contested. Could struggle to separate against tight, press coverage. A bit straight-linish with some stiffness in his hips and body affects his gear change and agility. Could be more disciplined in his routes. Has some prima donna traits and does not always compete for the ball when double coverage is rolled his way. Can be frustrated and let his emotions get the best of him. Did not interview well with teams at the Combine.

Future: A big, strong, ultra-competitive, physical receiver with similar talent, swagger and competitiveness as Cowboys WR Dez Bryant, Treadwell compensates for his lack of stopwatch speed with functional football-playing speed and physicality.

Draft projection: Mid- to-late first-round pick.

Scout's take: "Treadwell is better than Anquan Boldin. He is a talented (player), man. All I can say is, if he tested as well as he plays, he is a top-five pick hands down. He has pieces of some of the top receivers that have come out. He comes down with 50-50 balls like Megatron (Calvin Johnson). He runs routes like Julio Jones. He blocks like Mike Evans. I know he's not going to run fast, but he plays fast."

WR [Z] D'HAQUILLE "DUKE" WILLIAMS, #1 (Sr-4)
EX-AUBURN ▶ GRADE: 5.01
Ht: 6-2 1/4 | Wt: 229 | 40: 4.69 | Arm: 32 1/2 | Hand: 9 1/4

History: First name is pronounced "DAH-keel." Was raised — with seven siblings — by a single mother. Prepped in Louisiana, where he began high school playing basketball. Transferred to another school in order to play football — was a football junior, but three years shy of graduating. Finished his high school career in 2010. Got his GED in '11 then was a two-time All-American at Mississippi Gulf Coast College. Played 11 games in '12 and posted 67 receptions for 1,295 yards (19.3-yard average) and 17 touchdowns. D'haquille's 16-year-old cousin was shot and killed in May '13. In the fall, played nine games and caught 51-733-9 (14.4). Missed one game (sprained left shoulder). Originally committed to LSU, but signed with Auburn in order to distance himself from the gangs, violence and drugs of his hometown. Was used as a "Y" (slot) receiver by the Tigers. In '14, started 7-of-10 games played and grabbed 45-730-5 (16.2). Sprained his right MCL against Texas A&M and missed two games then was suspended for the Outback Bowl against Wisconsin (violation team rules). Was suspended for six days during '15 fall camp for an undisclosed discipline issue then tweaked an ankle during a scrimmage. On the season, managed 12-147-1 (12.3) in five starts. Was dismissed from the team after the San Jose contest, reportedly for an incident at an Auburn bar. According to al.com, Williams was upset when a member of his party was kicked out of the bar for not removing his sunglasses. Williams, who appeared intoxicated, allegedly verbally attacked security guards, threw a drink at a woman and threw punches at four people, including a teammate. Will be a 24-year-old rookie.

Strengths: Big, strong and physical. Competitive attacking the ball in the air. Makes demanding catches in traffic and willingly enters the middle. Withstands some big hits and holds onto the ball. Very good concentration. Ultra-tough and does not back down from a challenge. Has a passion for the game and has been praised by coaches for his practice habits and commitment to the game when he is in the football facility.

Weaknesses: Stiff route runner with tight hips. Does not pop out of his breaks. Is not a consistent blocker. Limited run-after-the-catch strength. Registered 15.6 body-fat percentage at the Combine, the highest measure for any receiver at the Combine and indicative of a poorly conditioned athlete at the WR position. Lacked maturity during the interview setting. Has required a lot of maintenance with multiple off-field issues and can invite distractions in the locker room.

Future: A second-round physical talent based on 2014 evaluation that will likely spiral down multiple rounds after running into trouble off the field as a senior and being kicked off the team. Would benefit from a strong veteran locker room and a patient, demanding positional coach in a town away from his native Louisiana where he has too many negative influences. Character concerns have removed him from consideration on many NFL draft boards and could leave him undrafted, though he has the talent to become a rags-to-riches success story if he ever can find a way to stay focused and out of trouble. Has starter-caliber potential for a patient coaching staff willing to provide

WIDE RECEIVERS

the hard coaching he needs to thrive.

Draft projection: Fourth- to fifth-round pick.

Scout's take: "(Williams) might be a free agent. Think about it for a minute. He has character (concerns). He didn't play this season. He didn't work out well. He's not worth the risk for a lot of teams. ...He will be the guy that Cincinnati signs, makes the team and becomes an all-pro."

WR [Z] JORDAN WILLIAMS, #8 (Sr-4)

BALL STATE   ▶ GRADE: 5.07

Ht: 6-2 1/2 | Wt: 226 | 40: 4.60e | Arm: 32 7/8 | Hand: 9 7/8

History: Also competed in basketball and track and field as an Indianapolis prep. As a true freshman in 2012, appeared in eight games without recording receiving stats. Began '13 on the second team, but injuries opened the door for him to start the final eight games. Overall, hauled in 72 catches for 1,050 yards (14.6-yard average) and 10 touchdowns. In '14, started all 11 games played at the "X" receiver and totaled 56-753-6 (13.4). Sustained a high left ankle sprain in the season opener and did not play against Indiana State. Started 11-of-12 games at the "X" in '15 and produced 72-920-8 (12.8). Graduated with a risk management degree.

Strengths: Experienced, three-year starter. Outstanding size. Good leaping ability. Has a wide catching radius and will climb the ladder and lay out for the ball. Uses his body well to get positioning and shield defenders from the ball. Good football smarts.

Weaknesses: Inconsistent hands. Not aggressive attacking the ball and struggles to separate — most of his catches are contested. Backside blocking temperament is passive and would expect to be more physical for his size. Does not operate well in the middle of the field. Not creative after the catch. Has not yet figured out what it means to prepare like a pro and is at his best with hard coaching. Has not regularly matched against top competition. Has no special teams experience.

Future: Well-built, athlete with enough strength to create some yardage after the catch and battle for a job as a backup in a West Coast offense. Limited special teams experience could diminish his chances of making a roster.

Draft projection: Priority free agent.

Scout's take: "I don't see the speed, toughness or passion for the game. He's missing an 'it' factor. His effort is different when the ball is coming his way — that's why he is covered like a blanket. He jogs on the backside when the ball isn't going to him. He doesn't make any plays."

WR [Z] / TE DE'RUNNYA WILSON, #1 (Jr-3)

MISSISSIPPI STATE   ▶ GRADE: 5.09

Ht: 6-4 5/8 | Wt: 224 | 40: 4.84 | Arm: 33 7/8 | Hand: 9 1/4

History: Birmingham native who only played football his freshman and senior years — won a pair of state championships on the hardwood, a Parade All-American, Alabama's Mr. Basketball was a D1-caliber prospect. As a true freshman in 2013, had 27 catches for 248 yards (9.2-yard average) and three touchdowns in 13 games (one start). Played seven games on the basketball team, but focused solely on football thereafter. Was used inside and outside in Dan Mullen's multiple, power-spread system. Was the Bulldogs' leading receiver in '14 when he started 10-of-12 games played and caught 47-680-9 (14.5). Was hurt against Alabama and held out for precautionary reasons against Vanderbilt. Was arrested for marijuana possession in March '15. On the season, started all 13 games and totaled 60-918-10 (15.3). Was carted off the field with an apparent neck injury against Alabama, but did not miss a start. Did not bench press at the Combine because of a right shoulder injury or perform the shuttles because of a left hamstring injury.

Strengths: Rare size with long arms and an 80 1/2-inch wingspan that translates to a wide catching radius. Good ball skills. Uses his body well to shield defenders from the ball. Powers through the jam and shows very good sideline awareness. Presents a huge target and security blanket for a quarterback and has been a reliable, chain-moving, third-down producer. Outstanding size to cover up defensive backs as a perimeter blocker in the run game.

Weaknesses: Comes off the ball upright and struggles to separate with speed or route savvy. Lets the ball into his frame too much. Recorded the slowest 40-yard dash time (4.89 seconds) of any receiver at the Combine, revealing his heavy feet and lack of burst. Also posted the lowest vertical jump (28 inches), which correlates to his non-explosive, monotone movement skill.

Future: Big, long-limbed, physical red-zone target capable of creating mismatches with his outstanding length and body control. Lack of foot speed could hinder his chances and force teams to take a look at him as a tight end conversion.

Draft projection: Late draftable pick.

TIGHT ENDS

Nawrocki's TOP 10

1. **HUNTER HENRY**
2. **Austin Hooper**
3. **Nick Vannett**
4. **Tyler Higbee**
5. **Jerell Adams**
6. **Thomas Duarte**
7. **Temarrick Hemingway**
8. **Beau Sandland**
9. **David Morgan**
10. **Ben Braunecker**

TE [F] JERRELL ADAMS, #89 (Sr-4)

SOUTH CAROLINA ▶ GRADE: 5.36

Ht: 6-5 1/8 | Wt: 247 | 40: 4.64 | Arm: 34 3/8 | Hand: 9

History: South Carolina native who played all over the field for the football team and won a state championship with the basketball team. Spent 2011 at Fork Union (Va.) Military Academy. With the Gamecocks in '12, saw limited action in nine games and caught four balls for 90 yards (22.5-yard average) and one touchdown. An ankle injury hampered him during '13 fall camp and into the season, but he managed to play all 13 games (one start) and log 13-187-2 (14.4). Played all 13 games in '14, drawing five starts after Rory Anderson was injured, and caught 21-279-1 (13.3). Dealt with a strained hamstring the week of the '15 season opener, but started 9-of-12 games and posted 28-421-3 (15.0). Graduated with a public health degree. Did not bench press at the Combine because of a right shoulder injury.

Strengths: Has a solid base with a sturdy build. Scrappy, competitive playing temperament — attacks the ball in a crowd and is very willing as a blocker. Is tough enough to mix it up against bigger bodies at the line of scrimmage and functional in-blocking in the run game. Solid showing finishing blocks against linebackers in Senior Bowl drills. Efficient second-level blocker — engages and runs his feet on contact. Urgent with the ball in his hands, turning up the field after the catch and displaying creativity in space to avoid tacklers. Sleek enough to stretch the seam and create some separation downfield. Adjusts well to the ball outside his frame and will sacrifice his body in a crowd. Has special teams experience and is aggressive covering kicks. Measured the second-longest wingspan (82 1/4 inches) of any tight end at the Combine.

Weaknesses: Very small hands for as big-framed as he is. Lacks bulk strength and weight-room strength to match up with power and could stand to add some mass to his frame. Rolls off the line with little suddenness and builds to speed. Needs to learn how to sharpen his routes and become more crafty shaking coverage — lacks polish sifting through zones on stick routes and rounds too much. Average run strength after the catch. Raw, developing positional instincts and feel for the game.

Future: Developmental athlete operated most heavily from the slot, yet surprisingly has the base, toughness and desire to effectively contribute as an in-line blocker and could emerge as a well-balanced, complete tight end with a few years of seasoning and continued physical development.

Draft projection: Third- to fourth-round pick.

Scout's take: "Adams is extremely talented, arguably the best all-around talent at the position in the draft when it comes to athletic ability, size, hands, strength — he is the best blocker. The only concern is going to be his questionable mental aptitude and instincts. That's where he doesn't measure up."

TE [F]/WR STEPHEN ANDERSON, #89 (Sr-5)
CALIFORNIA ▶ GRADE: 4.92
Ht: 6-2 1/8 | Wt: 230 | 40: 4.65e | Arm: 32 | Hand: 9 1/4

History: High school receiver who also played basketball as California prep. Walked on and redshirted in 2011. Saw very limited action in four games in '12. Played 10 games in '13, starting five at the "Y," and totaled 14 receptions for 125 yards (8.9-yard average) and zero touchdowns. Was put on scholarship Christmas Day. Suffered a hip flexor injury against Washington State and missed two games. Sprained his right MCL during '14 fall camp and missed the first two games. On the season, started 8-of-10 games played at the "Y" position and produced 46-661-5 (14.4). Missed much of '15 spring practice (illness) and had his right thumb surgically repaired before the season, but started 12-of-13 games and caught 41-474-2 (11.6). Graduated with a public health degree. Did not run the 40 or shuttles at the Combine after pulling his hamstring on a route in positional drills.

Strengths: Very good movement skill for the TE position — fires off the line and is quick into his routes. Can mismatch heavy linebackers and separate with speed. Is tough enough to work across the middle and shown he can withstand big hits. Understands how to sift through zones and keep working to come

free. Recorded a 38-inch vertical jump at the Combine, best among tight ends.

Weaknesses: Lacks bulk and physicality. Tips off his routes and gives up break points to defensive backs — is not sudden changing direction or popping out of his breaks and could do a better job setting up defenders in coverage. Too undersized to factor as an in-line blocker in the pros and could do a better job sustaining second-level blocks — too much of a one-hit positional blocker. Only bench-pressed 16 reps at the Combine despite measuring the shortest arms (32 inches) of any tight end.

Future: A big, possession receiver most effective running simple sit routes, Anderson has the receiving skills to warrant an opportunity in a camp, though he lacks the size, strength and girth to be effective as a blocker.

Draft projection: Priority free agent.

TE [H] BEN BRAUNECKER, #48 (Sr-4)
HARVARD ▶ GRADE: 5.19
Ht: 6-3 3/8 | Wt: 250 | 40: 4.72 | Arm: 32 3/4 | Hand: 9 1/2

History: Receiver-defensive back who also returned kicks and played basketball and competed in track and field as an Indiana prep. Missed the last two games of his senior season with a high ankle sprain. Was valedictorian of his graduating class. Did not see action in 2012. Played eight games in '13, recording nine receptions for 91 yards (10.1-yard average) and one touchdown. In '14, caught 11-227-1 (20.6) in seven games (five starts). Suffered an ankle injury against Lafayette and missed three games, and was a non-factor in the final two. Started all 10 games at H-back in '15 and produced 48-850-8 (17.7). Scheduled to receive his degree in molecular and cellular biology.

Strengths: Functional base strength. Creates good extension and lockout as an in-line blocker. Understands angles and leverage and how to torque defenders. Very good receiving production. Good hand-eye coordination and concentration in a crowd to make contested catches. Tough and competitive.

Smart and versatile — lines up all over the field. Registered a 11.32-second 60-yard shuttle at the Combine, best among the TE group and indicative of outstanding lateral agility. Produced a TE-best 1.59-second 10-yard split at the Combine, reflecting good short-area burst. Has a 35 1/2-inch vertical jump, indicative of outstanding athletic ability.

Weaknesses: Has very small hands and too often body-catches the ball. Not a crafty route

TIGHT ENDS

runner and lacks the top-end speed and agility to separate vs. NFL defensive backs. Shows no creativity after the catch and usually goes down on contact. Limited body control and leaping ability. Was not regularly challenged by Ivy League competition.

Future: Strong, steady consistent Ivy League producer most ideally suited for an H-back role in the pros. Has the toughness, competitiveness and intelligence to fend for a job as a No. 3 tight end and find ways to stick on a roster.

Draft projection: Late draftable pick.

Scout's take: "They have had had a number of players sign NFL contracts the last few years. They say (Braunecker) is the most explosive tight end they have had."

TE [F]/WR THOMAS DUARTE, #18 (Jr-3)
UCLA　　　　　　　　　▶ GRADE: 5.28
Ht: 6-2 1/8 | Wt: 231 | 40: 4.69 | Arm: 33 | Hand: 10

History: Mater Dei (Calif.) receiver-linebacker who garnered USA Today and Parade All-American honors. Manned the "Y" position in offensive coordinator Noel Mazzone's spread, up-tempo offense. As a true freshman in 2013, had 16 receptions for 214 yards (13.4-yard average) and three touchdowns in 13 games (four starts). Missed time during '14 fall camp because of a hamstring injury. On the season, started 7-of-11 games played and caught 28-540-4 (19.3). Re-aggravated the hamstring injury against California and missed the next two games. Started 11-of-13 games in '15 and produced 53-872-10 (16.5). Did not practice the week leading up to the Washington State contest (flu). Opted not to run the 60-yard shuttle at the Combine.

Strengths: Can set up defenders in man coverage and create some separation with savvy at the top of his routes. Has a knack for identifying and sinking into soft spots in zone coverage. Reliable red-zone target with outstanding production. Has deceptive speed to stretch the seam and track the ball downfield, making some difficult outstretched catches. Hauled in the ball very effortlessly in Combine receiving drills and is a natural catcher. Produced the second-fastest 10-yard split (1.60 seconds) of any tight end at the Combine.

Weaknesses: Lacks bulk and functional football playing strength to factor in-line and does not have the frame to support much growth. Only bench-pressed 225 12 times, the lowest among the TE group. Was not asked to block often and did not show a lot of desire blocking on the move. Not sudden or quick

off the line of scrimmage and builds to speed. Tweener traits.

Future: An oversized receiver deployed out of the slot, Duarte lacks ideal speed to escape NFL cornerbacks and does not have the size, strength or blocking ability desired as a true Y-type tight end. What he can do is create some mismatches on linebackers and safeties as a move or Joker tight end for a team such as the Redskins, Packers or Patriots. Has natural hands and athletic traits to contribute in a passing game.

Draft projection: Late draftable pick.

Scout's take: "He's a big receiver. That's what he plays, but he's too slow to help us. He's not better than our fifth receiver. He has to be a tight end, and he's not very big or strong. He's an average blocker. I'm not sure what you do with him, at least for us. Teams are hot and cold on the kid. True evaluators will accentuate his positives and find a spot for those traits to be used. He's a flex tight end."

TE [Y] DAVID GRINNAGE, #86 (Jr-4)
NORTH CAROLINA STATE　　　　▶ GRADE: 4.89
Ht: 6-5 1/4 | Wt: 248 | 40: 4.89 | Arm: 34 1/2 | Hand: 10 1/8

History: Last name is pronounced "GRINN-edge." High school tight end-defensive end who also played baseball as a Delaware prep. Redshirted in 2012. Played all 12 games in '13, starting the final seven, and had 14 receptions for 131 yards (9.4-yard average) and one touchdown. Started 11-of-13 games in '14 and recorded 27-358-5 (13.3). Was sidelined during '15 spring practice with a back injury. On the season, started 7-of-13 games and caught 25-290-3 (11.6). Did not bench press at the Combine because of a left elbow injury and a right hamstring injury prevented participation in the shuttles.

Strengths: Has good size with long arms and a frame to continue growing into. Rose to the occasion against better competition and had his best performances against Clemson and Florida State and finished the season strong against North Carolina.

Weaknesses: Does not adjust well to poorly thrown or low balls. Not explosive — gets stuck in his breaks and is a plodding mover. Can't separate vs. man coverage. Stiff, upright route runner — struggles to separate. Lacks bulk and does not play with any power or physicality as a blocker. Tied for the lowest vertical jump (29 1/2 inches) among tight ends at the Combine, confirming the average athletic ability and lower-body explosion with which he plays. Average production. Limited run-after-the-catch ability.

Future: A decent-sized, long-limbed, non-descript tight end with few redeeming qualities to warrant developing. Could warrant an opportunity in a camp.

Draft projection: Free agent

Scout's take: "He was playing with the third team when I went through there (early). He is sort of heavy footed but he has really soft hands. He's not much of a blocker — he should be much better for his size. I graded him as a free agent for someone else. ... He has a kid on the way. That's why he came out early. He could have used another year."

TE [F] **TEMARRICK HEMINGWAY**, #87 (Sr-5)
SOUTH CAROLINA STATE ▶ GRADE: 5.27

Ht: 6-4 7/8 | Wt: 244 | 40: 4.71 | Arm: 34 | Hand: 10

History: South Carolina native played receiver, linebacker and defensive end in high school. Redshirted in 2011. Played nine games in '12 and caught 11 balls for 164 yards (14.9-yard average) and one touchdown. Started 9-of-12 games played in '13 and collected 25-241-0 (9.6). Sat out against Bethune-Cookman (thigh). Started 11-of-12 games in '14 — despite a November concussion — and grabbed 18-257-1 (14.3). Started 9-of-11 games in '15 and pulled in 38-418-1 (11.0). Graduated.

Strengths: Very athletic build with long arms — looks the part. Fluid movement skills. Good speed to stretch the seam and separate. Adjusts well to the path of the ball. Catches in a crowd and can take a hit and hold onto it. Fearlessly works across the middle and is urgent turning upfield after the catch. Ran a TE-best 6.88-second 3-cone drill time at the Combine, indicative of superb quickness and lateral agility.

Weaknesses: Average hand size. Double-catches the ball and could do a better job securing it cleanly. Not a polished or crafty route runner. Lacks run strength after the catch and breaks few tackles in space with an inefficient spin move. Was not regularly challenged in the Mid-Eastern Athletic Conference. Needs to improve as a base blocker and on the move — inconsistent sustaining blocks.

Future: A better athlete than football player at this stage of his career, Hemingway operated heavily out of the slot in a spread offense and ran a lot of stick (option) routes, working well in the middle of the field. Possesses the athletic talent to develop into a solid contributor in the receiving game.

Draft projection: Fourth- to fifth-round pick.

Scout's take: "(Hemingway) was the best

tight end at the NFLPA (all-star) game. He was intriguing. He has size, length and upside. Someone is going to give him a shot to develop."

TE [F] **HUNTER HENRY**, #84 (Jr-3)
ARKANSAS ▶ GRADE: 5.92

Ht: 6-4 7/8 | Wt: 250 | 40: 4.80e | Arm: 32 3/4 | Hand: 9 1/4

History: Father, Mark, was an offensive tackle and team captain for the Razorbacks (1988-91). Henry is an Arkansas native who won a state championship, garnered Parade All-American honors and was a blue-chip recruit. As a true freshman in 2013, started 7-of-12 games and recorded 28 catches for 409 yards (14.6-yard average) and four touchdowns. Started 10-of-13 games in '14 and produced 37-513-2 (13.9). Won the Mackey Award in '15 — racked up 51-739-3 (14.5) in 13 starts. Opted not to run at the Combine.

Strengths: Outstanding production and dependability — did not drop a pass in 2015. Clutch performer — 38-of-39 (98 percent) career receptions on third down (36) have gone for a first down or TD (2). Catches without breaking stride and adjusts very well to the flight of the ball over his shoulder — terrific tracking, concentration and receiving instincts. Understands how to work through zones and where to settle. Has a knack for uncovering against tight coverage. Creates mismatch problems against linebackers and defensive backs. Can make an average quarterback look good. Functional position/sustain blocker — is capable in-line and more effective on the move. Is aggressive working to the second level and creating fits on linebackers.

Weaknesses: Has small hands and short arms. Is not a blazer and lacks top-end speed to separate from man coverage with ease. Only bench-pressed 225 pounds a mere 13 times, fewer than many wide receivers and needs to get physically stronger to hold up as a blocker in the pros. Too easily gets controlled and pushed aside as a run blocker (see Alabama).

Future: An athletic, receiving tight end, Henry was an immediate impact performer upon his arrival in college and has drawn some comparisons from evaluators to Ravens 2001 first-round pick (31) Todd Heap and even Chicago Bears 2007 first-round pick (31) and Panthers TE Greg Olsen, though Hunter is not in the same echelon as Olsen as an athlete with a smaller catching radius. Outstanding body control, sure hands and

TIGHT ENDS

clutch plays in critical situations are Henry's trademark. An exceptional receiving talent and solid football player.

Draft projection: Top-50 pick.

Scout's take: "Henry is arguably the top tight end in the class, but it is a weak tight end class, and he will get overdrafted. He's not a very good blocker. He's weak at the point of attack and gets tossed around. His best attributes are as a receiver and route runner."

TE [F] TYLER HIGBEE, #82 (Sr-5)

WESTERN KENTUCKY ▶ GRADE: 5.38

Ht: 6-5 3/4 | Wt: 249 | 40: 4.75e | Arm: 33 1/4 | Hand: 10 1/4

History: Also played baseball as a Florida prep. Entered the program as a 190-pound receiver as a true freshman in 2011 when he had two catches for 92 yards (46.0-yard average) and one touchdown in 11 games (one start). Suffered a broken right collarbone during fall camp, forcing him to redshirt in '12. Converted to tight end in '13 — caught 13-169-1 (13.0) in seven games (three starts) before stress fractures in his right footed ended his season. Was the Hilltoppers' No. 2 tight end in '14 when he played 11 games, drawing three starts, and tallied 15-230-4 (15.3). Missed two games with a left knee sprain. In '15, started 8-of-9 games played and pulled in 38-563-8 (14.8). Sprained his left MCL against North Texas — sat out four games then reinjured the knee in the Conference USA championship game against Southern Mississippi and missed the bowl game against South Florida. Was a medical exclusion from working out at the Combine because of left knee injury.

Strengths: Very dependable, high-percentage hands-catcher with a wide-catching radius. Catches with confidence and plays with a lot of emotion. Good job finding soft spots in zone coverage and concentrating in a crowd between the hash marks. Secures the ball cleanly outside his frame and can make difficult snags. Turns upfield urgently after the catch and can shake off the first tackler and weave through traffic. Tracks the ball well. Functional second-level, positional blocker able to mirror his man. Battles and competes. Max-effort performer on special teams. Versatile and lines up at multiple positions.

Weaknesses: Has a lean build, lacks in-line blocking strength to match up against power and cannot generate power through his lower half. Lacks weight-room strength. Could do a better job releasing cleanly off the line of scrimmage and escaping the jam. Average

separation speed. Not nifty-footed to elude tacklers and takes some direct hits. Durability has been an issue, missing multiple games every season of his college career and being slowed by multiple knee injuries. Did not regularly match up against top competition in Conference USA. Could learn to adopt a more professional approach to preparation.

Future: A converted receiver with outstanding hands and natural receiving skills, Higbee could factor readily in the passing game with continued focus and durability.

Draft projection: Fourth-round pick.

Scout's take: "He's a lot like (Broncos 2006 second-rounder) Tony Scheffler. He can be a weapon in the passing game, if he can stay healthy. He's a Clearwater, Florida kid who enjoys the nightlife."

TE [F] AUSTIN HOOPER, #18 (Soph-3)

STANFORD ▶ GRADE: 5.64

Ht: 6-3 3/4 | Wt: 254 | 40: 4.71 | Arm: 33 3/4 | Hand: 10 5/8

History: Also lettered in track and field at California powerhouse De La Salle, where he won three state Open Division titles. Redshirted in 2013. Started 10-of-13 games in '14 and produced 40 receptions for 499 yards (12.5-yard average) and two touchdowns. Was a Mackey Award finalist in '15 after starting all 14 games and hauling in 34-438-6 (12.9).

Strengths: Good size with big mitts — hands measured the largest of any tight end at the Combine. Has a good feel for coverage and understands where to settle in zones. Keeps working to uncover. Deceptively eats the cushion of DB's with smooth strides — can get on top of coverage. Has enough speed to threaten the field vertically. Well-versed in a pro-style offense. Aligns all over the field — in the slot, on the line and in the backfield. Solid base as a blocker. Functional second-level, wall-off blocker.

Weaknesses: Lacks physicality as a blocker. Has build-up speed and is not overly crafty in his routes, changing direction or popping out of his breaks. Not sudden or explosive. Lacks creativity with the ball in his hands. Stumbled through some of Combine drills and hand placement was awkward catching the ball. Only bench-pressed 225 pounds 19 times at the Combine and needs to get stronger.

Future: An athletic, pass catcher who had two years of eligibility waiting his turn behind a host of Stanford tight ends currently playing well in the NFL. Could have benefitted from another year of seasoning in college, yet has the athletic traits to develop into a mismatch

TIGHT ENDS

option-route receiver.

Draft projection: Second- to third-round pick.

Scout's take: "Hooper is just not as big or fast as (Arkansas TE) Hunter Henry, but he competes better at the point of attack as a blocker. He is extremely smart because they use him as an H-back — a motion/move/ slide guy. Even when you see him blocking out on the perimeter on receiver hitches, he is smart adjusting and finding guys to block. Henry just has better length. But all-around, the Stanford kid is probably the better player. And they are still third- or fourth-round type talents in a normal draft, but they will go in the second (round) because there are no (elite) tight ends (in this draft)."

TE [F] RYAN MALLECK, #88 (Sr-5)

VIRGINIA TECH ▶ GRADE: 5.12

Ht: 6-4 1/2 | Wt: 247 | 40: 4.80e | Arm: 32 1/2 | Hand: 9 3/8

History: Prepped in New Jersey. As a true freshman in 2011, appeared in 14 games (mostly on special teams). Started 7-of-13 games in '12 and had 17 catches for 174 yards (10.2-yard average) and zero touchdowns. Sat out the '13 season with a torn left rotator cuff and labrum. Started all 12 games played in '14, recording 24-195-2 (8.1). Injured his ankle in Week Three against East Carolina — sat out against Georgia Tech and was hobbled the rest of the season (aggravated in the Western Michigan game). Started all 13 games in '15 and chipped in 21-289-2 (13.8). Team captain was recognized as the Hokie who demonstrated the highest quality of leadership and character. Opted not to run the 40 at the Combine.

Strengths: Is willing to enter traffic, cross the middle of the field and catch on contact. Understands body positioning and how to shield defenders from the ball. Scrappy, competitive blocker — locates his target and can get in the way of linebackers. Accountable leader by example. The game is very important to him.

Weaknesses: Has a narrow frame. Underpowered with modest weight-room strength. Lacks bulk and is overwhelmed at the line of scrimmage by power — lacks the base and point-of-attack strength to sustain blocks. Only bench-pressed 225 pounds 18 times at the Combine, indicating average weight-room strength. Does not have ideal foot speed to threaten the seam. A bit upright and tight in his routes and shows some rigidity adjusting to the ball.

Future: An undersized move tight end,

Malleck played a complimentary role to the more physically talented Bucky Hodges for the Hokies and has the dependability, toughness and work ethic to become a solid role player in the pros. Similar to 49ers TE Garrett Celek and could fend for a No. 3 role.

Draft projection: Priority free agent.

Scout's take: "He's an overachiever. He's just a good football player. He's not very flashy. He's going to do the dirty work unselfishly and give you everything he's got."

TE [H] JAKE McGEE, #83 (Sr-6)

FLORIDA ▶ GRADE: 5.09

Ht: 6-5 1/2 | Wt: 250 | 40: 4.85e | Arm: 32 3/8 | Hand: 9 5/8

History: Quarterback-safety who also played basketball at Collegiate School in Richmond (Russell Wilson's alma mater), where he won a pair of state titles. Began his college career at Virginia, where he redshirted in 2010. Played all 13 games in '11 and tallied eight special teams tackles. Played all 12 games in '12, starting three, and caught 28 balls for 374 yards (12.4-yard average) and five touchdowns. Played 11 games in '13, starting three, and had 43-395-2 (9.2). Did not play against Georgia Tech (left MCL sprain). Decided to join the Gators as a graduate transfer in order to play in an offense better suited to his skill set. However, in the '14 season opener against Eastern Michigan, suffered a broken left tibia and fibula (granted medical hardship waiver). In '15, started all 13 games played and produced 41-381-4 (9.3). Recurring hamstring injuries have been an issue — missed 23 of 30 spring practices his last two years at UVA, sat out the Citrus Bowl against Michigan in January and was sidelined for the Senior Bowl. Was a medical exclusion running and jumping at the Combine because of a hamstring injury.

Strengths: Has a big frame with broad shoulders. Adequate second-level blocker — understands angles and fits well on linebackers. Good concentration in a crowd. Reliable hands — can make the difficult one-handed snag and practices it as an art form. Good ball skills. Quickly came to be respected as a leader at Florida and has some natural leadership traits as a former prep quarterback.

Weaknesses: Limited athlete. Straight-line, mechanical, upright route runner. Lacks speed to threaten the seam. Marginal hip snap on contact. Lacks explosive power in his body and is late out of breaks. Durability is a glaring concern— has struggled to stay healthy throughout his career with leg, knee, shoulder and hamstring injuries that have consistently

TIGHT ENDS

affected playing time. Only bench-pressed 225 pounds 17 times at the Combine and needs to get stronger.

Future: Functional short-to-intermediate receiver lacking the strength to factor in-line as a blocker and would fit best in a move role in the pros. Strong leadership traits could help him win a No. 3 role. Will have to contribute on special teams and find a way to avoid injury to make it.

Draft projection: Priority free agent.

TE [Y] DAVID MORGAN II, #82 (Sr-5)

TEXAS-SAN ANTONIO ▶ GRADE: 5.21

Ht: 6-41/8 | Wt: 262 | 40: 4.96 | Arm: 335/8 | Hand: 101/2

History: Texas native who played receiver in high school, where his basketball prowess convinced UTSA to offer a scholarship. As a true freshman in 2011, played all 10 games, drawing two starts, and recorded 13 catches for 214 yards (16.5-yard average) and two touchdowns. Missed the '12 season because of a chipped right femur (required surgery) — had an osteochondral defect which limited blood flow and softened his bone. Originally hurt the knee lifting weights, then aggravated the injury playing golf. Missed time during '13 spring practice (ankle). In the fall, logged 7-69-0 (9.9 in 11 games (two starts). Started 6-of-9 games played in '14, catching 20-255-1 (12.8). Missed three October contests (ankle). Became the Roadrunners' first All-American in '15 after producing 45-566-5 (12.6) in 12 starts. Sprained his knee during East-West Shrine Game practice and did not play in the game. Team captain will graduate with a degree in business management and a minor in athletic coaching.

Strengths: Outstanding size. Aggressive, face-up blocker who strikes with good initial pop and jars defenders on contact. Plays with a dogged determination, catching in traffic, running after the catch and sacrificing his body as a cut blocker. Aligns in-line, flexed in the slot and out wide, in the backfield and as an H-back — very versatile. Produced the fastest 20-yard shuttle time (4.19 seconds) and third-fastest 3-cone drill time (6.93 seconds) among tight ends at the Combine, indicative of outstanding lateral agility and short-area burst. Physically strong — paced all tight ends with 29 bench-press reps of 225 pounds. Plays with confidence. Solid producer.

Weaknesses: Lacks ideal foot speed to challenge the field vertically. Hit-and-whitt blocker on the move — could do a better job of sustaining blocks after initial contact and

too often let his man work to the ball against better competition (see Arizona and Oklahoma State). Average lower-body explosion, as confirmed in 30-inch vertical jump at the Combine.

Future: May not look pretty getting the job done, yet is consistently productive as an in-line blocker, after-the-catch runner and short-to-intermediate target. Needs to refine his technique, yet has the desire and enough physical talent to work with and could earn a role as a functional no. 2 blocking tight end with continued refinement.

Draft projection: Late draftable pick.

Scout's take: "There were some great tight ends at Miami. He was set to be one of the next great ones in line."

TE [Y] BEAU SANDLAND, #85 (Sr-5)

MONTANA STATE ▶ GRADE: 5.24

Ht: 6-41/2 | Wt: 253 | 40: 4.69 | Arm: 341/4 | Hand: 101/8

History: Prepped in California — high school team won four games in seven years and Sandland was a non-qualifier. At Pierce College (Calif.) in 2011, had 20 receptions for 265 yards (13.3-yard average) and two touchdowns (nine games). In '12, caught 24-267-3 (11.1) in eight games. Was highly recruited coast to coast before joining Miami (Fla.), where he was third on the depth chart in '13 — chipped in 9-94-1 (10.4) in 13 appearances. Seeking a change of scenery more like home and more playing time, transferred to FCS Montana State and redshirted in '14. Started all 11 games in '15 and produced 37-632-9 (17.1).

Strengths: Very well-built with well-defined muscularity, long arms and a powerful trunk. Measured the longest wingspan (82 3/4 inches) of any tight end at the Combine. Recorded a 35-inch vertical jump at the Combine, indicative of outstanding athletic ability. Good speed to work the seams and challenge the field vertically. Solid drive blocker in-line — runs his feet on contact. Strong after the catch to run through arm tackles. Book smart.

Weaknesses: Lets the ball into the fleshy part of his body too much and got beat up by the ball in the gauntlet drill at the Combine. Mechanical route runner. Raw positional instincts and overall awareness recognizing and adjusting to the blitz. Is not battle-tested against top competition.

Future: Physically has all the tools to compete in the NFL and develop into a functional starter. However, it could require some time for Sandland to adapt. Is most ideally suited

TIGHT ENDS

for a No. 2 in-line blocking role.

Draft projection: Fifth- to sixth-round pick.

TE [Y] **NICK VANNETT**, #81 (Sr-4)

OHIO STATE ▶ GRADE: 5.56

Ht: 6-6 | Wt: 257 | 40: 4.75e | Arm: 34 1/4 | Hand: 10

History: Ohio native also played basketball in high school. Redshirted in 2011. Played all 12 games for the undefeated Buckeyes in '12, starting two, and caught nine balls for 123 yards (13.7-yard average) and zero touchdowns. Played through a broken right pinky finger in October. Missed the '13 spring game (concussion). In the fall, contributed 8-80-1 (10.0) in 13 appearances. Played all 15 games in '14 (one start) and grabbed 19-220-5 (11.6). After backing up Jeff Heuerman (Broncos '15 third-rounder), emerged to start 12-of-13 and catch 19-162-0 (8.5) in '15. Graduated with a sports and industry degree. Was medically excluded from running the 40-yard dash at the Combine because of a lumbar injury.

Strengths: Exceptional size and length with a wide catching radius. Passes the eyeball test with a well-muscled, athletic build and long arms. Aligns all over the field — in-line, as a lead blocker in the backfield and detached in the slot. Has a good feel for coverage and understands where to find soft spots in zones. Highpoints the ball. Is capable of threatening the seam and catches on contact in a crowd. Strong runner after the catch. Has enough base strength to match up against power and anchor in pass protection. Delivers some knockout shots on the move. Can create red-zone mismatches. Caught the ball very cleanly in the gauntlet drill at the Combine, adjusting to the ball with ease and snagging a catch one-handed. Very strong all-around Senior Bowl showing. Smart, tough, competitive and very coachable. Takes a serious approach to the game and has strong personal and football character. Unselfish, team player.

Weaknesses: Could do a better job of using his hands to fend off the jam and play with more consistent aggression in the run game. Only a one-year, full-time starter with below-average career receiving production (was not heavily targeted in a deep supporting cast with rotating quarterbacks). Only bench-pressed 225 pounds 17 times at the Combine, and could improve his weight-room strength. Produced a 30 1/2-inch vertical jump, indicative of average athletic ability.

Future: A versatile, well-rounded tight end capable of factoring readily in the pros, Vannett's greatest strength is as a blocker, yet he has also proven to be a when opportunities

have presented and could be a mismatch piece in the red zone.

Draft projection: Second- to third-round pick.

Scout's take: "He was better than (Broncos 2015 third-round pick) Jeff Heuerman when he was backing him up last year. (Vannett) didn't catch a lot of balls with a revolving door at quarterback. He's a good receiver, though, and I really like the way he blocks."

TE [Y] **BRYCE WILLIAMS**, #80 (Sr-5)

EAST CAROLINA ▶ GRADE: 5.16

Ht: 6-5 3/4 | Wt: 257 | 40: 4.89 | Arm: 33 5/8 | Hand: 9 5/8

History: Also earned letters in track (four) and basketball (two) as a North Carolina prep. Began his college career as a preferred walk-on at Marshall, where he redshirted in 2011 and did not play in '12. Transferred to ECU — where his parents and brothers attended — and walked onto the team in '13, catching 20 balls for 220 yards (11.0-yard average) and five touchdowns in 13 games (one start). In '14, caught 18-237-4 (13.2) in 13 games (five starts, including two at fullback). Started all 12 games in '15 and hauled in 58-588-4 (10.1). Graduated with a degree in criminal justice.

Strengths: Very good size with a frame still to grow into. Versatile and aligns all over the field — in-line, in the slot, split wide and as a lead-blocking fullback. Willingly enters traffic and shows good concentration in congestion — effective on underneath drag routes and shallow crossers. Attacks the ball in the air. Functional stalk blocker effective sealing defensive backs and some linebackers.

Weaknesses: Lacks bulk strength and power to move any one off the line of scrimmage or anchor in pass protection. Double-catches too much. Lost track of the ball when turning up the field at the Combine and can do a better job securing the ball before turning upfield. Allowed defender to win at the break point vs. Florida and interception was returned for a TD. Is not a crafty route runner — tends to drift too much. Could do a better job selling patterns. Only a one-year, full-time starter. Recorded the slowest 20-yard shuttle time (4.53 seconds) and 3-cone time (7.19) of any tight end at the Combine, revealing marginal agility. Also tied for the lowest vertical jump (29 1/2 inches), indicating below-average athletic ability and lower-body explosion.

Future: A lanky, dependable receiving tight end capable of moving the chains and factoring in the red zone. Willing blocker on the perimeter, but lacks the girth and power to function in-line.

Draft projection: Late draftable pick.

TIGHT ENDS

OFFENSIVE LINE

Nawrocki's TOP 10

1. **LAREMY TUNSIL**
2. **Ronnie Stanley**
3. **Jack Conklin**
4. **Taylor Decker**
5. **Jason Spriggs**
6. **Cody Whitehair**
7. **Ryan Kelly**
8. **Germain Ifedi**
9. **Evan Boehm**
10. **Christian Westerman**

ORG/ORT VADAL ALEXANDER, #74 (Sr-4)

LSU ▶ GRADE: 5.30

Ht: 6-5 1/4 | Wt: 326 | 40: 5.58 | Arm: 35 | Hand: 10 1/2

History: Played all 13 games as a true freshman in 2012, drawing starts at right tackle in the final nine contests — notched 49.5 knockdowns in 656 snaps. In the spring of '13, had back surgery to repair a herniated disk. Shifted to left guard in the fall when he started all 13 games and posted 71 knockdowns. At the end of the season, played through right knee pain which required a scope. In '14, started all 12 games played at OLG and notched 75.5 knockdowns. Did not play against Arkansas because of a broken left hand. Reportedly shed 15 pounds before senior season and manned the ORT spot in '15 (with the exception of Ole Miss contest in which he played the left side) — started all 12 games and racked up 115.5 knockdowns (through regular season). Team captain shared the Tigers' Outstanding Offensive Player Award with Leonard Fournette.

Strengths: Naturally thick-bodied with excellent overall size, mass and body length. Efficient pulling. Can cover up defenders in the run game and handle power in pass pro. Three-and-a-half-year starter. Has played right- and left-handed at guard and tackle. Is at his best when he gets his hands on defenders and can maul in the run game.

Weaknesses: Tends to play upright and is on the ground too much. Average foot technician. Marginal peripheral awareness. Plays on his heels and cannot adjust easily to speed, allowing too many pressures (see Alabama vs OLB Tim Williams). Is sluggish reaching the second level, as confirmed at the Combine with the slowest 10-yard time (2.03 seconds) and 40 (5.62) of any offensive lineman at the event. Average finisher on the edges. Lacks awareness to pick up stunts. Weight has fluctuated considerably throughout his career.

Durability has been an issue with chronic knee soreness that limits practice time.

Future: Heavy-legged, heel-pounding, straight-line, power blocker. Graded more highly at left guard the previous two years than he did as a right tackle as a senior and projects best to right guard in the pros for a man-blocking scheme. Long-term durability must be considered and could affect draft value.

Draft projection: Fourth- to fifth-round pick.

Scout's take: "I'd take him as one of our eight offensive linemen. He can start for you. He can be on varsity because he's a two-position player. You can save a roster spot that way. He might only be a marginal starter, but I would not be afraid to put him in if someone got hurt."

C/OLG JACK ALLEN, #66 (Sr-5)
MICHIGAN STATE   ▶ GRADE: 5.31
Ht: 6-1 1/4 | Wt: 294 | 40: 5.29 | Arm: 32 1/4 | Hand: 10 1/8

History: Also was a state champion wrestler (285 pounds) in west suburban Chicago. Redshirted in 2011. Started 12-of-13 games in '12 — seven at center, five at left guard — and recorded 59 knockdowns, including a team-leading 14 "dominators," also known as decleaters. Missed the first two games of the '13 season because of turf toe before starting the final 12 at center, tallying 68 knockdowns, including 17.5 "dominators." In '14, started all 11 games played at center — did not allow a sack, led the Spartans with 18.5 "dominators" and amassed 85.5 knockdowns. Sat out against Wyoming and Indiana while nursing an ankle injury. Started all 12 games played at center in '15 for the Big Ten champs (also saw action at left tackle against Purdue and played fullback and tight end vs. Iowa in the Big Ten championship game). Scored a nine-yard rushing touchdown against Penn State in his final home game. Sustained a right ankle sprain against Rutgers and sat out against Michigan and Indiana. Team captain and two-time Rimington finalist graduated with a degree in hospitality business. Was not flagged for a penalty as a senior.

Strengths: Experienced, four-year starter in the Big Ten described within the program as the most respected player on the team. Makes all the line calls and has good awareness to blitz concepts. Has a good football temperament and seeks to finish blocks past the whistle. Understands angles and leverage and gets good fits in the run game. Functional pulling and walling off. Can generate a short surge in the run game. Dependable pass protector

(only allowed three career sacks). Flashes a jolt in his hands. Good base and balance — is seldom on the ground.

Weaknesses: Marginal arm length shows up in play — tends to grab and has an average blocking radius. Late to cut off linebackers at the second level and reach the block point. Marginal adjusting in space. Average foot athlete — struggles matching up against interior quickness and allows defenders to work edges. Can be moved by power. Has missed two games each of the last three seasons to injury and must prove durable.

Future: Tough, scrappy, strong-handed technician with the mental fortitude, football intelligence and leadership traits to earn a starting job and play a long time in the league if he can stay healthy. A gritty grinder lacking ideal length and feet for a zone scheme, yet will still find a way to get the job done.

Draft projection: Fourth- to fifth-round pick.

OLT/OLG WILLIE BEAVERS, #70 (Sr-5)
WESTERN MICHIGAN   ▶ GRADE: 5.19
Ht: 6-4 5/8 | Wt: 321 | 40: 5.28 | Arm: 34 | Hand: 10

History: Intended to play at Illinois, but had borderline grades and was victimized by oversigning, leading him to join WMU and then-head coach Bill Cubit. Redshirted in 2011. Appeared in eight games in '12, starting two at left guard. Took ownership of the left tackle job as a sophomore — started 38 games from 2013-15. Team captain.

Strengths: Excellent size and body mass. Very athletic and graceful mover. Is quick off the ball and into blocks in the run game. Efficient maintaining positioning in pass protection — can shuffle, slide and mirror. Can climb to the next level, run the field and connect with defensive backs. Effective cut blocker. Active and energetic. The game is important to him.

Weaknesses: Unrefined technician — opens his shoulders too early, offering a soft edge and inviting counter moves. Lacks ideal core strength and power. Is underdeveloped in the weight room, especially in the lower body. Can be overpowered at the point of attack and waylaid vs. the blitz (see Michigan State). Catches too much in pass protection and needs to become a more consistent finisher in the run game. Average eyes and blocking instincts — can be late to feel and diagnose stunts and blitzes and will will be targeted by aggressive defensive coordinators. Does not play with violence in his hands and can learn to a better job replacing them.

Future: A big, light-footed athlete at his

OFFENSIVE LINE

73

best with simple assignments. Possesses the prerequisite physical traits to man the OLT position and might even be ripe for a move inside, yet must continue to mature physically in the weight room. Would benefit most from extra one-on-one instruction in the pros and will require some time for the game to slow down for him to handle the interior. A finesse, positional blocker, Beavers is most ideally suited for a zone-slide protection scheme such as the Broncos, Packers or Seahawks.

Draft projection: Fifth- to sixth-round pick.

Scout's take: "I didn't think he was draftable, but he will get drafted. They tried him at guard at the Senior Bowl. It sounded like he generated some buzz there. …I still think he's a developmental project and a long ways away. He'd need a few years on the practice squad before our coaches would trust him."

ORG/ORT CALEB BENENOCH, #74 (Jr-3)

UCLA   ▶ GRADE: 5.16

Ht: 6-5 1/2 | Wt: 311 | 40: 5.09 | Arm: 34 1/8 | Hand: 10

History: Last name is pronounced "ben-en-KNOCK." Born in Nigeria and emigrated when he was eight. Brother, Josh, walked on and played at Baylor in 2011. As a true freshman in 2013, Caleb started the final nine games at right tackle. Started all 13 games at ORT in '14. In '15, started all 13 games (nine at ORT, four at right guard), and flagged 13 times for penalties. Opted not to bench press at the Combine.

Strengths: Good size and overall length with a long torso and short trunk. Can generate some movement in the run game. Plays hard and competes. Flashes some power in his hands. Recorded a 1.68-second 10-yard split at the Combine, the fastest of any offensive lineman, which translates to initial quickness, short-area burst and acceleration into blocks on the second level and as a puller. Versatile — has played inside and outside.

Weaknesses: Marginal technician — hands and feet do not work in unison and tends to bend at the waist and overextend, leading to balance deficiencies. Lacks awareness in pass protection to anticipate pressure. Too grabby and undisciplined. Plays small and lets defenders cross his face on inside counters. Does not yet understand blocking angles and leverage. Limited core strength. Soft finisher. Recorded a 5.14-second 3-cone drill time at the Combine, second slowest among OTs, and revealing marginal lateral agility.

Future: Long-limbed, developmental project with the requisite physical tools to war-

rant an opportunity to compete for a backup role. Has the length, athletic frame and intelligence to mature with continued technique work. Appears best suited for the inside.

Draft projection: Fifth- to sixth-round pick.

Scout's take: "(Benenoch) has some upside but he's not strong. He's better than a free agent because he's a dual guard/tackle. He actually didn't look bad playing guard. He'll go in the fifth (round) where you take developmental guys."

C/OG AUSTIN BLYTHE, #63 (Sr-5)

IOWA   ▶ GRADE: 5.21

Ht: 6-2 1/8 | Wt: 298 | 40: 5.36 | Arm: 31 1/2 | Hand: 9 1/2

History: Married. Iowa native who also competed in track and field and wrestling — won three state wrestling titles. Had his right knee scoped prior to his junior season in high school. Redshirted in 2011. Started 9-of-10 games played at right guard in '12 — sat out two games while nursing a high left ankle sprain. Shifted to center in '13, when he started all 13 games. Showed versatility in '14 when he started all 13 games — first six at center, one at ORG and the final six at left guard. Was a Rimington Trophy finalist in '15 after starting all 14 games at center. Team captain graduated with a communications degree.

Strengths: Experienced, four-year starter. Excellent feet and initial quickness off the ball to zone off areas. Explosive climbing to the second level and sealing linebackers, with good body control to adjust to moving targets. Runs his feet through contact. Very efficient pulling and operating in space. Extremely intelligent and football smart — makes all the line calls and is a very quick study. Versatile — has played all three interior line positions. Works hard, is highly competitive and respected as a team leader (four-year member of the leadership council). Can power clean 400-plus pounds and is a weight-room phenom, bench-pressing 225 pounds 29 times at the Combine, more than any other center.

Weaknesses: Undersized with small hands and extremely short arms that create some issues engaging and sustaining blocks. Lacks bulk and can be overpowered by big-bodied nose tackles and walked back in pass protection. Has some lower-body stiffness and could stand to play with more consistent knee bend in-line. Limited punch.

Future: Feisty, explosive zone-blocking center who compensates for his lack of mass and length with exceptional quickness, grit and work habits. Is wired to quickly earn a

OFFENSIVE LINE

starting job and make a living overcoming his physical limitations.

Draft projection: Fifth- to sixth-round pick.

C/ORG EVAN BOEHM, #77 (Sr-4)

MISSOURI ▶ GRADE: 5.54

Ht: 6-2 1/8 | Wt: 302 | 40: 5.34 | Arm: 32 1/2 | Hand: 10 1/4

History: Received scholarship offer to Missouri before entering high school and was a highly recruited Missouri prep who played for his father, earned all-state honors three times, and won state titles in football, wrestling and discus. As a true freshman in 2012, started all 12 games at left guard. Took ownership of the center position and started all 40 games from 2013-15. Suffered a sprained right ankle in the '15 opener and continued to play through the injury all season with his ankle spatted. Team captain's 52 career starts established a school record. Graduated with an agriculture degree.

Strengths: Experienced, four-year starter in the Southeastern Conference. Outstanding anchor strength — can latch on, steer and control defenders in the run game and stop blitzing linebackers stone-cold in their tracks in pass pro. Plays square and can match up against power. Has superb lower-body strength with a 700-pound squat and can physically overpower defensive lineman and put fright into linebackers at the second level. Has a nasty playing temperament and very good finishing strength. Highly respected team leader. Extremely competitive. Physically and mentally tough and very durable.

Weaknesses: Average height. Plays shortarmed with limited extension. Does not consistently finish blocks the way he is capable. Could stand to do a better job of keeping his head on a swivel and feeling pressure. Average lateral agility and recovery speed. Was on the ground more than he should be (as a senior) and stressed the further he traveled.

Future: Big, barrel-chested, physically strong mauler with a proven pedigree and track record of immediate success on the football field. An exemplary, trusted team leader and coaching favorite. Would be most effective in a power-blocking scheme where he could blast defenders off the line and grade roads, though moves well enough to handle zone assignments.

Draft projection: Third- to fourth-round pick.

Scout's take: "The best player at Missouri is the center. He has starter traits. He played on a bad high ankle injury all year but gutted it out. I think he's the second-best center in the draft and gave him a third-round grade. When

he's healthy, he's got it all. He's 6-2 with a 315-pound frame and can handle a nose."

C JAKE BRENDEL, #54 (Sr-5)

UCLA ▶ GRADE: 5.01

Ht: 6-4 1/8 | Wt: 303 | 40: 5.04 | Arm: 31 5/8 | Hand: 9

History: Last name is pronounced "BREN-dul." Prepped in Texas. Redshirted in 2011. Took immediate ownership of the Bruins' center position — started all 27 games 2012-13. Missed the '14 season opener against Virginia (MCL sprain), but started the next 12 games. Started all 13 games in '15. Three-time captain is UCLA's all-time leader in games started (52). Was a Campbell Trophy finalist, as well as a nominee for the Wuerffel, Senior CLASS Award and AFCA Good Works team. Graduated with an economics degree.

Strengths: Experienced, four-year starter with alpha-leadership qualities. Takes good angles. Tough competitor — battles, scraps and fights for positioning. Can bump and steer. Has enough anchor strength to hold a charge. Produced the best 20-yard shuttle time (4.27 seconds) of any offensive lineman at the Combine, indicating superb quickness and lateral agility. Stellar football and personal character. Was a pseudo player-coach in the spring (while UCLA OL coach was suspended). Very durable.

Weaknesses: Does not look the part. Has small hands that invite grip issues and disproportionately short arms for his height. Limited athlete. Short-stepping, plodding mover. Tends to play upright and straight-legged and lacks functional football-playing strength and power. One-position player.

Future: Tough, try-hard overachiever who will struggle to overcome his physical limitations in the pros. Has make-it toughness and leadership qualities and is the type of player that is difficult to cut, yet is the type of athlete teams will always be looking to replace. What you see is what you get and has limited upside to develop. Looks destined for a coaching career.

Draft projection: Priority free agent.

ORG JOSEPH CHEEK, #79 (Sr-5)

TEXAS A&M ▶ GRADE: 5.12

Ht: 6-6 | Wt: 295 | 40: 5.35e | Arm: 32 3/4 | Hand: 9 1/4

History: Father, Louis, was also an Aggie lineman before playing in 45 NFL games with the Dolphins, Cowboys, Eagles and Packers (1988-91). Texas native. Redshirted in 2011. Was a reserve/special teams contributor 2012-13 when he appeared in all 26 games. In '14,

OFFENSIVE LINE

started 9-of-12 games at right guard. Started all 13 games at ORG in '15. Graduated with an architecture degree. Was medically excluded from running at the Combine.

Strengths: Excellent body length. Very good effort. Efficient switching off defenders to pick up the blitz. Good awareness in pass protection. Blue-collar worker and people-pleaser. Smart, assignment-sound and has been extremely durable. Team comedian — adds to locker-room chemistry. Has NFL pedigree.

Weaknesses: Underpowered and lacks core strength. Not a glass-eater. Too easily ragdolled (see Alabama vs. Jonathan Allen). Operated heavily out of a two-point stance. Tends to set tall and play narrow-based, negating power. Average lateral agility to adjust to moving targets. Marginal finisher — pinballed too easily. Plays soft-handed.

Future: A big-bodied, developmental zone blocker with enough athletic talent to stick in the league as a swing backup if his processing speed and blocking instincts continue to ascend. A green talent who has shown some bright flashes in pass protection.

Draft projection: Late draftable pick.

ORT/OLG Le'RAVEN CLARK, #62 (Sr-5)
TEXAS TECH ▶ GRADE: 5.52
Ht: 6-5 1/4 | Wt: 316 | 40: 5.13 | Arm: 36 1/8 | Hand: 11

History: Redshirted in 2011. Sustained a concussion during '12 fall camp, but started all 13 games at right guard. As a sophomore, moved to left tackle and started all 38 games 2013-15. Had his right knee rolled up on against Kansas and sat out the second half, but did not miss the following week. Team captain who graduated with a General Studies degree. Pulled his left hamstring on his first 40 at the Combine and did not finish his workout.

Strengths: Proven, four-year starter with experience playing inside and outside. Looks the part. Outstanding size with wide base, vines for arms and huge mitts. Very functional run blocker once engaged and can collapse his side of the line. Effective stretch-zone blocker — seals off lanes. Can run defenders wide of the pocket. Enough mass to stop a charge. Good recovery quickness (enhanced by unique length).

Weaknesses: Operated out of a two-point stance in a pass-heavy offense and plays upright, negating his power. Can be overpowered and walked back when he sets tall. Marginal upper-body strength to press and control defenders. Inconsistent hand use — tends to

grab a lot. Struggled matching up with speed at the Senior Bowl, giving up a sack to Sheldon Day and also getting flagged for holding. Challenged by the speed of Oklahoma State's Emmanuel Ogbah in the regular season. Is late to reach linebackers and cut off at the second level, displaying average body control. Soft-handed finisher. Average processing speed. Only bench-pressed 18 reps at the Combine, second fewest among tackles.

Future: A giant, long-limbed tackle at his best when he short sets or gets his hands on defenders in the run game. Accomplished speed rushers will be able to have their way with him working inside or outside. Despite his unique physical talents, he will require time to acclimate in the pros, though most of his flaws are correctable and he could flourish under the tutelage of a crafty O-Line teacher. Could fit best at right tackle in a zone-blocking scheme.

Draft projection: Second- to third-round pick.

Scout's take: "He's not ready yet, but I really like his talent. He's a good football player with a high ceiling."

ORT SHON COLEMAN, #72 (Jr-4)
AUBURN ▶ GRADE: 5.48
Ht: 6-5 1/2 | Wt: 307 | 40: 5.40e | Arm: 35 1/8 | Hand: 10 5/8

History: Memphis native was part of the 2010 recruiting class, but treatment for leukemia sidelined him until '12, his redshirt season. In '13, backed up Rams '14 first-rounder Greg Robinson, seeing action in eight games. Stepped in at left tackle in '14, starting all 13 games. Started all 12 games played at left tackle in '15. Sat out against Idaho (right knee). Earned his undergraduate degree in Public Administration and master's degree in Adult Education. Will turn 25 during his rookie season. Was medically excluded from working out at the Combine because of right knee injury.

Strengths: Is a mountain of a man with power in his body and heavy jolt in his punch. Very good functional strength to mash defenders off the ball and drive undersized pass rushers into the ground with power (see Mississippi). When he gets his hands on defenders, say good night. Good enough foot athlete to ride pass rushers wide of the pocket. Has dealt with and overcome a lot of adversity in his life, spending three years beating leukemia, and mental fortitude runs deep.

Weaknesses: Stiff-bodied and is not an elite foot athlete. Tends to set tall, overextend and bend at the waist — too much of a leaner. Hands and feet do not always work in unison

OFFENSIVE LINE

and pass-pro technique could use more refinement — is too aggressive seeking kill shots and must learn the finesse art of pass protection (clean feet, squared shoulders and staying frontal vs speed). Medical evaluation and overall longevity needs to be weighed carefully given leukemia history. Overaged.

Future: Straight-line power blocker most effective driving defenders off the ball and paving lanes as a run blocker. Similar to Chargers 2006 second-round pick (50th overall) Marcus McNeill, another heavy-bodied waist-bender, Coleman is a capable pass protector more suited for the right side than the left. Will require several years of seasoning similar to Greg Robinson, yet possesses intriguing physical traits that cannot be taught. Medical evaluation will determine draft status.

Draft projection: Second- to third-round pick.

Scout's take: "I know some scouts have stamped top-10 grades on him. That's mighty rich for me. He's sitting in the back of the third (round) on our board. The problem when you take those kind of guys — you expect a lot more from them and it's hard for them to live up to it, like the second round talent that Miami took in the first (Ja'Wuan James) a few years ago. If you are going to draft an offensive lineman in the first round, to me, they've got to be able to dominate."

OLT/OLG JACK CONKLIN, #74 (Jr-4)

MICHIGAN STATE ▶ GRADE: 6.32

Ht: 6-5 3/4 | Wt: 308 | 40: 4.99 | Arm: 35 | Hand: 10 3/8

History: Played for his father as a prep in Michigan, where he also averaged 17 points and 10 rebounds as a basketball player. Redshirted in 2012. Started all 13 games in '13 — 10 at left tackle, three at right tackle — and recorded 55 knockdowns. Started all 13 games at left tackle in '14, tallying 113 knockdowns (nine "dominators"). Started all 12 games played at left tackle in '15, notching 65 knockdowns in the regular season. Injured his left knee against Central Michigan, causing him to sit out against Purdue and Rutgers. Allowed four sacks in 39 career games. Entered MSU as a preferred walk-on before earning a scholarship prior to his redshirt-freshman season.

Strengths: Looks the part with long arms. Good athlete with natural knee bend. Very good hand placement to steer and control blocks. Flashes some nastiness running his feet though the whistle and sticking with blocks 10 yards downfield, notably vs. Oregon and Ohio State. Scrappy, competitive

and highly driven. Understands angles and positioning. Effective torqueing and sealing defenders. Solid anchor strength to dig his heels in the dirt and stop a charge. Switches off blocks to pick up the blitz and shows very good awareness in pass protection. Gets stronger as the game goes on and wears down opponents. Tested, measured and performed very well athletically in drills at the Combine, displaying both the feet and length desired at left tackle.

Weaknesses: Gives some ground against top power, and base could stand to be more sturdy (knees buckle and legs give out at times). Looks thin from the knee down and plays too narrow-based. Can do a better job clearing his feet through traffic climbing to the second level.

Future: A very functional college left tackle, Conklin has the toughness, competitiveness and blocking instincts to become an excellent pro. Has the temperament of an all-pro guard, yet showed good enough feet and movement skill at the Combine to handle either edge. Has some similarities to Jaguars OLT and 2013 second overall pick Luke Joeckel at Texas A&M in terms of his technique, movement skill and temperament.

Draft projection: Top-20 pick.

Scout's take: "He pushed around (Oregon DE DeForest Buckner) pretty good. (Conklin) will be in the first (round) when all is said and done. Our OL coach had him graded at the top of the group and thought he was better than (Redskins 2015 fifth overall pick Brandon) Scherff. (Conklin) will be a guard in the pros. He can play outside, but he will be best inside."

ORT FAHN COOPER, #74 (Sr-5)

MISSISSIPPI ▶ GRADE: 5.12

Ht: 6-4 1/2 | Wt: 303 | 40: 5.19 | Arm: 34 3/4 | Hand: 10

History: Prepped in Illinois. Began his college career at Bowling Green, where he redshirted in 2011. Started all 13 games at left tackle in '12 (wore jersey No. 79). Was unhappy at BGSU, prompting a transfer to College of DuPage (Ill.), where he started 10 games at left tackle in '13 while serving as a team captain. Transferred to Ole Miss in '14 and started all 13 games (11 at right tackle, two at OLT). Shed 30 pounds entering '15, when he started all 13 games — the first seven at OLT in place of suspended starter Laremy Tunsil, the final six at ORT. Was awarded the Kent Hull Trophy as Mississippi's top offensive lineman.

Strengths: Experienced, four-year starter.

OFFENSIVE LINE

Good size and arm length. Functional movement skill to shadow and mirror. Strong enough to hold a charge, and athletic enough to work up a level to fit on linebackers. Plays on his feet and keeps battling. Has played left- and right-handed. Coachable.

Weaknesses: Tight-hipped and plays too upright. Underdeveloped lower-body strength. Limited lateral agility to cut off the rush and efficiently handle edge speed. Catches too much and feet too often go stagnant on contact. Needs to improve as a finisher and learn to do a better job of striking with his hands. Below-average blocking instincts. Takes time to process the blitz.

Future: A good-sized, developmental tackle who proved capable of playing on either side and has enough physical talent to warrant consideration as a backup swing tackle in the pros with continued technique refinement.

Draft projection: Late draftable pick.

OLG JOE DAHL, #56 (Sr-5)

WASHINGTON STATE ▶ GRADE: 5.14
Ht: 6-4 1/8 | Wt: 304 | 40: 5.19 | Arm: 33 1/8 | Hand: 9 1/8

History: Also played basketball as a Montana prep. Began his career at Montana, where he redshirted in 2011. Transferred to WSU and sat out the '12 season per NCAA rules, initially walking on before earning a scholarship. Suffered a herniated disk while working out in the weight room during the '12 offseason. Healthy in '13, started all 13 games — played left guard every week until shifting to left tackle for the New Mexico Bowl against Colorado State. Started all 12 games at OLT in '14. Managed nine starts at OLT in '15, missing four games because of a broken left foot. Allowed four sacks his last two seasons. Graduated with a marketing degree.

Strengths: Functional pass protector capable of sliding and mirroring — well-versed from operating in Mike Leach's pass-heavy, Air Raid offense. Good balance. Tough, effortful competitor. Takes good angles. Very good work habits. Respected as a line leader. Versatile — has played guard and tackle. Intelligent and football smart. Very quick learner. Has played through injuries. Outstanding personal character.

Weaknesses: Average size. Has extremely small hands and short arms for the outside. Plays compact with limited reach and extension. Limited power in his body. Marginal punch strength. Lacks the agility and length to match up with edge speed. Marginal recovery quickness when defenders attack his edges. Struggled with the power of Vernon Butler

and Jihad Ward at the Senior Bowl. Does not do squat lifts in the weight room because of back issues, hindering lower-body strength development, and back injury history requires medical evaluation.

Future: Smart, self-made, positional blocker with enough desire and intellect to contend for a roster spot as an interior backup in a zone-blocking scheme. Tough, try-hard overachiever.

Draft projection: Late draftable pick.

Scout's take: "He is a tight-skinned (maxed out), short-armed, developmental guy, one you would love to have as a classic backup. If he's starting, your line is probably in trouble. I don't ever see him being more than a subpar starter."

OLT / OLG TAYLOR DECKER, #68 (Sr-4)

OHIO STATE ▶ GRADE: 6.25
Ht: 6-7 | Wt: 310 | 40: 5.23 | Arm: 33 3/4 | Hand: 10

History: Ohio native who also excelled on the hardwood in high school. Was a reserve/special teams player as a true freshman in 2012 when he saw action in all 12 games. In '13, started all 14 games at right tackle and played 941 snaps, tops on the Buckeyes. Sprained his left MCL against Purdue. Shifted to left tackle as a junior, and started all 28 games 2014-15. Allowed two sacks as a senior when he was named the Rimington-Pace Award winner as the Big Ten's Offensive Lineman of the Year. Team captain and three-time "Iron Buckeye" award winner, which is awarded to six players bi-annually for unquestioned physical training dedication, determination, toughness and leadership.

Strengths: Has rare size with exceptional body length and good body control. Launches defenders with explosive punch. Eye-catching grip strength to ragdoll and control linebackers. Carries a swagger, is ultra-competitive and has a feisty football temperament. Can drive defenders off the ball with power and re-establish the line of scrimmage. Creates a surge in goalline situations and can wash defenders down the line. Good anchor strength to latch on and steer defenders in pass protection. Sound technician — efficient set and footwork in kickslide. Athletic enough to recover when he is outmaneuvered. Nasty finisher — plays to the echo of the whistle. Very workman-like with a blue-collar approach to the game. Displays alpha-leadership qualities on the field and in the locker room. Book smart with a high football IQ. Very durable and has not missed any time to injury.

Weaknesses: Has relatively short arms for

as tall as he is and does not create extension. Can be overaggressive to the second level and allow blockers to undercut his blocks. Inconsistent adjusting at the second level — has room to improve anticipating angles and maintaining lower pad level on the move. Falls off some blocks. Does not have elite feet to reach and seal speed rushers on stretch runs. Can be susceptible to quick, inside counter moves. Could more consistently sustain blocks.

Future: Giant-sized, ornery run blocker with the toughness and physicality desired on the right side of the line and enough length, agility, bend and movement skill to evolve into a sound blind-side protector. Tenacious and aggressive, Decker was the heart of the Buckeyes' offensive line and plays the game like a true throwback, old-school football player. Can be a plug-and-play starter with ability to fit in a zone- or man-blocking scheme on either edge.

Draft projection: First-round pick.

Scout's take: "What I don't like is that he plays short-armed too often. For that long frame, he doesn't have long arms. He's always playing with bent elbows and catching guys — I just don't see the punch and lockout."

ORG **SPENCER DRANGO**, #58 (Sr-5)

BAYLOR   ▶ GRADE: 5.12

Ht: 6-5 5/8 | Wt: 315 | 40: 5.29 | Arm: 33 3/4 | Hand: 9 1/2

History: Diagnosed with dyslexia following fourth grade. Prepped in Texas, where he posted 144 knockdowns while allowing zero sacks as a senior. Redshirted in 2011. Started all 13 games at left tackle in '12, grading out at 89.2 percent with 76 knockdowns. In '13, duplicated his 89.2 percent coaches' grade while tallying 43 knockdowns in nine starts at OLT. Missed four games (and the following spring practices) because of a herniated disk. Started all 13 games at OLT in '14, averaging 88.5 percent with 39 knockdowns. In '15, was an Outland Trophy finalist, Campbell Trophy finalist and the Big 12's Offensive Lineman of the Year — graded out at 90.3 percent with 48 knockdowns (regular season). Graduated with a Finance degree.

Strengths: Four-year starter. Outstanding size and weight-room strength. Can squat 600-plus pounds. Has strong hands to control defenders when he gets his hands on them. Can get in the way and seal lanes. Understands football concepts and is quick to sort out the blitz. Very gritty, workman-like, O-Line leader.

Weaknesses: Does not look the part —

narrow-hipped with a lean lower body and no power base. Short-armed and plays with little extension. Limited hip flexibility, bend and lateral agility. Stiff, linear mover — lumbers to the second level and struggles to initiate contact with linebackers. Flagged twice for holding in the Senior Bowl and struggled to match up against better competition or handle speed.

Future: A top-heavy, stiff, barrel-chested college left tackle whose only chance will come inside in the pros ideally in a gap-blocking scheme. Does not look the part, yet has the size, strength and grit to find ways to get the job done in the run game and was surprisingly productive protecting the pass. A better college football player than pro prospect, Drango has the makeup to fight his way into a starting lineup, but will always have limitations.

Draft projection: Fifth- to sixth-round pick.

Scout's take: "I didn't like him. I gave him a seventh-round grade. I don't care if he was a finalist for the Outland Trophy. He doesn't help us. He can't make our team, and we need help on our line."

ORG **PARKER EHINGER**, #78 (Sr-5)

CINCINNATI   ▶ GRADE: 5.10

Ht: 6-6 1/4 | Wt: 310 | 40: 5.34 | Arm: 33 | Hand: 9 7/8

History: Last name is pronounced "anger." Also competed in shot and discus as a Michigan prep. Redshirted in 2011. In '12, started 12-of-13 games at right guard — stepped into the lineup in Week Two and didn't look back. Started all 39 games the next three seasons — manned right tackle in '13; ORG in '14; and left tackle in '15. Team captain graduated with a criminal justice degree. Suffered springtime injuries to his left ankle, left MCL and right foot during his career, but did not miss any games. Lost his father in the summer prior to his junior season in an accident. Was medically excluded (left shoulder) from bench-pressing at the Combine and did not run shuttles because of a right hamstring injury.

Strengths: Very good size. Experienced, four-year starter. Versatile and has played inside and outside. Alert to pick up stunts and blitzes in pass protection. Can shadow and mirror in pass protection. Has a blue-collar work ethic and leads by example.

Weaknesses: Average arm length and agility for the edges. Does not sustain blocks after initial contact, leaving his man free to run to the ball too often. Very inconsistent finisher. Raw technician in pass pro — tends to lunge and overextend and does not keep his cleats in the ground. Marginal functional football-

OFFENSIVE LINE

playing strength.

Future: Pear-shaped, hit-and-whiff blocker lacking the feet to play outside and the base strength to play inside. Will be challenged against better competition. Has some similarities to former Broncos undrafted free agent Mike Remmers, a vagabond journeyman who found a home starting at right tackle for the Panthers on his sixth NFL stop in four years.

Draft projection: Priority free agent.

Scout's take: "He's all fluff. He plays small. He's not on our front (draftable) board. ...I know some bad scouts that have big grades on him though. If he winds up going in the second round, let's say I won't be shocked. I wouldn't draft him."

OLG JOSH GARNETT, #51 (Sr-4)

STANFORD ▶ GRADE: 5.42

Ht: 6-4 3/8 | Wt: 312 | 40: 5.31 | Arm: 33 7/8 | Hand: 10 1/8

History: Father, Scott, appeared in 27 NFL games with the Broncos, Chargers, 49ers and Bills (1984-85, 1987). Josh was highly recruited out of Washington before seeing action in all 14 games as a true freshman in 2012, including one start at left guard against Washington State. In '13, played all 14 games and drew four starts — four as a "jumbo" tight end, one at OLG. Became a fixture in '14 when he started all 13 games at OLG (lined up at TE against Notre Dame). Was the Outland Trophy winner in '15 after starting all 14 games at OLG. Team captain is on pace to graduate with a biology degree.

Strengths: Has a thick trunk and good lower-body strength to knock defenders off the ball and operate in a phone booth. Effective pulling and kicking out defensive ends. Has strong hips to twist, torque and wall off defenders. Can create a surge in short-yardage situations, playing with very good pad level. Good anchor strength to handle power and control defenders. Has NFL pedigree. Football is very important to him.

Weaknesses: Heavy-legged mover. Is stressed moving laterally and spends more time on the ground than he should. Does not generate force through his lower half. Late to reach the block point at the second level. Catches and absorbs contact too much in pass protection and could stand to do a better job recoiling his hands. Weight has fluctuated and ballooned earlier in his career.

Future: A big, strong, physical mauler who showed gradual improvement as a senior and has the size, strength and sheer mass to be effective in a man-blocking scheme. Profiles as a functional starter with pass-pro deficiencies — could always be challenged to handle speed.

Draft projection: Third- to fourth-round pick.

Scout's take: "He played better later in the season if you watch from Arizona on. If you watch him early in the year, he looks like a free agent. I wound up grading him at the back of (the third round)."

ORG/C GRAHAM GLASGOW, #61 (Sr-5)

MICHIGAN ▶ GRADE: 5.26

Ht: 6-5 7/8 | Wt: 307 | 40: 5.14 | Arm: 33 5/8 | Hand: 10

History: Prepped in Illinois before walking on at Michigan. Redshirted in 2011. Appeared in five games in '12. Earned a scholarship prior to the '13 season when he started all 13 games (nine at center, four at left guard). Busted for DUI in March '14 — pleaded guilty to misdemeanor driving a vehicle while visibly impaired, agreeing to probation which included alcohol education classes and random drug and alcohol testing. After serving a one-game suspension against Appalachian State, started all 11 games played (three at right guard, eight at center). In March '15, violated his probation by consuming alcohol and was given additional conditions, including probation through January '16, twice-a-day breathalyzer testing and five days on a jail work program. Was suspended from the team in the spring, but started all 13 games at center. Scheduled to graduate with an economics degree.

Strengths: Excellent size. Tenacious run blocker. Plays with an attitude and competes hard. Feisty football temperament. Natural knee bender. Generates power from his lower body and packs power in his punch. Strong finisher. Can work off blocks and fit at the second level. Good football smarts to handle multiple positions. Diligent weight-room worker. Very durable.

Weaknesses: Too tall for the center position. Could be overmatched by speed and quickness. Is overaggressive climbing to the second level and falls off too many blocks — lunges too much and needs to learn to play more under control and maintain his base. Will require a strong support system to avoid trouble (moved in with 81-year-old grandma as a senior at Michigan as a contingent of Jim Harbaugh following repeated alcohol issues).

Future: An ideal swing interior backup most ideally suited as a power guard in the pros. Off-field troubles could affect draft status and could require maintenance in the pros, yet has enough physical talent and competi-

OFFENSIVE LINE

tiveness to emerge as a valued contributor.

Draft projection: Fourth- to fifth-round pick.

Scout's take: "He might have to be a guard in my opinion. He's scrappy. I wouldn't take him until the fifth (round). He had a good year and learned how to block, but I need to know if grandma is still part of the package. (Harbaugh) made him live with his grandma to get his (act) together."

ORG/C DARRELL GREENE, #72 (Sr-5)

SAN DIEGO STATE ▶ GRADE: 4.82

Ht: 6-2 3/4 | Wt: 321 | 40: 5.18 | Arm: 31 5/8 | Hand: 9 5/8

History: First name is pronounced "duh-RELL." Also played basketball as a California prep. Redshirted in 2011. Appeared in two games in '12. Played all 13 games in '13, starting the final 12 at right guard. Started all 13 games at ORG in '14. Served a six-game suspension (failed drug tests) to begin the '15 season before returning to start the final seven regular season contests at ORG. Was academically ineligible for the bowl game against Cincinnati.

Strengths: Outstanding mass. Can squat 600-plus pounds. Is strong at the point of attack and functional as a run blocker once he gets his hands on a defender. Can seal off running lanes. Athletic enough to pull and maneuver in space.

Weaknesses: Lacks ideal height and arm length. Marginal body control and balance. Plays upright and relies too much on his upper-body strength in pass pro. Soft puncher — absorbs too much and does not keep his cleats in the dirt. Limited blocking instincts — does not play with awareness and is late to identify targets. Inconsistent finisher. Lacks discipline in his approach. Will require additional time to acclimate to complexities of an NFL offense.

Future: Squatty, short-limbed, base blocker best in a phone booth with man-blocking assignments. Similar to Raiders 2013 undrafted free agent Lamar Mady and could provide depth in a camp.

Draft projection: Priority free agent.

OLT JOE HAEG, #59 (Sr-5)

NORTH DAKOTA STATE ▶ GRADE: 5.23

Ht: 6-6 | Wt: 304 | 40: 5.18 | Arm: 33 3/4 | Hand: 9 5/8

History: Also played hockey as a Minnesota prep. Redshirted in 2011 at 268 pounds. Started all 15 games at right tackle in '12. Started all 14 games played at ORT in '13, missing just the Ferris State contest (right MCL sprain). Healthy in '14, started all 16 games at ORT. Moved to left tackle in '15 to replace Dolphins third-round pick Billy Turner and started all 15 games, winning his fourth straight FCS national championship. Two-time FCS Offensive Linemen of the Year (2014, 2015). Walk-on-turned-captain is scheduled to graduate in the spring with a civil engineering degree.

Strengths: Four-year starter. Good agility and foot speed to position and wall off. Patient pass-protector, with ability to shuffle, slide and mirror. Active and energetic hands. Intelligent and football smart. Played in a championship program. Recorded a 4.47-second 20-yard shuttle and 7.41-second three-cone drill time at the Combine, tied for second-best among offensive tackles and indicative of outstanding quickness and lateral agility.

Weaknesses: Has a lean, linear frame with little definition. Plays short-armed and too often locks his knees and chicken fights with his upper body. Lacks weight-room strength and functional, football-playing core strength. Needs more sand in his pants — does not have the anchor to handle NFL power. Average contact balance — spends more time on the ground than he should, slipping off blocks. Lacks pop in his punch. Has not consistently faced top competition or been challenged much at the FCS level.

Future: Developmental zone blocker with upside to be molded with continued strength gains. Will be overwhelmed by NFL speed and power and require time to acclimate to the NFL game. Could emerge as a functional starter in several years.

Draft projection: Fourth- to fifth-round pick.

Scout's take: "(Haeg) has a lot of upside. He's tough and smart. It's just the level of competition that scares you, though he played well against it. He probably lands in the fifth round. Someone could reach and take him sooner like the Dolphins did a few years ago with the other kid (Billy Turner) from that program."

ORT JERALD HAWKINS, #65 (Jr-4)

LSU ▶ GRADE: 5.32

Ht: 6-5 5/8 | Wt: 305 | 40: 5.23 | Arm: 34 1/4 | Hand: 9 5/8

History: Louisiana native who also competed in basketball, baseball and track and field as a prep, winning a 2A state championship in the shot put. Redshirted in 2012. Started all 26 games at right tackle 2013-14. Shifted to left tackle in '15 when he started all 11 games played. Sprained his ankle against Arkansas and sat out against Ole Miss. Team captain totaled 81 knockdowns his last two seasons. Allowed four sacks in '15.

Strengths: Very good length and overall size. Efficient zone blocker capable of sealing and Solid anchor strength to handle power and bull defenders. Regularly matched up against top SEC competition and proved he could stand up to the power of Alabama's talented front. Efficient kickslide.

Weaknesses: Is tight in the hips and upper body and sets tall in pass pro. Dips his head and bends at the waist when overmatched by speed. Does not adjust easily to quick, inside counters and stunts. Struggles with short power-leverage rushers naturally built to get underneath his pads. Too grabby. Could stand to do a better job finishing blocks. Recorded a 23 1/2-inch vertical jump at the Combine, which translates to very modest athletic ability.

Future: A long-limbed, narrow-based, tight-hipped OT prospect with surprisingly functional knee bend, Hawkins is built better to handle power on the right side where he played earlier in his career than he is capable of handling speed on the left, yet is most ideally suited for a swing backup tackle role.

Draft projection: Fourth- to fifth-round pick.

Scout's take: "I really thought (Hawkins) should have stayed in school. ...If you watch him this year, he looks like a free agent at times. He grades out as a fifth-rounder. You watch him (in 2014) at right tackle, he grades out like a fourth (rounder). ... He's big, but I don't think he is powerful. Watch it closely, because (many scouts) will disagree, but he has really good bend when you see him at practice. He can play either side. You can win with him. I know (scouts) are killing him, but there's a lot worse playing in the league right now."

ORT / ORG **GERMAIN IFEDI**, #74 (Jr-4)

TEXAS A&M ▶GRADE: 5.72

Ht: 6-5 3/4 | Wt: 324 | 40: 5.32 | Arm: 36 | Hand: 10 3/4

History: Brother, Martin, was drafted by the Rams in the seventh round in 2015 and currently plays for the Buccaneers. Houston native. Redshirted in 2012. Started all 13 games at right guard in '13. Moved to right tackle in '14 to replace Cedric Ogbuehi, who moved to the left side, and started all 11 games he played in '14. Sprained his left knee against Louisiana-Monroe, and did not play against Auburn or Missouri. Started all 13 games at ORT in '15, allowing five sacks on the season and being flagged for 12 penalties. Did not perform the 3-cone drill at the Combine because of a right ankle injury.

Strengths: Exceptional size, length and body mass — is very thick throughout his frame and built like a scout would draw up a tackle. Surprisingly athletic for a 325-pounder. Can climb to the second level and initiate contact with moving targets. Plays with a chip on his shoulder and will drive defenders into the ground (see Alabama). Can lock down defenders once he gets his hands on them.

Weaknesses: Operated predominantly out of a two-point stance in a pass-heavy, spread offense and will need to adjust to playing with his hand in the dirt. Appeared high-hipped at the Combine. Pads tend to rise in his kickslide, negating his anchor strength and allowing ends to leverage the edge. Footwork will need refinement. Hand placement is inconsistent — more of a grabber than a puncher. Too undisciplined and prone to mental mistakes. Too inconsistent in pass protection — could be overwhelmed by NFL pressure packages and exposed by elite speed rushers.

Future: Massive, thick-bodied, well-built college right tackle who could warrant the most consideration inside in the pros. Plays with a heaviness and has an intimidation factor with his ability to wear down defenders. Has first-round physical talent that cannot be coached and many of his flaws are correctable, though he must prove more disciplined, hone his technique and cut down on weekly penalties. Could ideally fit as a power right guard and also plug readily at right tackle.

Draft projection: Top-50 pick.

Scout's take: "I liked him. He is a monster. He is a first-round talent. He is long and looks the part. There is some tape that doesn't look good the way they vertical set in that spread offense. He has all the tools though."

ORG **DOMINICK JACKSON**, #76 (Sr-4)

ALABAMA ▶GRADE: 4.90

Ht: 6-5 | Wt: 313 | 40: 5.41 | Arm: 33 | Hand: 9 3/4

History: Has a daughter, Aiyana. Prepped in California, but was a non-qualifier coming out of high school. Played at College of San Mateo 2012-13, where he blocked in a triple-option offense and started all 20 games. With the Crimson Tide in '14, provided depth and was used as a jumbo-blocking back in goal-line situations. Started all 14 games played at right tackle for the '15 national champs. Sustained a high right ankle sprain against Tennessee and sat out against Charleston Southern. Graduated. Did not run at the Combine because of a right hamstring injury.

Strengths: Excellent size. Plays with a chip on his shoulder and seeks to finish. Good leg drive to create some surge in the run game. Tough and effortful.

Weaknesses: Not a natural knee-bender. Lunges and spends too much time on the ground. Over reliant on his upper-body strength. Marginal foot quickness and lateral agility — is stressed by edge speed and cannot cut off the edge. Very limited in pass protection. Late to process what he sees. Will require extra time to handle NFL complexities. Known to scrap and scuffle a lot in practice. Lack of agility was exposed in the national championship game vs. Clemson.

Future: Tough, gritty, college right tackle whose only chance will come inside in the pros. Lacks the versatility desired in a backup. Camp body.

Draft projection: Free agent.

Scout's take: "He got beat by (Kevin) Dodds for three sacks in the national championship game. He won't survive at tackle in our league. He has to be a guard. ...We had some concerns about his make-up. He still has some JUCO (junior college) traits."

OLT TYLER JOHNSTONE, #64 (Sr-5)
OREGON ▶ GRADE: 5.03
Ht: 6-5½ | Wt: 301 | 40: 5.19 | Arm: 34 | Hand: 10 3/8

History: Prepped at Arizona powerhouse Hamilton High, where he won a pair of state titles. Redshirted in 2011. Stepped into the lineup and started all 13 games at left tackle in '12. Tore his left PCL during '13 spring practice, but started all 13 games at OLT in the fall. However, tore his right ACL and meniscus against Texas in the Alamo Bowl, then re-tore the ligament at the beginning of '14 fall camp, causing him to miss the season. On the first day of camp in '15, left the field on a cart with back spasms. Returned to start all 13 games at OLT in '15. Graduated.

Strengths: Is a scrappy competitor and flashes a mean streak. Can swing his hips in the hole and cut off defenders. Runs feet on contact and is effective sealing and climbing to the second level. Effective cut blocker. Recorded the fastest 3-cone drill time (7.31 seconds) of any offensive tackle at the Combine, revealing good agility.

Weaknesses: Does not look the part. Very light-framed and lacks bulk strength and power in his body. Tends to play too tall and get driven back by power. Has little core strength. Plays short-armed, bends at the waist and overextends. Durability has been an issue with injuries to both knees.

Future: A developmental zone blocker who must prove durable to warrant an opportunity

as a backup.

Draft projection: Priority free agent.

Scout's take: "He's a free agent for someone else. He's all finesse. He has zero power. He has a bad back. I don't know what you do with him."

ORG NILA KASITATI, #54 (Sr-5)
OKLAHOMA ▶ GRADE: 4.84
Ht: 6-3¼ | Wt: 317 | 40: 5.32 | Arm: 32 | Hand: 10½

History: Has a daughter. Name is pronounced "NEE-luh kah-sih-TAH-tee." Grew up poor in American Samoa with 10 siblings. Lost his father when Nila was in eighth grade. Moved to Texas during his sophomore year. Suffered a knee injury during the '09 playoffs. Verbally committed to Baylor, but signed with OU at the behest of his mother, who wanted Nila to play for then-defensive coordinator Brent Venables. Redshirted in 2011. Appeared in four games in '12 before suffering a season-ending torn right ACL injury. Started 7-of-13 games at right guard in '13. Was held out of the '14 season opener against Louisiana Tech with a minor injury, but started 6-of-12 games played at ORG. In '15, started all 13 games at ORG despite spraining his ankle against Tennessee and playing sparingly against Tulsa. Graduated with a public relations degree.

Strengths: Has thick calves and a stout base. Good grip strength to lock up defenders when he gets his hands on them. Functional positional run blocker. Good weight-room work ethic and practice habits.

Weaknesses: Average arm length. Heavy-legged, foot pounder. Gets overextended and spends more time on the ground than he should. Limited lateral agility and lower-body flexibility to be effective pulling. Marginal reactionary recovery quickness sliding to cut off speed in pass pro. Only bench-pressed 225 pounds 12 times, the fewest of any offensive lineman at the Combine and needs to get stronger.

Future: Squatty, compact positional blocker lacking the agility and feet to match up against inside speed, though is functional enough in the run game to compete for a backup job.

Draft projection: Priority free agent.

C/OG/OT RYAN KELLY, #70 (Sr-5)
ALABAMA ▶ GRADE: 5.74
Ht: 6-4 | Wt: 311 | 40: 5.04 | Arm: 33 5/8 | Hand: 9 5/8

History: Prepped in Ohio. Suffered a torn left ACL and LCL at the end of his senior

OFFENSIVE LINE

season. Redshirted in 2011. Saw backup duty in 10 games in '12. Inherited Barrett Jones' center spot in '13 when he started all nine games played. Was sidelined for four games because of a right MCL sprain. Started all 12 games played in '14, but suffered another right MCL sprain and missed two games. Healthy in '15, won the Rimington Trophy after starting all 15 games for the national champs and not allowing a sack or being called for a penalty. Team captain obtained his master's degree.

Strengths: Excellent size with an 80-plus inch wingspan. Efficient pulling and maneuvering in space. Good snap-and-step quickness to get his hands on defenders quickly and steer them. Very consistent, assignment-sound and aware. Has a solid base and plays on his feet. Understands angles and positioning. Extremely versatile, five-position player. Highly respected team leader who elevates the play of his teammates. Smart, tough and extremely competitive. Makes all the line calls. Outstanding personal and football character.

Weaknesses: Has a history of knee injuries to both knees that have forced him to miss games during multiple seasons. Not explosive off the line of scrimmage and does not generate a lot of movement in the run game. Lacks pop in his punch and could strike with more violence in his hands.

Future: Big, strong, smart, versatile, tough veteran center who can be mismatched by speed at times, yet has been a model of stability on a national championship team and is capable of instantly contributing anywhere on the line.

Draft projection: Second-round pick.

Scout's take: "The best center in the draft is from Alabama. He can make all the blocks on every level. He's quick, smart as a whip and can play every position. He has the length to play tackle. He only played at 300 pounds, but he plays strong. He is a good football player. He's an NFL starter."

ORG/ORT DENVER KIRKLAND, #55 (Jr-3)
ARKANSAS ▶ GRADE: 5.34
Ht: 6-4 1/2 | Wt: 335 | 40: 5.52 | Arm: 34 5/8 | Hand: 9 5/8

History: Miami prep won a state championship at Booker T. Washington. Played all 12 games as a true freshman in 2013, drawing starts at guard in the final eight games. Started all 13 games at right guard in '14 — graded out at 79 percent while allowing one sack and committing three penalties. Moved to left tackle in '15 and started all

13 games — posted an 82 percent regular-season grade.

Strengths: Outstanding size and body mass. Rolls defenders off the ball and can take them for a ride once he gets his hands on them. Enough base anchor strength to withstand a charge in pass protection.

Weaknesses: Doesn't play to his size — pad level consistently rises and is more of a catcher than a puncher. Lacks foot quickness to match up with speed rushers. Technique fades late in the games with diminished stamina, as his Combine-worst 31.5 body-fat percentage indicates it would. Only bench-pressed 225 pounds 19 times at the Combine and needs to get stronger.

Future: Big, thick-bodied, duck-footed, position-sustain blocker looked much more natural inside his first two years than he did trying to handle speed on an island in 2015. Possesses the size and enough core strength to eventually fend for a starting job in a man-blocking scheme.

Draft projection: Fourth- to fifth-round pick.

Scout's take: "(Kirkland) got rocked against Alabama. He doesn't play with as much power as a 330-pounder should. He needs to move inside."

OLT/OLG ALEX LEWIS, #71 (Sr-6)
NEBRASKA ▶ GRADE: 5.27
Ht: 6-6 | Wt: 312 | 40: 5.24 | Arm: 34 | Hand: 10

History: Father, Bill, was a center for the Raiders, Cardinals and Patriots (1986-88, 1990-93). Alex also played lacrosse as an Arizona prep. Began his college career at Colorado, where he grayshirted in 2010. Appeared in all 12 games in '11, starting three (two at tight end, one at left tackle). Started all 12 games at left guard in '12, allowing just two sacks. Decided to transfer to Nebraska in order to play in a better/winning atmosphere. In May of '13 — while still in Boulder, was arrested on two felony assault charges after he got drunk and knocked out an Air Force cadet (witnesses said Lewis slammed the cadet's head into a brick wall and punched him repeatedly). Ultimately pleaded guilty to misdemeanor assault, served a month in jail and was sentenced to two years' probation, which included anger management, alcohol counseling and 100 hours of community service. Did not play in '13 (was not allowed contact with the team for a semester), but met conditions to regain his scholarship prior to the '14 season. Started all 26 games at left tackle 2014-15. Team captain graduated with a sociology degree. Was flagged for nine penalties in 2015.

Strengths: Outstanding size with good body and arm length to fend off edge rushers. Very good balance in his feet — is seldom on the ground. Flashes aggression in the run game. Good movement skills in Combine drills. Very competitive. Vocal leader. Has NFL pedigree and takes pride in his craft. Coachable, emotional leader.

Weaknesses: Lacks lower-body strength and explosion ideally sought on the inside. Lets his hands go wide and outside the target. Could do a better job of anticipating angles and coordinating his punch. Needs to become more stout in pass protection — rises out of his stance and plays tall. Is late to reach the second level. Lacks core power and is a bit top-heavy — bench-presses nearly as much as he squats.

Future: Narrowed-shouldered, thin-framed converted prep tight end still growing into his body. A better pass protector than run blocker, Lewis must continue to get stronger in the lower body to match up against NFL defensive linemen and power-leverage rushers. Developmental left tackle with eventual starter potential.

Draft projection: Fourth- to fifth-round pick.

Scout's take: "He is a tackle all the way. I couldn't see taking him anywhere before the fourth (round). He doesn't have any strength. He's tough and will try to maul, but (I thought) he struggled at times at the East-West (all-star) game when guys got on top of him. He will battle, but he doesn't have power."

C/ORG NICK MARTIN, #72 (Sr-5)

NOTRE DAME ▶ GRADE: 5.37
Ht: 6-4 1/8 | Wt: 299 | 40: 5.22 | Arm: 32 1/2 | Hand: 9 3/4

History: Brother, Zack, is an All-Pro guard for the Cowboys selected 16th overall in 2014. Nick, an Indiana native, won a state title at Bishop Chatard. Redshirted in 2011. Appeared in 13 games as a backup in '12. Started the first 11 games at center in '13 before suffering a season-ending torn left MCL injury. Returned to start all 13 games in '14 — first three at center, final 10 at left guard. Started all 13 games at center in '15, drawing seven penalties and not allowing a sack. Played thru an ankle injury as a senior. Two-year team captain graduated with a degree in management consulting.

Strengths: Outstanding size. Very football smart —good anticipation to recognize stunts, loops and inside pressure. Good shuffle, slide and mirror to cut off the rush. Flashes pop in his punch. Good finishing strength. Takes

good angles to the second level. Experienced, three-year starter. Versatile and can play any of the three interior OL positions. Good weight-room strength — bench-pressed 28 reps at the Combine. Outstanding personal and football character. Physically and mentally tough. Has NFL bloodlines.

Weaknesses: Has some tightness in his body and tends to lock his knees and grab too much, in turn struggling to adjust quickly to pressure at times. Average snap-and-step quickness and recovery speed — allows gap penetrators to pierce his edges too quickly. Has some limitations in space — can be half-step late to reach moving targets. Had an abnormally high 27.5 body-fat percentage at the Combine and played with a heaviness in his feet.

Future: More strong than quick, Martin is a smart, tough, versatile pivot who battled through an ankle injury all year. Has desirable toughness, football smarts and grit to eventually earn a starting job and play a long time in the league, yet could be overwhelmed initially if thrust into the lineup too soon. Will warrant looks as a guard.

Draft projection: Third- to fourth-round pick.

Scout's take: "(Martin) is a tough mauler, but he can't recover when he's off balance and not very good when he is in space. He relies on his upper-body too much. …I know he's being talked up (by the media). I'm not a big fan of last year's tape. I thought he was a fifth (rounder). I'm still not sold on him."

ORT/ORG TYLER MARZ, #61 (Sr-5)

WISCONSIN ▶ GRADE: 5.08
Ht: 6-6 3/4 | Wt: 316 | 40: 5.52 | Arm: 33 1/2 | Hand: 10

History: Last name is pronounced "MARE-itz." Was a defensive lineman as a Minnesota prep, where he also lettered in basketball and baseball. Tore his right ACL in October 2010. Redshirted in '11, earning Offensive Scout Team Player of the Year. Was a reserve in '12 when he appeared in 11 games. Was a fixture at left tackle, where he started all 40 games 2013-15. Graduated with a degree in life sciences communication.

Strengths: Outstanding size to cover up defenders in the run game and get in the way. Enough mass to lock on and seal off defenders once he gets his hands on them. Experienced, three-year starter in the Big Ten. Plays hard. Keeps working to sustain. Good football smarts.

Weaknesses: Average athlete. Struggles to handle edge speed and cut off the wide rusher, as was confirmed in slow kickslide in

OFFENSIVE LINE

85

Combine drills. Lunges too much and doesn't bring his feet with him. Gives up too much inside pressure in pass pro. Only bench-pressed 225 pounds 19 times at the Combine. Recorded a plodding, 8.38-second 3-cone drill time, translating to very limited agility. Labors to initiate contact with linebackers at the second level.

Future: Slow-footed, heavy-bodied college left tackle most ideally suited for the right side in the pros and could warrant some interest inside. Classic phone-booth blocker — the further he is asked to travel, the more he will struggle.

Draft projection: Priority free agent.

ORG/ORT CONNOR McGOVERN, #60 (Sr-5)
MISSOURI ▶ GRADE: 5.29
Ht: 6-4 1/4 | Wt: 306 | 40: 5.06 | Arm: 32 7/8 | Hand: 10 3/8

History: Decorated high school player from North Dakota. Won two state championships and was the Gatorade Player of the Year after earning all-state honors on both sides of the ball. Also wrestled. Redshirted in 2011. Missed time during '12 spring practice (right labrum), but appeared in nine games as a reserve guard during the fall. In '13, started all 14 games at right guard. Suffered a torn pectoral muscle while weight lifting prior to the '14 season. In the fall, started all 14 games — first four at right tackle, final 10 at ORG. Sprained his right MCL during '15 spring practice. Moved to left tackle in the fall and started all 12 games. Graduated with a degree in agricultural economics. Suffered a hamstring injury at the Senior Bowl.

Strengths: Three-year starter in the Southeastern Conference. Passes the eyeball test. Good base and balance. Plays under control. Sturdy base. Good eyes and awareness in pass protection to recognize the blitz. Has good feet to pull and maneuver in space. Enough reactionary quickness to recover when he gets out of position. Smart and assignment-sound. Versatile — has played guard and tackle. Outstanding weight-room worker — can squat a small house.

Weaknesses: Average arm length. Needs to learn how to use his hands more forcefully and strike with his punch. Not a natural knee bender and overextends and leans too much, negating the power in his body. Lets his base narrow at times and does not translate his immense weight-room strength to the field. Can be overaggressive on the move and struggle to connect with linebackers.

Future: Extremely strong, smart, mechanical college left tackle who looked more comfortable at right guard earlier in his career than he did playing the edges. An effective run blocker better in pass protection, would be best with help on both sides inside. Has eventual starter potential and would be most ideally suited for a zone-slide protection scheme.

Draft projection: Fourth- to fifth-round pick.

ORT KYLE MURPHY, #78 (Sr-4)
STANFORD ▶ GRADE: 5.10
Ht: 6-6 3/8 | Wt: 305 | 40: 5.45e | Arm: 33 1/2 | Hand: 9 3/4

History: Brother, Kevin, plays for the Minnesota Vikings. Blue-chip recruit who also threw shot put as a California prep. Appeared in all 14 games as a true freshman in 2012, drawing a pair of starts as a "jumbo" tight end. Wore jersey Nos. 78 when on the line of scrimmage and 94 when off the line. In '13, appeared in 13 games as a reserve/"jumbo" blocker. Manned right tackle in '14 when he started all 13 games. Following the departure of Andrus Peat (Saints '15 first-rounder), shifted to left tackle in '15 and started all 14 games. Did not work out at the Combine because of a left hamstring injury.

Strengths: Has a short trunk and long torso and plays with natural leverage. Is quick off the ball and gets good positioning to reach and seal. Has a good understanding of angles and leverage. Solid technician. Good wide base in pass pro. Takes the game seriously and it is very important to him.

Weaknesses: Does not play strong or physical or generate power thru his lower half. Can be steered and controlled too easily by power and lacks the lateral agility to handle speed and quick, inside counters. Was overwhelmed in Senior Bowl one-on-one's and susceptible to swim moves, as he was beat by Penn State DE Carl Nassib in the Senior Bowl game.

Future: Tough, try-hard, positional blocker lacking ideal strength for the right side and agility for the left. Does not have the foot quickness desired for a zone-slide protection scheme or the power sought to handle man-blocking assignments.

Draft projection: Priority free agent.

ORT STEPHANE NEMBOT, #77 (Sr-5)
COLORADO ▶ GRADE: 5.23
Ht: 6-6 3/4 | Wt: 322 | 40: 5.34 | Arm: 34 5/8 | Hand: 10 3/4

History: Name is pronounced "steff-on name-bot." Born in Cameroon. Speaks three languages and 11 different African dialects. Also played basketball, soccer and volleyball as a California prep. Redshirted in 2011 when he transitioned from defensive end to offensive line. Played all 12 games in '12, starting seven at right tackle — graded out at 74.6 percent and recorded 30 "will-breaker" blocks while allowing 5 1/2 sacks. Started all 24 games at ORT the next two seasons — totaled 45 knockdowns while allowing 7 1/2 sacks and 20 pressures in '13; and 47 knockdowns while allowing 14 pressures and three sacks and grading out at 81.6 percent in '14. Started all 13 games in '15 — first five at ORT, final eight at left tackle in place of the injured starter. Earned a 85.2 percent season grade — collected 25 knockdowns while yielding 4 1/2 sacks and 24 pressures. Was penalized five times. For his career, was credited with 18 touchdown blocks, as well as 42 "perfect plays" on touchdown passes as an upperclassman. Nembot, who will have two degrees (international affairs and ethic studies with a minor in business) from Colorado, will turn 25 during his rookie season. Aspires to open an orphanage when his playing days are over.

Strengths: Outstanding size and arm length with a naturally big bone structure and big mitts. Powerfully built and looks the part. Led all tackles at the Combine by bench-pressing 225 pounds 32 times and is very strong when he latches on. Very durable — has not missed any time to injury. Quick learner — progressed rapidly for not having played the game until senior year of high school. Outstanding personal character — well respected by all in the program.

Weaknesses: Very raw technician still learning the nuances of the game. Hands and feet do not always work in unison. Does not play big and too often gives up the edge against speed rushers. Developing positional instincts. Can be overwhelmed by stunts, loops and zone blitzes. Slips off blocks too easily opening up his hips and allowing defenders to run by. Can be late off the ball and do a better job of anticipating moves. Footwork will require refinement. Produced the slowest 20-yard shuttle time (5.19 seconds) and 3-cone drill time (8.62) of any tackle at the Combine, revealing a lack of lateral agility. Overaged.

Future: Entered the country at a young age intent on playing basketball and emerged from Colorado as a three-and-a-half-year starter protecting the quarterback's blind side. Developmental right tackle with similar upside as Vikings 2015 fourth-round pick T.J. Clemmings, though not as light-footed and may have a floor as a backup more similar to New

York Jets 2010 second-round pick (61) and Chicago Bears backup OLG Vladimir Ducasse. Possesses the physical talent to compete right away in the pros and could eventually earn a starting job if the game slows down for him. Many of his flaws are correctable.

Draft projection: Late draftable pick.

Coach's take: "He's a specimen. He's doing a good job at left tackle, and I definitely think he has a future in the NFL. Where he gets drafted, I don't know. Do I think he'll make a team and play for a long time? Yes, because he's built well, he's intelligent, he can play a few different spots on the offensive line. I think the NFL team, whoever gets him, will really like him because he's very mature, very articulate, very smart, and he's played in every game. He just keeps playing, and that's something you look for — the durability, especially for NFL linemen."

– Colorado head coach Mike MacIntyre

ORG/ORT REES ODHIAMBO, #71 (Sr-5)
BOISE STATE ▶ GRADE: 5.31

Ht: 6-3 7/8 | Wt: 314 | 40: 5.30e | Arm: 33 1/4 | Hand: 9 5/8

History: Born in Kenya. Father passed when he was 6 years old, leading mother to move to the United States to start over. She passed during his junior year of high school while working to be a pharmacist. Rees and his sister moved in with an uncle. Prepped in Texas. Redshirted in 2011. Was a reserve in '12 when he appeared in six games. Started all eight games played at right tackle in '13, though he missed five games because of a right ankle sprain. After the season, had a rod inserted in his leg to address a stress fracture. Moved to left tackle in '14 when he started nine of 10 games played. Suffered a torn calf muscle against Colorado State and missed four games. After the season, had surgery to alleviate compartment syndrome in his legs. Started the first eight games at OLT in '15 before suffering a season-ending broken left ankle injury against Wyoming. Did not work out at the Combine because of ankle injury.

Strengths: Thick-framed, powerful athlete. Looks the part of prototype power guard. Outstanding weight-room worker with very good core strength. Latches on and can take defenders for a ride as a run blocker — can pave lanes with power. Works to cut off linebackers at the second level and takes them out. Shocks defenders with his punch and jars defenders off their feet at times. Scrappy competitor — stays after blocks. Good football intelligence. Accountable, unselfish teammate with terrific football character.

Weaknesses: Lacks ideal length to handle the outside and slips off blocks in pass protection. Could stand to improve footwork, hand use and overall awareness in pass pro — too inconsistent. Does not consistently convert his strength to the field. Durability is a concern — has missed at least a quarter of the season each of the last four years and could struggle to make it through a 16-game season.

Future: The anchor of Boise's offensive line, Odhiambo has the natural power and strength highly desired in a man-blocking scheme. Would be more ideally suited on the right side than the left in the pros and ripe for a move inside. Has overcome a lot of adversity in his life to get where he is and is the type of player you root for. Long-term durability concerns will push him down draft boards. Could prove to be an ideal backup always stressed to handle a full-time role.

Draft projection: Fourth- to fifth-round pick.

Scout's take: "He's very talented and has starter potential. It's way too risky to take a chance on him early though because of the durability issues."

OLG/C **ALEX REDMOND**, #51 (Jr-3)

UCLA ▶ GRADE: 5.07

Ht: 6-4 3/4 | Wt: 294 | 40: 5.27 | Arm: 33 1/4 | Hand: 10 1/2

History: California native who also excelled as a wrestler. Started all 13 games at right guard as a true freshman in 2013. In '14, started 8-of-10 games played at guard. Missed three mid-season contests and did not play while nursing an ankle injury, then did not start against Colorado or Arizona. Started all 11 games played at left guard in '15. Was suspended against Colorado, then left the team and signed with an agent in December (four days prior to the Bruins' bowl game), though he was not expected to be academically eligible for his final game. Was flagged for eight penalties in 2015.

Strengths: Is light on his feet and plays with good balance. Quick climbing to the second level — gets good fits on linebackers. Very good to shuffle, slide and mirror in pass pro and uses his hands well to create torque, maintain control and recover. Good movement skill.

Weaknesses: Thin-framed and underpowered. Lacks bulk and gives up a lot of ground against power. Tends to lock his knees and plays upright and could not unlock his hips easily during Combine drills. Lacks discipline on and off the field and has a defiance at a

blue-collar position that invites closer investigation into his coachability and understanding of the team concept.

Future: Light-framed, zone-blocking left guard with enough foot quickness and reactive agility to fend for a roster spot and compete for a backup job with continued physical development.

Draft projection: Priority free agent.

ORT/ORG **DOMINIQUE ROBERTSON**, #75 (Sr-4)

WEST GEORGIA ▶ GRADE: 5.26

Ht: 6-4 5/8 | Wt: 324 | 40: 5.34 | Arm: 36 | Hand: 10 3/8

History: Prepped in California. Spent 2012-13 at Riverside (Calif.) Community College — as a sophomore, graded out at 96 percent and notched 42 pancakes and 54 knockdowns. Signed with Texas Tech, where he wore jersey No. 76 in '14 — appeared in four games, drawing one start at right guard. Was suspended against Arkansas ("in-house situation") then dealt with a concussion in October before leaving team before Week Nine. Transferred to Division II West Georgia. Was arrested in January '15 and charged with felony obstruction and simple assault and battery. Was present at an apartment complex where a fight was reported. When a police officer who lived in the complex responded to the disturbance and told the crowd to disperse, Robertson "just stared at the officer" and, according to the officer, said there would be repercussions because the officer was alone. When backup officers arrived, Robertson fled. Upon being apprehended, an officer attempted to handcuff Robertson, but he resisted, pushing the officer back and struggling before being cuffed. On the season, started all 13 games played at left tackle, earning All-American recognition and the first Combine invite in school history. Did not play against Shorter.

Strengths: Exceptional size and mass with rare arm length and a wingspan (86 1/4 inches) the size of an aircraft carrier. Packs an angry punch and has proven capable of dominating lesser competition. Strong drive blocker — moves defenders off the line of scrimmage. Outstanding anchor strength — is seldom inverted. Flashes some nastiness and will finish blocks.

Weaknesses: Duck-footed short-stepper with tight ankles and raw technique. Was not regularly challenged against Division II competition, and will coast and play down to the competition. Character issues need to be investigated closely and have already eliminated him from consideration for some teams. Has had issues with anger management

Future: Big, strong, physical, straight-line blocker with the mass to generate movement in the run game. Has the girth, length and strength to eventually fend for a starting ORT job in the pros if he could stay focused.

Draft projection: Fifth- to sixth-round pick.

Scout's take: "He looked okay at the NFLPA (all-star) game. He was one of the best players there, if not the best. He's a triple-transfer with a lot of issues. A lot of teams will kill his character. Somebody will probably take a chance on him in the fifth round where you could think about taking chances."

OLG/C ISAAC SEUMALO, #56 (Jr-4)

OREGON STATE ▶ GRADE: 5.27

Ht: 6-3 7/8 | Wt: 303 | 40: 5.19 | Arm: 33 | Hand: 9 7/8

History: Corvallis native comes from an athletic family — father, Joe, is the defensive line coach at UNLV; brother, Andrew, was an OSU grad assistant during Isaac's senior year; and sister, Jessi, plays volleyball at OSU. Isaac was the top recruit in Oregon after garnering all-state honors on both sides of the ball two years in a row. In 2012, started all 13 games at center — was one of just two true freshman centers to start a season opener, as well as the first freshman to start at center for the Beavers since 1978. Missed the '13 season opener (left knee sprain), but started 12 games — 10 at center, two at right tackle. Broke his left foot in the Beavers' bowl game, and the injury required two surgeries and a prolonged recovery period in which he was instructed not to put weight on his foot for 10 months. After sitting out the '14 season, returned to start all 12 games in '15 —nine at right guard, three at left tackle. Two-year captain. Was medically excluded from bench-pressing at the Combine because of a left elbow injury.

Strengths: Good base, balance and agility. Recorded a 1.75-second 10-yard split at the Combine, the fastest of any offensive guard and indicative of good short-area burst and quickness. Also led the pack in the 20-yard shuttle (4.52 seconds) and 3-cone drill (7.40). Has the feet to climb to the second level and efficiently pull and trap. Effective cut-blocking. Versatile and has played almost every position on the line.

Weaknesses: Plays too small on the outside and was overmatched by the power of Oregon's defensive line. Lacks ideal length for a tackle. Wrestles more than strikes with his hands and could do a better job of punching and replacing his hands. Is late to arrive at the second level and plays out of control.

Future: A swing interior player who is not yet the technician he will need to be in the pros to match up with power. Clearly showed the feet and movement skill to function well in a zone-blocking scheme. Has some upside to be molded and has eventual starter potential.

Draft projection: Late draftable pick.

Scout's take: "(Seumalo) is an enigma with underachiever tendencies. He's a big stiff and bad at the second level. I thought he was better at center where he played the first two years, and he's average to below-average there. I think he would look interesting in the fifth round."

ORT BRANDON SHELL, #71 (Sr-5)

SOUTH CAROLINA ▶ GRADE: 5.32

Ht: 6-5 3/8 | Wt: 324 | 40: 5.19 | Arm: 34 3/8 | Hand: 10 3/4

History: Great nephew of NFL Hall of Famer Art Shell. South Carolina native was a Parade All-American. Redshirted in 2011 after having surgery to repair a torn left labrum. In '12, started 10-of-13 games — the season opener at left tackle and Weeks Five through 13 at right tackle. Started all 26 games at ORT 2013-14. Sat out '15 spring practice while recovering from right labrum surgery. In the fall, shifted to left tackle and started all 12 games. Team captain graduated with a sociology degree. Pulled his left quad on his first 40 at the Combine and did not finish drills or positional workouts.

Strengths: Excellent size and body length. Produced the best 20-yard split (2.80 seconds) of any offensive lineman at the Combine, indicative of terrific short-area burst. Capable shuffling and mirroring his man in pass pro. Efficient working to the second level and sealing off linebackers. Stood out in the East-West Shrine game. Experienced, four-year starter in the Southeastern Conference. Has NFL bloodlines.

Weaknesses: Leggy and high-hipped, which often results in playing tall. Has some tightness in his body and struggles to unlock his hips. Tends to play straight-legged and gets overextended, creating balance issues. Could play with more awareness — is late to recognize and react to some stunts and games. Gives up the inside too easily on spin moves. Motor runs hot and cold. Could require some time to acclimate to an NFL playbook.

Future: A big-bodied, strong, functional college left tackle lacking ideal bend, balance and lateral agility to consistently handle NFL speed rushers on the left side and lacking the strength and power desired on the right. Has

OFFENSIVE LINE

enough tools to function as a marginal starter on either side and could be most ideal suited for a role as a swing backup.

Draft projection: Third- to fourth-round pick.

Scout's take: "(Shell) is a developmental guy. He's raw. He has some size. Someone might take a chance on him in the third. He's really a fourth-round value."

C MATT SKURA, #62 (Sr-5)

DUKE ▶ GRADE: 5.19

Ht: 6-3 3/8 | Wt: 305 | 40: 5.34 | Arm: 33 3/8 | Hand: 10 1/8

History: Engaged — scheduled to get married just prior to training camp. Also competed in track and field as an Ohio prep. Redshirted in 2011. Was a reserve guard in '12 when he saw action (125 snaps) in 10 appearances. Took ownership of the center position as a sophomore — started all 40 games 2013-15. Team captain completed his undergraduate degree.

Strengths: Extremely long arms for a pivot, helping pick up stunts and loops in pass pro. Good blitz recognition. Understands angles and positioning and consistently seals off his man. Latches on and is gritty sustaining. Made the line calls in David Cutcliffe's pro-style offense. Good practice habits and leadership skills — teaches incoming freshman and will embrace the team concept in the locker room. Tough and durable. Steady run blocker.

Weaknesses: Limited athlete. Tends to play tall and short-armed with very limited explosion to knock defenders off the ball. Lacks core strength and shock in his punch. Struggles unlocking his hips — comes off the ball upright. Marginal finishing strength.

Future: Gritty mauler lacking ideal agility and core strength to contribute readily in the pros, yet has the size, football smarts and work habits to become a functional starting positional/sustain blocker in the pros.

Draft projection: Late draftable pick.

Scout's take: "He's the type of kid who is going to be successful at whatever he does in life. (The coaches) love him at the school. I kind of liked him as a player on the early tape that I did. He has a chance."

ORT PEARCE SLATER, #71 (Sr-4)

SAN DIEGO STATE ▶ GRADE: 5.09

Ht: 6-6 3/4 | Wt: 329 | 40: 5.43 | Arm: 35 1/4 | Hand: 10

History: California native played just two years of high school ball. Did not play in 2011. Spent 2012 at El Camino (Calif.) Community College — missed a chunk of his redshirt freshman season because his appendix burst. In July '13, committed to Kansas and then-head coach Charlie Weis in the form of a non-binding grant-in-aid agreement. At the time, was considered a recruiting coup for the Jayhawks, who incentivized Slater by informing him he could finish his JUCO classes and be eligible to play that season, beating the likes of Oklahoma and Utah to the punch. However, Slater left campus in August (KU called it a "family medical emergency"), did not keep the coaching staff abreast of his situation and wound up back at El Camino, where he played all 11 games as a sophomore. Signed with the Aztecs and started all 27 games at right tackle 2014-15. As a senior, was the best blocker on a line which paved the way for a school single-season record 3,059 rushing yards. Team captain.

Strengths: Rare size — thick-bodied with extremely long arms and a long torso. Is a $25 cab ride to get around. Effective when he latches on, especially as a drive blocker. Engulfs defenders and is capable of generating some movement with sheer size. Understands positioning and angles.

Weaknesses: Long-legged, tight-hipped and too narrow-based, allowing speed rushers to get up and underneath his pads and turn the corner. Too often late off the ball and to cut off defenders, allowing the game to get on top of him too quickly. Too much of a leaner — plays tall, negating power. Raw hand technician — tends to push and shove more than strike. Could require additional time to acclimate to NFL complexities. Only bench-pressed 225 pounds 17 times at the Combine and needs to get stronger.

Future: A monster-sized, lumbering right tackle with a similar frame as Bears 1991 undrafted free agent James "Big Cat" Williams. Right tackle only. Needs to play in a power scheme and will require TE help outside in pass protection to handle NFL speed rushers. Could develop into a solid pro with continued maturity.

Draft projection: Priority free agent.

OLT JASON SPRIGGS, #78 (Sr-4)

INDIANA ▶ GRADE: 6.06

Ht: 6-5 5/8 | Wt: 301 | 40: 4.89 | Arm: 34 | Hand: 10 1/8

History: Also competed in basketball, lacrosse and track and field as an Indiana prep. Established himself as a fixture at left tackle for the Hoosiers. In '12, set an IU true freshman offensive lineman record by starting all 12 games — led the team with 80 knockdowns while allowing just two sacks in 961 snaps. Started all 12 games in '13. Was lim-

OFFENSIVE LINE

ited by an abdominal tear during '14 spring practice. In the fall, started 10-of-11 games played and tallied 45 knockdowns while allowing two sacks in 689 snaps. Suffered a right MCL tear against Maryland which sidelined him against North Texas. Incurred a helmet-to-helmet hit against Michigan State and was carted off the field before being discharged from the hospital that night. Did not start against Penn State. Started all 13 games in '15, logging 72 knockdowns and two sacks allowed (regular season) in 1,024 snaps. Team captain.

Strengths: Experienced, four-year starter in the Big Ten conference. Understands positioning and angles and is efficient walling off defenders in pass pro and hooking ends on stretch-runs. Good feet to climb a level and run the field. Flashes a mean streak as a run blocker. Enough anchor strength to handle the bull rush. Matched up well against Ohio State DE Joey Bosa in limited opportunities when squared off and will rise to the occasion against better competition. Solid showing in OL drills at the Senior Bowl, showing improved hand use. Outstanding Combine performance. Recorded a 4.44-second 20-yard-shuttle time, the best of any offensive tackle at the event, and appeared extremely quick-footed and athletic moving through drills. Also bench-pressed 225 pounds 31 times, second-best among tackles. Well-conditioned athlete. Strong personal and football character.

Weaknesses: Lacks physicality. When he sets too tall, can be overpowered and knocked back on speed-to-power moves at times, losing his balance, getting out-leveraged and struggling to recover. Tends to overset, does not transition cleanly and occasionally gives up the inside. Does not consistently play to this size. Could sharpen consistency handling stunts and twists. Could stand to add some bulk to his frame.

Future: A more eye-popping athlete than nuanced football player at this stage of his career, Spriggs is a poor man's version of Eagles OT Lane Johnson, possessing elite feet, agility and explosion desired in an up-tempo, zone-based blocking scheme. A Day-One starter with some correctable technique deficiencies, Spriggs can learn to sustain longer and translate his superb athletic talent to the field. Has a lot of upside and his best football is ahead of him.

Draft projection: Top-40 pick.

Scout's take: "I graded Spriggs at the back of (the) 2(nd round). I still don't like him. We set him at the top of the third (round) on our (pre-Combine) board. He's too soft — he got rolled back a couple times at the Senior Bowl. He intrigues you and then he has some really awful plays where you think he is (extremely soft). I wish he had more bite to him."

OLT RONNIE STANLEY, #78 (Jr-4)

NOTRE DAME ▶ GRADE: 6.74

Ht: 6-5 3/4 | Wt: 312 | 40: 5.22 | Arm: 35 5/8 | Hand: 10 5/8

History: Prepped at Las Vegas Bishop Gorman, one of the top programs in the country. Won four state championships (three football, one basketball) and was the top-rated recruit in Nevada. Saw limited action in two games as a true freshman in 2012, redshirting following a left elbow injury that required surgery. Started all 13 games at right tackle in '13. Following the departure of Cowboys '14 first-rounder Zack Martin, Stanley started all 26 games at left tackle from 2014-15, allowing one sack as a sophomore and three as a junior. Had arthroscopic surgery on his right knee following the 2014 spring game. Was not allowed to "accept his captainship" by head coach Brian Kelly. When asked about the punishment, Stanley explained by saying, "parking reasons." Was enshrined as the 2015 Polynesian College Football Player of the Year award. Was medically excluded from bench-pressing at the Combine because of a left wrist injury and did not perform the broad jump because of a right knee injury.

Strengths: Excellent size and overall length in his body and arms. Very good athlete with lower-body flexibility, natural knee bend and lateral agility that often make pass protection look effortless. Efficient, fluid mover pulling and climbing to the second and third levels. Plays with good extension and controls defenders. Very intelligent. Understands angles and leverage — walls off and steers defenders. Can anticipate the blitz, with good recognition to twists and stunts. Versatile enough to handle either edge.

Weaknesses: Underdeveloped weight-room strength is noticeable in soft football playing temperament. Not a glass-eater or fiery run blocker and lacks power in his body and the hip snap to drive defenders. Gets beat on some up-and-under moves to the inside (see Clemson). More of a catcher than a puncher. A white-collar blocker at a blue-collar position — has some underachiever tendencies and must prove willing to put in the grunt work required to be a great pro. Could stand to improve on-field discipline — was flagged 11 times for penalties in 2015, among the

OFFENSIVE LINE

highest of any blocker in this year's draft.

Future: An athletic, college left tackle with prototypical size well-versed in a slide-protection scheme. Possesses the athletic ability, length, balance and footwork to step into a starting job readily on either side and is very similar to Jaguars 2009 eighth overall pick and Ravens left tackle Eugene Monroe.

Draft projection: Top-10 pick.

Scout's take: "I have a high grade on the guy — about as high of a grade as I can go. He has good tape. Anyone who watches the tape will feel comfortable selecting him. I have been watching him for three years now. I am comfortable with what he is. He is going to be a starting left tackle for a long time."

OT JOHN THEUS, #71 (Sr-4)

GEORGIA ▶ GRADE: 5.14

Ht: 6-6½ | Wt: 313 | 40: 5.18 | Arm: 34½ | Hand: 10⅛

History: Elite prospect coming out of Florida, where he garnered Parade and USA Today All-American honors and competed in track and field (throws). As a true freshman in 2012, started all 14 games at right tackle. Following the season, had surgery to repair a broken fifth metatarsal on his right foot. Was a reserve the first portion of the '13 season — started 8-of-13 games, including the final seven. Started all 14 games at left tackle in '14. As a senior in '15, started all 13 games — the first eight at OLT, the final five at ORT. Team captain. Did not bench press at the Combine because of an injury.

Strengths: Experienced, three-and-a-half-year starter in the Southeastern Conference. Understands angles, positioning and leverage. Has enough size and length to get positioning against speed and power. Effective short-setting and locking out in pass protection. Is fairly light on his feet and capable of climbing to the second level efficiently.

Weaknesses: Needs more glass in his diet. Plays too tall with limited body control and base strength, and occasionally will allow defenders to cross his face. Has no shock in his hands. Could stand to bulk up and strengthen his base to withstand power. Not a rugged or tough finisher and is too easily controlled, even ragdolled at times (see Alabama). Needs to improve his core power and functional, football-playing strength.

Future: Smart, versatile college tackle lacking ideal strength for the right side and ideal feet for the left, though has proven capable of filling in on either side and could ideally fit as a swing backup in a zone-based blocking scheme. May never be good enough

to win with on the front lines, yet versatility and intelligence could allow him to hold a roster spot.

Draft projection: Late draftable pick.

OLG/C JOE THUNEY, #54 (Sr-5)

NORTH CAROLINA STATE ▶ GRADE: 5.25

Ht: 6-4⅝ | Wt: 304 | 40: 4.99 | Arm: 32¼ | Hand: 9⅝

History: Last name is pronounced "TOO-nee." Was president of his graduating class in Ohio, where he won two state football titles and played basketball. Entered NC State at 245 pounds. Redshirted in 2011. Was a back-up center in '12, appearing in eight games. As a sophomore in '13, was elected to the Wolfpack's Leadership Council, then voted the team's most valuable offensive lineman after starter all 12 games — played right guard in the season opener, right tackle in Week Two and left tackle the rest of the way. In '14, started 8-of-9 games played at left guard. Missed four games because of mono. In '15, started all 13 games at OLT, becoming the first NC State offensive lineman All-American in 36 years. Did not allow a sack in conference play. Earned his fist diploma in three years — graduated cum laude with an accounting degree, and will also obtain a second degree in international studies with a minor in Spanish.

Strengths: Good football-playing temperament — comes off the ball with aggression and attacks defenders in the run game. Scrappy and competitive and seeks to sustain and finish. Recorded a 7.47-second 3-cone drill time, second-best among tackles at the Combine, as well as a 4.54-second 20-yard shuttle indicative of outstanding agility. Flashed power at the East-West Shrine game. Intelligent and assignment-sound — scored a 39 on his Wonderlic test. Smart, versatile, accountable jack-of-all trades. Unselfish, team player. Graded well against Clemson.

Weaknesses: Marginal arm length and flexibility in his body. Plays too upright and gets overextended bending at the waist. Not a natural knee bender. Overly muscled and mechanical in his movement. Has tight hips and stumbles too much, as he also showed during Combine drills. The further he travels, the more his lack of athletic ability is exposed. Struggled with the speed of Eastern Kentucky's Noah Spence and will require chip help to handle playing on the outside.

Future: A five-position player in college, Thuney finished his career at left tackle and serviceably handled the edges against better competition. However, he profiles best as a zone-blocking left guard in the pros. For as stiff and upright as he plays, he is surprisingly light on his feet and plays with a chip on his shoulder that could allow him to eventually earn a starting job. Often does not look pretty, but consistently produces and compensates for his stiffness with grit. Smart, tough, versatile and more concerned about production than appearance, Thuney looks destined for a role with a zone-blocking team such as the Patriots. Best position might be at center.

Draft projection: Fourth- to fifth-round pick.

Scout's take: "Thuney actually did a good job shutting down (Clemson DE Shaq) Lawson. ... He's a short-armed, stiff, upright blocker. We have him in the fifth (round). A lot of teams have him (graded) as a (priority) free agent. He'll play in the league."

ORT **COLE TONER**, #78 (Sr-4)
HARVARD　　　　　　　　　　▶ GRADE: 5.16
Ht: 6-5 1/4 | Wt: 306 | 40: 5.29 | Arm: 33 1/8 | Hand: 9 3/4

History: Did not receive an FBS scholarship offer. As a true freshman in 2013, appeared in seven games and drew five starts at right tackle as an injury replacement. Did not see action in the season opener, and was sidelined the final two games because of a left MCL sprain. Missed the first two games of the '13 season while nursing a high right ankle sprain, but started the final eight contests at ORT. Started all 14 games at ORT in '14. Despite missing the Lafayette contest because of a soft tissue foot injury, started nine games at ORT in '15. Was Harvard's nominee for the National Football Foundation Scholar-Athlete Award, and is scheduled to graduate in the spring with a degree in government with a secondary in economics (has political aspirations).

Strengths: Extremely intelligent and the game comes easy to him. Plays with awareness and anticipates pressure. Takes good angles and understands leverage. Posted a 4.59-second 20-yard shuttle time at the Combine, one of the five best among offensive tackles and indicative of solid lateral agility.

Weaknesses: Tends to play tall and bend at the waist — is stressed by edge speed. Does not have power in his punch and hands often go wide of the target. Lacks lower-body strength to drive defenders off the ball. Not strong at the point of attack and could stand to add bulk to his frame. Was not regularly challenged against Ivy League competition and struggled matching up one-on-one against

speed and power at the Senior Bowl.

Future: Developmental positional blocker ideally suited for a zone scheme. Has the intelligence, agility and length to eventually develop into a functional swing backup tackle with continued physical maturity.

Draft projection: Late draftable pick.

ORG **SEBASTIAN TRETOLA**, #73 (Sr-5)
ARKANSAS　　　　　　　　　▶ GRADE: 5.20
Ht: 6-4 1/4 | Wt: 314 | 40: 5.46 | Arm: 31 | Hand: 10 3/8

History: Also played basketball as a California prep. Began his college career at Nevada, where he greyshirted in 2011. Appeared in 11 games in '12, starting four games at guard. "Flunked out" of Nevada and spent '13 at Iowa Western Community College, where he started 12 games. Lost 50 pounds when he arrived at Arkansas. With the Razorbacks in '14, started 11-of-13 games at left guard — graded out at 79 percent while allowing zero sacks and committing four penalties in 690 snaps. Was co-recipient of the Jacobs Blocking Trophy (Southeastern Conference's best blocker) in '15 when he started all 13 games at left guard, posting an 84 percent blocking grade (regular season).

Strengths: Outstanding body mass to anchor in pass protection. Good awareness to stunts and blitzes. Is difficult to move once he gets his hands on defenders. Can generate some push in the run game. The game is important to him. Has a very likeable personality that blends easily in the locker room.

Weaknesses: Extremely short arms. Struggles when defenders work his edges and gives up some inside pressure to gap penetrators (see Kansas State). Loses stamina late in games and technique begins to fall apart, tending to bend more at the waist and get overextended.

Future: Thick-bodied mauler who is at his best straight-line mauling, but struggles when defenders get outside his cylinder and work the edges. Will be challenged by NFL speed and would be better suited on the right side than left in the pros.

Draft projection: Late draftable pick.

C/OG **MAX TUERK**, #75 (Sr-4)
USC　　　　　　　　　　　　▶ GRADE: 5.46
Ht: 6-5 | Wt: 298 | 40: 5.15e | Arm: 32 1/2 | Hand: 10 3/4

History: California native. As a true freshman in 2012, appeared in all 13 games and started five of the final six — four at left tackle, one at left guard. Started all 14 games in

OFFENSIVE LINE

'13 (13 at OLG, one at right tackle). Slid to center in '14, when he started all 13 games. In '15, managed five starts at center before suffering a season-ending torn right ACL injury against Washington. Two-year captain was voted the Trojans' Most Inspirational Player. Was medically excluded from running and positional workouts at the Combine because of knee injury.

Strengths: Good body length. Very good athlete. Comes off the ball quickly and under control. Good knee bend and recovery speed. Plays with awareness and is alert to stunts and blitz. Good agility to pull and trap and hit a moving target. Plays hard. Battles and competes. Easy to coach and absorbs the game quickly. Good football intelligence. Very versatile — has experience at every position on the line. Consistent performer.

Weaknesses: Is not naturally big-boned and has struggled to hold weight. Lacks bulk and could improve his functional football-playing strength to match up better against big-bodied nose tackles. At times gets out-leveraged and lets defenders come underneath him. Has short arms for the OT position. Bench-pressed 225 pounds only 22 times at the Combine, the fewest of any center. May not be ready for training camp coming off knee surgery.

Future: A smart, versatile, finesse, zone-blocking pivot with starter potential when healthy. Surprisingly showed up at the Combine weighing 298 pounds after injuring his knee late at mid-season and weighing 269 less than a year ago. Versatility will enhance his draft value, yet could slide a round or two while he is still rehabbing from his season-ending knee injury.

Draft projection: Third- to fourth-round pick.

Scout's take: "The USC center has no power. He is really lean and long. I don't think he can play center. I wrote him as a tackle only. He's sitting in the fourth round for me."

OLT **LAREMY TUNSIL**, #78 (Jr-3)

MISSISSIPPI   ▶ GRADE: 7.50

Ht: 6-5 | Wt: 310 | 40: 5.15e | Arm: 34 1/4 | Hand: 10

History: Elite prospect coming out of Florida — USA Today All-American and consensus No. 1 offensive tackle in his recruiting class. As a true freshman in 2013, started 9-of-12 games played at left tackle. Injured his left knee in the Egg Bowl against Mississippi State and did not play in the Rebels' bowl game. Started all 11 games played at OLT in '14. Did not play against Auburn or Presbyterian because of partially torn biceps,

then suffered a fractured right fibula and dislocated ankle in the Peach Bowl versus TCU. Missed '15 spring practice while recovering from surgery. Served a seven-game suspension to begin the season after an NCAA investigation determined Tunsil received impermissible extra benefits and was not forthcoming when questioned. Upon returning, started the final six games at left tackle. Scored a two-yard touchdown in the Rebels' Sugar Bowl victory over Oklahoma State. Did not perform the bench press at the Combine because of an injury and opted not to run the 40 or shuttles.

Strengths: Has well-proportioned dimensions for a left tackle. Very athletic and fluid for a big man. Natural bender with outstanding hip flexibility and ankle flexion. Plays with great balance and consistent pad level. Has very clean footwork and technique, as confirmed during Combine positional drills, and easily mirrors speed rushers. Can put on a clinic in pass protection, with a natural kickslide and strong power step to stop inside moves and cut off the speed rush. Outstanding recovery speed. Has a powerful six-inch punch. Shut down Texas A&M sack artist Myles Garrett and dominated against Arkansas and Mississippi State. Very good recovery quickness. Efficient pulling, locating his target and maneuvering in space — can run the field and look up defenders on the second and third levels. Battle-tested in the Southeastern Conference. Scheme diverse and can fit any style of ground game.

Weaknesses: Has some room to grow as a drive blocker rolling defenders off the line of scrimmage. Will let defenders get underneath his pads and can be walked back some — had fits against Auburn's Carl Lawson and could be challenged by power-leverage rushers. Lower-body and core functional strength could be improved. Has missed games each season for an assortment of reasons including some improprieties and collectively has missed too many games throughout his career.

Future: A big, strong, athletic prototypical left tackle with the balance, agility, recovery speed and technique to become a perennial Pro Bowler. Very similar to Jets 2006 fourth overall pick D'Brickashaw Ferguson, though even more stout, Tunsil makes the game look easy. Immediate impact starter who looks destined for the top overall pick

Draft projection: Top-10 pick.

Scout's take: "He is very talented. The only physical flaw you can ding him for — I was a little disappointed with the way his lower

OFFENSIVE LINE

body looked (on the school visit). He has very good natural bend. ...It was a shame he was suspended. A lot of it has become public knowledge now. His step-dad turned him in for recruiting violations and made up a lot of stories. After the third accusation was found untrue, they stopped investigating."

ORG **LANDON TURNER**, #78 (Sr-5)

NORTH CAROLINA ▶ GRADE: 5.07

Ht: 6-3 7/8 | Wt: 330 | 40: 5.58 | Arm: 32 7/8 | Hand: 10 3/8

History: Uncle, Jim Braxton, was a full-back for the Bills (1971-1978). Landon prepped in Virginia, overcoming serious injury during his sophomore season — broke his left ankle and incurred ligament damage in his foot, which required insertion of a metal plate and three screws. Was recruited by then-head coach Butch Davis. Redshirted in 2011. Shed 30 pounds and appeared in all 12 games in '12, starting the final four at right guard in place of the injured Brennan Williams. Started all 13 games at ORG in '13. Started all 11 games played at ORG. Did not play against East Carolina or Clemson because of a left MCL sprain. Started all 14 games at ORG in '15. Graduated after studying English and exercise and sport science. Pulled his right hamstring at the Combine while running his first 40-yard dash and did not perform shuttles or positional drills.

Strengths: Outstanding body mass to move defenders off the line of scrimmage when he is aligned over the top of them. Solid anchor strength to handle power. Can bump and steer defenders once he gets his hands on them.

Weaknesses: Not a natural knee bender. Hands too often go wide and outside of target. Is too easily stressed by speed — struggled to match up against the talented front of Clemson. Struggles to get off the track on the second level and cut off linebackers. Recorded the lowest vertical jump (19 inches) of any offensive lineman at the Combine, indicating limited athletic ability. Loses stamina and tends to wear down late in games, as confirmed by 26.8 percent body fat. Weight has fluctuated throughout his career.

Future: Sluggish, straight-linish mover lacking core strength, agility and recovery speed to sustain blocks. Lack of foot quickness could limit his opportunities. Would be most ideally suited for a team that employs a lot of man-blocking schemes such as the Lions, Titans and Bills.

Draft projection: Priority free agent.

ORT **HALAPOULIVAATI VAITAI**, #74 (Sr-4)

TCU ▶ GRADE: 5.04

Ht: 6-6 | Wt: 320 | 40: 5.26 | Arm: 34 1/4 | Hand: 10 5/8

History: Pronounced "hah-lah-poo-li-VAH-tee VIE-tie." As a true freshman in 2012, saw limited action in five games. In '13, started 7-of-12 games (five at right tackle, two at left tackle). Started all 13 games at right tackle in '14. Missed '15 spring practice while recovering from surgery to repair a torn left labrum. In the fall, started 11-of-12 games played at left tackle. Hurt his right knee against West Virginia, which cost him a start against Oklahoma State and sidelined him against Kansas.

Strengths: Outstanding size with excellent overall length. Has sufficient feet to climb a level in a straight line and seal lanes. Plays hard and competes. Very strong personal and football character. Coachable, driven to succeed and well-respected as a leader.

Weaknesses: Plays with too much finesse and is inverted too easily for as big as he is. Plays upright, carries his hands low and does not strike with power. Lacks core strength and gets tossed to the ground. Has limited lateral agility, as confirmed in subpar shuttle times at the Combine, and struggles to cut off the speed rush. Very raw technique.

Future: Developmental positional blocker with enough foot quickness to help in a pinch on the left side. More ideally suited for the right side in the pros and could fend for a chance to become a swing backup.

Draft projection: Priority free agent.

OLG/C **CHRISTIAN WESTERMAN**, #55 (Sr-5)

ARIZONA STATE ▶ GRADE: 5.53

Ht: 6-3 1/8 | Wt: 298 | 40: 5.21 | Arm: 33 1/2 | Hand: 11

History: USA Today All-American and elite offensive line recruit coming out of Arizona — won three state championships at Hamilton High and had offers from coast to coast. Began his college career at Auburn, where he redshirted in 2011. Was bothered by an ankle injury in '12 when he saw action in two games (one start). Transferred to ASU and sat out the '13 regular season (NCAA transfer rules) before appearing in the Holiday Bowl against Texas Tech. Stepped into the lineup in '14, starting all 12 games played at left guard. Sprained his left knee against Washington and sat out against Utah. Started all 13 games at OLG in '15.

Strengths: Broad-shouldered and rocked up with muscle. Has huge hands, the biggest of any guard at the Combine, and uses them well to latch on and steer defenders in the run

OFFENSIVE LINE

game. Bench-pressed 225 pounds 34 times, leading all guards at the Combine. Very good movement skill. Plays with a mean streak and urgently climbs the second level seeking contact. Takes pride in finishing blocks. Active and intense. Showed very well in drills at the Senior Bowl. Very serious and business-like in his approach and is ultra-focused on improvement. Good practice and preparation habits.

Weaknesses: Has some tightness in his ankles and body that leads him to fall off blocks and struggle sustaining. Lacks bulk and can be controlled and tossed around by power (see Oregon). Could do a better job of using his hands and striking with authority. Too often overaggressive and plays out of control. Winds up on the ground more than he should looking for the knockout shot.

Future: A gritty competitor with the natural girth, toughness and finishing power to contribute readily and as a guard or center in a zone-blocking scheme. Has a very football-centric approach with tunnel vision that could allow him to become a very solid pro for a long time.

Draft projection: Third- to fourth-round pick.

Scout's take: "I like the way (Westerman) is wired. He's all ball. ... He's one tough hombre."

OLG/OT CODY WHITEHAIR, #55 (Sr-5)

KANSAS STATE ▶ GRADE: 5.86

Ht: 6-3 3/4 | Wt: 301 | 40: 5.07 | Arm: 32 3/8 | Hand: 10 1/8

History: Kansas native recorded 140 pancakes as a high school senior. Redshirted in 2011. Started 12-of-13 games in '12 — the season opener at right tackle, nine at left guard and the final two at right guard. Shifted to left guard for the next two seasons, starting all 26 games 2013-14. In order to get the Wildcats' best five linemen on the field, was used at left tackle in '15 when he started all 13 games. Team captain graduated with a sociology degree.

Strengths: Experienced, durable four-year starter with experience inside and outside — has never missed a game. Plays with great awareness and good grip strength. Quick but patient and controlled maneuvering to the second level and squaring up on linebackers — locates his target and seals lanes. Very good body control, foot quickness and balance. Recorded a 1.75-second 10-yard split at the Combine and has outstanding short-area burst. Also registered a 4.58-second 20-yard shuttle and a 7.32-second 3-cone, second best among all tackles at the even — has superb agility. Outstanding personal and football

character. Respected team leader.

Weaknesses: Marginal arm length. Only bench-pressed 16 reps, the second-fewest of any OG prospect at the Combine, and needs to continue to develop his weight-room strength. Can be knocked around at times and controlled vs. power ends. Does not consistently finish blocks like he is capable. Will struggle to handle elite edge speed on an island in the pros.

Future: A college left tackle lacking ideal length for the outside, Whitehair will fit best at left guard in the pros for a zone-blocking scheme such as the Patriots, Texans, Broncos or Redskins.

Draft projection: Top-50 pick.

Scout's take: "He's probably the best guard I have seen (this year). I don't think he can play left tackle. He's got to be a guard."

ORG/ORT AVERY YOUNG, #56 (Jr-4)

AUBURN ▶ GRADE: 5.38

Ht: 6-4 5/8 | Wt: 328 | 40: 5.41 | Arm: 33 3/4 | Hand: 10 1/2

History: Brother, Willie, is a defensive end for the Bears, and cousin, Thomas Davis, is a linebacker for the Panthers. Played high school ball in Florida. As a true freshman in 2012, arrived with a damaged left shoulder, but started the first three games at right tackle before undergoing season-ending surgery to repair a torn labrum. Played 10 games in '13, starting the final nine at right tackle. Was a backup until Week Six. In '14, started all 13 games — seven at ORT, three at right guard and three at left guard. Manned ORT in '15 when he started all 11 games played. Sat out against Jacksonville State (ankle).

Strengths: Has a big power base and functional anchor strength. Plays with aggression in the run game and battles and scraps. Runs his feet on contact. Versatile and has lined up at inside and outside. Has NFL pedigree.

Weaknesses: Long-legged with a short torso and bends at the waist too much, gets overextended and falls off blocks, both in-line and in space. Hands and feet do not work in unison. Struggles with speed-to-power rushers (see Arkansas) when they get underneath his pads and will be stressed by NFL speed on the edges. Struggles keeping his cleats in the ground. Could do a better job finishing blocks.

Future: Lined up mostly at right tackle, but will be best suited to play in confined quarters where he has outside help in the pros. Will require some development time, yet has the power to create running lanes as a right guard and has eventual starter potential.

Draft projection: Third- to fourth-round pick.

OFFENSIVE LINE

DEFENSIVE LINE

Nawrocki's TOP 10

1. JOEY BOSA
2. DeForest Buckner
3. Sheldon Rankins
4. A'Shawn Robinson
5. Robert Nkemdiche
6. Kevin Dodd
7. Jarran Reed
8. Austin Johnson
9. Shaq Lawson
10. Vernon Butler

DEFENSIVE LINE

DLE MEHDI ABDESMAD, #45 (Sr-5)

BOSTON COLLEGE ▶ GRADE: 4.92

Ht: 6-6 1/4 | Wt: 284 | 40: 5.11 | Arm: 33 3/8 | Hand: 9 3/4

History: Pronounced "Ab-des-MAHD, Meh-DEE." Born to Tunisian parents. Lost his father during high school. Prepped in Montreal. Saw limited action in eight games as a true freshman in 2011 when he notched three tackles, zero for loss and zero sacks. Started 8-of-12 games at defensive end in '12, collecting 25-3-0 with one batted pass and one forced fumble. In '13, managed 17-31/2-2 in four starts at defensive tackle before suffering a season-ending torn left patellar tendon injury. Started 2-of-3 games played at DT in '14 (4-0-0), but was not 100 percent, aggravated his left knee injury and was shut down in order to have it scar tissue surgically repaired. Returned to started 8-of-12 games at defensive end in '15, notching 49-15-5 1/2. Graduated with a finance degree. Will be a 25-year-old rookie. Rated a top-5 CFL prospect.

Strengths: Outstanding size. Flashes some strength to control blockers vs. the run. Has a nice swim move.

Weaknesses: Average instincts — is late to locate and find the ball. Plays short-armed with slow hands. Takes choppy steps and covers little ground. Marginal bend. Struggles to anchor vs. the double team and gets washed out of his gap. Can be run at. Lacks variety of pass-rush moves. Was never a full-time starter. Durability has been an issue throughout his career with recurring left knee injuries.

Future: Size prospect who could provide some depth in an NFL camp. Best chance to develop will likely come in his native CFL.

Draft projection: Priority free agent.

Scout's take: "I didn't care for the big, tall, basketball-looking, 6-5, 280-pound end. He looks like he's 250 (pounds) and doesn't play strong or physical. He has a narrow base. He's not effective as a pass rusher. He covers a limited area as a run stopper. I was not impressed. The light has not really come on yet."

5T STERLING BAILEY, #58 (Sr-5)

GEORGIA ▶ GRADE: 5.07

Ht: 6-4 | Wt: 285 | 40: 5.16 | Arm: 33 3/8 | Hand: 10 1/4

History: Also played basketball and threw shot put as a Georgia prep. Had surgery to

DEFENSIVE LINE

repair a right labrum tear prior to entering UGA. Redshirted in 2011. Had torn ligaments in his right foot surgically repaired in December, forcing him to sit out '12 spring practice. In the fall, saw very limited action in three games and recorded one tackle, zero for loss and zero sacks. Had right thumb surgery in October. Played all 13 games in '13, starting the first eight as a 3-4 defensive end, and logged 34-1-1 with three batted passes. Played with a hurt right ankle against Kentucky. Had his left ring finger surgically repaired in January '14. In the fall, played all 13 games, drawing the start at defensive tackle in the opener, and was credited with 27-1/2-1/2 with two batted passes. Started 10-of-13 games at DE in '15 and produced 46-21/2-1 with two batted passes. Graduated with a history degree.

Strengths: Very good size. Good balance. Plays on his feet. Flashes some straight-line power to create a push. Solid tackler. Plays hard and competes.

Weaknesses: Very heavy-footed, lumbering mover. Struggles unlocking his hips. Average lower-body strength to hold the point against double teams. Straight-linish. Limited pass-rush potential. Marginal production.

Future: Big, strong, 3-4 defensive end capable of providing some depth as a rotational two-down, run stuffer. Could provide some depth in a camp.

Draft projection: Priority free agent.

Scout's take: "I thought he was just a guy. He looks the part, but doesn't produce. Something is missing. He's average across the board in quickness, athleticism and strength. His instincts are borderline or questionable. He passes the eyeball test; he just doesn't play it."

DLE-OLB JIMMY BEAN, #92 (Sr-5)

OKLAHOMA STATE ▶ GRADE: 5.06
Ht: 6-5 | Wt: 264 | 40: 4.90e | Arm: 33½ | Hand: 9¾

History: Prepped at Denton (TX) Guyer. As a true freshman in 2011, was credited with three tackles, zero for loss and zero sacks in three appearances. Lost his '12 season to a dislocated knee (medical hardship). Started all 26 games at defensive end the next two seasons — totaled 34-91/2-41/2 in '13; and 42-6-31/2 with two batted passes, one interception and three blocked kicks. In '15, logged 25-101/2-51/2 in eight starts at DE before suffering a season-ending torn ACL injury. Received the Vernon Grant Award, given to a player who shows outstanding leadership,

spirit and enthusiasm. Was a medical exclusion at the Combine because of a left knee injury and did not run or jump.

Strengths: Experienced, three-year starter. Good body length. Good effort to push the pocket. Reliable tackler inside the box.

Weaknesses: Plays too upright, negating his leverage and gets washed by double teams. Needs to do a better job of using his hands, creating extension and locking out to control blockers. Lacks short-area burst and closing speed to reach the quarterback. Instincts are still developing — could do a better job feeling blocking pressure and locating the ball more quickly.

Future: A big, stiff, finesse rusher lacking ideal bend and strength to set the edge and the burst to trim the corner. Could warrant some consideration as a developmental outside linebacker from teams employing "30" fronts, but profiles as a backup base end for a "40" front. Could always struggle with durability issues given his body stiffness.

Draft projection: Late draftable pick.

Scout's take: "He's a high effort, tough overachiever. He might be too stiff to be anything but a left end for even fronts. He has good length, decent strength and a high motor. He is just stiff and does not have a lot of production. He's a late-round pick for an even front (defense). I don't think he is big or strong enough for a 3-4 (front). He's too stiff and tight to be an outside linebacker."

NT ANDREW BILLINGS, #75 (Jr-3)

BAYLOR ▶ GRADE: 5.56
Ht: 6-0 5/8 | Wt: 311 | 40: 5.04 | Arm: 33 | Hand: 10

History: Waco native was an all-state football player and record-setting powerlifter. As a true freshman in 2013, broke his nose during fall camp before recording 30 tackles, four for loss and one-half sack in 11 games (started final two). Did not play against Buffalo or West Virginia (ankle). Took ownership of the nose tackle spot in '14 when he started all 13 games and posted 37-111/2-2 with one forced fumble. Was the Co-Big 12 Defensive Player of the Year in '15 when he notched 40-15-51/2 with one forced fumble in 12 starts. Did not play against Iowa State (left ankle sprain). Will be a 21-year-old rookie.

Strengths: Exceptional body mass and overall strength. Is square-cut, thick-bodied and looks like a small tank. Deceptively athletic. Can clear his feet through trash. Very strong to hold the point of attack and stack double teams. Is seldom inverted and can create a good push. Flashes power in his hands. Plays hard and flattens down the line. Good strength on a rail. Is tough and will battle through injuries.

Weaknesses: Lacks ideal height and body length. Stiff in his ankles and hips. Cannot play half a man. Lacks the hip fluidity and short-area burst to pierce gaps. Struggles matching up against power. Marginal range outside the tackle box. Average lateral agility, as confirmed with below-average shuttle times at the Combine.

Future: Big, strong plugger played through an ankle injury late in the year and did not look like the same player he was at the start. A true nose tackle lacking pass-rush ability to be an impact player. Could play on a shade in an even front, but lacks the twitch to factor as a gap-penetrating three technique the way he thinks he can. Can be a three-down rotational player most effective defending the run.

Draft projection: Second- to third-round pick.

Scout's take: "He's a nose only. He (received) a lot of pub early — he's a media fabrication. If you watch him against Oklahoma and better teams in the conference, he disappeared. Early on, he was playing very well against Texas Tech and West Virginia. When you watch him against some decent offensive linemen, he is a mid-round talent. He is a nose all the way. ... There were some arguments and discussion about whether he is a two- or three-down player in our (draft) room. He is a two-down player, and he was not as productive as the kid from Washington that the Browns (Danny Shelton) drafted that didn't do anything this year."

DLE-3T RONALD BLAIR, #49 (Sr-5)

APPALACHIAN STATE ▶ GRADE: 5.19
Ht: 6-2 1/8 | Wt: 284 | 40: 5.16 | Arm: 34 | Hand: 10 1/4

History: Prepped in Georgia. As a true freshman in 2011, started all 12 games at right defensive end and amassed 40 tackles, 11 1/2 for loss and 3 1/2 sacks with one batted pass and one forced fumble. Started all 12 games at DE in '12, producing 60-8 1/2-3. In '13, managed 7-11 1/2-1 in two starts at DE before a left thumb injury (ended his season — tore chipped a bone and tore ligaments. Was arrested in September and charged with driving after consuming alcohol underage (blood alcohol content was 0.04) and driving without a license. Healthy in '14, started all 12 games at DE and totaled 43-13-6 with one batted pass. Was the Sun Belt Defensive Student-Athlete of the Year in '15 after racking up 71-19-7 1/2

with a 30-yard interception return touchdown and one forced fumble. Two-year captain. Only ran one 40 at the Combine due to an unspecified injury.

Strengths: Very good arm length. Experienced, four-year starter. Good motor. Outstanding weight-room worker. Bench-pressed 225 pounds 32 times, best among all defensive ends at the Combine. Solid showing against better competition (see Clemson). Registered a 1.76-second 10-yard split, indicating good short-area burst. Can create pressure and split double teams effectively on stunts and loops. Solid overall run defender.

Weaknesses: Lacks ideal height. Very tight-hipped and comes off the ball upright. Plays narrow-based, relying too much on his upper body strength, and lacks true anchor strength. Registered the slowest 3-cone drill time (7.96 seconds) of any defensive end at the Combine, indicating a lack of body control and short-area burst. Needs to do a better job of using his hands to shed blocks. Production is inflated from facing inferior production. Must prove alcohol will not be an issue.

Future: A strong, five-technique who exceled playing multiple positions along a "30" front, Blair has the size, brute strength and enough agility to warrant interest as a developmental, rotational five-technique in an aggressive, zone-blitzing scheme such as the Bills, Titans or Ravens. Questions about alcohol require closer scrutiny and could affect draft status.

Draft projection: Late draftable pick.

DLE-DT-LOLB JOEY BOSA, #97 (Jr-3)

OHIO STATE ▶ GRADE: 6.94
Ht: 6-5 1/4 | Wt: 269 | 40: 4.86 | Arm: 33 3/8 | Hand: 10 1/4

History: Father, Joe, was a Dolphins first-round pick in 1987, and uncle, Eric Kumerow, was a Dolphins first-round pick in '88. Joey prepped at Florida powerhouse St. Thomas Aquinas, where he won a state championship and garnered USA Today All-American honors. As a true freshman in '13, started 10-of-14 games at strong-side defensive end and recorded 44 tackles, 13 1/2 tackles for loss and 7 1/2 sacks with one batted pass and one fumble recovery touchdown. Was the Big Ten's Defensive Player of the Year in '14 — notched 55-21-13 1/2 with one batted pass, four forced fumbles and one fumble recovery touchdown in 15 starts. Was suspended for the '15 season opener against Virginia Tech before starting all 12 games played and totaling 51-16-5 with four batted

DEFENSIVE LINE

passes, one interception and one forced fumble. Was ejected from the Fiesta Bowl versus Notre Dame (targeting penalty). Led the Big Ten with 13 1/2 tackles for loss in conference play. Two-time conference defensive lineman of the year.

Strengths: Well-built with good muscularity and superb functional football-playing strength. Has quick and strong hands. Can convert speed to power, get underneath the pads of blockers and leverage them back to the quarterback. Strong lockout and extension to control defenders. Has a strong swat and rip move and keeps working to come free. Disruptive kicking down to the inside and mismatching guards on third down, with the burst to pierce inside gaps and surprising strength and hand violence to stack and shed against bigger bodies. Physically and mentally tough. Competes hard and makes plays in pursuit. Athletic enough to fall back into coverage, and did not look out of place in LB coverage drops at the Combine. Scheme diverse — can fit in either a 30 or 40 front and play anywhere along the line. Has NFL pedigree.

Weaknesses: Does not have elite edge burst or upfield speed to scream off the edge. Gets overextended and stumbles and trips too much, as he also did going through the bag drills at the Combine. Could stand to be more disciplined timing the snap — gets caught jumping offsides trying to anticipate too much. Likes to party.

Future: Though he may not have produced the sacks expected of an elite pass-rusher, Bosa's upfield presence was consistently felt by quarterbacks all season, and he was far more dominant than the stat sheet shows, continually harassing passers, creating inside pressure and stuffing the run. Has a very similar skill set to New York Giants Hall of Famer Michael Strahan and could make an immediate impact in the pros.

Draft projection: Top-10 cinch.

Scout's take: "We could put Bosa at rush end because he is better than anything we have there, but he's really a 4-3 base end or an outside backer in a 3-4. (Scouts) are comparing him to (Rams 2008 2nd overall pick) Chris Long. I don' think Chris Long was as talented as Bosa."

5T-3T DeFOREST BUCKNER, #44 (Sr-4)

OREGON ▶ GRADE: 6.70

Ht: 6-7 | Wt: 291 | 40: 5.06 | Arm: 34 3/8 | Hand: 11 3/4

History: Also an all-state basketball player as a Hawaii prep. Partially tore his left PCL as a senior, costing him part of his football and basketball seasons. Recruited to Eugene by then-head coach Chip Kelly. As a true freshman in 2012, Buckner was named the Ducks' top first-year player — played all 13 games, starting two at defensive tackle, and recorded 29 tackles, 2 1/2 for loss and one sack with two batted passes. Played all 13 games in '13, moving into the starting lineup for the final eight contests, and produced 39-3 1/2-2 1/2 with a batted pass and a forced fumble. In '14, was deployed as a 3-4 defensive end opposite 49ers '15 first-rounder Arik Armstead — tallied 81-13-4 with four batted passes and a forced fumble (14 starts). Had his left knee scoped and was limited during '15 spring practice. Was the Pac-12 Defensive Player of the Year and a Hendricks Award finalist in '15 when he amassed 83-17/10 1/2 with five batted passes. Sprained his right wrist against Arizona State. Earned his criminology degree. Two-time team captain. Opted not to bench press at the Combine.

Strengths: Rare size, with very long arms and monster-sized, nearly 12-inch hands, the largest of any player at the Combine. Excellent edge-setting strength — locks out and presses defenders into the backfield and resets the line of scrimmage. Brandishes a powerful club move to swat blockers out of the way, uses a strong arm-over and swim moves. Can collapse the pocket. Outstanding effort — motor always runs hot. Can shock blockers with his punch. Outstanding production. Excellent tempo at practice.

Weaknesses: Gets in trouble when he comes up out of his stance too tall, getting overwhelmed by the double team (see pancaked against Oregon State). Could stand to play with more consistent knee bend. At times can be a tick late to locate the ball. Is a long strider and struggles to make sharp cuts — at times plays out of control and can't come to balance, as confirmed in Combine drills rounding corners. Average body control. Leaves his feet too much. Does not have elite explosion for an inside penetrator in a 40 front. Lacks weight-room strength and has room to get stronger.

Future: A prototypical 3-4 defensive end with exceptional size, strength and length to set the edge, Buckner also has the agility to beat guards one-on-one from the inside on third down. A big man who plays big. Emerged as a disruptive force against the run and pass and has immediate impact potential in the pros. Best fit will come in a 30 front.

Draft projection: Top-10 pick.

Scout's take: "(Buckner) is more of a two-gap type of guy. He's a defensive tackle in an even front, but he's not as athletic as you would like a three-technique to be. And he's not quick enough to play the edge in an even front. He's a 30 defensive end and maybe he kicks down in sub-packages. He is a strong and powerful wardaddy."

5T JONATHAN BULLARD, #90 (Sr-4)
FLORIDA ▶ GRADE: 5.58
Ht: 6-3 | Wt: 285 | 40: 4.93 | Arm: 33 5/8 | Hand: 10

History: Highly recruited out of North Carolina. As a true freshman in 2012, recorded 27 tackles, five for loss and 11/2 tackles for loss with one batted pass in 13 games (two starts at defensive end). In '13, started 8-of-11 games played — five at DE, three at defensive tackle — and tallied 33-21/2-11/2. Did not play against Georgia Southern (right knee sprain). In '14, started all 12 games — nine at DT, two at DE, one at NT — and posted 52-81/2-21/2 with two batted passes. Started all 14 games in '15 — six at NT, five at DT, 3 at DE — and totaled 66-171/2-61/2 with two batted passes. Hurt his right knee against Florida Atlantic, but did not miss a start.

Strengths: Outstanding size with good arm length. Has a strong power base to stack blocks and stuff the run. Locks out and presses blockers into the backfield. Excellent controlling blockers and making plays run at him. Locates the ball quickly and works off blocks to flatten and come free. Very active. Feels blocking pressure and reacts to it. Versatile and aligns inside and out and could warrant some consideration for an even front.

Weaknesses: Lacks ideal hip flexibility to work the edges and bend around blockers. Plays too upright. Is not explosive off the ball to pierce gaps or dynamic to penetrate on stunts and loops. Struggles to hold his ground against the double team. Needs to develop more variety as a pass-rusher. Average closing speed.

Future: Appears to be a prototype three-technique on paper and could even wind up being drafted to fill that role. However, his inflexible hips and body stiffness often force him to rise and make him most ideally suited to stack the corner as a straight-line, edge-setting, power rusher for a "30" front, where he excels defending the run. A much better run

defender than pass rusher.

Draft projection: Second- to third-round pick.

Scout's take: "He can't be a three-technique for us. No way. He's too stiff. He's a 3-4 defensive end all the way."

3T-5T VERNON BUTLER, #9 (Sr-4)
LOUISIANA TECH ▶ GRADE: 5.88
Ht: 6-3 5/8 | Wt: 323 | 40: 5.32 | Arm: 35 | Hand: 10

History: Mississippi native who also played basketball and ran track in high school before choosing Louisiana Tech over offers from Ole Miss and Mississippi State, among others. As a true freshman in 2012, recorded 21 tackles, 11/2 tackles for loss and zero sacks in 11 games. Did not play against Utah State. Played 11 games in '13, starting once, and tallied 43-41/2-1. Did not play against Florida International (back). Switched from jersey No. 45 to No. 9 and started all 27 games the next two seasons — totaled 56-131/2-1 with one batted pass and one forced fumble in '14 (14 games); and 50-10-3 with two batted passes in '15 (13 games). Team captain. Is only 21 years old.

Strengths: Has an NFL body with a big-bone structure, extremely long arms and pure strength to push the pocket. Has an aircraft carrier wingspan measuring seven feet. Is light on his feet for as big as he is and capable of flipping his hips and working in gaps or stacking blockers and two-gapping. Plays faster than his timed speed. Good closing burst to the quarterback. Very good strength to hold his ground against the double team. Stout and physical and flashes the ability to dominate. Good power in his punch. Flashes a mean streak. Strong, wrap tackler. Improved steadily throughout his career and is brimming with upside. Solid Senior Bowl performance. Versatile and can play anywhere along a "30" front.

Weaknesses: Recorded the slowest 40-yard dash (5.40 seconds) of any defensive lineman at the Combine. Is still very raw and learning how to harness and deploy the innate power in his body. Motor does not always run hot. Not a consistent finisher. Marginal sack production — only five career sacks.

Future: Possessing unique versatility to line up in an even or odd front, Butler has the size, strength, arm length and power to become a very solid starter with continued refinement. A big-bodied late bloomer that could thrive with NFL coaching. Ideally fits as a one-gap, penetrating nose tackle in a slanting odd front, with strength to handle the five-technique. Is

DEFENSIVE LINE

best insuited inside in the pros.

Draft projection: Top-50 pick.

Scout's take: "Vernon Butler made some money (at the Senior Bowl). He is a big, athletic guy. He got a little too big. They have him on creatine at the place where he is training. He's north of 320. His ideal playing weight is 310. He has a big, big upside."

DRE-ROLB SHILIQUE CALHOUN, #89 (Sr-5)

MICHIGAN STATE   ▶ GRADE: 5.45

Ht: 6-4 3/8 | Wt: 251 | 40: 4.84 | Arm: 34 1/4 | Hand: 9 7/8

History: Defensive end-tight end who also played basketball (averaged 18 points and 10 rebounds) as a New Jersey prep. Redshirted in 2011. Was a reserve in '12 when he notched six tackles, 2 1/2 for loss and one sack with two batted passes. Had a breakout season in '14 when he was the Big Ten Defensive Lineman of the Year, College Football Performance Awards National Defensive Performer of the Year and a Hendricks Award finalist — amassed 37-14-7 1/2 with two forced fumbles and one interception in 14 starts at weak-side defensive end. Scored three touchdowns — two fumble recovery scores and a 56-yard INT return against South Florida. In '14, started all 13 games and collected 39-12 1/2-8 with one forced fumble and a blocked field goal attempt. Was a Hendricks finalist again in '15 after starting all 14 games and posting 49-15-10 1/2 with three batted passes, one forced fumble and one blocked field goal attempt. Two-time captain and the only Spartan defensive lineman in school history to earn first-team All-Big Ten honors. Graduated with a criminal justice degree.

Strengths: Experienced, three-year starter. Good size with long arms. Good eyes and instincts to locate the ball quickly. Athletic mover. Very good bend to trim the corner and generate pressure off the edge — consistently harasses the quarterback. Quick-handed to play off blocks and disengage. Good closing speed. Recorded the second-fastest 3-cone drill time (6.97 seconds) of all defensive ends at the Combine, indicative of good body control, balance and lateral agility. Has a 35-inch vertical jump. Very good football intelligence. Outstanding personal and football character. Very coachable.

Weaknesses: Lacks ideal anchor strength to defend the run and can be moved off the line of scrimmage. Does not play strong or physical and allows blockers to steer him too much. Overmatched against the double

team and cannot dig his heels in the dirt and anchor. Uses too much finesse and plays too nice. Does not sacrifice his body around piles. Could stand to do a better job anticipating the snap — too jumpy and undisciplined trying to beat blockers off the ball.

Future: A long-limbed, rangy, athletic pass rusher most ideally suited for an open-side end, rushing role in a 4-3 front, Calhoun can bring consistent energy to pressure the quarterback and has consistently been productive. Has room to continue improving as a run defender. Could warrant some interest as an outside linebacker in a "30" front. Strong work ethic and character should allow him to maximize his potential and reach his ceiling.

Draft projection: Third- to fourth-round pick.

Scout's take: "I still like him. He was taken in similar in a way to the Michael Oher situation (in the movie The Blind Side). It's an incredible story. I'm rooting for the kid."

NT KENNY CLARK, #97 (Jr-3)

UCLA   ▶ GRADE: 5.62

Ht: 6-2 5/8 | Wt: 314 | 40: 5.07 | Arm: 32 1/8 | Hand: 10 1/2

History: Also wrestled as a California prep. Was deployed as a 3-4 nose tackle during his UCLA career. As a true freshman in 2013, collected 31 tackles, four for loss and one sack in 13 games (three starts). Started all 26 games the next two seasons — totaled 58-5 1/1-0 with one batted pass in '14; and 75-11-6 with five batted passes in '15. Team captain. Did not perform the 3-cone drill at the Combine because of left foot injury. Will be a 20-year-old rookie.

Strengths: Outstanding size — rocked up with muscle and has very good strength. Good body control and balance. Smooth mover. Fluid ankles. Plays with power in his hands — jolts defenders with his punch and rips off blocks. Has bull strength to push the pocket. Plays low to the ground with natural leverage and can anchor vs. the double team. Good awareness to locate the ball quickly and sniff out screens. Good Combine showing in positional drills.

Weaknesses: Lacks ideal length. Short-legged in proportion to his body with a long torso, which negates his agility and closing burst. Takes short, choppy strides and misses tackles. Lacks explosive lower-body power. Plays down to the level of competition.

Future: An ideal nose tackle for a one-gapping "40" front, Clark is a strong, straight-line plugger with enough quickness to slide to a

DEFENSIVE LINE

three-technique in sub-packages. Is one of the youngest players in the draft and has a lot of upside. Must learn to become more consistent and avoid taking plays off to reach his potential. Marginal stamina.

Draft projection: Second- to third-round pick.

Scout's take: "USC put (Clark) on his back a number of times. I'm not sure if he was quitting. All I know is that he looked like he was dominating early on in the season. He beat up on Arizona. Towards the end of the year, he looked like just a guy. His stats dropped. When you have a guy who is supposed to be an interior nose getting put on his back by (bad) offensive lineman, it's not good. He had a good workout at the Combine. That should help him."

3T MALIEK COLLINS, #7 (Jr-3)
NEBRASKA ▶ GRADE: 5.68
Ht: 6-1⅞ | Wt: 311 | 40: 5.02 | Arm: 33⅛ | Hand: 9½

History: Prepped in Missouri, where won the Class 2A state wrestling championship with a 48-0 mark. As a true freshman in 2013, tallied 12 tackles, two for loss and one sack with one forced fumble in 12 games (one start against Georgia in the Gator Bowl). Did not play against Michigan. Was Nebraska's Defensive co-MVP in '14 when he started all 13 games and recorded 45-14-4½. Started 12-of-13 games in '15, posting 29-7-2½ with one batted pass. Incurred a regrettable personal foul penalty at the end of the Northwestern game — did not start the following week against Purdue (entered the game on the third defensive snap). Team captain will be a 21-year-old rookie.

Strengths: Has a thick trunk with a good base and balance. Very quick off the ball with good lateral agility, as confirmed with 4.52-second 20-yard shuttle time and 7.53-second 3-cone drill time. Has quick, active hands and an assortment of pass-rush moves — a good swim, arm-over, rip, slap, push-pull and tug and can win one-on-one battles. Feels blocking pressure and plays off blocks. Very energetic and keeps working to the quarterback.

Weaknesses: Could play with more consistent knee bend — tends to raise tall, negating his leverage and power. Is not overly stout. Could stand to do a better job of anticipating the snap and throwing his hips in the hole.

Future: A quick, active one-gap penetrator most ideally suited to shoot gaps as a three-technique in a "40" front. Could warrant some developmental interest as a 3-4 defensive end in a "30" front. Ability to consistently create pressure is his calling card.

Draft projection: Second- to third-round pick.

Scout's take: "Collins is a little undersized, but he is powerful. He reminded me a lot of (Tampa Bay DT) Gerald McCoy when he was a sophomore. I saw him live in the fall, and it looked like he had some ankle issues. That could be why his production was down."

DLE-LOLB JAMES COWSER, #53 (Sr-7)
SOUTHERN UTAH ▶ GRADE: 5.23
Ht: 6-3⅛ | Wt: 248 | 40: 4.79 | Arm: 32⅞ | Hand: 10¼

History: Also played basketball as a Utah prep. Did not get an FBS scholarship offer. Redshirted in 2009. Served a two-year LDS mission in Hong Kong. Started all 48 games of his SUU career. Made an immediate impact in '12 when he posted 61 tackles, 13½ for loss and 7½ sacks (school freshman record) with one batted pass, one interception and one forced fumble in 13 games. In '13, had 77-19-10½ with four batted passes, one interception, two forced fumbles and two blocked kicks in 13 games. Set the Big Sky single-season record for tackles for loss in '14 — amassed 87-29-11½ with two batted passes, three forced fumbles and two blocked kicks in 12 games. In '15, was the FCS Defensive Player of the Year (Athletic Directors Association) after piling up 68-19-13 with one batted pass, four forced fumbles and a one fumble recovery touchdown. Broke Jared Allen's Big Sky records for career tackles for loss (80) and sacks (43.5). Three-time team captain obtained an undergraduate degree in psychology and a master's in communication. Will be a 26-year-old rookie.

Strengths: Experienced, four-year starter. Good instincts and feel for blocking pressure. Has strong hands to control and rip past tight ends. Flashes pop in his punch. Produced the fastest 3-cone drill time (6.80 seconds) of any defensive lineman at the Combine, indicative of outstanding lateral agility and body control. Record-breaking production. Very tough, smart and competitve with a great motor. Has stood out on special teams throughout his career, blocking four kicks.

Weaknesses: Does not look the part. Has a 31 1/2-inch vertical jump, indicating below-average lower-body explosion. Has some stiffness in his hips and ankles and is not natural dropping. Is seldom asked to play man coverage and lacks the hip flexibility and foot speed to match up. Plays upright and is a bit robotic in his movement. Overaged.

Future: A stiff, try-hard, overachieving base

DEFENSIVE LINE

end ideally suited for a "40" front but also could fit as a rush outside linebacker in a "30" front. Has also played some inside linebacker in nickel packages where he has been very effective blitzing. Miminally will find a way to contribute on special teams and could turn out to be a pleasant surprise as a pass rusher. Looks like Jane, plays like Tarzan.

Draft projection: Fifth- to sixth-round pick.

Scout's take: "One of the reasons he has been so productive is that you're matching up a 26-year-old against 18-year-olds. There is a big difference in physical maturity when you're the big kid playing against pee-wees. I'll give him credit for what he is— he can win a lot of different ways, with quickness, effort, toughness and power. He finds the ball quickly and runs to it, but he is an average athlete. Then again, Jared Allen was invited to an all-star game as a long snapper. He didn't have a great body either. Look what he has done. Opinions are all over the place on (Cowser)."

3T SHELDON DAY, #91 (Sr-4)

NOTRE DAME ▶ GRADE: 5.25

Ht: 6-0 5/8 | Wt: 293 | 40: 5.09 | Arm: 32 5/8 | Hand: 9 5/8

History: Prepped at Indianapolis Warren Central, where he was runner-up to Gunner Kiel for the state's Mr. Football award. As a true freshman in 2012, collected 23 tackles, 31/2 for loss and two sacks with one batted pass. Was deployed as a 3-4 defensive end in '13 when he started 8-of-11 games played and tallied 33-51/2-1/2 with one batted pass. Sustained a high right ankle sprain against Purdue — did not play against Oklahoma and Michigan State, then aggravated the injury against Navy. After playing in Bob Diaco's 3-4, was used as a 4-3 defensive end by Brian Van Gorder. Started all 11 games played in '14, totaling 40-71/2-1 with two batted passes. Did not play against Louisville or USC (right MCL sprain). Played defensive tackle in '15 when started all 13 games and notched 45-151/2-4 with four batted passes and two forced fumbles. Two-time captain on track to graduate with a degree in information technology management.

Strengths: Experienced four-year starter. Very agile and quick. Produced a 7.44-second 3-cone drill time, tied for second-fastest among defensive tackles at the Combine and indicative of outstanding body control and short-area burst. Plays with good balance and is effective slanting, stunting and looping into gaps. Has a relentless motor and keeps working to come free. Showed very well in

pass-rush drills at the Senior Bowl, displaying violence in his hands. Doubled his career sack total as a senior and consistently moved quarterbacks off the spot. Very solid personal and football character.

Weaknesses: Lacks ideal height and bulk strength. Is not stout against the run. Leaves production on the field because of his lack of length. Wears down late in games and is not an every down player. Only bench-pressed 21 reps of 225 pounds at the Combine. Has been nicked up with a lot of injuries.

Future: An undersized, one-gap penetrator with a knack for beating one-on-one blocks, Day possesses a skill set most ideally suited to create penetration in sub-packages from the interior of a "40" front similar to those being run in Dallas, Seattle and Jacksonville. Lack of size will lessen draft value, though has the agility, balance and burst to develop into a functional role player.

Draft projection: Fourth- to fifth-round pick.

Scout's take: "Sheldon Day doesn't fit a 3-4 defense. His only fit is as an outside linebacker, and that's not what he is. He has to be a 4-3 under tackle. That's how he's going to make his money. ... I thought he was a sixth-rounder as a nickel rusher. He would have been perfect for the old Tony Dungy, Tampa 2 defense. ...He came in with 22 percent body fat and got down to 13, but he's still not as good as (Eagles 2008 second-rounder) Trevor Laws or (Seahawks 2013 third-rounder) Jordan Hill — those undersized guys are so short they can't finish plays, but they produce a lot of TFL's because they penetrate so quickly."

DLE-3T-LOLB KEVIN DODD, #98 (Jr-4)

CLEMSON ▶ GRADE: 6.12

Ht: 6-5 | Wt: 277 | 40: 4.84 | Arm: 34 | Hand: 10

History: South Carolina native who also competed in track and field (throws) as a prep. Spent 2011 at Hargrave Military. Saw limited action in '12, recording six tackles, zero for loss and zero sacks. In '13, managed 7-1/2-0 in four games before suffering a season-ending injury. Appeared in 12 games in '14, notching 8-21/2-0 while backing up Corey Crawford. Did not play against Louisville (coach's decision). Posted a breakout season in '15 — started all 15 games and racked up 62-231/2-12 with one batted pass, one forced fumble and one blocked kick. Opted not to bench press at the Combine and did not complete jumps or shuttles because of a left hamstring injury suffered second 40 attempt.

Strengths: Outstanding size and body length

with long arms. Instinctive with disciplined eyes — is quick to locate the ball and run to it. Feels blocking pressure developing and plays off it. Competes hard. Good strength to set the edge and anchor vs. the run. Plays with good discipline and understands block-to-ball relationships. Strong tackler. Is quick enough to win with inside moves. Has a long second step and good playing speed and bend to take the corner for as big as he is. Is able to disrupt the quarterback's vision with long levers. Showed gradual improvement throughout his career and has enough size and quickness to kick down to the inside on third downs and mismatch offensive guards. Played big on the biggest stages and notched three sacks in the national championship game.

Weaknesses: Is not an elite athlete and is still growing into his body. Only a one-year full-time starter. Lacks a variety of pass-rush moves and could stand to use his hands with more authority. Is not yet a sophisticated or nuanced pass-rusher.

Much of production came against inferior competition. Gets stymied by the double team and needs to learn how to split it. Outstanding overall character.

Future: A strong, base end who benefitted from extra attention being dedicated to teammate Shaq Lawson, Dodd is a smart, assignment-sound, productive pass rusher who wins with quickness, length, strength and discipline. An ascending talent whose best football is still ahead of him. May require some patience initially but has huge upside.

Draft projection: Top-50 pick.

Scout's take: "No. 98 jumps out at you the most of any player on that defense when you're breaking them down. You can see some of his flaws — he has some tightness, but he is a solid football player. He has a big upside."

DLE-LOLB **JASON FANAIKA**, #51 (Sr-6)

UTAH ▶ RADE: 5.23

Ht: 6-1 3/4 | Wt: 271 | 40: 4.89 | Arm: 32 5/8 | Hand: 9 7/8

History: Married with a daughter, Loumaile. Cousin, Paul, is a guard for the Chiefs. Utah native who began his college career at Utah State. Wearing jersey No. 90 in 2010, recorded 15 tackles, one for loss and zero sacks with one batted pass and one forced fumble in 10 games (one start on the defensive line). In '11, was scheduled to embark on his two-year LDS mission, but discontinued and returned to the team in Week Two because his father was diagnosed with colon cancer. One the season (wore jersey No. 5), had 14-2-1/2 in 12

games (four starts at outside linebacker). In order to be closer to his family, transferred to Utah and redshirted in 2013. Started 8-of-13 games in '14 — six at outside linebacker, two at defensive end — and produced 55-911/2-5 with one forced fumble and one interception. Started 10-of-13 games at right end in '15, totaling 53-101/2-4 with four batted passes and two forced fumbles.

Strengths: Solid instincts. Very good competitor. Plays with urgency and confidence and can inspire teammates. Functional edge-setting strength —flashes the ability to bore through contact. Versatile and has played multiple positions, lining up at the DE, DT, OLB and ILB positions. Produced a 35 1/2-inch vertical jump at the Combine, indicating good athletic ability. Strong, drive-thru tackler. Beat Indiana's Jason Spriggs with an inside move in one-on-one drills at the Senior Bowl and has showed he can outmaneuver talented blockers one-on-one. Has an effective swim move. Film junkie. Can squat a small house. Universally praised for his character within the program.

Weaknesses: Does not have ideal height. Has never been a full-time, every-game starter. Struggles to win up the field with speed and burst and cannot turn the corner. Lacks the hip flexibility and body control to to trim the corner. Needs to become a more secure open-field tackler. Let weight balloon as a senior and could stand to cut down body fat and improve stamina.

Future: A shorty, thick-framed, smooth-muscled base end most ideally suited for a "40" front, Fanaika lacks great burst and bend to consistently bring pressure. However, he has enough functional strength, effort, toughness and competitiveness to produce and be a solid run defender. Could warrant some interest as a 3-4 strongside leverage/power rusher.

Draft projection: Fifth- to sixth-round pick.

Scout's take: "Everyone in the program to a man says he is the best leader on the team, that guys respond to him. His character checks out through the roof. They are honest there and don't sugarcoat the truth. It doesn't match up when you see his body though. He doesn't look the part. It makes you feel like you're drinking the kool-aid. I still have to come to terms with that. I liked the football player."

5T-3T **ADAM GOTSIS**, #96 (Sr-4)

GEORGIA TECH ▶ GRADE: 5.37

Ht: 6-4 1/2 | Wt: 287 | 40: 4.95e | Arm: 34 1/8 | Hand: 10 3/4

History: Born in Australia, where he played Australian Rules Football for eight years.

DEFENSIVE LINE

Gotsis delayed enrollment at an Australian college in order to pursue a scholarship opportunity in the U.S. Gotsis was recommended to GT head coach Paul Johnson by Paul Manera, who was recruited by Johnson to Hawaii in 1989. As a true freshman in 2012, notched five tackles, 11/2 for loss and one sack with one batted pass in 12 games (one start as a 3-4 defensive end). Played nose tackle in '13 when he started all 13 games and posted 38-141/2-51/2 with one interception. Played defensive tackle in '14 when he started all 14 games and logged 36-61/2-3 with three batted passes and one interception. In '15, managed 31-5-3 with a fumble recovery touchdown in nine starts at nose tackle before suffering a season-ending left knee injury. Team captain. Graduated with a business degree. Was a medical exclusion (knee) form the Combine.

Strengths: Outstanding size with big hands. Is quick and athletic enough to cross the face of blockers and dart into the backfield. Good movement skill when healthy. Very solid point-of-attack strength. Is seldom inverted or moved off a spot. Exceptional wing span measuring 84 3/8 inches. Extremely hardworking. Takes pride in his craft. Outstanding personal and football character. Tough and highly competitive. Versatile and has played inside and outside.

Weaknesses: Has some stiffness in his body. Needs to continue getting stronger and learn how to use his hands with more savvy and strength. Struggles to hold his ground against the double team — rises out of his stance and plays a bit tall. Lacks short-area burst to penetrate. Eyes and instincts are still developing.

Future: An underdeveloped, raw talent with the two-gapping strength to factor inside for a "40" front and outside for a "30 front". Durability concerns could affect his draft status. Though he lacks the same length as Bengals 2013 second-round pick Margus Hunt, Gotsis' overall skill set and rawness has drawn some comparisons to him from scouts.

Draft projection: Third- to fourth-round pick.

Scout's take: "(Gotsis) doesn't know how to play yet. He's raw technique-wise. He has the physical traits you're looking for, but instinctively, he is more of a ready-aim-fire type. It's not instant, and he doesn't trigger fast."

Anchored the nose tackle spot for the FCS Bulldogs. Started 9-of-11 games in '12 and posted 45 tackles, 41/2 for loss and two sacks. Missed the first two games of the '13 season (left ankle sprain), but started 9-of-11 games played and tallied 52-121/2-51/2 with four forced fumbles. Started 11-of-12 games in '14 despite playing through a sprained left MCL, racking up 55-231/2-16 with two batted passes, three forced fumbles and a 61-yard fumble recovery score. Put himself on the national radar by notching six sacks against Bethune-Cookman (despite not starting because of a minor knee injury). Earned Mid-Eastern Athletic Conference Defensive Player of the Year honors for the second straight year in '15 after registering 59-22-131/2 with two forced fumbles. Graduated with a sports management degree. Earned invitations to the East-West Shrine and Senior Bowl all-star games.

Strengths: Outstanding body mass. Experienced, four-year starter. Dominant at the FCS level of competition. Has a low center of gravity and plays with leverage and power. Agile for a 310-pounder. Very competitive and will strain to finish. Exceptional weight-room strength — bench-pressed 225 pounds 29 times at the Combine and has a 650-pound squat. Dominated one-on-one drills at the East-West Shrine game, disrupted in the game with sheer power and competed hard in the Senior Bowl where he notched a sack. Outstanding career production from the interior (37 career sacks).

Weaknesses: Lacks ideal body and arm length. Will stay blocked too long and take some plays off. Eyes and instincts are still developing. Struggles to come free against the double team. Has a history of nagging ankle injuries. Could require some additional time to acclimate to an NFL defense.

Future: Very squatty, strong, quick and powerful interior presence capable of creating an interior push and factoring readily as a 25-play, rotational contributor. Compares favorably to Falcons 2015 fifth-round pick Grady Jarrett. Is most ideally suited to play on a shade in an aggressive, one-gapping "40" front where he could slant, penetrate and disrupt.

Draft projection: Fourth- to fifth-round pick.

3T JAVON HARGRAVE, #97 (Sr-5)
SOUTH CAROLINA STATE   ▶ GRADE: 5.31
Ht: 6-13/8 | Wt: 309 | 40: 4.87 | Arm: 32 | Hand: 95/8

History: Prepped in North Carolina, where he also won a state basketball championship. Was not academically eligible in 2011.

DT JOEL HEATH, #92 (Sr-5)
MICHIGAN STATE   ▶ GRADE: 5.02
Ht: 6-51/4 | Wt: 293 | 40: 5.04 | Arm: 341/2 | Hand: 101/2

History: Married. Prepped in Ohio, where he was named AP Division II Co-Defensive Player of the Year. Redshirted in 2011. Ap-

DEFENSIVE LINE

peared in five games in '12 without recording any stats. In '13, saw limited action in nine games and tallied a batted pass and three quarterback hurries. Bulked up 30 pounds and transitioned from defensive end to three-technique in '14 when he started 12-of-13 games and logged 29 tackles, five for loss and 2½ sacks. Did not start the Sugar Bowl against Baylor. In '15, started all 12 games played and logged 31-5½-2-2 with one batted pass and one forced fumble. Sat out against Central Michigan (elbow?). Hurt his right ankle on the first drive of the second half against Nebraska, which sidelined him against Maryland and limited him against Ohio State. Graduated with a degree in interdisciplinary studies in social science.

Strengths: Excellent size and length with an 84-inch wingspan. Flashes some strength to drive blockers and quickness to play in gaps. Plays hard and competes. Mature, focused and willing to put in the work to improve.

Weaknesses: Very tight hips that he struggles to unlock, forcing him to play tall and stumble too much. Below-average balance and body control. Gets collapsed by the double team (see Ohio State). Does not play sudden or to timed speed. Struggles clearing his feet through trash. Lacks functional strength. Limited burst to close to the ball. Lacks a pass-rush plan. Marginal sack production.

Future: Stiff-bodied, high-hipped converted defensive end lacking the functional strength to battle inside. Height-weight-speed prospect with a chance to develop into a role player.

Draft projection: Priority free agent.

3T WILLIE HENRY, #69 (Jr-4)

MICHIGAN   ▶ GRADE: 5.20
Ht: 6-2¾ | Wt: 303 | 40: 4.99 | Arm: 33⅜ | Hand: 10⅞

History: Prepped at Cleveland Glenville, where he also played basketball. Redshirted in 2012. Started 6-of-12 games played in '13 and was credited with 32 tackles, three for loss and one-half sack with one blocked kick. Did not play against Notre Dame. Started 6-of-10 games played in '14 and recorded 20-5½-3 with a 7-yard interception touchdown. Sat out two mid-season contests because of an arm injury. In '15, started 10-of-13 games and totaled 34-10-6½ with two batted passes. Will be a 21-year-old rookie.

Strengths: Good size with big, strong hands. Solid point-of-attack strength. Functional run defender. Flashes some power in

his hands and plays with enough strength to two-gap (see Utah). Versatile and plays inside and out. Effective stunting.

Weaknesses: A bit high cut and takes choppy steps. Plays too upright. Gives up his legs and can be cut too easily. Average balance and body control. Spends too much time on the ground. Has a tendency to dip his head and rely too much on bull-rush move. Lacks variety in his pass-rush arsenal to win one-on-one battles. Much of his production is schemed.

Future: Developmental three-technique with enough mass to line up as a five-technique in an odd front. Does not play with the explosion, quickness or savvy desired in a penetrator and best asset is as a plugger against the run. Has the physical tools to be molded into a solid contributor, but lacks any elite trait.

Draft projection: Fifth- to sixth-round pick.

Scout's take: "He didn't excite me. He's really not a great fit for us (in a 3-4 defense)."

3T-5T MATT IOANNIDIS, #9 (Sr-4)

TEMPLE   ▶ GRADE: 5.18
Ht: 6-3½ | Wt: 299 | 40: 5.06 | Arm: 32⅜ | Hand: 10⅛

History: Last name is pronounced "I-an-NYE-dis." Prepped in New Jersey. As a true freshman in 2012, appeared in the final six games of the season, recording three tackles, zero for loss and zero sacks in six appearances. In '13, started all 12 games — four at defensive tackle, three at defensive end — and had 26-7½-3 with one forced fumble. Wore jersey No. 95 prior to his junior season when he was given No. 9, signifying his status as one of the toughest players on the team. Started all 26 games at DT his final two years — totaled 46-11-3½ with three batted passes in '14 (12 games); and 42-11½-3½ with five batted passes in '15 (14 games). Gaduated with a communications degree.

Strengths: Experienced, three-year starter. Good weight-room strength. Bench-pressed 225 pounds 32 times at the Combine. Flashes some violence in his hands. Strong tackler. Very good effort — plays hard. Tough, physical and highly competitive. Good pursuit production. Very durable. Football is very important to him.

Weaknesses: Plays too upright, loses leverage and does not consistently push the pocket. Not quick or explosive off the ball. Limited body control. Lacks creativity as a pass rusher. Gets stalled on spin moves. Does not show much burst or bend to the quarterback. Is not sudden changing direction, as confirmed in below-average shuttle times at the Combine. Could stand to improve against the double team.

Future: Developmental gap penetrator most ideally suited for a backup role. Has enough size, length and quickness to be considered as a developmental 3-4 defensive end.

Draft projection: Fifth- to sixth-round pick.

DLE-LOLB BRANDEN JACKSON, #9 (Sr-5)
TEXAS TECH ▶ GRADE: 4.82
Ht: 6-3 7/8 | Wt: 273 | 40: 5.06 | Arm: 33 3/8 | Hand: 10 1/4

History: Prepped in Pennsylvania, where he also played basketball. Redshirted in 2011. Played all 13 games in '12, drawing two starts at left defensive end, and collecting 19 tackles, zero for loss and zero sacks with one forced fumble and one batted pass. Was deployed as a 3-4 defensive end in '13 when he started all 13 games and tallied 44-9-4 with three batted passes. Started all 12 games in '14 and produced 44-10 1/2-5 with two batted passes and one forced fumble. Also recovered a fumble for a score. Played 4-3 defensive end in '15 — started 11-of-13 games and chipped in 31-41/2-2 with one batted pass and one forced fumble. Team captain graduated with a sociology degree.

Strengths: Very good size for a base end and length for an outside linebacker. Flashes some strength to hold his ground.

Weaknesses: Slow-footed and stiff-hipped. Soft football temperament. Lacks functional strength and physicality taking on blocks. Questionable toughness to dig his heels in the dirt and anchor against the run. Average closing and finishing burst. Looked like a fish out of water in linebacker drills at the Combine, showing limited body control and agility while moving in reverse.

Future: A well-built, broad-shouldered base end with just enough strength to compete for a backup job. Projects to outside linebacker for "30" fronts. Practice-squad candidate.

Draft projection: Priority free agent.

Scout's take: "(Jackson) is not tough enough to play for our defensive coordinator. We projected him to outside linebacker and kept him alive late as draftable."

3T-5T QUINTON JEFFERSON, #99 (Jr-4)
MARYLAND ▶ GRADE: 5.42
Ht: 6-3 7/8 | Wt: 291 | 40: 4.94 | Arm: 33 3/8 | Hand: 8 7/8

History: Married with three daughters. Pittsburgh native prepped at powerhouse Woodland Hills, where he had 16 sacks as a senior and also played basketball. Arrival at Maryland was delayed by a broken jaw. As a true freshman in 2012, recorded 13 tackles, one-half for loss and zero sacks with one forced fumble in nine appearances. Was deployed as a 3-4 defensive end in '13 when he started all 13 games and produced 47-71/2-3 with one forced fumble. In '14, managed 8-1-1 in three starts at DE before suffering a season-ending torn right ACL injury. Started all 12 games in '15, totaling 39-121/2-61/2 with one batted pass, one interception, one forced fumble and one blocked kick. Graduated with a family science degree. Opted not to perform the broad jump at the Combine.

Strengths: Is quick off the ball and can create some inside penetration. Recorded second-fastest 20-yard shuttle (4.37) among defensive tackles at the Combine, indicative of outstanding quickness and lateral agility. Understands leverage and how to walk back blockers. Versatile and has played inside and outside.

Weaknesses: Has the smallest hands (8 7/8 inches) of any defensive lineman at the Combine. A bit narrow-based and tight-hipped, which tends to bring him off the ball too upright and allow blockers to wash him down the line at times. Needs to improve base, lower-body strength. Lacks variety as a pass rusher.

Future: High-hipped, athletic gap penetrator with the ability to create inside pressure and stack the run. Still did not appear fully recovered from 2014 ACL injury and is developing athletically. Has enough strength to fit as a right defensive end in a "30" front in the pros, though best opportunity will likely come in an even front.

Draft projection: Third- to fourth-round pick.

DLE-DT AUSTIN JOHNSON, #99 (Jr-4)
PENN STATE ▶ GRADE: 6.04
Ht: 6-4 3/8 | Wt: 314 | 40: 5.29 | Arm: 32 3/4 | Hand: 9 7/8

History: Also an all-state basketball player as a New Jersey prep. Redshirted in 2012. Played all 12 games in '13, drawing two starts, and recorded 27 tackles, three for loss and one sack. Started all 26 games the next two seasons — totaled 49-6-1 with three batted passes in '14; and 78-15-6 1/2 with two batted passes and one forced fumble. Graduated with a journalism degree.

Strengths: Very stout with a thick trunk and sturdy base. Plays with good balance and leverage and can walk blockers back to the quarterback. Relatively light on his feet for a

315-pounder. Can cross the face of blockers and beat reach blocks. Can dig his heels in the dirt and hold his ground vs. the double team. Outstanding effort production. Feels blocking pressure and keeps working to the ball. Sniffs out screens. Plays disciplined, smart, assignment-sound football. Showed steady improvement.

Weaknesses: Below-average arm length. Stays tied up with blockers too long and needs to do a better job of using his hands to disengage from blockers. Is not quick off the snap and lacks closing burst to finish plays.

Future: A thick-trunked, strong, well-muscled, top-heavy power player with enough strength to bore through underpowered blockers and handle the dirty work between the tackles. One of the best run defenders in the draft, Johnson is strong, savvy and effortful enough to push the pocket and create some inside pressure.

Draft projection: Top-50 pick.

Scout's take: "He played both three-technique and nose. He reminded me of one of those Pittsburgh guys that plugs in and plays 12 years — a Casey Hampton-type."

DT CHRIS JONES, #98 (Jr-3)
MISSISSIPPI STATE ▶ GRADE: 5.56
Ht: 6-5 3/4 | Wt: 310 | 40: 5.03 | Arm: 34 1/2 | Hand: 10 3/4

History: Also played basketball as a prep in Mississippi, where he was a five-star recruit after piling up 235 tackles his last two high school seasons. Played all 13 games in each of his three seasons in Starkville. As a true freshman in 2013, recorded 32 tackles, seven for loss and three sacks with three batted passes (three starts). In '14, tallied 31-1-1 with one forced fumble. Was a 13-game starter in '15 when he produced 44-71/2-21/2 with four batted passes.

Strengths: Exceptional size and arm length with huge hands and very good movement skill for a big man. Recorded a 4.62-second 20-yard shuttle and 7.44-second 3-cone drill time, both superb for his size and indicative of very good agility. Flashes the ability to dominate when he wants to. Good strength in his hands and power in his body to walk offensive guards back to the quarterback. Pushes the pocket and commands a double team. Strong tackler who corrals backs with his long arms.

Weaknesses: Has underachiever tendencies. Lacks urgency and is late to locate the ball. Rises out of his stance and plays too tall, negating the the power in his body. Too often

plays as if he doesn't want to get his gloves dirty. Recorded a 24 1/2-inch vertical jump at the Combine, the lowest among defensive tackles and indicative of average athletic ability and lower-body explosion. Stamina appeared to wear down late in games.

Future: A classic underachiever who has yet to figure out just how good he could be, Jones is an exceptionally athletic big man ideally suited for a role as a slanting nose tackle in a movement front. Has the size and athletic talent to play anywhere along a "30" front and could be equally terrorizing in the middle of a "40" front.

Draft projection: Second- to third-round pick.

Scout's take: "His physical pro potential is much better than his production. He is a better athlete than football player. I didn't totally kill him. He is athletic as can be, but something was missing."

DLE MATT JUDON, #9 (Sr-6)
GRAND VALLEY STATE ▶ GRADE: 5.24
Ht: 6-3 | Wt: 275 | 40: 4.69 | Arm: 33 7/8 | Hand: 9 1/2

History: Has a child. Last name is pronounced "Jew-DON." Michigan native. Redshirted in 2010. Played in the final seven games in '11, collecting 14 tackles, two for loss and two sacks with one batted pass. Started all eight games played in '12 and had 37-7-31/2 with one batted pass, a 41-yard interception touchdown and one forced fumble. Missed four games because of a partially torn right MCL. His '13 season ended seven plays in, as he suffered a torn ACL and meniscus. Changed from jersey No. 99 to No. 9 in '14 when he started 9-of-11 games and produced 72-19-81/2 with five batted passes, four forced fumbles and one blocked kick. In '15, was the Division II Defensive Lineman of the Year and the Conference Commissioner's Association Defensive Player of the Year after leading all of college football in sacks and setting GVSU single-season records for tackles by a lineman, tackles for loss and sacks — registered 81-231/2-20 with three batted passes and three forced fumbles. Owns the Lakers' career sacks record (34). Team captain. Graduated.

Strengths: Very good size and length. Exceptional small-school production — dominated competition. Bench-pressed 225 pounds 30 times. Has a 35-inch vertical jump, indicative of very good lower-body explosion. Appeared athletic enough in LB drills at the Combine to make the converstion to outside linebacker and handle zone drops. Has experi-

DEFENSIVE LINE

ence as a four-phase, core special teamer.

Weaknesses: Recorded the slowest 60-yard shuttle (12.42 seconds) of any player at the Combine, indicating average dynamic agility. Much of his production was clear-view where he came unblocked. Limited hip flexibility. Average body control. Misses some tackles in space playing too recklessly and out of control. Only shows one gear and doesn't accelerate at the top of his rush or consistently finish, gearing down after being run wide out of plays.

Future: High-cut, athletic producer with intriguing developmental traits to be molded into a solid base end. Could even warrant some looks as a developmental five-technique for a "30" front.

Draft projection: Fifth- to sixth-round pick.

Scout's take: "(Judon) will be a little bit of a sleeper. He is intriguing. He was not highly rated at all coming into the season. He has some athletic ability. He is going to get bigger and stronger and is worth taking a gamble on, sort of like when the Newberry kid (OLB Edmond Robinson) came out last year."

5T UFOMBA KAMALU, #47 (Sr-4)

MIAMI (FLA.) ▶ GRADE: 5.10

Ht: 6-5 1/8 | Wt: 295 | 40: 5.01 | Arm: 35 | Hand: 10

History: Born in Nigeria. Prepped in Georgia. Spent 2012 at Butler Community College (Kan.), where he was credited with 54 tackles, 14 for loss and 71/2 sacks with three forced fumbles in 12 games. With the Hurricanes in '13, chipped in 13-31/2-31/2 in nine appearances. Played all 13 games in '14 (started at defensive tackle against Georgia Tech) and collected 34-4-31/2 with two batted passes. Was the Hurricanes' Defensive MVP in '15 after starting 9-of-13 games and producing 47-4-1 with one forced fumble and one interception.

Strengths: Looks every bit the part. Exceptional size and body length, with very long arms. Has the core strength to stack the point and two-gap. Versatile and has lined up at multiple positions along the front. Can close on the quarterback and move him off spots from the inside.

Weaknesses: Has very marginal instincts and is late to locate and find the ball. Plays too tall and gets steered and controlled by the double team. Not explosive and does not know how to use his hands to set up the rush or pierce gaps. Limited range to the perimeter. Effort wanes — too many backside loafs.

Future: Very green, developmental five-

technique still learning the game and growing into the position. Is at least several years away from contributing, but could turn dividends for a patient staff willing to develop him.

Draft projection: Priority free agent.

Scout's take: "He is body beautiful with length and core strength, but he has zero instincts and he's not naturally explosive. I thihk he is a free agent."

DLE-OLB BRONSON KAUFUSI, #90 (Sr-4)

BYU ▶ GRADE: 5.27

Ht: 6-6 1/2 | Wt: 285 | 40: 4.84 | Arm: 34 1/2 | Hand: 9 3/4

History: Married. Father, Steve, is BYU's defensive line coach. Bronson prepped at Utah powerhouse Timpview, where his final two seasons were truncated by injury — tore his right PCL in 2008, then tore his right ACL and meniscus in '09. Served a two-year LDS mission in New Zealand. Returned to the field in '12 when he appeared in all 13 games and recorded 23 tackles, 51/2 for loss and 41/2 sacks with one batted pass. In '13, was deployed as a left end in the Cougars' 3-4 front — produced 37-7-4 with six batted passes, one interception (touchdown) and one forced fumble in 13 starts. Started 10-of-11 games played at weak-side (outside) linebacker in '14, managing 43-111/2-7 with six batted passes and one forced fumble. Sustained a high ankle sprain against Texas and sat out against Houston and Virginia. Did not start against Savannah State. Went back to his natural defensive end position in '15 when he notched 64-20-11 with two batted passes, one interception, three forced fumbles and four blocked kicks in 13 starts. Team captain and AFCA Good Works Team nominee. Played on the BYU basketball during his freshman year.

Strengths: Moves very easily. Recorded a 4.25-second 20-yard shuttle and 7.03-second 3-cone drill time at the Combine, displaying exceptional quickness and agility for a 285-pounder. Exceptional shuttle times at the Combine, indicating very good strength. Good lateral pursuit and very good motor to flatten down the line and make plays. Good sack production. Unselfish team player who will do what's best for the good of the team. Outstanding personal and football character. Smart and football savvy enough to suggest defensive adjustments on the sideline.

Weaknesses: Has a narrow frame. Plays small. Developing instincts. Late reactor. Lacks lower-body strength.

Future: A former basketball player with

DEFENSIVE LINE

unique athletic ability for his size, Kaufusi has a frame that suggests he might be able to handle becoming a 3-4 defensive end, yet lacks the functional strength, physicality and instincts to handle playing a big-man's game. Is a well-conditioned athlete who moves well laterally. Has the type of movement skill, feet and athletic ability that could allow him to function as a rush linebacker for a team that employs a traditional "30" front such as the Bears or 49ers. Versatility could also be attractive to a multiple-front defense such as the Patriots.

Draft projection: Fifth- to sixth-round pick.

Scout's take: "He can add and drop weight like no one else. He was a totally different weight last spring (252) than he is now (285). I've never seen anything like it. He's an enigma that way. I initially thought he could only be an outside linebacker (in a 3-4 defense). Some other teams are saying he's a five-technique because he came in much heavier. I just don't think he is tough or physical enough."

DT-DE DARIUS LATHAM, #98 (Jr-3)
INDIANA ▶ GRADE: 5.07
Ht: 6-4 1/4 | Wt: 311 | 40: 5.31 | Arm: 34 3/4 | Hand: 10

History: Indiana native who lettered four times in football and basketball. Appeared in all 12 games as a true freshman in 2013, recording 22 tackles, three for loss and two sacks with three batted passes. Played all 12 games in '14, starting the final 10 as a five-technique in IU's 3-4 defense, and produced 26-5 1/2-1 1/2 with three batted passes. Was one of nine players suspended for the '15 season opener against Southern Illinois because he "did not live up to responsibilities to the program," then was suspended for the Ohio State contest because of a student ethics issue. On the season, started 10-of-11 games played at the five-technique and tallied 33-10-4 with one batted pass, one interception and two blocked PATs. Opted not to perform the bench press at the Combine.

Strengths: Looks the part with very good body and arm length, with nearly 35-inch arms. Has innate power in his body. Is heavy-handed and can control blockers in the run game. Flashes some pass-rush ability shooting gaps and working his hips around the edges. Solid run defender capable of pushing the pocket.

Weaknesses: Takes too many plays off. Lacks discipline and takes too many penalties. Tends to stand up and play too tall. Per-

sonal and football character need to be vetted closely — has been suspended multiple times and must prove that the game is important to him.

Future: Thick-bodied, top-heavy, see-and-go reactor with the size, strength and power to eventually earn a starting job for a team willing to mold troubled talent such as the Rams or Bengals.

Draft projection: Late draftable pick.

Scout's take: "He's off our board character-wise. If you're purely grading the talent, he'll get looks in the middle rounds. I liked him as a player. I didn't love him. He's big, long, has some strength and flashes playmaking ability."

NT NILE LAWRENCE-STAMPLE, #99 (Sr-5)
FLORIDA STATE ▶ GRADE: 5.13
Ht: 6-1 | Wt: 320 | 40: 5.35e | Arm: 32 3/4 | Hand: 9 7/8

History: Transitioned from linebacker to defensive lineman as a Florida prep. Redshirted in 2011. Saw limited action in eight games in '12, notching 10 tackles, one for loss and zero sacks. In '13, started 6-of-13 games alongside Timmy Jernigan (Ravens '14 second-rounder), contributing 15-1 1/2-0. Did not play against Syracuse (concussion). Tore his right labrum during '14 spring practice. In the fall, managed 10-1/2-0 in four games (two starts at nose tackle) — against Clemson suffered a torn pectoral muscle injury which sidelined him until the Rose Bowl. Shifted to the three-technique in '15 when he started 12-of-13 games and posted 36-3 1/2-2 1/2 with one batted pass. Sustained a concussion against Syracuse, and did not start against Clemson. Opted not to bench press and did not work out because of a tight Achilles' injury.

Strengths: Has a thick frame with wide shoulders and strong hips. Flashes power in his lower body to generate some movement. Strong enough to hold the point and anchor vs. double teams.

Weaknesses: Lacks ideal height. Marginal pass-rush ability. Can be late to locate the ball and get fooled by misdirection. Too straight-linish. Needs to improve his hand use and do a better job shedding blocks — stays blocked too long and struggles to come free. Only a one-year, full-time starter.

Future: Thick-bodied, barrel-chested 3-4 nose tackle with scheme versatility to factor in a rotation for an even or odd front. Uses a lot of finesse and would be best in a defense

DEFENSIVE LINE

where he is allowed to slant, stunt and shoot gaps. Has some moldable traits.

Draft projection: Late draftable pick.

DRE-ROLB SHAQ LAWSON, #90 (Jr-3)

CLEMSON ▶ GRADE: 5.98

Ht: 6-2 5/8 | Wt: 269 | 40: 4.68 | Arm: 32 3/4 | Hand: 10

History: Also played basketball as a prep in South Carolina — grew up minutes from Clemson. Totaled 200 tackles, 46 for loss and 22 sacks his last two high school seasons. Spent 2012 at Hargrave Military Academy (Va.). With the Tigers in '13, contributed 35-10-4 with one batted pass in 13 appearances. Played all 13 games (one start) in '14, logging 44-11-31/2 with one forced fumble and one blocked PAT. Following the departure of Vic Beasley (Falcons '15 first-rounder), broke out in a big way in '15 when he was a finalist for the Nagurski, Lombardi and Hendricks Awards — led the nation in tackles for loss by racking up 60-251/2-121/2 with one forced fumble. Sprained his left knee in the national semifinal win over Oklahoma. Was a medical exclusion from the bench-press test at the Combine because of a left shoulder injury.

Strengths: Strong, power-based edge setter. Presses the line and can jolt blockers with his punch. Has a strong bull rush. Strong-handed to play off blocks. Drive-through, wrap tackler. Chases backs down from behind. Defensive tempo-setter — consistently brings pressure and keeps fighting through multiple blockers. Scheme-diverse and versatile with the ability to play multiple positions and techniques in either an even or odd front. Good competitor. Makes plays when they are needed. Workman-like pass rusher.

Weaknesses: Below-average arm length — can be engulfed by bigger blockers. Is wound tightly and lacks ideal edge burst and acceleration to take the corner. Limited hip flexibility, which forces him to play tall, negating the power in his body. Played overweight and stamina consistently wore down late in games. Not a natural bender.

Future: Bided his time behind Vic Beasley and emerged as an impactful player in his first year as a full-time starter. Dropped 10-15 pounds from his playing weight and showed well in drills at the Combine. Can fit as a base end for a "40" front or an outside linebacker for a "30" front. Is at his best with his hand in the dirt moving forward, similar to Steelers

2007 second-round pick LaMarr Woodley.

Draft projection: Top-40 pick.

Scout's take: "He received a lot of hype because Clemson was No. 1 in the country. People are going to say he was an elite rusher. Maybe at 260 he could be. He played between 279 and 284 during the year, and he looked it."

DLE-DT DEAN LOWRY, #94 (Sr-4)

NORTHWESTERN ▶ GRADE: 5.14

Ht: 6-5 3/4 | Wt: 296 | 40: 4.83 | Arm: 31 | Hand: 9 3/8

History: Was part of back-to-back 14-0 teams at Rockford (Ill.) Boylan Catholic. As a true freshman in 2012, appeared in all 13 games and contributed 14 tackles, three for loss and one sack with one batted pass. Played 11 games in '13 — started the first eight at right end before sustaining a high right ankle sprain against Iowa — and logged 33-7-41/2 with three batted passes, two interceptions (one touchdown) and two forced fumbles. Sat out against Nebraska and didn't start the final three games. Started all 25 games at RDE 2014-15 — totaled 41-8-4 with eight batted passes and one forced fumble in '14 (12 games); and 52-131/2-3 with six batted passes, one interception and one blocked kick in '15 (13 games). Scheduled to graduate with an economics degree.

Strengths: Outstanding body length and overall mass. Very competitive and leaves all his effort on the field, chasing down plays from behind. Functional point-of-attack strength to hold ground. Has a knack for disrupting the quarterback's vision and batting down balls. Good weight-room work ethic.

Weaknesses: Extremely short arms, tied for the shortest of any defensive lineman at the Combine, and small hands for his size. Thin-legged. Limited core power. Tends to play upright and get controlled by double teams. Not quick-twitched or explosive off the ball penetrating gaps or creatively beating blockers one-on-one. Stays velcroed on blocks too long and needs to develop more variety in his pass-rush arsenal. Below-average agility and closing speed.

Future: A big, try-hard, tough, short-armed developmental five-technique with the toughness and football smarts to earn a contributing role in the pros.

Draft projection: Late draftable pick.

Scout's take: "(Lowry) looks like he belongs in a 3-4 defense. He might not be drafted highly, but he will make a team. With his mo-

DEFENSIVE LINE

tor and effort, he will be very difficult to cut."

DT-DE LUTHER MADDY, #92 (Sr-5)

VIRGINIA TECH ▶ GRADE: 5.09

Ht: 6-0 | Wt: 287 | 40: 5.12 | Arm: 33 1/4 | Hand: 9

History: Prepped in Florida. Played 13 games as a true freshman in 2011 — started the final seven as an injury replacement, logging 19 tackles, two for loss and one sack with one forced fumble. Started 9-of-13 games in '12 and collected 35-61/2-4. In '13, posted 55-131/2-61/2 with two batted passes in 13 starts. His '14 campaign lasted four starts — managed 9-1/2-0 — before he suffered a torn right meniscus, which required two surgical procedures (was granted medical hardship waiver). Returned to start all 13 games in '15 when he tallied 57-7-21/2. Was voted team captain and outstanding senior by teammates. Graduated with a degree in apparel, housing and resources with a concentration in residential property management. Did not work out at the Combine following arthroscopic surgery on his left knee.

Strengths: Flashes some quickness and explosion off the ball to play in gaps. Solid competitor — plays hard and chases the ball. Active and energetic. Has quick hands. Plays with emotion. Can take hard coaching.

Weaknesses: Has very small hands and measured the shortest (6-0) of any defensive lineman at the Combine. Not a creative pass rusher and gets hung up on blocks too often. Too jumpy trying to anticipate the snap and could stand to play with more discipline. Durability is a concern given history of knee injuries.

Future: Short, small-boned, knock-kneed, injury-prone one-gap penetrator with a chance to compete for a job in a wave role for a "40" front such as the Seahawks, Cowboys or Falcons. Concerns about size and durability could leave him undrafted.

Draft projection: Priority free agent.

NT CHRIS MAYES, #93 (Sr-5)

GEORGIA ▶ GRADE: 4.86

Ht: 6-3 1/8 | Wt: 338 | 40: 5.34 | Arm: 34 | Hand: 9

History: Georgia native also lettered in basketball in high school. Spent 2011 at Mississippi Gulf Coast College, where he was credited with 17 tackles, zero for loss and zero sacks with one forced fumble. Redshirted in 2012. With Georgia in '13, missed time during fall camp because of a concussion. Sat out the first two games, but started 8-of-11 games played at nose tackle and contributed 31-1-1 with two batted passes. Transitioned from defensive coordinator Todd Grantham to Jeremy Pruitt as a junior. Sat out the first two games in '14 (right MCL sprain). On the season, backed up Mike Thornton and was called upon in goal-line personnel — notched 7-1-0 in eight appearances. Started 11-of-12 games in '15 and produced 41-1-0 with one batted pass. Did not play against Missouri (knee) and did not start in the Bulldogs' bowl game against Penn State. Opted not to run the 3-cone drill. Will be a 25-year-old rookie.

Strengths: Rare size — measured the heaviest (338 pounds) of any player at the Combine and produced the most bench-press reps (33) of any defensive lineman. Has a strong bull rush to walk back blockers. Workman-like and accountable.

Weaknesses: Extremely small hands. Very limited athlete with marginal playing range. Too much stiffness in his body. Recorded the lowest vertical jump (23 inches) of any defensive lineman at the Combine, indicative of poor lower-body explosion. Also produced the slowest 20-yard shuttle (5.18 seconds), indicative of marginal lateral agility. Overaged.

Future: Heavy-bodied, big-boned, long-framed run clogger with too much stiffness in his body to consistently play low and hold his ground as a nose tackle. Size prospect only for a "30" front.

Draft projection: Priority free agent.

PRS-ROLB ALEX McCALISTER, #14 (Jr-3)

FLORIDA ▶ GRADE: 5.10

Ht: 6-6 1/8 | Wt: 239 | 40: 4.76 | Arm: 36 | Hand: 9 3/8

History: Also played basketball as a North Carolina prep. Redshirted in 2012. Dealt with a shoulder injury in '13 when he saw limited action in six games and notched three tackles, zero for loss and zero sacks. Backed up Donte Fowler (Jaguars '15 first-rounder) in '14, chipping in 23-9-6 with one batted pass and one forced fumble. In '15, was suspended for the season opener against New Mexico State (violation program policy) before starting 6-of-9 games as a hybrid defensive end/rush linebacker and producing 26-91/2-61/2 with one batted pass and one forced fumble. Injured his right foot against South Carolina and missed three games before he was dismissed from the team for another violation of team rules. Did not perform the bench-press test at the Combine because of a right shoulder injury.

Strengths: Exceptional length, with rare

DEFENSIVE LINE

36-inch arms and a Combine-best 86 1/4-inch wingspan, tied for the largest of any player at the Combine. Produced the fastest 20-yard shuttle (4.00 seconds) and 60-yard shuttle (11.56 seconds) of any defensive lineman at the Combine, indicative of outstanding lateral agility and dynamic quickness. Has a long second step and is quick to beat blockers off the ball.

Weaknesses: Extremely lean with a narrow frame that is not built to hold weight. Lacks bulk strength and physicality to be an every-down player. Is easily moved off the line against the run. Was never a full-time starter. Durability could be an issue given slight frame. Character requires closer scrutiny and has knocked him off some draft boards.

Future: Very lean, wiry developmental pass rusher with the bend and burst to fend for a role as a situational pass rusher with continued physical maturity. Needs to prove more dependable for teams to be willing to take a chance.

Draft projection: Late draftable pick.

Scout's take: "He has some rush traits, but he has no strength, and there are some other issues that need to be dealt with."

DLE CARL NASSIB, #95 (Sr-5)

PENN STATE ▶ GRADE: 5.28

Ht: 6-6 7/8 | Wt: 277 | 40: 4.78 | Arm: 34 | Hand: 10 3/8

History: Brother, Ryan, is a quarterback for the Giants. Carl was a two-way lineman who also competed in basketball and track and field as a Pennsylvania prep. Entered Penn State as a preferred walk-on. Redshirted in 2011 and did not see action in '12. Appeared in 10 games in '13, recording 12 tackles, two for loss and one sack with one forced fumble and one batted pass. Played all 13 games in '14, collecting 7-31/2-1 with one forced fumble and one batted pass. In '15, took home the Lombardi, Hendricks and Lott IMPACT awards and was the Big Ten Defensive Player of the Year after leading the nation in sacks and forced fumbles — registered 46-191/2-151/2 with one batted pass, one interception and six forced fumbles in 13 starts. Played just a handful of snaps the final two regular season games because of a nagging hamstring injury. Also was a finalist for the Burlsworth Trophy (top player who started his career as a walk-on), Nagurski and Bednarik awards. Graduated with a biology degree. Did not play in the Senior Bowl because of injury.

Strengths: Exceptional size with long arms

to disrupt the quarterback's vision. Good straight-line speed. Plays with a sense of urgency. Very good effort and grit. Flattens down the line, hustles and chases. Outstanding effort production — terrific competitor. Very intelligent. Outstanding personal and football character.

Weaknesses: Narrow-framed. Lacks power. Very underdeveloped lower body. Cannot hold ground vs. double teams. Allows blockers to get into his frame too easily. Very raw hand usage. Not a strong or forceful tackler. Plays with too much finesse. One-year wonder. Has a 281/2-inch vertical jump, among the lowest of all defensive ends at the Combine, and indicative of average athletic ability.

Future: Late-blooming, self-made, high-motor overachiever lacking the core strength desired for the pro game. Has intriguing size but does not play big. Developmental five-technique with the tenacity to fend for a job. Effort is his most defining trait and will only carry him so far. Will require some time to acclimate to the physicality of the pro game.

Draft projection: Fourth- to fifth-round pick.

Scout's take: "(Nassib) leads the nation in sacks but made his plays against Buffalo and San Diego. He had nothing against Ohio State. Once he got into the meat of the schedule, he cooled off. Talk about being narrow-waisted. He has no strength. To me, he is nothing but a developmental guy. We've drafted guys like him before and you have to cut them to try to get them to your practice squad."

5T-DT GIORGIO NEWBERRY, #4 (Sr-5)

FLORIDA STATE ▶ GRADE: 4.83

Ht: 6-5 1/2 | Wt: 285 | 40: 4.94 | Arm: 34 | Hand: 9 1/2

History: Florida native. Redshirted in 2011. Was a reserve defensive end in '12, seeing limited action in 13 games and collecting 13 tackles, zero for loss and zero sacks. Was a backup tight end in '14 — played all 14 games, drawing one start, but did not record any stats. Provided defensive line depth again in '14 when he notched 2-0-0 in 14 appearances. Contributed in a rotational role in '15 when he chipped in 21-3-2 with six batted passes. Graduated with a social sciences degree. Will turn 25 during rookie season.

Strengths: Outstanding size. Good movement skill for a big man. Has a knack for disrupting a quarterback's vision with good body and arm length.

Weaknesses: Limited experience. Struggled settling into a position. Needs to get physi-

DEFENSIVE LINE

cally stronger and commit to the game. Over-aged

Future: Height-weight-speed prospect with raw dimensions to consider developing as a five-technique.

Draft projection: Free agent.

Scout's take: "(Coaches) could never find a position for him. They tried him at a bunch of different places — tight end, defensive end and defensive tackle. He'll get some looks as a five-technique at our level."

3T-DLE ROBERT NKEMDICHE, #5 (Jr-3)

MISSISSIPPI ▶ GRADE: 6.26

Ht: 6-3 1/2 | Wt: 294 | 40: 4.91 | Arm: 33 7/8 | Hand: 10 3/4

History: Last name is pronounced "kim-DEECH-ee." Consensus No. 1 overall recruit in America coming out of Georgia. Made an immediate impact in 2013 when he started 10-of-11 games played — six at defensive end, four at defensive tackle — and recorded 34 tackles, eight for loss and two sacks with two batted passes. Sat out against LSU and Idaho State while nursing a strained left hamstring. Started all 13 games at left tackle in '14, notching 35-4-2 with one batted pass. Was a finalist for the Paul Hornung Award (nation's most versatile player) in '15 when he posted had 29-7-3 with two batted passes and a blocked field goal attempt in 11 starts at defensive tackle. Sustained a concussion against Memphis and sat out against Texas A&M, then was suspended for the Sugar Bowl against Oklahoma State after he was arrested in December — fell 15 feet out of a hotel window (needed stitches in his back and leg) and was charged with possession of marijuana because police found approximately seven rolled marijuana cigarettes in the room. Was also used sparingly on offense — had nine career rushes for 34 yards (3.8-yard average) and two touchdowns, as well as a 31-yard touchdown reception — and served on special teams as a punt protector. Did not run any shuttles at the Combine after pulling his right groin on his final positional drill.

Strengths: Is built like Adonis and looks like he was born to play football, with a well-distributed, thick-bodied, muscular frame. Has the movement skill of a linebacker — great balance in his feet. Explosive knifing into gaps and disrupting the backfield. Strong enough to hold ground against the double team and quick enough to split it. Recorded a 35-inch vertical jump, tied for best among defensive tackles at the Combine and indicative of outstanding athletic ability. Matched

up very well against Alabama C Ryan Kelly. Outstanding Combine workout.

Weaknesses: Production has yet to live up to immense potential and consistently leaves some on the field. Marginal sack production. Is not an accomplished hands-fighter and needs to develop more variety in his pass-rush arsenal. Takes some plays off and disappears for long stretches. Too easily stymied if his initial move is taken away and does not keep working to the ball.

Future: A dynamic three-technique with Pro Bowl-caliber talent for a team with a track record of successfully rolling the dice on boom-or-bust talent such as the Redskins, Chiefs, Seahawks or Broncos.

Draft projection: First-round pick.

Scout's take: "(Nkemdiche) is explosive as (expletive), strong, fast and powerful. He has (Ndamukong) Suh's power. Suh was bigger and used his hands so much better. (Nkemdiche) was a one-man wrecking crew against Alabama. He had a very good game. He kicked the (expletive) out of them. He had some problems against Arkansas. ... He is an eccentric (person). He is weird. He is kind of a nerd. I don't think he is a bad kid. His brother is a big-time (mess) with two arrests and a lot of issues, but he idolizes him and it drags him down. Wherever big bro goes, little bro follows. That's how Mississippi got him there. They signed the big brother knowing his younger brother was coming up."

DLE SHAWN OAKMAN, #2 (Sr-5)

BAYLOR ▶ GRADE: 5.37

Ht: 6-7 5/8 | Wt: 287 | 40: 4.91 | Arm: 35 3/4 | Hand: 10 5/8

History: Philadelphia native also won a Pennsylvania basketball championship. As a youth, spent time in a homeless shelter and saw his mother become addicted to cocaine and get sent to prison. Was placed in the care of an uncle at age 10. Began his career at Penn State, where he redshirted in 2011. Was dismissed by then-head coach Bill O'Brien in March '12 — at a campus convenience store, pocketed a sandwich, then tried to pay for a drink using an ID card that with no meal points on it. When questioned about the sandwich, Oakman asked, 'What sandwich?' When he tried to take his card back, he grabbed the cashier's wrist, incurring a misdemeanor and fine. The incident was Oakman's "third strike" in the eyes of O'Brien, the first being a missed class, the second being the robbery of a pizza delivery man Oakman was wrongly accused of (Oakman did not know the men who committed the crime and was not present for the crime). Oakman later told Philly.com, "I was at a bad point at Penn State. My grades were bad. I was a disciplinary problem. I had anger issues. . . It was my fault. I didn't know it then, but I wasn't ready. I just thought I'd be there a while and go play in the NFL. It was like the rules didn't apply to me. I really felt that way until it was too late." Oakman transferred to Baylor, where Brian Norwood, a former Penn State assistant, was on staff. Sat out the '12 season per NCAA rules. Was a reserve in '13 when he recorded 33 tackles, 121/2 for loss and two sacks with two forced fumbles in 13 games. Broke out in '14 when he set Baylor's single-season sack record — posted 51-191/2-11 with three batted passes and three forced fumbles in 13 starts at defensive end. Sat out '15 spring practice while recovering from surgery to repair a torn left wrist ligament. Was suspended for the opener against SMU for a violation of team rules. On the season, started all 12 games played at DE and totaled 43-141/2-41/2 with two forced fumbles. Graduated.

Strengths: Imposing physical specimen with rare arm length and height, the largest of any player at the Combine — has a 7-foot-plus wingspan. Extremely lean with only 11 percent body fat. Big strong hands. Plays with emotion. Tough, physical and aggressive. Flashes big-play ability knifing into the backfield. Strong, physical tackler. Very good strength to set the edge. Has the sheer mass to collapse the pocket. Good football character. Plays hard and competes.

Weaknesses: Long-legged and slew-footed with stiffness in his body. Very tight ankles. Tends to stand up tall out of his stance, negating leverage and power. Not a natural bender. Is not a nuanced pass rusher and needs to develop some counter moves and learn how to use his long arms to leverage blockers. Too often allows defenders to get their hands on him. Is late to recognize and feel blocking pressure. Needs to become more disciplined in his approach and a better student of the game. Added 18 pounds from the Senior Bowl to the Combine and did not look as athletic in drills as he did moving around during the season.

Future: A better athlete than football player, Oakman is a flash player with physical traits to develop. Could fit as a right defensive end in a "30" front or a monster-sized base end in a "40" front. Has a high ceiling if the light bulb quits flickering and stays on. Is still very

much a raw developmental project.

Draft projection: Third- to fourth-round pick.

Scout's take: "I interviewed him. He has quack feet — he'll probably pull a muscle running because his feet point 10 and 2. He is Spiderman. ... But I'll tell you this — he won me over. Listen to him tell it, I'm not sure how the (expletive) he is alive. It's scary. He is crazy. But I'm sticking with him."

DRE-ROLB **EMMANUEL OGBAH**, #38 (Jr-4)
OKLAHOMA STATE ▶ GRADE: 5.82
Ht: 6-4 1/4 | Wt: 273 | 40: 4.62 | Arm: 35 1/2 | Hand: 10

History: Last name is pronounced "AWG-buh." Born in Nigeria and moved to Houston at age nine. Redshirted in 2012. Appeared in all 13 games in '13, tallying 20-51/2-4. Was the Big 12 Defensive Lineman of the Year in '14 when he started all 13 games and produced 49-17-11 with five batted passes and one forced fumble. Was the Big 12's Co-Defensive Player of the Year and a Hendricks Award finalist in '15 when he registered 64-171/2-13 with four batted passes and three forced fumbles, as well as an OSU single-season record 19 quarterback hurries. Team captain.

Strengths: Extremely long arms. Outstanding burst to beat blockers one-on-one and take the corner. Produced the fastest 10-yard split (1.56 seconds) of any defensive lineman at the Combine and tied for the fastest 40-yard dash (4.56 seconds). Has strong hands and can leverage the edge and convert speed to power. Outstanding disruptive production. Solid point-of-attack strength. Good personal and football character.

Weaknesses: Needs to cultivate his pass-rush arsenal and develop more counter moves. Clocked a 4.54-second 20-yard shuttle at the Combine, revealing of very tight hips and limited lateral agility. Effort too often wanes. Inconsistent down-to-down compete level. Is a bit high-hipped and struggles to sink his hips and anchor against the run.

Future: An excellent-sized, straight-line speed rusher most effective from a wide-nine alignment where he has room to crash the corner. Has some similarities to Chargers 2015 second-round pick (50th overall) Jeremiah Attaochu and could warrant interest as a rush linebacker in a "30" front or a speed rusher in a "40" front. Impressive Combine showing created a buzz and could elevate his draft standing beyond his inconsistent performance.

Draft projection: Top-50 pick.

Scout's take: "He is a sometime player. He

is strong, but I didn't think he was as good against the run. They just widen his alignment and let him go. I know he had a lot of sacks, but I thought a lot of them came against average tackles. He could play left end and kick inside, but he's not going to be as good against the run. He has to learn how to play it."

DLE-LOLB ROMEO OKWARA, #45 (Sr-4)
NOTRE DAME ▶ GRADE: 5.16
Ht: 6-45/8 | Wt: 265 | 40: 4.87 | Arm: 341/8 | Hand: 101/8

History: Born in Nigeria. Prepped in North Carolina. As a true freshman in 2012, saw limited action in all 13 games and was credited with seven tackles, 11/2 for loss and zero sacks with one forced fumble. Played all 13 games in '13, drawing one start at defensive end, and recorded 19-11/2-1/2. Played in defensive coordinator Bob Diaco's for two years, providing depth at DE, "Cat" (rush linebacker) and "Dog" (drop linebacker). Started all 26 games his final two years as a defensive end in Brian VanGorder's 4-3 scheme — totaled 39-4-4 with one batted pass and two forced fumbles in '14; and 48-121/2-8 with one blocked kick in '15. Graduated with a degree in accountancy. Will be a 21-year-old rookie.

Strengths: Outstanding size with very good arm length. Very active hands. Flashes strength at the point of attack. Forceful tackler. Plays hard with good effort production. Solid overall character.

Weaknesses: Comes off the ball too upright and cannot trim the corner. Marginal awareness and feel for the game. Gets hung up on blocks and is slow to shed. Needs to develop some counter moves. Does not translate his weight-room strength to the field.

Future: A stiff, straight-linish base end with developing instincts. Could warrant looks as a strong-side outside linebacker in a 3-4 front or even a "Sam" linebacker in a "40" look.

Draft projection: Late draftable pick

3T-NT SHELDON RANKINS, #98 (Sr-4)
LOUISVILLE ▶ GRADE: 6.42
Ht: 6-11/8 | Wt: 299 | 40: 4.99 | Arm: 33 3/8 | Hand: 9 3/8

History: Prepped in Georgia. Played defense tackle in Vance Bedford's 4-3 scheme his first two seasons in Louisville. As a true freshman in 2012, notched five tackles, one for loss and one sack in nine appearances (one start). Missed three games because of a sprained left MCL. Had both his labrums repaired prior to the '13 season when he collected 15-4-3 with two batted passes and one forced fumble in 10 games (started the Cardinals' bowl game against Miami). Sat out the season opener against Ohio (high left ankle sprain), as well as games against Kentucky and Central Florida (shoulder). Started all 26 games in defensive coordinator Todd Grantham's 3-4 scheme the next two seasons — totaled 53-131/2-8 with one batted pass, two interceptions and one forced fumble in '14 (13 starts at left end); and 58-13-6 with one batted pass and a 46-yard fumble recovery touchdown in '15 (13 starts at right end). Sprained his knee during Senior Bowl practices. Two-time team captain graduated with a health and human performance degree.

Strengths: Clocked a 1.69-second 10-yard split, indicating excellent short-area burst for a 300-pounder. Very good hip snap and suddenness to penetrate gaps. Good instincts to feel blocking pressure. Outstanding weight-room strength and functional playing strength at the point of attack. Has a 34 1/2-inch vertical jump and a 9-foot, 10-inch broad jump (tops among all defensive tackles), demonstrating excellent athletic ability and lower-body explosion. Plays with solid base and is seldom on the ground. Excellent showing in one-on-one drills at Senior Bowl. Outstanding personal and football character. Is the first player in line and has natural leadership qualities to take youth under his wing and elevate the play of those around him. Smart and football smart.

Weaknesses: Has below-average arm length and is not naturally big. Can be neutralized by the double team and has to give ground to get off blocks when matched against top power. Injuries (shoulder, ankle, knee) have consistently been an issue throughout his career.

Future: An active, strong and quick one-gap penetrator most ideally suited to line up as a three-technique in a "40" front, though he is strong and powerful enough to play the nose in an even or odd front. An ascending talent with Pro Bowl potential.

Draft projection: First-round pick.

Scout's take: "(Rankins) plays with great pad level. He has a lot of power in his body. It showed up at the Senior Bowl in one-on-one drills, and it transferred to the team period. ... He is a versatile player. When you have strength, power and quickness, you can fit any scheme."

NT-OG **D.J. READER**, #48 (Sr-4)

CLEMSON ▶ GRADE: 5.10

Ht: 6-2 5/8 | Wt: 327 | 40: 5.31 | Arm: 33 | Hand: 9 1/2

History: North Carolina prep who played four years of varsity in football, baseball and basketball. As a true freshman in 2012, recorded 40 tackles, zero for loss and zero sacks with one batted pass in 13 games. In '13, tallied 43-5-3 in 13 games (three starts). Reader's father, David Sr., died from complications of kidney failure in the summer of '14. On the season, played 12 games (one start) and had 27-21/2-11/5. Was suspended against North Carolina State (violation team rules). Took a leave of absence (personal reasons) at the beginning of the '15 season. Missed six games, but returned to start 6-of-9 games played and chip in 13-11/2-1/2. Graduated with a communications degree.

Strengths: Has a strong base and is not easily moved. Bench-pressed 225 pounds 30 times and has outstanding weight-room strength. Flashes some quickness. Takes the game seriously.

Weaknesses: Marginal production resulting from never having been a full-time starter. Stays blocked too long and struggles to disengage. Very limited closing burst. Weight has fluctuated and affects stamina. Inconsistent motor. Has been injured a lot.

Future: A big, strong powerful space occupier with enough size and strength to function as a nose tackle in an even front. Could warrant some consideration as a developmental offensive guard.

Draft projection: Priority free agent.

5T-DT **JARRAN REED**, #90 (Sr-4)

ALABAMA ▶ GRADE: 6.12

Ht: 6-2 7/8 | Wt: 307 | 40: 5.17 | Arm: 33 3/8 | Hand: 10 1/2

History: First name is pronounced "JER-in." Prepped in North Carolina and originally committed to Division II Fayetteville State before spending 2011 at Hargrave Military Academy (Va.). Played two seasons at East Mississippi Community College — totaled 35 tackles, five for loss and one sack in '12 (nine games); and 66-51/2-31/2 with two batted passes for the NJCAA national champions in '13 (12 games). Committed to North Carolina, Ole Miss and Florida before landing at Alabama. Was charged with a DUI in July '14 — was suspended for nearly a week of fall camp and temporarily demoted to the third team. With the Crimson Tide, started 13-of-14 games at 3-4 defensive end in '14,

producing 55-61/2-1 with five batted passes. In '15, started all 15 games at DE for the national champs, notching 57-41/2-1 with two batted passes. Graduated. Did not bench press at the Combine because of a left shoulder injury.

Strengths: Very well built. Exceptional strength — is a 500-pound bench-presser. Very stout at the point of attack to steer blockers. Strong run defender rips off blocks and strikes ballcarriers with intent. Packs a powerful punch. Can stack the double team. Is instinctive and alert to sniff out screens. Very productive tackler with a great feel for blocking pressure.

Weaknesses: Lacks ideal height and arm length. Has some tightness in his body and is not natural working the edges. Is not a nuanced pass rusher and lacks the agility and burst to close to the quarterback and finish at the top of his rush. Not sudden or quick-twitched in his movement. Marginal sack production. Was immature early and must prove that he could avoid the trappings of the game in the pros.

Future: A two-gapping, straight-line, power rusher with fencepost strength to ward off blockers, Reed can make an immediate impact in the pros as a run defender. However, his inability to create pressure as a pass rusher diminishes his value.

Draft projection: Top-40 pick.

Scout's take: "Reed plays the game with the tenacity of a junk-yard dog. He's a very strong two-gap player. He is tight in the hips with above-average bend. When it comes to balance and feet, he has all that."

3T-5T **HASSAN RIDGEWAY**, #98 (Jr-4)

TEXAS ▶ GRADE: 5.33

Ht: 6-3 3/8 | Wt: 303 | 40: 5.01 | Arm: 33 | Hand: 9 3/8

History: Grew up in California before moving to Texas at age 14. U.S. Army All-American also played basketball as a prep. Recruited by then-head coach Mack Brown. Redshirted in 2012. Was a reserve in '13 when he recorded 13 tackles, one for loss and zero sacks with one batted pass in 12 appearances. Was injured and did not play in the Longhorns' bowl game against Oregon. Played all 13 games in '14, starting the final 10 at nose tackle, and produced 43-11-6. Missed part of '15 fall camp because of a back injury which kept him out of the starting lineup until Week Four — on the season, started 8-of-11 games played and collected 36-61/2-31/2 with one fumble recovery touchdown. Hurt his shoulder against Oklahoma, but did not miss a start thanks to a bye week. Missed the season finale against Baylor because of a left ankle injury.

Strengths: Good size. Has a 32-inch vertical jump and is athletic and light on his feet for a 300-pounder. Locks out and get good extension. Flashes quickness to slice gaps and swat past blockers. Solid strength at the point of attack. Plays with some pop in his hands.

Weaknesses: Has underachiever tendencies. Disappears for stretches and takes plays off. Intermittent intensity. Does not create much push. Weight has fluctuated throughout his career, affecting his stamina and leading to injuries and inconsistency. Produced the slowest 3-cone drill time (8.29 seconds) of any defensive lineman at the Combine. Durability has been an issue.

Future: Surprisingly declared for the draft following a ho-hum junior season in which he regressed playing through injuries. A one-gap penetrator with enough athletic talent to emerge as a solid starter in the pros in time. Has enough strength to play end in a 30 front. Questionable durability and stamina could affect draft status.

Draft projection: Third- to fourth-round pick.

Scout's take: "I thought he played really well against Oklahoma. Then he had a stinger and his arm dropped. I started to get excited. Then I put the West Virginia game on, and he couldn't get off the ball. He was a flasher and an enigma. I don't know if injuries got to him. That's what where you have to be sure to go to the school to find out what makes the guy tick."

5T-3T A'SHAWN ROBINSON, #86 (Jr-3)

ALABAMA ▶ GRADE: 6.33

Ht: 6-3 5/8 | Wt: 307 | 40: 5.17 | Arm: 34 1/2 | Hand: 10 1/2

History: Prepped in Texas, where he was a USA Today All-American and five-star recruit on both sides of the ball. Appeared in all 13 games as a true freshman, drawing two starts at nose tackle, and recorded 38 tackles, 8 1/2 for loss and 5 1/2 sacks with a blocked kick. Missed nearly two weeks of '14 fall camp because of a left knee sprain. On the season, started 13-of-14 games at nose guard and tallied 49-6 1/2-0 with three batted passes and one forced fumble and a blocked PAT. Did not start against Florida Atlantic. Missed time during '15 spring practice because of an ankle injury, but was an Outland Trophy finalist — started all 15 games (12 at DE, three at NG) — after posting 46-7 1/2-3 1/2 with two batted passes and a blocked PAT in 15 starts

as a 3-4 defensive end.

Strengths: Big-boned. Has outstanding length to disrupt the vision of quarterbacks and bat down balls or block kicks (see LSU). Looks every bit the part with a frame that is trim at 307 pounds and could easily hold another 15. Has natural power in his body to control and steer blockers. Very good movement skills for his size. Can push the pocket and walk blockers back to the quarterback. Very strong tackler. Flashes shock in his punch.

Weaknesses: First move is up — tends to play too upright. Needs to improve pad level and leverage. Average finishing speed and burst. Lacks a pass-rush arsenal and is very raw in his technique. Motor runs hot and cold and is too complacent staying blocked. Only bench-pressed 225 pounds 22 times at the Combine, indicating below-average strength. Marginal production. Immature and still learning what it takes to be a pro.

Future: Big-boned, naturally strong and powerful anchor capable of playing anywhere along a "30" front. Has not yet figured out how to unlock his hips and cut loose his athletic potential. Did not produce heavily while playing in a very deep front-seven rotation. Has the talent to emerge as an impact run defender. However, has a long ways to go."

Draft projection: Top-20 pick.

Scout's take: "He is 6-4, 305 pounds and he looks like he is 290 when you see him in person. He is an excellent athlete. It's almost freakish for as big as he is. He's just a big block of man — big wrists, big knees, big everything. As a player, the only thing that is concerning is there's not a lot of production. They rotate them a lot. Their front seven is really good. I wanted to see more toughness, physicality and fight in him, but he's super, super strong to stack the point."

NT DEVAUNTE SIGLER, #8 (Sr-5)

JACKSONVILLE (ALA.) STATE ▶ GRADE: 4.87

Ht: 6-3 1/2 | Wt: 298 | 40: 5.14 | Arm: 33 3/4 | Hand: 9 7/8

History: Has a daughter. Played linebacker as an Alabama prep. Began his college career at Auburn, where he played defensive tackle and defensive end. As a true freshman in 2011, tallied 10 tackles, 1 1/2 tackles for loss and one sack in 13 games. Produced just 2-0-0 in '12 (five appearances), as a concussion rendered him a virtual non-factor. Appeared just five times in '12 — notched 2-0-0. Was dismissed from the team in the spring of '13 by Gus Mulzahn. Did not play that season,

DEFENSIVE LINE

instead working as a brick layer. Transferred to JSU in '14 (wore jersey No. 92) and made an immediate impact — was the Ohio Valley Conference Defensive Player of the Year after starting 9-of-10 games as a five-technique and logging 37-9-3.5 with two batted passes, one interception, two forced fumbles and one blocked kick. Missed two games because of a broken left hand. After the season, had his left shoulder surgically repaired. Wore jersey No. 8 in '15 when he started 8-of-10 games played as a five-technique and notched 32-21/2-2 with four batted passes. Sustained a high ankle sprain in the season opener which cost him three games and a start. Also missed a pair of late-season contests (knee?). Graduated with a public administration degree. Opted not to perform the broad jump at the Combine.

Strengths: Outstanding size. Good arm length. Solid core strength to occupy space. Has a strong bull-rush move. Very tough and competitive. Chases hard. Football smart and aware. Has a passion for the game.

Weaknesses: Not quick or sudden off the ball. Is late to find it — lacks awareness. Could stand to do a better job of using his hands to play off blocks. Pad level is very inconsistent. Very average Combine workout. Limited athlete. Is not a natural knee bender. Marginal closing burst to the ball. Spends too much time on the ground. Is not a strong tackler. Cannot handle the double team. Durability has been an issue.

Future: Size prospect with some strength to warrant an opportunity in a camp.

Draft projection: Priority free agent.

DLE CHARLES TAPPER, #91 (Sr-4)

OKLAHOMA ▶ GRADE: 5.26

Ht: 6-2 5/8 | Wt: 271 | 40: 4.59 | Arm: 34 3/8 | Hand: 11

History: Charles' father died when his son was four. Also played basketball as a Baltimore prep (didn't play football until junior year). Saw limited action in five games as a true freshman in 2012, notching two tackles, zero for loss and zero sacks. In '13, was used as a defensive end in Mike Stoops' 3-3-5 scheme 6 produced 49-9-51/2 with one batted pass. Was ejected against Baylor for throwing a punch, causing him to be suspended for the first half of the Iowa State contest. Started all 26 games at DE the next two years — totaled 37-71/2-3 with two batted passes and one forced fumble in '14; and 50-10-7 with three batted passes and four forced fumbles in '15. Team captain. Graduated. Did not perform

shuttles at the Combine because of a right hamstring injury.

Strengths: Very good body mass with long arms and big hands. Has a knack for batting down passes and disrupting the vision of quarterbacks. Produced the second-fastest 10-yard split (1.58 seconds) of any defensive linemen at the Combine, indicative of outstanding short-area burst, and tied for the fastest 40-yard dash (4.56) of any defensive lineman. Has strong hands to steer and control blockers. Good effort to flatten down the line of scrimmage. Very good anchor strength. Very durable.

Weaknesses: Tight-hipped with marginal lateral agility and burst. Inconsistent effort and motor — does not consistently chase and looks too content getting just getting his job done. Does not play with urgency and disappears for stretches. Needs to learn how to work an edge and develop a better pass-rush plan. Sickle cell trait could affect conditioning and stamina.

Future: A naturally big, strong, straight-line fast power rusher better playing the run that rushing the passer. Eye-opening Combine workout could allow him to be drafted more highly than he grades on tape and provide more of an opportunity to earn a role. Is best suited for a job as a base end in a "40" front.

Draft projection: Fourth- to fifth-round pick.

Scout's take: "He plays in that crouched, four-point stance so you never really see his athletic ability. He shocked everyone with the way he ran (fast at the Combine). The question is still, where do you play him? He doesn't have 4.6 play speed. You don't see burst. I didn't anyway. He struggles to get off blocks. He has some core strength and length but he did not do much."

DT-DLE LAWRENCE THOMAS, #8 (Sr-5)

MICHIGAN STATE ▶ GRADE: 5.12

Ht: 6-31/2 | Wt: 286 | 40: 4.96 | Arm: 32 3/4 | Hand: 10 1/8

History: Detroit native racked up 54 tackles for loss his last two high school seasons. Redshirted in 2011 while recovering from a shoulder injury. Sustained a concussion during '12 fall camp. Transitioned from linebacker to defensive end to fullback between fall camp and Week Two — appeared in all 13 games, drawing three starts at FB, and recorded seven receptions for 78 yards (11.1-yard average) with three special teams tackles. Played defensive tackle in the bowl game against TCU.

Sustained another concussion against Indiana. Was back on defense in '13, but was a non-factor after missing the first half of the season because of a back injury — made one tackle in seven appearances. Primarily played nose tackle in '14 when he had 30 tackles, 41/2 for loss and three sacks with one batted pass in 13 starts. Started all 14 games in '15 (13 at defensive end, one at defensive tackle) and notched 38-5-3 with six batted passes. Graduated with a sociology degree. Did not complete the bench press test at the Combine because of a right shoulder injury and opted out of the shuttles.

Strengths: Has exceptional size. Good motor. Plays hard and competes. Recorded a 35-inch vertical jump, tied for best among defensive tackles at the Combine and indicative of outstanding athletic ability. Good job occupying blockers. Has good vision to see the quarterback and a knack for batting down balls.

Weaknesses: Below-average arm length. Is late to locate the ball. Marginal instincts. Plays too recklessly and out of control, struggling to come to balance in the open field. Consistently plays too tall. Stiff and non-explosive. Does not have a variety of pass-rush moves. Marginal production.

Future: An intriguing athlete with enough athletic ability to function as an interior penetrator or as a two-down, base power end.

Draft projection: Late draftable pick.

NT VINCENT VALENTINE, #98 (Jr-4)

NEBRASKA   ▶ GRADE: 5.13
Ht: 6-3 5/8 | Wt: 329 | 40: 5.19 | Arm: 33 1/8 | Hand: 9 5/8

History: Prepped in Illinois. Was recruited to Nebraska by then-head coach Bo Pelini. Redshirted in 2012. Manned the nose for the Huskers. Started 6-of-13 games in '13, collecting 21 tackles, five for loss and one sack. Started 11-of-13 games in '14, producing 45-7-3 with two batted passes and one forced fumble. Did not start against Rutgers or Purdue while coping with a hyperextended elbow. Started 7-of-10 games played in '15, tallying 10-4-3. Missed three contests and did not start three more while nursing a high left ankle sprain. Graduated with a journalism degree.

Strengths: Good body mass and strength with a thick trunk to hold his ground and occupy space. Flashes some pop in his hands. Is tough and will battle through injuries.

Weaknesses: Only bench-pressed 225 pounds 17 times, the lowest total of any de-

fensive tackle and indicative of marginal weight-room strength. Clocked a 8.05-second 3-cone drill time, indicating limited body control and burst. Initially moves as if he is pulling a wagon — slow power. Has yet to learn how to use his hands. Durability has been an issue that could be worsened by carrying too much weight. Motor idled too much.

Future: Surprisingly departed school early after an injury-plagued season that left him little to show for it. Will need to return to full health and re-establish his sophomore form to warrant an opportunity to develop.

Draft projection: Fifth- to sixth-round pick.

DLE-3T JIHAD WARD, #17 (Sr-4)

ILLINOIS   ▶ GRADE: 5.62
Ht: 6-5 1/8 | Wt: 297 | 40: 5.12 | Arm: 33 7/8 | Hand: 9 3/8

History: First name is pronounced "juh-HODD." Philadelphia native played safety and receiver in high school, but did not qualify academically. Spent two years at Globe Institute of Technology (N.Y.) — recorded 55 tackles and eight sacks in 2012 (nine games) and 26-3-2 in '13 (eight games). Missed one contest (stinger). With the Illini in '14, started all 13 games at defensive end and produced 51-81/2-3 with one batted pass and two forced fumbles. Also ranked second in FBS with four fumbles recovered. Suffered a stress reaction in his left foot, prompting surgery in April '15. Had minor knee surgery during fall camp, but returned in time for the season — started all 12 games (first eight at DE, final four at defensive tackle) and posted 53-31/2-11/2 with two batted passes and one forced fumble. Wore jersey No. 17 because that's how old his mother was when she gave birth to him.

Strengths: Outstanding size, lower-body girth and power in his hands, displaying the most hand violence swatting bags in individual drills at the Senior Bowl. Is not yet done filling out his frame and has still has room to grow, especially in the upper body. Great motor and pursuit effort flattening down the line and chasing (see Iowa). Surprisingly light on his feet for 300-pounder. Has overcome a lot of adversity in his life and is very determined and driven to succeed.

Weaknesses: Instincts are still developing. Stays blocked too long. Too often his first move is up, and he plays tall and narrow. Does not lock out and create extension and is not a natural stack-and-shed player. Can improve his upper-body strength — only bench-

DEFENSIVE LINE

121

pressed 225 pounds 20 times at the Combine. Had a 25-inch vertical jump, indicative of below-average lower-body explosion.

Future: A powerfully built defensive lineman with both strength and quickness to play anywhere along an even or odd front. Ward is still developing physically and filling out his frame after days of being a high school receiver. Has unique tools that cannot be taught and has as much upside as any player in the draft.

Draft projection: Second- to third-round pick.

Scout's take: "I like Ward; I didn't love him. I liked when he was kicking down to three-technique, where I think he will wind up fitting. He has some technique issues, but he has good strength. He's not explosive. He plays (tall). I don't see a lot of violence or pop in his hands. I do see strength and power to torque guys and make plays. There is some rawness in him. The question is how much better he can get. I put him in the third (round). I think he is still two years away, though those defensive linemen with big (butts) and wide hips always go a lot higher."

DEFENSIVE LINE

3T ADOLPHUS WASHINGTON, #92 (Sr-5)
OHIO STATE ▶ GRADE: 5.36
Ht: 6-3 3/8 | Wt: 301 | 40: 5.16 | Arm: 34 1/2 | Hand: 9 7/8

History: Cincinnati native whose 43 sacks over two seasons garnered five stars and Parade All-American honors. Also starred on the hardwood, as he was named Ohio's Gatorade Player of the Year after averaging 23 points and 14 rebounds. As a true freshman in 2012, played 10 games and recorded nine tackles, 3 1/2 for loss and three sacks with one forced fumble. In '13, started 5-of-12 games played — three at defensive end, one at "Viper," one at nose guard — and managed 36-4-2. Injured his right groin muscle in the season opener against Buffalo, aggravated the injury the next week against San Diego State and missed the next two games. Also sprained his ankle against Northwestern. Transitioned to defensive tackle full time in '14 when he started 14--of-15 games for the national champs, producing 48-101/2-41/2 with one forced fumble. Did not start against Michigan State (350-pounder Cris Carter played the first snap of the game based on MSU's formation/personnel). Started all 12 games played at DT in '15, logging 49-7-4 with one batted pass, one interception and one forced fumble. Was suspended for the Fiesta Bowl against Notre Dame —was arrested and charged with misdemeanor solicitation for prostitution (busted as part of a police sting operation at a Columbus hotel).

Strengths: Outstanding arm length and body mass. Quick and light on his feet. Has advanced hand use to jolt and lock out blockers. Has a good feel for blocking concepts. Can get skinny, rip, swim and counter to come free. Flashed quickness in Senior Bowl one-on-one drills.

Weaknesses: First move is too often up. Average anchor strength. Underwhelming Combine workout. Produced the lowest broad jump (7-foot, 4 inches) of any defensive lineman at the Combine, indicative of marginal lower-body explosion. Also recorded one of the slowed 20-yard shuttles (4.84 seconds) and only bench-pressed 225 pounds 21 times. Measured 25 percent body fat at the Combine, reflecting limited stamina that shows up in tired play, especially late in games. Character requires closer scrutiny following end-of-season suspension.

Future: Is most ideally suited for a role as a gap-penetrating, three-technique or situational one-technique for an aggressive front such as the Cowboys, Seahawks or Jaguars. Has some boom-or-bust qualities.

Draft projection: Third- to fourth-round pick.

Scout's take: "(Washington's) motor and effort needs to become more consistent. He's a flash player who disappears a lot."

NT ANTWAUN WOODS, # 99(Sr-5)
USC ▶ GRADE: 4.77
Ht: 6-0 1/8 | Wt: 318 | 40: 5.40e | Arm: 31 | Hand: 9 5/8

History: Los Angeles native. Redshirted in 2011. Played all 13 games in '12, starting the first four at nose tackle, and recorded 16 tackles, 41/2 for loss and three sacks. In '13, started 6-of-13 games played at NT and logged 19-2-1 with one batted pass. Did not play against Arizona. Started 10-of-12 games played at NT in '14 and had 37-1-1 with one batted pass. Missed the Holiday Bowl against Nebraska because of a torn pectoral muscle, which required surgery and sidelined him for '15 spring practice. In the fall, was a 13-game starter at NT — posted 41-7-3. Sprained his left shoulder against Stanford and did not play against Arizona State. Team captain graduated with a sociology degree. Injured his right pectoral muscle during the bench-press test and missed the rest of his workout.

Strengths: Good eyes to locate the ball. Plays hard and competes. Flashes some shock in his hands. Football smart. Film junkie. Unselfish, team player.

Weaknesses: Tied for measuring the shortest arms (31 inches) of any defensive lineman at the Combine. Too easily stalled at the line of scrimmage and gets stuck in place. Marginal lower-body strength. Very limited playing range and pass-rush ability.

Future: Short, squatty, round-bodied, top-heavy, two-down run stuffer with enough mass to engulf backs and clog running lanes. Lacks ideal dimensions for the NFL game. Camp body.

Draft projection: Free agent.

Scout's take: "He looks like a sawed-off fire hydrant, very low to the ground. He doesn't make plays."

NT CONNOR WUJCIAK, #90 (Sr-5)
BOSTON COLLEGE ▶ GRADE: 5.10
Ht: 6-2 1/2 | Wt: 291 | 40: 4.93 | Arm: 33 1/4 | Hand: 10

History: Last name is pronounced "woe-JACK." Father, Alan, was on the 1973 Notre Dame national championship team, and older brother, Alex, was an All-Atlantic Coast Conference linebacker at Maryland (2006-10). Connor also played basketball as a New Jersey prep. Had a torn left labrum in 2011, his redshirt year. Played 10 games in '12, starting five at defensive tackle, and had 24 tackles, one for loss and zero sacks. Started 8-of-13 games at DT in '13, recording 24-2-0 with two batted passes and one forced fumble. Started all 25 games at nose tackle the next two seasons — totaled 33-71/2-3 with one forced fumble and one blocked field goal attempt in '14 (13 games); and 31-11-41/2 with one batted pass and one forced fumble in '15 (12 games). Graduated with a communication degree.

Strengths: Recorded a 341/2-inch vertical jump. Also recorded the fastest 20-yard shuttle time (4.27 seconds) and 3-cone drill time (7.32) of any defensive tackle at the Combine, indicative of outstanding lateral agility. Plays stout with a good base. Has strong hands to rip off blocks.

Weaknesses: Average anchor strength vs. the double team — gets walked and driven five yards off the ball (see Florida State). Limited pass-rush ability to work the edges. Disappears for stretches. Marginal production. Not a strong finisher. Below-average upper-body strength.

Future: Very stocky, compact inside plugger with a powerful base and good effort. Can fit as a two-down, rotational, backup over tackle in a 40 front. Must improve his strength to earn a roster spot.

Draft projection: Late draftable pick.

Scout's take: "I liked the defensive tackle.

He's a two-down player though. He really doesn't have a skill set as a pass rusher."

3T-DLE ANTHONY ZETTEL, #98 (Sr-5)
PENN STATE ▶ GRADE: 5.12
Ht: 6-3 7/8 | Wt: 277 | 40: 4.81 | Arm: 31 1/8 | Hand: 9 1/2

History: Last name is pronounced "ZET-tull." Prepped in Michigan, where he also lettered in basketball, baseball and track and field — set the state record in the shot put (61 feet, 8 inches). Redshirted in 2011. Was a defensive end his first two seasons. In '12, recorded 15 tackles, four for loss and four sacks with two batted passes in 12 games. Played all 12 games in '13, drawing two starts, and tallied 16-6-4 with two batted passes. Shifted to defensive end and started all 26 games the next two seasons — totaled 42-17-8 with five batted passes, three interceptions and one forced fumble in '14; and 47-11-4 with six batted passes and one forced fumble in '15 (was voted Nittany Lions' outstanding senior player). Lost his father to cancer prior to the San Diego State contest. Team captain graduated with a kinesiology degree. Was a candidate for the Senior CLASS Award.

Strengths: Good instincts to locate the ball. Steady career sack production (20). Produced a 4.39-second 20-yard shuttle, indicating very good lateral agility. Very good hand use to rip, pull, tug and come free. Much of production comes in chase mode pursuing down the line of scrimmage. Hustles and competes. Terrific motor and energy. Outstanding weight-room worker. Football smart and versatile. Ultra-tough battler.

Weaknesses: Lacks bulk and base strength and does not have a frame to get much bigger. Is moved off the line by double teams. Has very short arms and gets hooked on blocks. Has some stiffness in his body that negates bend and flexibility to function well on stunts, loops and games.

Future: An intense, try-hard overachiever lacking ideal bulk and length for the NFL game, yet possesses the desire and determination to win the hearts of coaches and will be very difficult to cut given the energy he brings to a locker room. Could have the most value in the pros as a situational inside rusher.

Draft projection: Late draftable pick.

Scout's take: "I graded him in the sixth (round). He is a high-motor guy. He plays hard. You want guys like him in the locker room. But he's a short-armed guy. He didn't have his best year."

DEFENSIVE LINE

LINEBACKERS

Nawrocki's TOP 10

◀ 1. **MYLES JACK**
2. **Reggie Ragland**
3. **Leonard Floyd**
4. **Jaylon Smith**
5. **Noah Spence**
6. **Darron Lee**
7. **Kamalei Correa**
8. **Jordan Jenkins**
9. **Kyler Fackrell**
10. **Yannick Ngakoue**

ILB DOMINIQUE ALEXANDER, #1 (Jr-3)

OKLAHOMA ▶ GRADE: 5.04

Ht: 6-0 | Wt: 232 | 40: 4.76 | Arm: 32 1/4 | Hand: 9

History: Oklahoma native played all over the field in high school. An injury to Broncos 2014 seventh-rounder Corey Nelson thrust Alexander into the lineup at outside linebacker in 2012, and he was named Big 12 Defensive Freshman of the Year for his efforts — started 8-of-13 games and totaled 80 tackles, 3 1/2 for loss and one sack with one pass breakup and two forced fumbles. Moved to inside linebacker, started all 26 games the next two seasons and led Sooners tacklers — produced 107-6-11/2 with one forced fumble in '14; and 103-7-11/2 with two pass breakups and one interception in '15. Sat out '15 spring practice (wrist surgery). Did not run at the Combine because of an unspecified injury.

Strengths: Very solid production. Will shoot gaps and step downhill aggressively. Flashes some pop on contact. Fairly athletic movement skill. Makes a lot of tackles in pursuit.

Weaknesses: Undersized with limited bulk. Non-instinctive. Late to locate the ball, is easily pulled by misdirection and takes false steps. Gets stuck on blocks and cannot shed or disengage quickly. Marginal take-on strength. Needs to get stronger. Has a Combine LB-low 8-foot, 6-inch broad jump and a 28 1/2-inch vertical jump, tied for the lowest of any inside linebacker at the Combine and indicative of below average athletic ability. Best fit might be as a "Jack" linebacker in a "30" front.

Future: A surprise early entry, Alexander is an undersized, non-instinctive 'backer lacking ideal strength and physicality for the inside and the speed and athletic ability desired on the perimeter. Ticket must come on special teams.

Draft projection: Priority free agent.

Scout's take: "If you look at his tackle production, you would think he's a good player. That's where analytics get you in trouble. I didn't think he was draftable. I have no idea why he decided to leave school a year early."

SLB DEVANTE BOND, #23 (Sr-5)

OKLAHOMA ▶ GRADE: 5.12

Ht: 6-1 1/8 | Wt: 235 | 40: 4.66 | Arm: 32 3/8 | Hand: 9 1/4

History: California native struggled academically early in his high school career and played just one season of varsity football. Spent two years at Sierra College (wore jersey No. 52). In 2011, logged 49 tackles, 10 1/2 for loss and seven sacks with one pass breakup and one forced fumble in nine games. In '12, tallied 77-27-17 with four pass breakups and three forced fumbles. Originally committed to Miami, but did not qualify academically and sat out '13. Dealt with ankle and shoulder injuries during '14 fall camp, but recorded 29-4-0 in 12 games (three starts at outside linebacker). Started 5-of-9 games played at OLB in '15 and had 43-7-3 with two pass breakups and one forced fumble. Missed four October contests while nursing a high left ankle sprain. Graduated.

Strengths: Very good speed to accelerate off the edge. Good enough functional strength to hold ground against tight ends. Recorded a 37 1/2-inch vertical jump at the Combine, indicative of outstanding athletic ability.

Weaknesses: Tight-hipped. Raw eyes and positional instincts — gets lured in by play-action and is late to see plays developing. Lacks bulk to stack the corner and anchor against big-bodied tackles. Lacks variety in his arsenal as a pass rusher. Was never a full-time starter. Has not been a core special teams player.

Future: A developmental Sam linebacker with athletic traits to compete on special teams and fend for a roster spot. Will require patience but has enough talent to ascend into a contributor.

Draft projection: Late draftable pick.

MLB KENTRELL BROTHERS, #10 (Sr-5)
MISSOURI   ▶ GRADE: 5.23
Ht: 6-0 3/8 | Wt: 245 | 40: 4.86 | Arm: 30 3/4 | Hand: 9 3/4

History: Linebacker-receiver out of Oklahoma. Redshirted in 2011 after he broke his fibula and tore ankle ligaments during fall camp. Was a reserve in '12 when he tallied 14 tackles, zero for loss and zero sacks with one forced fumble in 11 appearances. Started all 14 games at weak-side linebacker in '13 — produced 70-61/2-1 with three pass breakups and three interceptions. Had surgery to repair a torn right labrum in late March '14. In the fall, was the Tigers' leading tackler after starting all 14 games at WLB and piling up 122-5-1 with four pass breakups and three forced fumbles. Was the nation's leading tackler in '15 when he started all 12 games at WLB and registered 152-12-21/2 with three pass breakups, two interceptions, one forced fumble and three blocked kicks. Graduated with a sociology degree.

Strengths: Good size and bulk strength. Plays with good awareness and is around the ball a lot. Enough strength to take on blocks.

Very smart, determined and dedicated to the craft. Outstanding career production. Solid special teams contributor.

Weaknesses: Has very short arms and gets hung up on blocks. Average strength — only bench-pressed 225 pounds 19 times at the Combine. Not explosive through his knees (average bend) and legs too often go dead on contact. Marginal foot speed to reach the perimeter. See-and-go reactor (not instant or anticipatory). Limited range in zone coverage and will be stressed by NFL tight ends and backs in man coverage. Late to arrive on the blitz and does not time it up very well.

Future: Compact, thickly built weakside linebacker who projects most ideally to middle in the pros, where his lack of foot speed could be better concealed. Has the football smarts, toughness and overall character to earn a back-up job. Is wired to fight his way into a lineup

Draft projection: Fifth- to sixth-round pick.

Scout's take: "I didn't like him. He is tight. He can't change direction. He doesn't have any real pop for his size. He gets hung up in trash a lot. He can't run very well. I like the person more than the player. I don't think he would make our team."

SLB BENIQUEZ BROWN, #42 (Jr-4)
MISSISSIPPI STATE   ▶ GRADE: 4.80
Ht: 6-0 3/4 | Wt: 229 | 40: 4.73 | Arm: 31 3/8 | Hand: 9 1/8

History: First name is pronounced "ben-KNEE-quez." Safety-running back who prepped in Alabama. Redshirted in 2012. Played strong-side linebacker for the Bulldogs. Played all 13 games in '13, drawing three starts, and recorded 39 tackles, 41/2 for loss and zero sacks. Started 12-of-13 games in '14 and produced 62-7-2 with two pass breakups and two interceptions. Did not start against Vanderbilt (Senior Night). Started all 13 games in '15 and registered 99-11-4 with two pass breakups, one interception and two blocked kicks, including one against Arkanas in the final seconds that preserved a win.

Strengths: Solid production. Has some strength. Has some straight-line speed. Functional special teams contributor.

Weaknesses: Short-stepper. Plays too straight-legged and tall, negating quickness, power or explosion. Plays flat-footed. Limited movement skills — is often late to arrive and out of position. Too easily pulled by play-action. Too much body stiffness. Marginal eyes and anticipation. Struggles to shed and disengage. Easily mismatched by tight ends in coverage.

Future: An undersized, short-armed strong-

LINEBACKERS

side linebacker only. Will be overmatched by good tight ends. Will have to earn his way on special teams to stick on a roster.

Draft projection: Priority free agent.

Scout's take: "He's another junior that I thought should have stayed in school. He doesn't make our team better. I don't know what you do with him. He's not fast enough to be a will and doesn't have the length you want on the strong side. I don't see any power to play inside. He's a free agent for us."

WLB-SS JATAVIS BROWN, #1 (Sr-4)

AKRON   ▶ GRADE: 5.10

Ht: 5-10 3/4 | Wt: 221 | 40: 4.49 | Arm: 31 7/8 | Hand: 9

History: Glades Central (Fla.) product. Was suspended for playoff games his senior year for his role in a sexual incident — allegedly was part of a group of players who pressured a freshman girl into sex acts. As a true freshman in 2012, recorded 23 tackles, one-half for loss and zero sacks with one forced fumble in 11 games (one start). Took ownership of the "Will" linebacker position in '13 — was the Zips' Defensive MVP after starting all 12 games and producing 107-61/2-2 with two pass breakups and two forced fumbles. Switched from jersey No. 53 to No. 1 as a junior. Was voted team MVP after starting all 12 games and registering 99-141/2-4 with one pass breakup and three forced fumbles. Was the Mid-American Conference Defensive Player of the Year in '15 after setting Akron single-season records for tackles for loss and sacks — racked up 116-20-12 with one pass breakup, one interception and four forced fumbles in 13 starts. Owns the school record for career tackles for loss (411/2). Team captain graduated with his organizational supervision degree.

Strengths: Three-year starter. Very good eyes and playing instincts. Superb motor and pursuit effort. Explosive closing speed — smells blood. Natural knee-bending, impact striker — uncoils on contact and drives through ballcarriers. Strong pound-for-pound and can bench-press nearly twice his weight. Has enough speed to match up in space with receivers. Very tough and battles through injuries. Excellent career production. Film junkie. Alpha leader in the locker room. Makes defensive calls and adjustments. Stood out at the NFLPA Collegiate Bowl.

Weaknesses: Small-framed and measured the smallest wingspan (75 1/8 inches) of any linebacker at the Combine, limiting his ability to wrap and secure as a tackler, which is more

exposed on the perimeter. Lacks ideal size and bulk to take on blocks. Gets velcroed to some blocks in tight quarters and struggles to disengage. Did not regularly face top competition in the Mid-American Conference.

Future: An undersized strong-side college linebacker who projects to the weak side in a 40 front or nickel linebacker. Has enough speed, burst and range to warrant consideration as a box safety.

Draft projection: Late draftable pick.

SLB-ROLB De'VONDRE CAMPBELL, #26 (Sr-5)

MINNESOTA   ▶ GRADE: 5.34

Ht: 6-3 5/8 | Wt: 232 | 40: 4.56 | Arm: 33 5/8 | Hand: 9 5/8

History: Has a daughter, born last October. Defensive end-tight end who also ran track as a Florida prep. Was a qualifier out of high school, but went the JUCO route to attract more offers. Went to Hutchinson (Kan.) Community College, where he redshirted in 2011 while distancing himself from a concussion. Played 12 games at linebacker in '12 and registered 83 tackles, eight for loss and 31/2 sacks with four pass breakups and a 34-yard interception return touchdown. With the Gophers in '13, was used primarily on passing downs — logged 41-3-0 with one pass breakup and one forced fumble in 13 appearances (three starts on the weak side). Started all 13 games at WLB in '14 and produced 75-61/2-21/2 with one pass breakup, one interception and one blocked kick. In '15, started 11-of-13 games at WLB and totaled 92-61/2-4 with three pass breakups, one interception and one forced fumble. Was benched the first quarter against Colorado (violation team rules) and was limited against Nebraska days after the birth of his daughter. Reportedly failed one drug test while at Minnesota. Graduated with a business and marketing degree and was working on his master's degree during the season. Opted not to run the 3-cone drill at the Combine.

Strengths: Looks the part. Outstanding body and arm length with exceptional speed for his size. Smart and versatile. Understands run fits. Loose-hipped and athletic in space. Exceptional speed and closing burst to the ball. Has lined up with his hand in the dirt in sub-packages to rush the passer and has the edge speed to disrupt off the edge.

Weaknesses: Only bench-pressed 225 pounds 16 times at the Combine and lacks functional strength and power in his hands to control tight ends. Lacks physicality at the point of attack — more of a catcher than a striker. Is late to shed and disengage from

LINEBACKERS

blockers. Overruns the ball and could stand to take better angles. Has a limited feel for routes — below-average coverage awareness. Could be challenged by the sophistication of a complex defense.

Future: High-cut, long-limbed athletic weakside linebacker with the frame that looks ideally suited for rushing the passer on third down if he could continue to add bulk and improve functional strength. Developmental prospect with intriguing athletic traits to fit at multiple positions.

Draft projection: Fourth- to fifth-round pick.

Scout's take: "He's a lengthy linebacker. He moves around well. I have a good grade on him that equates to the third or fourth-round based on his athletic traits. He is still developing as a football player, but he has physical traits that are not easy to find."

ROLB-DRE KAMALEI CORREA, #8 (Jr-3)
BOISE STATE ▶ GRADE: 5.64
Ht: 6-2 5/8 | Wt: 243 | 40: 4.69 | Arm: 31 5/8 | Hand: 9 3/8

History: Also played basketball as a Hawaii prep. Played the "Stud" position (hybrid defensive end/linebacker) and did not miss a game during his three-year Broncos career. As a true freshman in 2013, had 12 tackles, 11/2 tackles for loss and one sack in 13 appearances. Started all 27 games the next two seasons — totaled 59-19-12 with two batted passes, two forced fumbles and a blocked punt in '14 (14 games); and 39-11-7 with three forced fumbles in '15 (13 games). Did not run shuttles at the Combine because of right calf cramping.

Strengths: Good athlete with natural bend and rush instincts to locate the ball while trimming the corner. Plays hard with a sense of urgency and competes every down. Very good closing speed when he triggers and plays with discipline on the backside. Consistently disruptive creating pressures and hurrying the quarterback — can beat blockers one-on-one. Athletic enough to split wide and zone drop. Outstanding motor, effort and desire. Interviewed very well at the Combine, being described as a pleaser.

Weaknesses: Has short arms and gets hung up on blocks vs the run. Needs to develop more variety in his pass-rush arsenal and disengage more quickly. Lacks ideal bulk and needs to get stronger. Recorded a 9-foot broad jump, indicating modest lower-body explosion. Lacks power in his body. Production dipped as as junior.

Future: An undersized, athletic edge rush-er with very good bend, burst and desire to contribute readily as a sub-package pressure player. Must continue to get stronger to become a complete every-down player, though has the potential to emerge as a very solid starter.

Draft projection: Second- to third-round pick.

Scout's take: "No. 8 can bend and has some burst to him. He's in the same category as (Cowboys 2015 early second-round pick) DeMarcus Lawrence. (Correra) could be an undersized end, but I think he'll fit best as an outside linebacker in a 3-4. He's more athletic than Lawrence."

ILB STEVEN DANIELS, #52 (Sr-4)
BOSTON COLLEGE ▶ GRADE: 5.08
Ht: 5-11 1/2 | Wt: 243 | 40: 4.93 | Arm: 32 5/8 | Hand: 10

History: Also played basketball as an Ohio prep. Recorded 25 tackles, one-half for loss and zero sacks in 10 appearances (one start at weak-side linebacker) as a true freshman in 2012. Had surgery to repair a torn right labrum prior to the '13 season. In the fall, started 12-of-13 games at WLB and produced 88-61/2-3 with two pass breakups, one interception and one forced fumble. Moved to middle linebacker in '14 and notched 72-7-1/2 with one pass breakup and one interception in 13 games (10 starts). In '15, was the leading tackler for one of the nation's top defenses — posted 82-16-6 with two pass breakups and one interception in 12 starts at MLB. Opted not to run the 60-yard shuttle at the Combine.

Strengths: Experienced, three-year starter with solid production. Aggressive taking on lead blockers and is quick to fill downhill. Strikes with some power in his body on contact to knock back ballcarriers. Plays hard and competes.

Weaknesses: Short and slow-footed with marginal playing speed and range to make tackles outside the box. Allows blockers to get into his frame and is late to disengage. Only bench-pressed 225 pounds 16 times at the Combine and needs to get physically stronger. Can be outleveraged to the sideline and take some questionable angles. Lacks the hip flexibility and feet to handle quick tight ends in man coverage. Recorded the slowest 3-cone time (7.35 seconds) of any linebacker at the Combine, indicative of average body control and burst.

Future: Thickly-built, tough, two-down thumper most ideally suited to play inside. Lack of foot speed will create limitations in coverage. Ideally suited as a backup, though lacks ideal

LINEBACKERS

speed and agility to factor on special teams.

Draft projection: Priority free agent.

Scout's take: "(Daniels) is decent. I did like him. He is smart, competitive and aware. He fits the 3-4 (defense) as a 'Will' more than he fits as a 4-3 'Mike.' He's not really a fit for us. He's a backup with some skill."

ROLB-SLB KYLER FACKRELL, #9 (Sr-5)
UTAH STATE   ▶ GRADE: 5.52

Ht: 6-5 | Wt: 245 | 40: 4.64 | Arm: 33 | Hand: 10 1/8

History: Married with a daughter named Delaney. Linebacker-receiver who also played basketball and volleyball as an Arizona prep. Redshirted in 2011. Started every game of his career as a 3-4 outside linebacker. In '12, recorded 87 tackles, eight for loss and three sacks with three pass breakups, three interceptions and one forced fumble in 13 games. In '13, totaled 82-13-5 with one pass breakup, one interception (99-yard score) and two forced fumbles in 14 games. Also caught a four-yard touchdown pass. Suffered a torn right ACL in the '14 season opener, and was granted a medical hardship waiver. Returned to start 13 games in '15 and post 82-15-4 with two forced fumbles. Also tallied 12 quarterback hurries and recovered five fumbles (one TD). Graduated with a business administration degree. Will turn 25 during his rookie season. Did not run the 3-cone drill at the Combine because of a right hamstring injury.

Strengths: Exceptional length with an 80-inch wingspan. Good initial quickness at the snap. Very good movement skill and playing range — keeps his feet clean through trash. Outstanding effort, motor and pursuit production. Flattens down the line and chases hard from the backside. Solid, wrap tackler. Mature, accountable, unselfish team player.

Weaknesses: Lacks ideal base strength to stack the corner vs the run. Only bench-pressed 225 pounds 16 times at the Combine, lowest among outside linebackers. Could improve finishing strength as a tackler. Is still learning how to use his hands and disengage from blockers — a bit of a one-trick pony. Instincts are still honing — can be late to react to the ball and does not instinctively feel plays developing. Overaged.

Future: A high-motor, hard-charging developmental talent with a chance to be molded into an excellent pro. Has the length, athletic ability and motor to produce and could shine with continue strength development. Early in his career reminded his coaching staff of a young Brian Urlacher and might be able to play on his feet for a "40" front and even offer some value as a situational Mike Vrabel-like goalline tight end.

Draft projection: Second- to third-round pick.

Scout's take: "(Fackrell) is very raw, but he has a big upside. I still graded him in the third (round), though I liked him a lot better before he got hurt. I'm not as big of a fan of him right now. I think he's more of (an NFL) backup. When he played Sam at the Senior Bowl, he didn't look comfortable at all, tripping in space. I like the person and the makeup — I just don't see a lot of pass-rush instinct."

SLB-ROLB TRAVIS FEENEY, #41 (Sr-5)
WASHINGTON   ▶ GRADE: 5.26

Ht: 6-3 5/8 | Wt: 230 | 40: 4.46 | Arm: 33 3/8 | Hand: 9 1/2

Notes: Also played basketball and baseball as a California prep — was drafted by the Oakland Athletics in the 48th round of the 2011 MLB draft. Redshirted as a safety in '11, earning Defensive Scout MVP before having off-season surgery to repair a torn left labrum. In '12, started 9-of-12 games as a 4-3 strong-side linebacker and contributed 76 tackles, six for loss and four sacks with two interceptions and one forced fumble. Did not play against Portland State (right labrum tear, which required off-season surgery). Played all 13 games in '13, drawing two starts, and notched 55-5-2 1/2 with six pass breakups. Started 8-of-14 games in '14 and had 60-4 1/2-1 with three pass breakups, two interceptions (touchdown) and one forced fumble. After the season had torn left labrum surgically repaired. The Huskies switched to a 3-4 scheme in '15 and Feeney was deployed as a "Buck" (hybrid linebacker/ rush end) — was named the Huskies' Most Outstanding Defensive Player after starting 12-of-13 games and registering 56-17 1/2-8 with two pass breakups and three forced fumbles. Hurt his right shoulder against Oregon — did not start against Stanford, aggravated the injury against Oregon State and did not bench press at the Combine, where it was revealed he was also dealing with a sports hernia. Team captain graduated with a communications degree. Had three defensive coordinators during his time at UW. Did not bench press at the Combine because of a right shoulder injury.

Strengths: Excellent straight-line speed and overall length. Can accelerate and close fast to the sideline and has very good playing range. Good striker. Measured the fastest 40-yard time (4.41 seconds) and most explosive vertical jump (40 inches) of any linebacker at the Combine. Stood out on special teams coverage

LINEBACKERS

at the East-West Shrine Game.

Weaknesses: Lacks bulk strength to match up with NFL tight ends at the point of attack. Has a thin frame that looks nearly maxed out. Is tight in the hips and too straight-linish. Marginal lateral agility, as confirmed with marginal shuttle times at the Combine, including a 4.45-second 20-yard shuttle that stacked among the slowest of linebackers. Needs to become a more secure tackler in space — leaves his feet too early and does not consistently wrap. Has not been a model of durability and could struggle to stay healthy in the pros.

Future: A long-framed, narrow-built, run-and-hit 'backer who lacks the strength and physicality desired to line up on the strong side in the pros. Could make an immediate impact as a special teams coverage player and might warrant some interest as a "Jack" linebacker in a "30" front, with intriguing length and outstanding initial burst to come off the edge if he could continue to develop physically.

Draft projection: Fifth- to sixth-round pick.

Scout's take: "(Feeney) weighed less than 220 pounds in the fall when I passed through there. I think he only fits in a 4-3 front. He is not big enough to play inside in a 3-4 defense, and he's not a pass rusher outside. He lit up his Combine workout, but I won't temper my grade."

ROLB-SLB LEONARD FLOYD, #84 (Jr-4)
GEORGIA ▶ GRADE: 6.23
Ht: 6-5 5/8 | Wt: 244 | 40: 4.59 | Arm: 33 1/8 | Hand: 10 1/8

History: Georgia native played defensive end in high school. Attended Hargrave Military Academy in 2012. With the Bulldogs in '13, started 8-of-13 games at 3-4 outside linebacker and produced 55 tackles, 9 1/2 for loss and 6 1/2 sacks with one pass breakup and two forced fumbles. As a 3-4 "Sam" in '14, was voted the team's defensive MVP after he started 11-of-12 games played and collected 55-81/2-6 with three forced fumbles. Played with shoulder pain the second half of the season then had surgery, knocking him out of the bowl game against Louisville. In '15, started all 13 games at "Sam" and totaled 74-101/2-41/2 with three pass breakups. Rushed from multiple alignments and was used occassionally as a "Star" defender (nickel slot defensive back). Played under defensive coordinators Todd Grantham and Jeremy Pruitt. Did not bench press at the Combine because of a left pectoral injury and pulled his left hamstring on his first 40 attempt and did no perform shuttles or positional drills.

Strengths: Exceptional, quick-twitch athlete with the short-area burst, acceleration and top-end speed to fly off the edge. Has a 39 1/2-inch vertical jump and explosive power in his body. Very good length — measured the tallest of any linebacker at the Combine. Outstanding closing burst and short-area explosion. Natural knee bender. Athletic enough to play on his feet and cover slot receivers. Can get skinny to pierce gaps and win with inside moves. Versatile — aligns all over the field, standing up as a rusher, covering the slot and and aligning inside the bubble.

Weaknesses: Extremely lean and underpowered to hold ground — can be pushed around easily, ragdolled and run at. Lacks functional strength to set the edge and gets overwhelmed at the point of attack. Gets stuck to blocks, hung up in traffic and can be engulfed. Has had multiple shoulder surgeries that require further evaluation and long-term durability should be a consideration. Average production.

Future: A long-limbed, fluid-moving athlete with an intriguing skill set that could transfer well to the ROLB position in a 3-4 front or an elephant end or "Sam" linebacker role in a 4-3 front. An ascending talent with superb explosion and pass-rush potential, Floyd is far from a polished product and must continue to get stronger and develop more variety in his pass-rush arsenal to emerge as a Pro Bowl performer. Has a similar skill set to Dolphins 2013 third overall pick Dion Jordan, and lack of strength and physicality could create difficult challenges to overcome in the pros. Has boom-or-bust potential.

Draft projection: Top-20 pick.

Scout's take: "Floyd is Barkevious Mingo. They are both excellent athletes with size and length. Maybe Floyd is a little smarter when it comes to learning. Look at the production. Mingo might have even had more. I think there is something missing with (Floyd's) instincts. He does not have the killer instinct to attack and go find it. He is super athletic. He is (getting drafted) in the first round. Coaches are going to say they will get the production out of him. It's going to be one of those deals. Sometimes you don't learn from history."

WLB JOSH FORREST, #45 (Sr-5)
KENTUCKY ▶ GRADE: 5.01
Ht: 6-3 1/8 | Wt: 249 | 40: 4.93 | Arm: 33 1/2 | Hand: 9 1/2

History: Defensive back-receiver who also played basketball and ran track as a Kentucky prep. Transitioned from a 210-pound receiver to hybrid linebacker/safety during his 2011 redshirt season. Wearing jersey No. 8 in '12,

LINEBACKERS

tallied 13 tackles, one for loss and zero sacks in nine appearances. Did not play against Kent State then missed two more September contests with a thigh bruise. Was a reserve/special teams player in '13 when he collected 16-1/2-0 with one interception and two blocked kicks (one field goal, one block) in 12 appearances. Moved to middle linebacker and started all 24 games the next two seasons, leading UK tacklers both seasons — totaled 110-8-1 with two pass breakups, two interceptions and one forced fumble in '14; and 93-6-31/2 with five pass breakups, two interceptions (one touchdown) and one forced fumble in '15. Graduated with a degree in community and leadership development. Opted not to run the shuttles at the Combine.

Strengths: Good size and arm length. Effective slipping and avoiding blocks when filling and as a blitzer. Flashes some striking ability. Athletic enough to run with backs in coverage. Gets good depth in his zone drops and plays the ball well in front of him. Is very active, competes hard and runs to the ball. Very good production.

Weaknesses: Plays too narrow-based and tall and gets hung up in traffic. Uses too much finesse. Average instincts. Takes false steps and is late to trigger. Lacks point-of-attack strength. Only bench-pressed 225 pounds 11 times, the fewest of any linebacker at the Combine and indicating a serious strength deficiency for a 250-pound linebacker. Tied for the slowest 10-yard split (1.75 seconds) of any linebacker at the Combine, indicating marginal short-area burst.

Future: A good-sized, slip-and-avoid backer who plays small, Forrest lined up on the weak side of a "30" front and is best in a position where he is protected and free to run to roam. Developmental prospect still growing into his body. Will have to make a mark on special teams to earn a roster spot.

Draft projection: Priority free agent.

WLB KRIS FROST, #17 (Sr-5)

AUBURN   ▶ GRADE: 5.03

Ht: 6-2 1/4 | Wt: 240 | 40: 4.92 | Arm: 32 1/2 | Hand: 10 1/2

History: U.S. Army All-American out of North Carolina. Redshirted in 2011 while recovering from surgery to repair a torn left labrum. Was a reserve weak-side linebacker in '12 when he tallied five tackles, zero for loss and zero sacks with one forced fumble in nine appearances. Rotated at middle linebacker in '13, collecting 59-6-0 with one pass breakup and two forced fumbles in 14 games

(one start). Was ejected for targeting against Arkansas State. Suffered a stinger against Tennessee. Started 12-of-13 games at WLB in '14 and produced 87-10-31/2 with three pass breakups, one interception and three forced fumbles. Did not start against LSU because of a left MCL sprain. In '15, started 10-of-13 games at WLB and amassed 96-3-0 with two pass breakups, two interceptions and one forced fumble. Was benched for disappointing effort along with two other starters following loss to LSU. Did not participate in the East-West Shrine game while nursing a "nagging injury." Graduated with an aviation management degree. Did not bench press at the Combine because of a left shoulder injury and opted out of running the shuttles.

Strengths: Good size — looks the part. Plays hard and competes. Closes fast to the ball. Athletic enough to protect his feet through traffic. Intelligent and football smart — makes the defensive calls. Respected defensive leader.

Weaknesses: Does not play strong. Falls off tackles and does not finish. Takes some questionable angles. Plays on his heels. Very stiff and upright in his pedal. Limited awareness in zone coverage. Marginal lateral agility. Tied for the slowest 10-yard split (1.75 seconds) of any linebacker at the Combine, indicating marginal short-area burst. Has a 29-inch vertical jump, reflecting average athletic ability.

Future: Good-sized, high-effort, productive, durable run defender with too many generic traits. Special-teams contribution could dictate his fate.

Draft projection: Priority free agent.

Scout's take: "(Frost) is not very physical at the point of attack. He's an average take-on guy. His instincts were off with his run fits. And he had a bad workout at the Combine."

OLB B.J. GOODSON, #44 (Sr-5)

CLEMSON   ▶ GRADE: 5.14

Ht: 6-0 5/8 | Wt: 242 | 40: 4.66 | Arm: 33 1/4 | Hand: 10

History: Also played basketball as a South Carolina prep. Redshirted in 2011. Was a reserve/special teams player in '12 when he notched four tackles, zero for loss and zero sacks in 13 appearances. In '13, dealt with a concussion in September and saw limited action in seven games, collecting 7-0-0. Started 6-of-12 games played at "Sam" in '14 (gave way to nickel back in non-starts) and totaled 34-31/2-1 with two pass breakups. Sat out against Georgia Tech (hip flexor). Moved to the "Mike" in '15 — was the Tigers' leading tackler with 108-14-51/2 with three pass

LINEBACKERS

breakups, two interceptions and one forced fumble in 15 starts. Team captain graduated with a sociology degree.

Strengths: Excellent straight-line speed. Outstanding weight-room strength — measured the most bench-press reps (30) of any linebacker at the Combine. Good effort. Competes on special teams.

Weaknesses: Tight in the hips and is late to trigger. Does not trust what he sees, translating to average functional football-playing speed. Eyes and instincts are still developing — gets caught up in trash and stays blocked. Tied for the slowest 20-yard shuttle time (4.53 seconds) of any outside linebacker at the Combine, indicative of limited lateral agility. Does not play with natural knee bend and lacks explosiveness. Only a one-and-a-half year starter.

Future: Overly muscled, thick-framed workout warrior lacking instincts, flexibility, agility and awareness for the LB position. A better athletic tester than functional football player who intrigues more on paper than he does on film. Is tough and competitive enough to fend for a special teams role.

Draft projection: Late draftable pick.

Scout's take: "(Goodson) is just a guy. He is not any better than the seventh-rounder the Colts took (in 2010) — Kavell Conner. He's small. He'll get drafted because there are few quality Mike's (middle linebackers). His instincts are off."

WLB-MLB-RB MYLES JACK, #30 (Jr-3)

UCLA   ▶ GRADE: 6.67

Ht: 6-1 | Wt: 245 | 40: 4.50e | Arm: 33 5/8 | Hand: 10 1/4

History: Linebacker-running back won three state titles at Washington powerhouse Bellevue, where he was also a key member of the track team (11.4 100 meters). As a true freshman in 2013, was a finalist for the Paul Hornung Award after Pac-12 coaches named him Offensive and Defensive Freshman of the Year — started 12-of-13 games (10 at left outside linebacker, one at left inside linebacker, one at running back) and amassed 75 tackles, seven for loss and one sack with 11 pass breakups, two interceptions (one touchdown) and a blocked punt. Also had 38 carries for 267 yards (7.0-yard average) and seven touchdowns as a running back. In '14, started all 13 games at LILB and produced 88-8-0 with seven pass breakups and one interception. Rushed 28-113-3 (4.0). In '15, managed 15-0-0 with one pass breakup and one interception with 2-7-1 (3.5) rushing in three starts before suffering a season-ending torn right meniscus injury. At that time, left UCLA and focused entirely on his

rehab and pro career. Signed an endorsement deal with Under Armour in February. Will be a 21-year-old rookie. Was a medical exclusion at the Combine because of right knee injury.

Strengths: Exceptional athlete with rare cover skills to impact the entire field. Very well-conditioned athlete. Plays with good pad level and drives through ballcarriers. Very explosive on contact. Extremely fluid movement skill to clear his feet through traffic and beeline to the ball. Fluid in his drops with loose hips and outstanding short-area burst and acceleration to close. Rare cover skills. Secure wrap tackler. Good strength to play off blocks. Has the range to play sideline-to-sideline. Is athletic enough to rip off the edge and rush the passer. Can be a mismatch piece as a blitzer. As a running back, has the strength, quickness and balance to power his way thru creases in short-yardage / goalline situations.

Weaknesses: At times will get out of position overrunning the ball and trying to do too much, and misses some tackles as a result. Could stand to learn how to play with more discipline. Was not a team captain at a key position of leadership and left the team and university early in the season following injury. Knee injury will require medical evaluation.

Future: A rare physical specimen who steps into a starting lineup from Day One and makes an immediate impact. Is uniquely talented with the size, strength and athletic ability to interchange between all three linebacker positions in a "40" front or play inside or even outside in a "30" front. Athletic enough to play safety and offers dual capabilities as a situational running back. A game-changing physical specimen in the same athletic category athletically as a Junior Seau or Patrick Willis.

Draft projection: Top-10 pick.

Coach's take: "You put him in the middle, and he's going to make plays all over the field. Of all the athletes I've ever been fortunate enough to be around — just pure athleticism — there's Michael Vick and Julius Peppers. Two different body types, but amazing athleticism. Myles is at their level as an athlete." (ESPN) – *UCLA Head Coach Jim Mora*

ROLB JORDAN JENKINS, #59 (Sr-4)

GEORGIA   ▶ GRADE: 5.57

Ht: 6-2 5/8 | Wt: 259 | 40: 4.82 | Arm: 34 1/4 | Hand: 11 1/4

History: Son of an Army man — lived in five states before attending high school in Georgia. Played defensive end and competed in track and field. As a true freshman in 2012, started 6-of-14 games at weak-side linebacker and contributed 31 tackles, eight for loss and

LINEBACKERS

five sacks with one forced fumble and two pass breakups. Began the year behind Jarvis Jones (Steelers '13 first-rounder), but played well enough when Jones was hurt that the Bulldogs kept Jenkins on the field and moved Jones to the strong side. Started all 13 games in '13 and produced 45-12-5 with one forced fumble and two pass breakups. Moved to the "Jack" linebacker in '14 and registered 70-91/2-5 with two forced fumbles and one pass breakup in 14 starts. Was the Bulldogs' Defensive MVP in '15 after starting 10-of-12 games played at "Jack" and posting 59-101/2-4 with two forced fumbles. Did not play against Missouri (groin). Team captain. Ranks fourth on UGA's tackles for loss list (40) behind David Pollack, Quentin Moses and Jones. Did not run shuttles at the Combine because of a right hamstring injury.

Strengths: Experienced, three-and-a-half year starter. Has a big frame with long arms. Measured the biggest hands and largest wingspan (80 3/8 inches) of any linebacker at the Combine. Good eyes and instincts. Plays with strength at the line of scrimmage and can lock out, press and control blockers. Has shown he could convert speed to power and turn the corner. Flattens down the line and runs to the ball. Good football intelligence. Tough and competitive. Has good balance and body control. Outstanding personal and football character.

Weaknesses: Only bench-pressed 225 pounds 16 times at the Combine and would benefit from more time in the weight room. Allows some separation in man coverage and can do a better job staying in phase. Seldom used in zone coverage. Average sack production.

Future: A big, strong, powerful linebacker that played a multitude of roles and is most ideally suited for a role as a strong-side or left outside linebacker in a "30" front. Played thru injury as a senior and showed more burst earlier in his career. Is very tough, competitive and instinctive and has the physical talent to readily become a very good pro.

Draft projection: Third-round pick.

Scout's take: "He was playing with a bad groin all year. You have to keep that in mind when you're evaluating him."

ILB C.J. JOHNSON, #10 (Sr-5)

MISSISSIPPI ▶ GRADE: 4.82

Ht: 6-13/4 | Wt: 234 | 40: 4.77 | Arm: 323/8 | Hand: 87/8

Notes: Full name is Christopher Jakensly Johnson. Highly recruited Mississippi native who garnered Parade and U.S. Army All-American honors. Committed to the Rebels and then-head coach Houston Nutt. As a true

freshman in 2011, had 32 tackles, four for loss and one sack with one forced fumble in 11 games (three starts at defensive end). In '12, started 10-of-13 games at DE and registered 55-8-61/2 with one batted pass. In '13, managed 12-4-0 in four starts at DE before breaking his right ankle and undergoing season-ending surgery (granted medical hardship). Started 12-of-13 games at DE in '14 and totaled 38-8-4 with one batted pass. Moved to "Mike" linebacker in '15 and recorded 43-3-2 with one pass breakup, two interceptions and one forced fumble in 10 games (nine starts). Was suspended for the season opener against Tennessee-Martin (violation team rules) then had surgery to repair a torn left meniscus — was sidelined against New Mexico State and Memphis and did not start against Texas A&M. Two-year captain graduated with criminal justice degree. Opted not to bench press or run shuttles at the Combine and did not perform any jumps because of a groin injury.

Strengths: Good length. Generates some pop on contact. Flashes some strength in his hands to control blockers. Times up the blitz well and has a knack for piercing gaps. Has some pass-rush ability.

Weaknesses: Developing instincts — bites on play-action and takes time to digest what he sees. Takes choppy strides, plays too upright and is not explosive. Tied for the slowest 10-yard split (1.75 seconds) of any linebacker at the Combine, indicating marginal short-area burst. Also produced the slowest 20-yard shuttle (4.59 seconds) of any linebacker at the event.

Future: Converted defensive end with physical limitations that will be difficult to overcome in the pros. Camp body.

Draft projection: Free agent.

Scout's take: "(Johnson) is knock-kneed and pigeon-toed and coming off a knee injury too. I could possibly see him drafted in the late rounds. I didn't like him."

WLB DEION JONES, #45 (Sr-4)

LSU ▶ GRADE: 5.42

Ht: 6-07/8 | Wt: 222 | 40: 4.58 | Arm: 323/8 | Hand: 91/4

History: Nicknamed "Debo." Also played basketball for three years as a prep in Louisiana, where he was the 5A Outstanding Defensive Player despite tearing his left labrum. Was an impact special teams player his first three years in Baton Rouge. Recorded 23 tackles, three for loss and zero sacks in 2012 (13 games); 15-1-0 in in '13 (13 games); and 27-31/2-0 with one pass breakup in '14 (13 games, one start at Will). In the spring of

'15 had surgery to repair a stress fracture in his left leg. In the fall, stepped into the lineup and thrived at WLB under Kevin Steele. Was a finalist for the Butkus Award, as well as the Tigers' leading tackler and Defensive MVP — produced 100-131/2-5 with three pass break-ups, two interceptions (one touchdown) and one forced fumble. Was flagged for targeting against Auburn and suspended the first half of the Syracuse contest. Team captain. Opted not to run shuttles or bench press at the Combine.

Strengths: Outstanding athlete with excellent speed to close to the ball and make plays to the perimeter. Clocked among the fastest 40 times of any linebacker at the Combine and is explosive on contact. Aggressive filling downhill. Understands run fits and plays with surprising discipline (for a one-year starter) and toughness to take on blocks at the point of attack. Four-phase, core special teams contributor. Strong personal and football character. Unselfish team player.

Weaknesses: Measured the lighest (222 pounds) of any linebacker at the Combine and has a frame that will be maxed out at 230 pounds. Needs to add some bulk. Can do a better job of using his hands to disengage blocks. Still learning how to pick up crossers and cling in zone coverage. Will be overwhelmed at the point of attack in the pros. Only a one-year starter.

Future: A lean, productive, undersized, run-and-hit "Will" linebacker who made his senior season his best. Has the explosiveness to make an immediate impact on special teams in the pros. Best football is still several years aways. Has the physical tools to become an exceptional football player.

Draft projection: Second- to third-round pick.

Scout's take: "I know he is only a one-year guy, but all the guys that were playing in front of him are in the league now. Jones is fast and can really run. I liked him."

ILB **RAPHAEL KIRBY**, #56 (Sr-4)
MIAMI (FLA.) ▶ GRADE: 4.97
Ht: 6-0 1/4 | Wt: 236 | 40: 4.75e | Arm: 31 | Hand: 9 7/8

History: U.S. Army All-American out of Stone Mountain, Ga. As a true freshman in 2012, broke his right fibula during fall camp and missed the first five games. Was a reserve/special teams player, tallying 16 tackles, zero for loss and zero sacks in seven appearances while learning Mark D'Onofrio's 3-4 hybrid scheme. Was the backup middle linebacker in '13 when he collected 10-21/2-1 with one pass breakup. In '14, started all 13 games at weak-

side linebacker and produced 54-41/2-0 with one pass breakup, two interceptions and two forced fumbles. Started the first six games at MLB in '15 — managed 44-11/2-0 — before suffering a season-ending torn right ACL injury. Team captain. Was a medical exclusion from running or jumping at the Combine because of a right lower extremity injury.

Strengths: Good weight-room worker. Produced the most bench-press reps (27) of any inside linebacker at the Combine. Stood out on special teams early in career. Good football intelligence and competitiveness.

Weaknesses: Foot pounder with marginal speed to the perimeter. Takes bad angles and gets outflanked to the edge. Lacks physicality at the point of attack. Gets engulfed easily and struggles to come free vs. bigger blockers. Durability has been an issue with lower extremity issues that might linger given his lack of fluidity.

Future: A stiff, try-hard, run-and-chase overachiever coming off injury whose only chance to stick on a roster will be special teams.

Draft projection: Priority free agent.

ILB **NICK KWIATKOSKI**, #35 (Sr-5)
WEST VIRGINIA ▶ GRADE: 5.40
Ht: 6-2 | Wt: 243 | 40: 4.68 | Arm: 31 3/4 | Hand: 9 1/2

History: Prepped in Pennsylvania. Had surgery to repair a broken right wrist prior to his senior season then missed the first two months of the season because of a back injury. Redshirted in 2011. Sustained a concussion during '12 fall camp, and sat out the opener against Marshall. On the season, recorded 28 tackles, zero for loss and zero sacks in 12 games (one start at "Sam" in the Mountaineers' 3-3-5 defense). Started all 10 games played in '13 — nine at "Will," one at "Sam" — and produced 86-61/2-2 with three interceptions and two forced fumbles. Pulled his right hamstring against Maryland and missed two games. Started all 13 games at "Mike" in '14 and posted 103-111/2-1/2 with four pass breakups. Moved to "Sam" in '15 and was the Mountaineers' leading tackler for the third straight year — registered 86-10-3 with seven pass breakups, three interceptions and one forced fumble in the Mountaineers' 3-3-5. Team captain graduated with multidisciplinary studies degree.

Strengths: Very productive, experienced three-year starter. Outstanding effort and motor — is around the ball a lot. Plays with urgency. Triggers fast and accelerates quickly. Takes on blocks, sheds and makes plays in the hole. Fine eyes in zone coverage to read

LINEBACKERS

the quarterback, locate the nearest receiver entering his zone and pick up crossers. Good closing speed to the ball. Reliable tackler. Can carry tight ends down the seam. Good football intelligence. The game is very important to him. Versatile — was able to interchange between all linebacker positions. Solid Senior Bowl showing.

Weaknesses: Has short arms and some stiffness in his body. Can be engulfed by bigger blockers. Takes some questionable angles to the ball and gets outflanked to the perimeter by speed backs. Does not cover a lot of ground in zone drops.

Future: Versatile, active, highly competitive 'backer who fits a throwback mold. Brings the type of dependability and lunch-pail mentality valued in the middle of a defense. Ability to interchange between any LB spot in a "40" front will endear him to coaches. Minimally contributes as a 4-phase core special teamer as a rookie and has eventual starter potential.

Draft projection: Third- to fourth-round pick.

WLB DARRON LEE, #43 (Soph-3)
OHIO STATE ▶ GRADE: 5.72
Ht: 6-0 3/4 | Wt: 232 | 40: 4.48 | Arm: 33 1/4 | Hand: 9 3/4

History: Played cornerback and quarterback as an Ohio prep. Redshirted in 2013. Was deployed as a "walkout" (in the slot) linebacker in Ohio State's 4-3 over scheme. Started all 15 games in '14 and produced 81 tackles, 16 1/2 for loss and 7 1/2 sacks with three pass breakups, two interceptions and one forced fumble for the national champs. Started all 13 games in '15 and posted 66-11-41/2 with two pass breakups, one interception and two forced fumbles.

Strengths: Exceptional short-area burst, confirmed by the fastest 10-yard split (1.54 seconds) of any linebacker at the Combine). Also produced the longest broad jump (11-foot, 1-inch) of any linebacker, indicative of excellent lower-body explosion. Explosive, quick-twitched movement skill with the fluidity of a defensive back. Has loose hips. Effective getting skinny, timing up the snap and darting through gaps as a blitzer. Can keep stride with backs and slot receivers down the field and handle some slot receivers in man coverage.

Weaknesses: Undersized and plays small. Does not drive thru contact and lacks physicality supporting the run. Needs to do a better job of keeping his head on a swivel and show more awareness in space (see decleated vs. Il-

linois). Is too easily knocked off balance and controlled in tight quarters. Plays out of control and could stand to become a more secure tackler.

Future: An extremely athletic, finesse, run-and-hit weakside linebacker at his best flying around the field and maximizing his coverage ability in the slot. Was more impactful as sophomore than he was as a junior and has flashed enough playmaking ability to warrant early consideration for a fast-flowing defense predicated on speed.

Draft projection: Top-50 pick.

Scout's take: "Darron Lee is a safety. I want a guy like him that can play safety, nickel and 'Will' linebacker. You don't have to substitute to go to nickel on first and second down — that is where his value is. He's probably a luxury — he's going to be drafted too highly for where I would like to take him. He might get into the first round. His value is in the second."

OLB CORY LITTLETON, #42 (Sr-4)
WASHINGTON ▶ GRADE: 5.12
Ht: 6-3 1/8 | Wt: 238 | 40: 4.78 | Arm: 33 3/8 | Hand: 10 1/8

History: High school defensive end also played basketball as a California prep. Appeared in nine games as a true freshman in 2012, drawing two starts at rush end, and tallied 14 tackles, 11/2 for loss and zero sacks with one forced fumble. Had surgery after the season to repair a torn left labrum. Started all 13 games at rush end in '13 and produced 62-10-5 with two pass breakups and one forced fumble. Transitioned to a 3-4 outside linebacker role in '14 when he had 37-31/2-1 with two pass breakups and one forced fumble in 14 games (four starts). Started all 13 games in '15 and totaled 65-11-6 with two pass breakups. Opted not to bench press at the Combine.

Strengths: Ideal length. Good cover skills. Very good effort — chases down plays from behind. Fluid mover. Versatile and plays multiple alignments and has stood out on special teams, possession enough speed and hip flexibility to affect coverage teams.

Weaknesses: Lacks bulk in the lower body. Marginal functional strength to set the edge. Struggles to disengage from blocks. Recorded a 29 1/2-inch vertical jump, indicating average athletic ability. Has difficulty holding weight and played closer to 220 pounds as a senior.

Future: Could intrigue coaches with his triangle numbers on paper but will leave them wanting more on the field. Might fit best as a developmental "Sam" linebacker, though lacks physicality and play strength to consistently match up with tight ends on the line of scrimmage.

Draft projection: Late draftable pick.

Scout's take: "I saw him play man, zone, rush and even play in the slot. Even though he ran slower than the other linebacker there (Travis Feeney), I thought (Littleton) was more fluid."

MLB STEVE LONGA, #3 (Jr-4)

RUTGERS   ▶ GRADE: 5.08

Ht: 6-0 5/8 | Wt: 241 | 40: 4.74 | Arm: 32 | Hand: 9 3/4

History: New Jersey native. Redshirted in 2012. Started all 13 games at middle linebacker in '13 and registered 123 tackles, 71/2 for loss and three sacks with four pass breakups and two forced fumbles. Moved to the weak side in '14 and amassed 102-41/2-2 with one pass breakup and one forced fumble in 13 starts. In '15, started all 11 games played at WLB and notched 117-5-2 with two pass breakups and two forced fumbles. Sat out against Army (minor injury). Was the Scarlet Knights' leading tackler the last three seasons and was voted the team's defensive MVP twice.

Strengths: Outstanding career production. Fills fast and is around the ball a lot. Capable of manning short zones. Tough and will battle through injury. Experienced, three-year starter.

Weaknesses: Plays too narrow-based. Lacks striking power on contact. Allows blockers to get on top of him too quickly, gets caught in trash and struggles to disengage. Inconsistent eyes. Produced the slowest 60-yard shuttle (12.03 seconds) and 3-cone drill (7.52 seconds) of any linebacker at the Combine, indicative of marginal dynamic quickness. Straight-linish. Tight and tall in his pedal. Struggles to match up with tight ends in coverage.

Future: Very productive, undersized, run-and-hit "Mike" linebacker who profiles as a better college football player than potential pro. Needs to play in a "40" front to have a chance.

Draft projection: Priority free agent.

SLB-LOLB CURT MAGGITT, #56 (Sr-5)

TENNESSEE   ▶ GRADE: 5.18

Ht: 6-3 1/4 | Wt: 247 | 40: 4.75e | Arm: 33 | Hand: 10 1/8

History: Last name is pronounced "muh-JIT." High school defensive end out of Florida. Played through a torn left labrum in 2009 (had surgery after the season). As a true freshman, started 8-of-11 games played at strong-side linebacker and recorded 56 tackles, 51/2 for loss and one-half sack with one forced fumble. Sat out against South Carolina (calf). Had off-season shoulder surgery and was sidelined during '12 spring practice. In the fall, started all nine games played at SLB and managed 30-5-2 with one pass breakup and two forced fumbles. Played with turf toe on his right foot (sat out against Georgia State in Week Two), and tore his right ACL in Week 10. Redshirted in '13. Returned to start 10-of-13 games at SLB in '14 and collect 48-15-11 with one forced fumble. Had off-season surgery and sat out '15 spring practice. In '15, notched 7-3-0 in two starts before chipping a hip bone and missing the rest of the season. Graduated with a communications degree. Involved in an ongoing lawsuit against the University of Tennessee — admitted to punching a former teammate who aided a woman who was allegedly raped by Vols players.

Strengths: Looks the part with a well-built frame. Outstanding effort and motor — flies around the field and makes plays. Good instincts. Quick to trigger. Aggressive attacking downhill. Good strength at the point of attack. Explosive on contact with good knee bend. Flashes the ability to convert speed to power. Outstanding work ethic. Alpha leader.

Weaknesses: Very stiff hips. Durability is a concern, having been slowed by hip, knee, toe and multiple shoulder surgeries. Limited cover skills — too leggy and narrow-based. Loses phase when redirecting. Is not natural moving in reverse. Can be overly emotional and too much of a locker-room enforcer.

Future: Extremely tough, high-motor, productive edge rusher with enough core strength and power to eventually earn a starting job in the pros if he can find a way to stay healthy. A poor man's version of Cowboys DE Jeremy Mincey when he exited as a sixth-round pick of the Patriots in 2006.

Draft projection: Fifth- to sixth-round pick.

Scout's take: "(Maggitt) is tough. His injury was bad. It was a freak injury. He planted his foot and fractured his hip against Oklahoma. It was a non-contact injury. It was gross on tape. He's had a bunch of injuries because he is ultra-stiff."

ILB BLAKE MARTINEZ, #4 (Sr-4)

STANFORD   ▶ GRADE: 5.31

Ht: 6-1 5/8 | Wt: 237 | 40: 4.69 | Arm: 31 5/8 | Hand: 10

History: Also played basketball and volleyball as an Arizona prep. Saw limited action as a true freshman in 2012, scratching three tackles, zero for loss and zero sacks in 14 appearances.

LINEBACKERS

Played 10 games in '13 and collected 11-0-0 with one forced fumble and one interception. Missed four early-season contests after injuring himself in practice. Suffered a broken right collarbone in the offseason, but was healthy for the '14 season. Stepped into the lineup at inside linebacker and produced 102-7-41/2 with two pass breakups, three interceptions and three forced fumbles in 13 starts. Broke his left hand against UCLA in Week 12. Was the Cardinal's leading tackler for the second straight year in '15 when he piled up 141-61/2-11/2 with six pass breakups, one interception and one forced fumble in 14 starts. Was hobbled by an ankle injury leading up to the Pac-12 championship against USC. Team captain will graduate with a management science and engineering degree.

Strengths: Good instincts and anticipation. Shoots gaps when he triggers and plays downhill. Good motor and effort production. Uses his hands well to play off blocks and protect his legs. Good technician. Matches up well in coverage with tight ends and backs. Shows awareness in zone coverage. Has been a productive special teams performer. Outstanding personal and football character. Interviewed extremely well at the Combine.

Weaknesses: Lacks ideal arm length. Can be overaggressive at times overrunning the ball. Recorded a 28 1/2-inch vertical jump, indicative of below-average athletic ability. Can be beat to the outside and take some bad angles. Somewhat rigid and mechanical in his movement. Does not have elite speed to hit the corner.

Future: A smart, tough, productive overachiever who consistently found ways to overcome his athletic limitations and make plays. A better football player than athlete, Martinez can contribute immediately on special teams and serve as a multi-positional backup as a "Mike" and "Sam" linebacker. Compensates for his lack of fluidity with superb instincts and discipline. Does not always look pretty, but consistently grades out highly and gets the job done.

Draft projection: Fourth- to fifth-round pick.

Scout's take: "I think Martinez is the complete package. His production is high. He makes plays against the run and pass. I graded him as a (second-year starter) when I went through the school. I don't know what there is not to like. Stanford just does not play against smashmouth teams like Alabama, and he's not explosively fast, but he's fast enough. He's so smart, he will do well."

MLB TYLER MATAKEVICH, #8 (Sr-4)

TEMPLE ▶ GRADE: 5.31

Ht: 6-0 | Wt: 238 | 40: 4.78 | Arm: 311/4 | Hand: 91/2

History: Linebacker-running back also played baseball as a Connecticut prep. Missed the first half of his senior season with a broken right foot. Attended Milford Academy (Conn.). Manned weak-side linebacker for the Owls. Sustained a concussion during '12 fall camp, but played all 11 games (wore jersey No. 32), starting the final eight, and racked up 101 tackles, three for loss and zero sacks with three pass breakups and one forced fumble. Was given jersey No. 8 in '13, symbolic of his status as one of the toughest players on the team. Started all 12 games in '13 and piled up 137-111/2-1 with one interception and three forced fumbles. Started all 12 games in '14 and totaled 117-101/2-11/2 with three pass breakups, one interception and one safety. In '15, posted the best individual statistical season by an Owl defender in school history. Took home the Bednarik and Nagurski Awards, was named American Athletic Conference Defensive Player of the Year, was a finalist for the Lott IMPACT Trophy and Senior CLASS Award and became the first defensive player in school history to earn All-American honors. On the season, started all 13 games and registered 126-15-41/2 with five pass breakups and five interceptions. Was the only player in FBS to lead his team in tackles every week. Owns Temple's career tackles mark (493). Three-time captain graduated with a degree in adult and organizational development.

Strengths: Triggers instantly and consistently makes plays. Always around the ball — exceptional effort, hustle and pursuit production. Advanced eyes and anticipation — reads through the triangle (OG-C-RB), feels blocking schemes develop and beats pullers to the hole. Terrific instincts and career tackle production. Exceptional personal and football character — leads by example and vocally and challenges his teammates to improve. Showed noticeable improvement in coverage as a senior. Very humble, grounded, natural born leader — inclusive of everyone on the team, sets the tone in practice with his attitude and galvanizes the locker room. Football smart — knows where everyone lines up on the field and has played all three LB positions.

Weaknesses: Average athlete with short arms, small hands and a small-bone structure. Lacks the foot speed and length to match up with athletic tight ends in man coverage. Struggles to beat speed backs to the corner

LINEBACKERS

and can be out-leveraged to the sideline, arriving a half-step late or an arm's length too short to make a tackle, and his deficiencies will be magnified in a game of inches in the pros. Tied for the slowest 20-yard shuttle time (4.53 seconds) of any outside linebacker at the Combine, indicative of marginal lateral agility.

Future: An excellent college football player lacking ideal length and foot speed for the NFL game, Matakevich has the makeup of a 4-phase, core special teams player and functional, trustworthy spot backup. Can immediately add a spark to any special teams' coverage unit. Classic overachiever who will find a way to overcome all odds and contribute.

Draft projection: Fourth- to fifth-round pick.

ILB-DE CASSANOVA McKINZY, #8 (Sr-4)
AUBURN   ▶ GRADE: 5.05
Ht: 6-1 | Wt: 248 | 40: 4.90e | Arm: 31 1/4 | Hand: 9 7/8

History: Birmingham native. Played eight games as a true freshman in 2012 (drew one start at middle linebacker), and recorded 23 tackles, one-half for loss and zero sacks with one forced fumble. Injured his right ankle against Georgia and missed the final two games. Started all 14 games at weak-side linebacker in '13 and was the Tigers' leading tackler — produced 75-8-2 with one pass breakup and one interception. Started 12-of-13 games at middle linebacker in '14 and racked up 91-11-11/2 with one interception and one forced fumble. Sustained a concussion against Louisiana Tech and did not start against LSU. In '15, started 10-of-13 games — two at linebacker before transitioning to "Buck" (hybrid defensive end/linebacker) — and notched 74-10-5 with one pass breakup and one forced fumble. Was benched against Mississippi State along with two other starters following disappointing effort in loss to LSU. Sprained his right knee in the Birmingham Bowl against Memphis. Played for three defensive coordinators in four years. Graduated with a public administration degree. Did not work out at the Combine because of a hamstring injury.

Strengths: Three-year starter. Very good bulk and take-on strength to fill on inside runs and knock back blockers. Times up blitzes, stunts and loops and can convert speed to power and flush the pocket. Good closing speed to the ball.

Weaknesses: Lacks ideal height and arm length. Very tight-hipped with too much stiffness in his body to re-direct or move in reverse without standing tall. Near liability in coverage — rarely used in man coverage and lacks fluidity to be effective in zones. Limited bend

off the edge. Overaggressive biting on play-action. Takes some questionable angles undercutting blocks and could stand to be more disciplined. Inconsistent motor.

Future: A strong, physical, downhill "Mike" 'backer with stiffness in his body that could make it difficult to stay healthy in the pros. Could compete for a job as a two-position backup as a "Mike" and "Sam", though may not be fluid enough to break down in the open field and contribute on special teams.

Draft projection: Priority free agent.

Scout's take: "He's stiff and can't run."

MLB ANTONIO MORRISON, #3 (Sr-4)
FLORIDA   ▶ GRADE: 5.29
Ht: 6-1 | Wt: 232 | 40: 4.75e | Arm: 9 3/8 | Hand: 9

History: Won a state championship and was a USA Today All-American at Bolingbrook (Ill.) High. Missed the state title game his senior year because of a Jones fracture in his left foot. As a true freshman in 2012, backed up Dolphins 2013 third-rounder Jelani Jenkins at 3-4 "Will" linebacker — recorded 34 tackles, two for loss and one sack with one forced fumble in 13 games (four starts). Was arrested in June '13 after punching a nightclub bouncer then arrested again in July for barking at a police dog. Charges were dropped after both incidents, but Morrison served a one-game suspension against Toledo. On the season, moved to the "Mike" and started 7-of-8 games, notching 56-1-0. Was sidelined the last three games with a torn right meniscus. Transitioned to a 4-3 scheme in '14 when he started all 12 games (11 at "Will," one at "Mike") and posted 101-6-1 with one pass breakup, one interception and one forced fumble. Tore his left ACL in the Gators' Birmingham bowl game on January 3, 2015 against East Carolina, but was back at 100 percent for the '15 season. Solidified the "Mike" 'backer spot and led Gators tacklers by amassing 103-12-21/2 with one pass breakup and one forced fumble. Had four defensive coordinators/co-defensive coordinators in four years. Graduated with criminology degree. Did not attend the Combine because of an infection from a medical procedure that was performed immediately following the Senior Bowl to alleviate minor knee discomfort involving the screws that had been previously inserted into his long-healed ACL.

Strengths: Experienced three-year starter. Plays with physicality and drives through ballcarriers. Strong tackler. Aggressive taking on blocks. Extremely competitive. Very good instincts. Attacks downhill. Plays with natural

LINEBACKERS

leverage. Surprisingly strong at the point of attack. Alpha locker room leader — plays with supreme confidence and carries a swagger. Outstanding work habits — lives in the facility and has a passion for the game.

Weaknesses: Small-framed with short arms. Can be engulfed by big blockers if they get their hands on him. Has some deficiencies in coverage, lacking ideal length and foot speed to match up with tight ends in man coverage. Marginal coverage production. Durability is a concern, as he did not play at full health after amazingly being ready for the season nine months after tearing his ACL, and knee injury must clear medically after suffering setbacks following the Senior Bowl.

Future: Undersized, hard-hitting middle 'backer who could be most ideal as a weak-side linebacker in a 4-3 front or on the inside as a "Jack" linebacker in a traditional 3-4 front where he would be protected and free to roam. Has the wiring to become a great pro. However, medical evaluations could have a significant impact on Morrison's draft status and longevity and could even potentially leave him undrafted.

Draft projection: Fourth- to fifth-round pick.

Coach's take: "Because he's an honest person, you may not like what he says, but he's up front and honest. A lot of people don't want to hear the truth. Antonio is that type of guy, but he's going to hold himself accountable, too. When he knows he's screwing up, he tells you he's screwing up. He'll apologize and say, 'Fellas, this was on me. I didn't do right. Don't let me go down the ropes like somebody else. Hold me accountable the same.' That's the greatest thing about Antonio. He's the pulse of the team because he's honest." – *Florida LB coach Randy Shannon*

OLB-DRE-PRS DADI NICOLAS, #90 (Sr-5)
VIRGINIA TECH ▶ GRADE: 5.38
Ht: 6-2 7/8 | Wt: 235 | 40: 4.71 | Arm: 34 3/4 | Hand: 10 3/8

History: First name is pronounced "Daddy." Born in Haiti. Prepped in Florida, where he was primarily a basketball player — played just one year of high school football. Redshirted in 2011. Was arrested in late June '12 — was charged with second-degree larceny stemming from a stolen bike on campus. Was suspended for two months before being reinstated to the team after pleading not guilty and receiving a deferred disposition plus 125 hours of community service. On the season, appeared in 12 games and tallied 17 tackles, 3 1/2 tackles for loss and two sacks with one batted pass and one forced fumble. Played all 13 games in '13, drawing on start at defensive end, and

recorded 32-7-4 with three batted passes and one interception. Stepped into the lineup in '14 when he started all 13 games at DE and produced 72-18 1/2-9 with one batted pass and two blocked kicks. In '15, started 12-of-13 games and totaled 45-7-21/2 with two batted passes and two forced fumbles despite being impaired by a broken finger on his left hand and jammed fingers on his right hand. Was suspended for the first half of the Virginia contest — against North Carolina, was called for offsides, then angrily slapped the arm of the referee while he was announcing the penalty. Graduated with a sociology degree.

Strengths: Has exceptional arm length. Recorded the most explosive vertical jump (41 inches) of any defensive lineman at the Combine, indicative of outstanding lower-body explosion and burst. Natural bender with good balance and body control. Very athletic. Good closing speed. Can be consistently disruptive. Produced a 7.04-second 3-cone drill time, indicative of very good body control and agility.

Weaknesses: Lacks bulk and bulk strength and too easily can be overmatched and pinballed defending the run. Produced the fewest bench-press reps (14) of any pass rusher at the Combine. Not comfortable moving in reverse. Is late to react to what he sees — eyes and instincts are still being honed. Durability is a concern.

Future: Sack production slipped heavily as a senior playing through multiple hand injuries as well as lining up as a five-technique in base packages, where he was out of position and not expected to heavily rush the passer. Still a better athlete than football player at this stage of his development. Compares in some ways to Chicago Bears 2006 fifth-round pick Mark Anderson exiting Alabama and could be most ideally suited for a situational nickel pass-rush role initially. Could also warrant looks as a developmental outside linebacker in a "30" front, with unique explosion to rush the passer. Evaluators need to revisit late 2014 film to fully appreciate Nicolas' talents.

Draft projection: Fourth- to fifth-round pick.

Scout's take: "He was playing with one broken hand and one ligament messed up in the other. How do you rush the passer without using your hands."

ROLB-DRE YANNICK NGAKOUE, #7 (Jr-3)
MARYLAND ▶ GRADE: 5.52
Ht: 6-2 | Wt: 252 | 40: 4.72 | Arm: 32 1/2 | Hand: 9 1/2

History: Name is pronounced "Ya-neek Ingah-kway." Parade All-American and Gatorade Player of the Year in Maryland. Provided depth at outside linebacker as a true freshman in 2013 when he collected 10 tackles, 4 1/2 tackles for loss and two sacks with one batted pass, one interception and one forced fumble in 13 appearances. In '14, started 11-of-13 games as a 3-4 outside linebacker and produced 37-13 1/2-6 with two batted passes. Was deployed as a 4-3 defensive end in '15 when he set the Maryland single-season sacks record — started 11-of-12 games and produced 38-15-13 1/2 with one batted pass and one forced fumble. Was banged up and limited against Rutgers, his lone non-start.

Strengths: Looks the part with a well-defined musculature. Comes out of the blocks low and presents a small target. Explosive hip snap to take on and rip through blocks. Bench-pressed 225 pounds 26 times, and plays with good grip strength to control and steer blockers. Outstanding motor. Good hand use — fine swim, up-and-under and stutter bull-rush moves. Flashes ability to convert speed to power with jolt in his punch. Highly motivated and driven to succeed. Very good sack production.

Weaknesses: Lacks ideal height and length. Very tight in the hips, leading to missed tackles in the open field. Too often leaves his feet on contact and does not drive through tackles. Could do a better job of anchoring against the run and developing more counter moves as a pass-rusher.

Future: Strong power-leverage rusher who looks destined for an aggressive odd front such as the Steelers, Ravens or Colts. Could factor readily on third downs with the ability to evolve into a solid, every-down starter with continued refinement.

Draft projection: Third- to fourth-round pick.

ILB JARED NORRIS, #41 (Sr-5)

UTAH　　　　　▶ GRADE: 5.19

Ht: 6-1 1/4 | Wt: 241 | 40: 4.83 | Arm: 31 1/2 | Hand: 10 1/8

History: Prepped in California. Redshirted in 2011. Saw very limited action in seven games in '12, scratching two tackles, zero for loss and zero sacks. Had arthroscopic surgery on his right wrist in the spring of '13. Teamed with Gionni Paul in Utah's 4-2-5 scheme. Started 7-of-10 games in the fall — first two at "Rover," five at "Mac" — and was credited with 64-4 1/2-2 with two pass breakups and two forced fumbles. Sustained a concussion against Arizona State, which rendered him a non-factor the final three games. Started all 13 games at "Rover" in '14 and racked up 116-13-4 with one pass breakup. Started all 12 games played at "Mac" 'backer in '15 and totaled 87-6 1/2-1 with five pass breakups and

two forced fumbles. Did not play against USC (undisclosed injury). Team captain graduated with economics degree. Opted not to run the 3-cone drill at the Combine.

Strengths: Active and energetic. Plays with intensity and has very good pursuit production. Very competitive and will sacrifice his body coming downhill to take on isolation-lead blocks. Matches up well with tight ends in coverage. Is physically tough and will battle through injuries.

Weaknesses: Naturally small-framed with a narrow bone structure and is tied for the smallest hands of any player at the Combine. Has short arms and struggles to disengage from blocks. Average athlete with a 29 1/2-inch vertical jump. Has some tightness in movement. Durability could be an issue given thin frame. Production dipped heavily as a senior.

Future: Good-sized, 'backer ideally suited to play inside. Could warrant looks as a two-position backup in a "40" front, with the ability to function as a "Sam" 'backer. An accomplished overachiever with a special teams temperament.

Draft projection: Fifth- to sixth-round pick.

Scout's take: "(Norris) came into the season with a lot of hype. I guess there's a lot of West Coast (scouts) reading his stat lines. He has some straight-line speed, but I did not see any other redeemable traits."

LOLB-DE VICTOR OCHI, #91 (Sr-5)

STONY BROOK　　　　　▶ GRADE: 5.21

Ht: 6-1 1/8 | Wt: 246 | 40: 4.87 | Arm: 33 3/4 | Hand: 10 1/8

History: Last name is pronounced "O-Chee." Lived in Nigeria from age nine to 12 before prepping in New York, where he also ran track. Redshirted in 2011. Played all 13 games in '12, drawing five starts at defensive end, and recorded 45 tackles, 7 1/2 for loss and three sacks. Started 9-of-11 games played at DE and tallied 33-10-5 1/2 with one forced fumble. Started all 11 games played at DE in '14 and notched 57-16 1/2-11 with two forced fumbles. Sat out against Rhode Island (high left ankle sprain). Sat out '15 spring practice while nursing a torn right labrum. Was the Colonial Athletic Association Co-Defensive Player of the Year after registering 47-16 1/2-13 with one forced fumble. Owns Stony Brook's career records for sacks (32.5) and tackles for loss (49). Team captain graduated with a health science degree. Did not bench press at the Combine because of a left pectoral injury. Voted a captain by teammates at the East-West Shrine game.

Strengths: Good arm length and functional playing strength. Plays bigger than his size

LINEBACKERS

and can anchor down in the run game and set a hard edge. Very active hands to control and shed blockers. Outstanding effort and tenacity. Good job anticipating the snap. Dominated lesser competition in college and stood out during the East-West Shrine practices, where he consistently outmatched blockers in one-on-one drills and made plays in the game. Experienced, four-year starter. Strong vocal leader. Outstanding career production. The game is very important to him.

Weaknesses: Mechanical mover with tight hips, even more noticeable stumbling during drills at the Combine. Recorded the slowest 10-yard split (2.10 seconds) of any player at the Combine, indicative of marginal short-area burst. Lacks ideal take-off speed to win at the snap. Was not asked to drop into coverage much and lacks the hip flexibility desired for zone drops. Lacks the speed and fluidity desired on special teams. Has run into some trouble off the field[RP2] and could require some maintenance.

Future: Tough, relentless, high-motor power rusher with a terrific football temperament. Could contribute readily as a situational pass rusher and has the strength, physicality and competitiveness to emerge as an eventual starter if he stays focused. Will require some time to acclimate to the speed and sophistication of the NFL game.

Draft projection: Fifth- to sixth-round pick.

Coach's take: "(Ochi) came in as an undersized, athletic kid who had somewhat limited football experience, and he's developed himself off the field physically, has learned the game, has paid a price, plays on the field at 100 percent, and he loves the game. The scouts say he's going to be a hybrid outside linebacker in a 3-4 who can pass rush. Every team has been here multiple times. He plays as fast on every play than anybody I've ever seen on the playing field that I've competed against or coached. There is a focus to it and there is a talent level that he has. He works very hard." (Newsday) — Stony Brook Head Coach Chuck Priore

WLB-SS DARRELL "MONTESE" OVERTON, #51 (Sr-5)

EAST CAROLINA ▶ GRADE: 5.08

Ht: 6-1 3/4 | Wt: 223 | 40: 4.56 | Arm: 32 3/4 | Hand: 9 1/2

History: First name is pronounced "monn-TEECE." North Carolina native. Redshirted in 2011. Played "Sam" linebacker in the Pirates' 3-4 defense. Sustained a concussion during '12 fall camp and did not play in the season opener against Appalachian State. On the season, recorded 29 tackles, 3 1/2 for loss and one sack

with one pass breakup and a 16-yard fumble recovery touchdown in eight games (three starts). Missed five games and was limited in two others the second half of the season because of a left MCL sprain. Was a backup/special teams player in '13 but played significant snaps — totaled 50-10 1/2-6 with two pass breakups and two forced fumbles. Stepped into the lineup and started all 13 games in '14 and produced 68-11 1/2-3 with four pass breakups. Started 11-of-12 games in '15 and totaled 70-10-71/2 with seven pass breakups. Did not start against Central Florida (disciplinary). Graduated with a degree in criminal justice. Will turn 25 during his rookie season.

Strengths: Outstanding straight-line speed. Very strong pound-for-pound. Throws his body around and chases hard to the outside and strings out perimeter runs. Covers a lot of ground. Excelled on special teams coverage earlier in career.

Weaknesses: Thin-legged with skinny ankles and a narrow bone structure that is nearly maxed out. Lacks strength and physicality and can be run at and overwhelmed at the point of attack. Can do a better job of shedding blocks. Lacks awareness in zone coverage. Freelances too much and disappears for stretches. Plays out of control. Marginal 20-yard shuttle time (4.47 seconds), indicating average lateral agility. Overaged.

Future: A tight-hipped, straight-linish athlete who lacked the bulk to hold up against the run, Overton was not ideally suited for the Pirates' 3-4 front and would be better suited playing on the weak side in a "40" front. Could even warrant some interest as a box safety. Special teams will have to be his ticket.

Draft projection: Priority free agent.

ILB GIONNI PAUL, #13 (Sr-5)

UTAH ▶ GRADE: 4.89

Ht: 5-10 1/8 | Wt: 231 | 40: 5.06 | Arm: 31 | Hand: 8 1/8

History: First name is pronounced "gee-ah-nee." Has a daughter named Skylar. Prepped in Florida, and began his college career at Miami (Fla.). As a true freshman in 2011 (wore jersey No. 36), notched four tackles, zero for loss and zero sacks in seven appearances. Started 7-of-10 games at outside linebacker in '12, recording 61-31/2-0 with two pass breakups and one forced fumble. Missed the first two games because of a hyperextended left knee, and was suspended against Florida State after he was late to a team meeting. Transferred to Utah and sat out '13 per NCAA rules. In the spring of '14, suffered a Lisfranc fracture in his left foot that delayed his debut until Week Three. Teamed with Jared Norris in the Utes' 4-2-5 scheme — started 7-of-8 games at the "Mac" linebacker and posted 61-3-1 with one pass breakup and four interceptions. The foot injury flared again in November, requiring surgery that sidelined him the final three games. Was the Utes' leading tackler in '15 when he started all 13 games and piled up 117-131/2-3 with three pass breakups, four interceptions and two forced fumbles from the "Rover" position. Also had a 54-yard fumble recovery touchdown. Team captain obtained two bachelor's degrees in sociology and economics. Opted not to perform the 3-cone drill at the Combine.

Strengths: Good pop and explosion. Plays with natural leverage and can surprisingly jolt big blockers off their feet. Good instincts and anticipation — made a lot of plays. Outstanding production. High-energy, vocal leader.

Weaknesses: Marginal size. Has very small hands and short arms. Struggles to disengage when blockers get their hands on him. Heavy-footed. Recorded the slowest 40-yard time (5.10 seconds) of any linebacker at the Combine. Wore down late in the season. Needs to become more accountable. Has a history of foot injuries.

Future: Stocky, strong, run-and-hit 'backer with size-speed deficiencies that needed to be covered up in college and would be exposed in the pros. Could add a lot of energy to a locker room if he could earn a spot on special teams, though lack of foot speed could be very restricting.

Draft projection: Priority free agent.

SLB JOSHUA PERRY, #37 (Sr-4)

OHIO STATE ▶ GRADE: 5.47
Ht: 6-3 3/4 | Wt: 254 | 40: 4.63 | Arm: 33 7/8 | Hand: 10

History: Ohio native. Primarily a special teams player in 2012 when he collected five tackles, zero for loss and zero sacks in 10 appearances. Played in an odd front in '13 — started 10-of-14 games (seven at "Sam" linebacker, final three at "Mike") and contributed 64-2-1 with two pass breakups. Sustained a concussion against Illinois. Was the "Will" linebacker in the Buckeyes' 4-3 over scheme the last two seasons. In '14, led the team in tackles by producing 124-81/2-3 with two pass breakups and one forced fumble. Lone non-start was the season opener against Navy, as he shared reps in the middle with Curtis Grant in a unique game plan designed specifically for the Mids' triple-option offense. Started all 13 games in '15 and totaled 71-1/2-0

with three pass breakups, three interceptions and one blocked kick. Sprained his right ankle early in the Penn State contest. Team captain graduated with degree in consumer and family financial services. Was recognized as an AFCA Good Works Team member. Did not play in the Senior Bowl (groin). Did not perform the shuttles at the Combine because of a left hamstring injury.

Strengths: Exceptional size and length. Experienced three-year starter. Strong, knockback hitter and reliable tackler. Extremely smart and football smart. Very good closing speed. Plays with physicality at the line of scrimmage and matches up well against tight ends in the run game. Alert in coverage. Very good weight-room work habits and presence on the field. Outstanding personal and football character. Has been durable and not missed any time.

Weaknesses: Has some tightness in his body and plays a bit upright, allowing blockers to gain inside positioning. Tends to be a tick late to trigger. Could stand to do a better job of using his hands to disengage. Average lateral agility.

Future: Exceptionally-sized, well-proportioned strong-side linebacker with the size, speed, secure tackling and football smarts to command the interest of defenses that place a premium on versatility and intelligence such as the Patriots and Eagles.

Draft projection: Third- to fourth-round pick.

Scout's take: "I graded Perry in the fifth round. He's a smart player. I don't think he is a naturally tough guy, but he has some production against a high level of competition. I might have been a little low on him grading him as a 'Sam'. It's become like a fullback to me in some ways. You better be able to rush the passer on third down to hold value at that position."

LOLB-DLE D.J. PETTWAY, #57 (Sr-5)

ALABAMA ▶ GRADE: 4.97
Ht: 6-2 1/8 | Wt: 265 | 40: 4.97 | Arm: 32 1/4 | Hand: 9 1/2

History: Prepped in Florida. Redshirted in 2011. Record eight tackles, four for loss and 21/2 sacks in 13 appearances in '12. Was dismissed from the team for his involvement in a February '13 robbery (drove teammates away from the scene of the crime). Played at East Mississippi Community College that year, logging 47-181/2-111/2 with one batted pass and one forced fumble. Had his right knee scoped after the season. Returned to Alabama in '14 — head coach Nick Saban vehemently defended Pettway's right to a second chance — and chipped in 23-3-2 with three batted passes in

LINEBACKERS

14 games (one start at defensive end). A situational pass rusher for the Tide in '15, Pettway notched 18-5-2 with two batted passes and two blocked kicks, including a field goal attempt in the national championship game against Clemson. Graduated in 31/2 years with a health and environmental sciences degree.

Strengths: Very tough and aggressive. Good lower-body strength. Strikes with power in his hands and can occupy and control blockers. Very good effort. Solid base anchor strength to defend the run at him.

Weaknesses: Limited foot speed and agility — labors to change direction, as confirmed with a 7.76-second 3-cone drill time. Lacks ideal length and gets stuck to blocks. Only bench-pressed 225 pounds 17 times at the Combine and recorded a 28-inch vertical jump. Overmatched against double teams. Marginal career production. Has never been a full-time starter. Limited special teams value.

Future: A big-bodied, stiff, heavy-footed base end who capably defends the run, but lacks pass-rush ability. Could find a role as a two-down, run defender in a "30" front.

Draft projection: Priority free agent.

ILB-OLB REGGIE RAGLAND, #19 (Sr-4)
ALABAMA ▶ GRADE: 6.30
Ht: 6-11/4 | Wt: 247 | 40: 4.66 | Arm: 32 | Hand: 9 7/8

History: Alabama native won a basketball state championship and was the No. 1 inside linebacker recruit in the country. Was a reserve/special teams player in 2012 when he was credited with eight tackles, zero for loss and zero sacks with one forced fumble in 11 appearances. Missed three September contests while nursing a right ankle sprain. In '13, logged 17-1/2-0 in 13 appearances, as his 11 special teams tackles were tops on the team. After backing up Ravens '14 first-rounder C.J. Mosley, Ragland stepped into the lineup at the "Will" linebacker in Alabama's 3-4 defense — started 13-of-14 games in '14 and produced 95-101/2-11/2 with one forced fumble, three pass breakups and one interception. Did not start against Southern Miss (Tide opened in dime package). Broke his left hand and had surgery prior to the LSU contest and sustained a concussion in the national championship against Ohio State. In '15, moved to the "Mike" and was named Southeastern Conference Defensive Player of the Year — led the team in tackles by registering 102-61/2-21/2 with seven pass breakups and two forced fumbles. Also was a finalist for the Bednarik, Nagurski and Butkus awards. Team captain

graduated with a degree in consumer affairs. Did not bench press at the Combine because of a right shoulder injury and opted out of the 3-cone drill because of cramping.

Strengths: Exceptional size and body thickness. Strong, physical, drive-thru tackler with knockback power in his body. Plays big in a big man's game and can stop isolation/lead blockers head on in their tracks. Packs a punch and sets the tone for the defense. Good instincts. Plays square to the line of scrimmage and is quick to trigger. Very athletic movement skill for as big as he is and can keep stride with tight ends in man coverage. Very secure tackler with great playing range. Studies the game. Versatile and can play multiple positions, showing that he could come off the edge and win some one-on-one battles against big bodies at the Senior Bowl. Strong personal and football character.

Weaknesses: Weight has tended to fluctuate throughout college and needs to be monitored — played at 265 pounds as a sophomore and has pushed close to 270. Lacks elite man cover skills and is much more natural moving forward than he is in reverse. A bit high-cut with some tightness in his hips and is not as productive making plays in space. Will need to hone his feet in zone drops.

Future: A big, strong, fast, athletic, instinctive 'Mike' linebacker who stands in a class of his own in this year's draft among true middle linebackers, Ragland has the skill set to make an immediate impact in the pros. However, it took some time to acclimate in college and might require an adjustment period in the NFL to transition to a complex system. Shed 12 pounds from the Senior Bowl to the Combine and has enough athletic talent to play any linebacker position, though is most natural in the middle.

Draft projection: Top-20 pick.

Scout's take: "Ragland is a full-grown man. When he hits people, he drops them. He is big and athletic. You should see him covering running backs and tight ends. I saw him lined up on the slot once. When it comes to physical traits, he has it all."

OLB JOE SCHOBERT, #58 (Sr-4)
WISCONSIN ▶ GRADE: 5.14
Ht: 6-13/8 | Wt: 244 | 40: 4.69 | Arm: 311/2 | Hand: 9 3/4

History: Last name is pronounced "SHOW-bert." Safety-running back who won a state championship as a prep in Wisconsin, where he also competed in basketball, baseball and track and field. Accepted a preferred walk-on invitation from then-head coach Bret Bielema. As a true freshman in 2012, saw limited action in five games without recording any stats. Was deployed as an outside linebacker in Dave Aranda's 3-4 scheme. Earned his scholarship in '13 — played all 13 games (one start) and collected 24 tackles, 21/2 for loss and one sack with three pass breakups. Started all 27 games the next two seasons — totaled 69-131/2-3 with seven pass breakups and two forced fumbles in '14; and 79-191/2-91/2 with two pass breakups, one interception and five forced fumbles in '15. Was named Big Ten Linebacker of the Year and the Badgers' MVP.

Strengths: Produced the fastest 60-yard shuttle (11.59 seconds) of any linebacker at the Combine, indicative of superb dynamic quickness. Good balance and body control. Outstanding disruptive production — keeps working to the quarterback and gives great second- and third-effort. Smart, disciplined and assignment-sound. Has special teams coverage ability.

Weaknesses: Has very short arms with a maxed-out, manufactured frame. Lacks ideal bulk and base strength to set the edge with authority — gets overwhelmed and moved off spots by big-bodied blockers. Lacks variety in pass-rush arsenal — does not have a plan and much of his production is schemed. Struggles to come to balance in the open field and secure tackles — misses too many tackles in space. Limited range in coverage.

Future: A high-effort, short-armed, outside leverage rusher ideally suited for a backup and special teams role in the pros. Could warrant an opportunity as a developmental rush linebacker for a team such as the Ravens or Steelers and make an immediate impact on special teams.

Draft projection: Late draftable pick.

Scout's take: "Schobert is real tight skinned. He has no pop to him. He's undersized. He gets engulfed a lot. I wasn't a fan when I went through the school. I didn't give him a draftable grade. Where do you play him?"

WLB JAYLON SMITH, #9 (Jr-3)

NOTRE DAME ▶ GRADE: 6.20

Ht: 6-2 | Wt: 223 | 40: 4.60e | Arm: 33 | Hand: 91/2

History: Brother, Rod, is a running back with the Cowboys. Jaylon was a linebacker-running back who won four Indiana state titles, was named Mr. Football and played basketball for three years. Consensus All-American and high school Butkus Award winner was rated the top outside linebacker recruit in the country before making an immediate impact. Became the first true freshman ND linebacker to start from Day One since 1995. In 2013, was deployed as a "Dog" (outside) linebacker in Bob Diaco's 3-4 scheme — started all 13 games and produced 67 tackles, 61/2 for loss and zero sacks with three pass breakups, one interception and one forced fumble. As a sophomore, transitioned to "Will" linebacker in Brian VanGorder's 4-3 scheme. Started all 13 games in '14 and registered 112-9-31/2 with two pass breakups and one forced fumble. In '15, took home the Butkus Award after leading the Irish in tackles for the second straight season — piled up 114-9-1 with five pass breakups and one forced fumble in 13 starts. Tore his left ACL and MCL in the Fiesta Bowl against Ohio State. Had reconstructive surgery in January, and subsequent Combine medical examination revealed nerve damage which could jeopardize his rookie season. Reportedly has a $5 million loss of value insurance policy which pays $700k if he doesn't get drafted in the first round and $100k per pick thereafter. Team captain. Was a medical exclusion at the Combine.

Strengths: Prior to Fiesta Bowl injury, was an exceptional athlete with terrific closing speed. Instinctive locating the football. Very good hip flexibility and fluidity in his movement. Explosive hitter. Makes plays all over the field. Clears his feet easily through trash. Moves as well in reverse as he does going forward. Can come off spots in coverage and close in a heartbeat. Shows good anticipation in coverage with the burst, twitch and transitional quickness to stay on the hip of tight ends, back and even receivers. Effective blitzer who can get to an edge and knife through the backfield. Outstanding production.

Weaknesses: Very light-framed and narrowly built. Not a strong take-on player. Lacks playing strength and needs to add more bulk to his slight frame. Needs to do a better job of securing tackles in space — overruns the ball at times. Did not make the defensive calls, needs some help getting lined up at times and could be challenged by overly complex defenses. Is often a tick late to react to what he sees and eyes are still developing. Freelances and does not always play within the scheme. Only has 4 percent body fat and could use more meat on his body to withstand the physicality of the NFL game. Long-term durability must be considered following the type of knee injury that can be career-ending. Not a take-charge leader at a position where teammates are looking to him for leadership.

Future: A very lean, fluid-moving, extreme-

LINEBACKERS

ly athletic playmaker with speed to make plays at every level of the field and contribute in all phases — as an aggressive run defender, pass rusher/blitzer and coverage defender. Has the athletic skill set to interchange between any of the three LB positions in a "40" front and could be equally effective in a "30" front most ideally as a "Jack" linebacker where he can scrape fast to the ball and accentuate his speed and playmaking ability.Was projected as a top-10 cinch prior to injury and could considerably based on medical evaluations.

Draft projection: First-round pick.

Scout's take: "The big question with him is whether the knee injury is going to be career-threatening. Our doctors will sort through that. …It started giving me flashbacks to that movie, 'The Program,' where Alvin Mack tears up his leg when he would have been the top pick in the draft. … There were scouts in our room that graded him as the top pick in the draft. He is very talented. The medical (evaluation) is going to knock him down. The question is where the risk meets the reward. Somewhere in the middle of the first round, I expect the value is going to be too great for a team not to take a chance."

ILB TERRANCE SMITH, #24 (Sr-5)
FLORIDA STATE ▶ GRADE: 5.19
Ht: 6-2 7/8 | Wt: 235 | 40: 4.71 | Arm: 32 3/4 | Hand: 9 7/8

History: Father, Terry, was a standout at Clemson, but was killed tragically when Terrance was four. Cousin of Texans All-Pro receiver DeAndre Hopkins. Terrance also competed in track and field as a Georgia prep. Arrived in the program under 200 pounds and appeared in two games in 2011, but took a medical hardship. Was a reserve/special teams player in '12 when he cobbled together nine tackles, 11/2 for loss and zero sacks in 13 appearances. Played all 14 games in '13, starting at "Mike" linebacker from Week Five on — produced 59-21/2-2 with three pass break-ups and one interception. Dealt with a left turf toe injury during '14 spring practice. On the season, started 10-of-12 games played at weak-side linebacker and totaled 87-41/2-1 with one pass breakup, two interceptions and two forced fumbles. Was suspended against Wake Forest (violation team rules), did not play against Louisville (pectoral strain) and played with a sprained right MCL the final two games (non-starts). In '15, managed 66-41/2-1 with one forced fumble in nine starts at WLB. Missed four October contests while nursing a high right ankle sprain. Hurt his hamstring in

the East-West Shrine Game. Graduated with a social science degree. Did not run the 3-cone drill at the Combine because of a left hamstring injury.

Strengths: Experienced, three-year starter. Good speed and playing range. Efficient slipping/avoiding blocks. Rangy and athletic enough to make plays to the perimeter. Good chase speed. Fine balance and body control. Fluid enough to carry tight ends down the field in man coverage. Has NFL pedigree.

Weaknesses: Average instincts. Not aggressive stepping downhill. Plays too passively — too many tackles are made downfield. Marginal strength at the point of attack. Effort runs hot and cold. Does not show much awareness in coverage — marginal ball skills. Lacks discipline. Has a narrow frame that is close to being maxed out. Durability has been a consistent issue throughout his career.

Future: A lanky, athletic 'backer who lined up inside for a 3-4 front and could potentially fit even better on the weak side for a "40" front. Underachiever tendencies will need to be eliminated to maximize his pro potential. Durability issues could linger and may affect his draft standing.

Draft projection: Fifth- to sixth-round pick.

ROLB-DRE NOAH SPENCE, #9 (Sr-4)
EASTERN KENTUCKY ▶ GRADE: 5.72
Ht: 6-2 1/2 | Wt: 251 | 40: 4.84 | Arm: 33 | Hand: 10 3/4

History: Was a Parade All-American, Pennsylvania's Gatorade Player of the Year and a five-star recruit coming out of high school. Began his college career at Ohio State, where he wore jersey No. 8. As a true freshman in 2012, contributed 12 tackles, one for loss and one sack with one batted pass in 11 appearances. Did not play against Michigan State. Started all 13 games played at defensive end in '13, producing 52-141/2-8 with two batted passes and one forced fumble. Tested positive for ecstasy and was suspended for the Orange Bowl and first two games of the '14 season. Tested positive again in September, at which point he was permanently banned by the Big Ten. Reportedly was scared straight and made a concerted effort to change his life. Attended a drug-treatment program at OSU — four hours per night, four days per week — through the end of October, ditched bad influences and opted against jumping to the NFL prematurely. "I felt like I hadn't proven enough off the field," Spence told foxsports. com, "and that I needed more time to show everybody that you could be a better person off the field and to show that that wasn't me — and that I can go for the rest of my life and be a straight-forward great person, and that I can do that, starting with disciplining myself enough to go down a level and not be ignorant and try and go straight to the NFL." Meyer recommended Spence to EKU head coach Dean Hood, signing off on Spence's character and worthiness of a second chance. Was arrested in May '15 — was charged with alcohol intoxication and second-degree disorderly conduct after he tried to throw a bottle into a garbage can when it shattered, catching the attention of a police officer. Ultimately completed community service and had the charge expunged. Lived up to expectations on the field (wore jersey No. 9) — was the FCS National Defensive Performer of the Year (College Football Performance Awards) and the Ohio Valley Conference Co-Defensive Player of the Year after piling up 63-221/2-111/2 with three forced fumbles and 15 quarterback hurries in 11 starts at defensive end (operated from a two- and three-point stance, usually lined up on the outside shoulder of the offensive tackle opposite of EKU's "Colonel" defender, a hybrid DE/outside linebacker). Passed at least five drug tests during his time with the Colonels. Graduated with a general studies degree.

Strengths: Outstanding initial quickness to beat blockers off the ball and take the corner. Has an explosive get-off and plays faster than his timed speed. Comes off the ball low, can dip and rip and come up and under blocks. Can run the arc and trim the corner. Very good bend and burst. Good pursuit effort. Can change games on third downs. Showed well at the Senior Bowl, including registering a sack in the game. Produced highly against better competition at Ohio State prior to transferring to Eastern Kentucky.

Weaknesses: Lacks ideal height, bulk and base strength to anchor against the run. Does not always compete hard at the point of attack. Did not eliminate concerns about his past transgressions during interviews with NFL teams at the Combine and still has maturing to do.

Future: One of the most gifted pure pass rushers in the draft, Spence is a havoc-wreaking disruptor who will make a living affecting the game on third downs. Has had to overcome a lot of adversity in his life to get where he is and must prove to teams that he is focused on a team to take a chance on his immense upside.

Draft projection: Top-50 pick.

Scout's take: "I didn't think he was quick enough to be a DPR (defensive pass rush specialist). He is a pass rusher that doesn't play the run well, and I didn't think he was a special rusher. He looked little to me on tape. Maybe you have to stand him up. He will jolt (blockers) and if he gets half-a-man, he can win. He'll get called early, but I didn't have him up there as high as he is being talked about."

OLB **ERIC STRIKER**, #19 (Sr-4)

OKLAHOMA ▶ GRADE: 5.17

Ht: 5-11 3/8 | Wt: 227 | 40: 4.78 | Arm: 31 1/4 | Hand: 10 1/8

History: Recorded 42 sacks and won a state championship as a Florida prep. Saw limited action in all 13 games in 2012 when he recorded six tackles (all against Kansas), zero for loss and zero sacks. Started all 39 games the next three seasons — totaled 50-101/2-61/2 with three pass breakups and one forced fumble from the "Jack" linebacker in '13; 68-17-9 with five pass breakups from the "Sam"/nickel in '14; and 67-19-71/2 with three pass breakups, one interception and one forced fumble as a rush LB in '15. On track to graduate in the spring.

Strengths: Experienced, three-year starter. Has a knack for beating blocks one-on-one off the edge and was very productive out-leveraging blockers with up-and-under moves. Outstanding motor — hustles and pursues. Very active and competitive and consistently brings pressure. Times the snap well and has good closing speed. Can trim the corner and create issues for blockers with his natural leverage. Athletic enough to zone drop and run with backs. Vocal, energetic leader. Football smart and instinctive.

Weaknesses: Exceptionally undersized for an edge rusher and can be run at. Lacks bulk and length and is overmatched at the point of attack. Not explosive as a rusher and needs to develop a better pass-rush plan. Much of his production is clear-view where he is unblocked.

Future: A gifted pass-rusher who could find a role for a creative coordinator as a subpackage zone blitzer. Will not fit a traditional mold but could become a very productive pro on third downs if used as a mismatch piece to create pressure. Skill set might be best defined more traditionally as a nickel safety, though he lacks ideal foot speed. Will be a schematic non-fit for many teams and draft stock could suffer as a result. A good football player.

Draft projection: Late draftable pick.

Scout's take: "I don't know what to do with

LINEBACKERS

him. He's not a linebacker. He is a special package sub-rusher. It's difficult to fight for him in such a limited role, but that's what he can do. … You have got to have a plan for him. He's kind of a luxury pick for a compensatory pick or a team with a strong roster already. He can rush the passer. Or do you wait and try to get him on his second contract."

ROLB-DE RON THOMPSON, #13 (Jr-4)

SYRACUSE ▶ GRADE: 5.44
Ht: 6-3 | Wt: 253 | 40: 4.92 | Arm: 32 1/4 | Hand: 9 3/8

History: Tight end-defensive end also played basketball as a Michigan prep. Was recruited to Syracuse by then-head coach Doug Marrone. Both the offensive and defensive coaches wanted him on their side of the ball, but Thompson chose to begin his college career as a tight end. Redshirted in 2012 when he underwent surgery to repair a blood-flow issue in his hip. With the Orange thin at defensive end, Thompson and a new coaching staff mutually agreed he should convert to DE. In '13, notched 20 tackles, 4 1/2 for loss and two sacks with one batted pass in 13 contests. Started all 24 games the next two seasons — totaled 32-7-3 with five batted passes and two forced fumbles at defensive tackle in '14; and 35-9 1/2-7 with four batted passes and four forced fumbles at defensive end in '15. Missed time during fall camp with a left foot injury.

Strengths: Has a solid frame with room to get bigger. Good athletic ability. Plays with natural knee bend. Is light on his feet and operates well in space. Effective looping inside on stunts. Stood out against Clemson. Has a nose for the ball and can be disruptive creating turnovers. Efficient blocking the quarterback's vision. Athletic enough to drop back into coverage.

Weaknesses: Lacks ideal strength — only bench-pressed 225 pounds 18 times at the Combine. Needs to be more stout against the run. Below-average shuttle times at the Combine, indicating a lack of agility. Lacks ideal short-area burst and acceleration and is too often a half-step late to arrive at the quarterback.

Future: A versatile athlete who contributed in multiple positions along the Orangemen's defensive line the last two years in a "40" front, yet is most ideally suited to rush the passer from the outside of a "30" front in the pros. Is still growing into his body and needs to get stronger and widen his pass-rush arsenal.

Draft projection: Third- to fourth-round pick.

ILB NICK VIGIL, #41 (Jr-4)

UTAH STATE ▶ GRADE: 5.29
Ht: 6-2 3/8 | Wt: 239 | 40: 4.67 | Arm: 32 3/8 | Hand: 10 1/4

History: Brother, Zach, also played at USU and is a linebacker for the Dolphins. Nick was a linebacker-running back who also played basketball as a Utah prep. Broke a bone in his left foot at the end of his senior season. Redshirted in 2012. Played all 14 games in '13, starting four as a 3-4 outside linebacker, and recorded 57 tackles, 8 1/2 for loss and 5 1/2 sacks with one pass breakup and one interception. Shifted to inside linebacker in '14 when he started 13 games (including one at running back) and piled up 123-16 1/2-7 with two pass breakups, one interception and five forced fumbles. Also carried 41 times for 152 yards (3.7-yard average) and three touchdowns and tossed two completions. Did not play against Hawaii (left hamstring). Ranked second nationally in tackles in '15 after registering 144-13 1/2-3 with two pass breakups and two forced fumbles. Added 6-17-1 (2.8) on the ground. Scheduled to graduate with a sociology degree. Did not bench press at the Combine because of a left pectoral injury.

Strengths: Good size. Plays with urgency and runs to the ball. Outstanding production. Produced a 4.00-second 20-yard shuttle and 6.73-second 3-cone drill, the fastest of any linebackers at the Combine and generally indicative of very good lateral agility. Can make plays to the perimeter. Good recovery speed.

Weaknesses: Lets linebackers get on top of him too quickly and does not play with consistent knee bend or use his hands well to shed. Struggles to make himself skinny and fit his shoulders through gaps, getting hung up and knocked off balance too much. Tight in the hips and will struggle to come to balance and secure speed backs in the open field. Struggles to come free from edge blockers when aligned outside and has no pass-rush plan. Does not consistently play to his workout numbers — eyes are still developing. Tall in his pedal.

Future: Good-sized, active middle 'backer with enough size and urgency to contribute with continued development. Has some similarities to Titans 2011 fourth-round pick Colin McCarthy and should be an immediate contributor on special teams.

Draft projection: Fourth- to fifth-round pick.

Scout's take: "I thought he would be a lot smaller, so I initially graded him lower. He looks small in person but came in bigger (at the Combine) than I thought he would. He was highly productive. No one really felt a strong

LINEBACKERS

conviction about him in our room or wanted to stamp him."

SLB-MLB STEPHEN WEATHERLY, #45 (Jr-4)
VANDERBILT　　　　　▶ GRADE: 5.18
Ht: 6-4 3/8 | Wt: 267 | 40: 4.54 | Arm: 34 1/2 | Hand: 10 1/4

History: Also competed in baseball and track and field as a prep in Georgia. Redshirted in 2012. On track to graduate. Rotated at defensive end in '13 when he chipped in 19 tackles, five for loss and 31/2 for loss in 12 appearances. Was used as a 3-4 outside linebacker his final two seasons. Started 9-of-12 games in '14 and recorded 55-121/2-41/2 with one pass breakup, one forced fumble and one blocked punt for touchdown. Started all 12 games in '15 and logged 46-91/2-31/2 with three pass breakups and two forced fumbles. Scheduled to graduate in the spring. Opted not to run shuttles at the Combine.

Strengths: Big-boned and measured the longest arms and most weight of any linebacker at the Combine, with the type of size that is difficult to find at the LB position. Very good straight-line speed to flatten down the line and make plays in pursuit.

Weaknesses: Marginal pass-rush arsenal and sack production. Cannot convert speed to power. Does not play fast. Lacks functional strength to escape blocks — and gets stood up too tall. Most of his production comes moving laterally. Is often the last linebacker to move. Too easily chopped down by the cut block. Not a physical tackler.

Future: Long-legged, high-hipped, stiff, straight-linish strong-side 'backer who prefers playing defensive end, yet lacks the knee bend and play strength desired to trim the corner as a speed rusher for a 4-3 front. Does not play to his workout numbers nor does he have the instincts and thump desired in a middle 'backer. Best chance could come as a backup "Sam" and "Mike" and special teams' contributor.

Draft projection: Late draftable pick.

ILB-FB PHILLIP "SCOOBY" WRIGHT III, #33 (Jr-3)
ARIZONA　　　　　▶ GRADE: 5.25
Ht: 5-11 3/4 | Wt: 239 | 40: 4.89 | Arm: 30 1/2 | Hand: 9 3/4

History: Lightly recruited as a California prep. As a true freshman in 2013, started 12-of-13 games at "Sam" linebacker in the Wildcats' 3-3-5 defense — produced 83 tackles, 91/2 for loss and one-half sack with one pass breakup and one interception. Accumulated most of his production on run downs. Moved to middle linebacker in '14 and was one of the best defenders in the nation. Took home the Nagurski, Lombardi and Bednarik Awards and was Pac-12 Defensive Player of the Year after ranking first nationally in tackles, tackles for loss and forced fumbles — racked up 163-29-14 with six forced fumbles. In '15, managed 23-31/2-2 in three starts, but his season was marred by injury. Tore his left meniscus in Week One against Texas-San Antonio — had arthroscopic surgery and returned two weeks later against UCLA, but suffered a Lisfranc injury and arch damage in his right foot. Was sidelined the rest of the regular season before returning for the bowl game against New Mexico, when he notched 15-31/2-2. Opted not to run the 3-cone drill at the Combine.

Strengths: Excellent motor. Very good strength. Has a chip on his shoulder and is extremely driven and motivated to succeed. Good anticipation and feel for the game. Times up the blitz well. Strong tackler who drives his legs through contact. Exceptional college production in 2014. Extremely hard-working in all facets of the game — in the weight room, on the practice field and watching film.

Weaknesses: Naturally small-boned and measured the smallest arms of any linebacker at the Combine, which limits the ability to wrap/secure as a tackler. Overly muscled and extremely rigid in his movement, resulting in frequent missed tackles. Mechanical and almost robotic lower-body movement that negates his lateral agility. Limited athlete. Marginal timed speed. Gets velcroed to blocks too easily and needs to do a better job of shedding. Plays too out of control and spends more time on the ground than he should.

Future: Stiff, try-hard overachiever who bulked up too much for his body in 2015 and put too much stress on his maxed-out frame, leading to injuries and restricting the All-American production he churned out as a sophomore. Looks like a nose tackle playing middle linebacker and might even be best projecting to fullback in the pros. Looks like a borderline reject on paper by NFL standards, yet consistently found a way to overachieve in college. A better college football player than pro prospect, Wright has been able to will his way to success in college, but will be more challenged doing so against the world's finest athletes.

Draft projection: Fourth- to fifth-round pick.

Coach's take: "Once he got on campus, we found that he could handle a lot physically and mentally. He's just a football player whether you put him at defensive end or linebacker. We could put him at fullback because he's great there, too. ... Tedy Bruschi was Scooby Wright before Scooby Wright." (ESPN) – *Arizona head coach Rich Rodriquez*

DEFENSIVE BACKS

Nawrocki's TOP 10

1. **JALEN RAMSEY**
2. **Vernon Hargreaves III**
3. **Mackensie Alexander**
4. **Darian Thompson**
5. **Vonn Bell**
6. **Kendall Fuller**
7. **Zack Sanchez**
8. **Eli Apple**
9. **Su'a Cravens**
10. **Keanu Neal**

LCB MACKENSIE ALEXANDER, #2 (Soph-3)

CLEMSON ▶ GRADE: 5.92

Ht: 5-10 3/8 | Wt: 190 | 40: 4.49 | Arm: 31 3/8 | Hand: 9 1/8

History: Heralded recruit also wrestled and ran track as a Florida prep. Redshirted in 2013 while recovering from groin surgery. Started all 13 games at field corner in '14 and collected 22 tackles, six pass breakups and zero interceptions with two tackles for loss. Started 13-of-14 games at FCB in '15 and logged 23-5-0 with two tackles for loss. Was benched for the first possession against Wofford for being "45 seconds late" to a meeting, according to head coach Dabo Swinney. Did not play against Wake Forest (knee). Played with a hurt right hamstring in the national championship against Alabama. Allowed 33 completions on 106 targets (31.1 percent) the last two seasons. Did not give up a touchdown in his final 23 games. At the Combine proclaimed himself the best corner in the draft despite not working out (left hamstring), where he was officially held out as a medical exclusion.

Strengths: Outstanding straight-line speed and short-area burst to react to the thrown ball in front of him and deter quarterbacks from making throws. Terrific reactionary quickness and recovery speed. Very good man and off-man cover skills to shadow and mirror receivers. Has a 37-inch vertical. Strong, aggressive tackler — fills fast and chops down receivers in the open field. Carries a swagger and plays with confidence. Is tough and will battle through injury as he tried doing early in the National Championship game.

Weaknesses: Lacks ideal size. Only bench-pressed 225 pounds 11 times at the Combine and has room to grow physically stronger. Chirps to the point of losing his own focus.

Marginal career production (11 passes defended and never recorded an interception). Can be pulled up by play-action and bites too much. Hamstring injuries have been nagging concern and are worrisome to NFL scouts, who fear he needs everything to be perfect for him to perform. Could require some time to acclimate to NFL terminology.

Future: Good-sized, physical corner most ideally suited to press receivers at the line of scrimmage. Commended for being one of the most entertaining interviews at the Combine and does not lack for confidence. Has the physical talent to develop into a solid starter in the pros.

Draft projection: Top-50 pick.

Scout's take: "I graded him in the back of the first (round). He is a confident, trash-talking corner who can run. His personality fits the position well. I don't like that he never had an interception in college, but he is one of the best in college football not letting passes be caught in front of him."

RCB ELI APPLE, #13 (Soph-3)

OHIO STATE ▶ GRADE: 5.72

Ht: 6-05/8 | Wt: 199 | 40: 4.42 | Arm: 313/8 | Hand: 93/8

History: Changed his last name from Woodard to Apple in December 2012 in order to recognize his stepfather's role in his upbringing. Cornerback-receiver prepped in New Jersey (suburban Philadelphia) and was a U.S. Army All-American. Redshirted in 2013 — discovered an iron deficiency which negatively affected his strength, energy and stamina. Played field corner for the national champs in '14 — started 14-of-15 games and produced 53 tackles, 10 pass breakups and three interceptions with 51/2 tackles for loss and one forced fumble. Didn't practice leading up to the Michigan State contest because of a hamstring injury. Played right corner in '15 when he started all 13 games and tallied 33-8-1 with two tackles for loss. Was Defensive MVP of the Fiesta Bowl against Notre Dame. Did not do jumps, shuttles or 3-cone drill at the Combine because of cramping. Will be a 21-year-old rookie.

Strengths: Outstanding size and overall length to match up with big receivers. Light on his feet with excellent combination of speed and quickness, particularly in short area. Smooth movement, backpedal and transition. Very athletic with natural man-cover skills to keep stride with receivers and carry them on short-to-intermediate routes. Showed soft hands at the Combine. Has experience matching up with NFL-caliber receivers.

Weaknesses: Average positional instincts and reactionary quickness. Suspect overall ball skills (see Penn State in 2015 and Cincinnati in 2014). Gets out of phase and is beat too often, displaying limited downfield awareness with his back to the ball. Too grabby — was flagged too often for pass interference/holding. Struggles locating the ball from the trail position. Takes some bad angles. Needs to hone his technique and get stronger to take away inside releases (see two TDs allowed zbe desired — too soft. Immature and could require some additional maintenance.

Future: A very good-sized, long-limbed corner that scouts have compared to Saints 2015 third-round pick P.J. Williams. Can eventually compete for a job as a No. 2 corner in an aggressive man-cover defense. However, his finesse style and questionable ball skills will turn off some teams, and his penalties could be a limiting factor in a league where defensive backs are penalized freely.

Draft projection: Second- to third-round pick.

Scout's take: "I like (Apple's) size and length. The two biggest negatives are his lack of physicality in run support and his ability to turn, track and locate the ball. Even on plays he made downfield, he was late getting turned around, almost as if he were faceguarding."

FS VONN BELL, #11 (Jr-3)

OHIO STATE ▶ GRADE: 5.82

Ht: 5-103/4 | Wt: 199 | 40: 4.53 | Arm: 323/8 | Hand: 91/2

History: Five-star recruit out of Georgia. Was busted for underage drinking the summer before arriving in Columbus. As a true freshman in 2013, served as the backup nickel and recorded 19 tackles, zero pass breakups and one interception with one tackle for loss in 14 games (started Orange Bowl vs. Clemson). Tore his left MCL during '14 spring practice (required surgery). In the fall, started 14-of-15 games at free safety and produced 92-6-6 with two tackles for loss and one sack. Started all 13 games at FS in '15 and posted 65-9-2 (one touchdown) with one tackle for loss and a 14-yard fumble recovery touchdown. Did not work out at the Combine (right hamstring).

Strengths: Starter-caliber movement skills and range. Outstanding short-area burst, acceleration and functional play speed. Instinctive playing the pass. Sudden off spots when he sees it. Jumps routes and has natural hands as an interceptor. Very good zone cover skills — reads the quarterback's eyes and adjusts to the flight of the ball.

Weaknesses: Has cornerback size and could be more susceptible to injury in the pros. Poor leaper (30 1/2-inch vertical). Can be overaggressive biting on play-action. Absorbs too much contact — is not an intimidating, blow-up striker. Tends to coast and pick his spots to exert himself. Does not play with abandon and could use more glass in his diet. Does not play big in the run game. Can be hesitant and soft-footed in his run fits. Quality of play fluctuated.

Future: A talented cover safety with range to roam the back end, Bell stood to benefit from another year in Columbus and his overall consistency, intensity and physicality leave you wanting more. However, he has the type of athleticism, burst and speed needed as NFL offenses continue spreading out. Has some similarities to Buffalo Bills 2006 first-round pick and current Browns S Donte Whitner, with versatility to potentially interchange as a nickel safety in the slot.

Draft projection: Top-50 pick.

Scout's take: "I don't think Von Bell wows you. He has straight-line speed and he's good coming downhill. He gets exposed in coverage and plays with a little bit of hesitation. He's always there to make the tackle but not make a play on the ball. There's just something missing."

NCB BRIEAN BODDY-CALHOUN, #29 (Sr-5)
MINNESOTA ▶ GRADE: 5.18
Ht: 5-9 1/2 | Wt: 193 | 40: 4.47 | Arm: 31 | Hand: 9 1/8

History: High school quarterback, defensive back and kick returner who competed in basketball and track as a Delaware prep. Was headed for a Division III school before Coffeyville (Kan.) Community College swooped in. Wearing jersey No. 20 in 2011, recorded 40 tackles, four pass breakups and four interceptions with one forced fumble and one blocked kick in 10 games. Committed to then-head coach Jerry Kill and the Gophers that fall. Was a backup/special teams player in '12, scratching 9-1-0 with one blocked kick. In '13, managed 5-0-1 (89-yard touchdown against UNLV) in two starts before suffering a season-ending torn left ACL injury. Returned to start 10-of-13 games (two at safety, final eight at cornerback) in '14 and produce 51-9-5 with two tackles for loss and two forced fumbles (strip of a Nebraska player saved a sure touchdown and preserved a win). Started 9-of-11 games played in '15 and totaled 48-6-4 with 1 1/2 tackles for loss and one-half sack. Did not play against Northwestern or Purdue and did not start against Nebraska or Michigan (right knee). Team captain graduated with a degree in elementary education.

Strengths: Aware in zone coverage. Jumps underneath routes. Good ball reactions — aggressive and competitive at the catch point. Serves as a gunner on special teams. Outstanding practice habits and overall football character.

Weaknesses: Undersized and needs to get stronger. Intermittent physicality supporting the run — ankle-biting tackler. Has man-cover limitations — lacks top-end speed and quickness. Recorded an 11.72-second 60-yards shuttle time at the Combine, indicative of deficient short-area burst and acceleration.

Future: Compactly built cornerback most ideally suited as sub-package slot defender or cover-2 boundary player given his average size and athleticism. Will have to earn his way on special teams, and intangibles increase his appeal.

Draft projection: Sixth- to seventh-round pick.

RCB-SS JAMES BRADBERRY, #21 (Sr-5)
SAMFORD ▶ GRADE: 5.26
Ht: 6-0 3/4 | Wt: 211 | 40: 4.52 | Arm: 33 | Hand: 9 1/8

History: Also played basketball as an Alabama prep. Began his college career at Arkansas State, where he redshirted as a safety in 2011. Transferred to FCS Samford in order to play cornerback. Did not miss a game during his college career. Made 11 starts in '12 (wore jersey No. 41) and contributed 32 tackles, two pass breakups and two interceptions with 1 1/2 tackles for loss. Started 12-of-13 games in '13 and tallied 26-10-2. Did not start against Furman. Started all 22 games the next two seasons — totaled 25-4-2 with three tackles for loss in '14; and 45-11-2 with four tackles for loss in '15. Team captain earned an invite to the Senior Bowl. Would be the fourth Samford defensive back drafted in the last five years.

Strengths: Outstanding size-speed combination. Is aggressive filling vs. the run. Caught the ball with ease very naturally in the gauntlet drill at the Combine. Held his own in press coverage at the Senior Bowl, jamming and knocking down receivers. Aggressive tackler. Good football intelligence — makes the defensive calls. Very durable and has not missed any time to injury.

Weaknesses: Raw technician still honing his footwork. Is a bit tight and leggy. Really struggled as a back-half safety at the Senior Bowl and looked like a fish out of water. Did not regularly match up against top competition and could be an adjustment period to covering elite speed. Could stand to benefit from an NFL strength and conditioning program.

Future: A very good sized, long-armed cornerback who looks every bit the part and has the press strength and movement skill to be a very effective bump-and-run corner for an aggressive defense such as the Ravens, Cardinals or Steelers. Could contribute as a nickel safety.

Draft projection: Sixth to seventh-round pick.

Coach's take: "We were a two-deep team and we mixed in some three-deep and a match-up zone. For a good portion, it was James and Jaquiski (Tartt) to take advantage of their abilities to play a matchup and play man within a zone concept." *(AP) – Samford Defensive Coordinator Bill D'Ottavio*

RCB ANTHONY BROWN, #9 (Sr-4)
PURDUE   ▶ GRADE: 5.10
Ht: 5-11 1/4 | Wt: 192 | 40: 4.34 | Arm: 31 3/4 | Hand: 8 1/4

History: All-purpose standout as a prep in Texas, where he also excelled in track (recorded 10.5 100 meters). As a true freshman in 2012, notched six tackles, zero pass breakups and zero interceptions in 10 appearances. Did not play against Illinois (right foot sprain). Played all 12 games in '13 — an injury to the starter opened the door for him to start the final 10 games at safety and produce 69-3-0 with three tackles for loss and one forced fumble. Started all 24 games at left cornerback the next two seasons — totaled 54-10-0 with 5 1/2 tackles for loss and 1 1/2 sacks in '14; and 59-6-4 with one tackle for loss and one blocked kick in '15. Graduated with a degree in organizational leadership and supervision.

Strengths: Well-conditioned athlete with four percent body fat. Outstanding straight-line speed and acceleration — recorded a 1.5-second 10-yard split at the Combine. Can keep pace vertically. Bench-pressed 225 pounds 19 times at the Combine, tied for the second most of any cornerback, and has good press strength to re-route receivers. Has been used as a gunner. Showed steady improvement at the East-West Shrine Game, indicating good coachability.

Weaknesses: Very small hands. Has too much body tightness, particularly in his hips (stiff transition). Too grabby. Loses phase and gets beat too easily over the top. Gave up too many big plays/touchdowns. Average balance and leaping ability. Not a playmaker. Struggled in run support. Weak tackler.

Future: Height-weight-speed prospect whose body stiffness limits his ceiling. Has speed to work as a gunner, but will have to prove he can tackle adequately to stick.

Draft projection: Late draftable pick.

Scout's take: "He is really, really tight and needs to loosen up his hips."

SS LaMARCUS BRUTUS, #42 (Sr-5)
FLORIDA STATE   ▶ GRADE: 4.97
Ht: 5-11 5/8 | Wt: 206 | 40: 4.74 | Arm: 31 1/2 | Hand: 8 3/4

History: Florida native. Redshirted in 2011. Saw limited action in six games in '12 without recording any stats. Was a reserve/special teams player the next two years — tallied 16 tackles, one pass breakup and one tackle for loss in '13 (11 games); and 15-1-2 in '14 (14 games). Stepped into the lineup at free safety in '15 when he produced 68-1-3. Broke his left ring finger against Florida. Was ejected for targeting against Central Florida. Graduated with a degree in social science.

Strengths: Football smart. Tough competitor. Aggressive in run support. Physical tackler. Good ball skills. Team-first player who waited his turn and accepted his role in an exceptionally deep and talented college secondary. Terrific intangibles.

Weaknesses: Small hands. Has coverage and overall athletic limitations. Marginal foot speed. Recorded a 9-foot broad jump and 12.28-second 60-yard shuttle, both lows among the DB group and indicative of a lack of lower-body explosion and dynamic quickness.

Future: A tough, productive overachiever lacking the foot speed, hip flexibility and cover skills to survive on the back end in the pros. Linebacker in a safety body. Could fight his way onto a roster contributing on special teams.

Draft projection: Priority free agent.

Scout's take: "He led the team in interceptions. He's slow, smart and stiff, but real consistent. He's a core (special) teams guy. He doesn't fit us, but he's draftable for a lot of teams."

RCB ARTIE BURNS, #1 (Jr-3)
MIAMI (FLA.)   ▶ GRADE: 5.37
Ht: 5-11 7/8 | Wt: 193 | 40: 4.46 | Arm: 33 1/4 | Hand: 9 1/2

History: Also an elite track athlete at Miami Northwestern — three-time 3A 110-meter hurdle champion who registered the best 110-meter and 300-meter hurdles times in America as a junior. As a true freshman in 2013, recorded 17 tackles, three pass breakups and one interception with one-half tackle for loss and one forced fumble in 11 appearances. In '14, started 11-of-13 games and contributed 40-6-0 with two sacks. Started all 12 games played in '15 and notched 36-5-6 with one-half tackle for loss. Also ran track for the Hurricanes —

DEFENSIVE BACKS

set a new American junior record by running a 7.68-second 60-meter hurdles. Artie's mother, Dana Smith, died of a heart attack in late October (sat out against Virginia), and Artie's father, Artie Sr., is serving a 25-year prison sentence for cocaine trafficking. Did not do jumps, shuttles or 3-cone drill at the Combine (left knee).

Strengths: Good size with very long arms. Good straight-line speed. Comfortable in press coverage. Very zone aware with good pattern recognition. Understands how to read quarterbacks and progressions and undercut routes. Can pluck the ball out of the air. Solid interception production (see Nebraska and Virginia Tech). Plays with confidence and has a swagger.

Weaknesses: Too much of a strider with stiffness in his body. Not an instant accelerator. Marginal transitional quickness, as confirmed in turn-and-run times at the event. Pedals upright and gets caught on his heels. Needs to be more physical against the run. Has a 31 1/2-inch vertical jump, reflecting average athletic ability.

Future: Good-sized, confident press corner. Flashes playmaking ability and has the ball skills to warrant developing as a No. 4 or 5 corner. Has endured a lot of adversity and is the type of person you root for.

Draft projection: Fourth to fifth-round pick.

Scout's take: "There are games where (Burns) looks like a seventh-rounder and some where he looks like a late third (rounder) depending on what game you are watching. The Virginia Tech game was probably his best game where he had two picks. Most of the rest, he plays like a fourth (rounder). The Clemson game, he looks like a free agent, but to be fair to the kid, it was to be expected. His mom just passed, he had his two brothers to take care of. He had a lot of stuff going on."

RCB JUSTON BURRIS, #11 (Sr-5)

NORTH CAROLINA STATE   ▶ GRADE: 5.27

Ht: 6-0 1/4 | Wt: 212 | 40: 4.49 | Arm: 31 1/2 | Hand: 8 7/8

History: North Carolina native. Redshirted in 2011. Served as the nickel back in '12 when he chipped in 43 tackles, eight pass breakups and zero interceptions with one tackle for loss in 13 games (five starts). Started all 38 games at right cornerback the next three seasons — totaled 54-11-1 with one tackle for loss in '13 (12 games); 29-5-1 with one tackle for loss in '14 (13 games); and 38-7-1 with three tackles for loss and one forced fumble in '15 (13 games). Sustained a concussion at the begin-

ning of his sophomore season. Graduated with sports management degree.

Strengths: Experienced, three-year starter. Looks the part — well-built and strong. Bench-pressed 225 pounds 19 times at the Combine, tied for second-most among cornerbacks and correlating to good press strength. Effective pressing and re-routing receivers. Very good timed speed. Productive. Willing tackler.

Weaknesses: Has small hands and only three career interceptions. Struggles to track and locate the ball downfield and is flagged too much for pass interference. Too grabby. Could stand to be more aggressive as a tackler. Recorded a 4.45-second 20-yard shuttle, indicative of very limited lateral agility.

Future: Big, physical, competitive, press corner who should appeal to teams like the Eagles, Cardinals, Seahawks, Ravens, Titans and Redskins.

Draft projection: Fifth- to sixth-round pick.

Scout's take: "I put (Burris) in the sixth round when I passed through the school. He was flagged for about four pass interference calls in the games I did. I liked how he played in press coverage. His sophomore year looked like his best season."

FS DEON BUSH, #2 (Sr-4)

MIAMI (FLA.)   ▶ GRADE: 5.40

Ht: 6-0 3/8 | Wt: 199 | 40: 4.59 | Arm: 30 7/8 | Hand: 9 1/4

History: Miami native. As a true freshman in 2012, started 6-of-10 games played at strong safety and recorded 34 tackles, three pass breakups and zero interceptions with one tackle for loss and three forced fumbles. Suffered a shoulder injury against Virginia Tech and missed two November contests. In April '13, learned his father had liver cancer then Deon had hernia surgery in June which sidelined him until Week Three. On the season, managed 31-1-1 with two sacks and one forced fumble in 11 games (three starts). Started all 11 games played in '14 and totaled 53-3-2 with four tackles for loss, two sacks and five forced fumbles. Suffered a hamstring injury against Florida State and sat out against Virginia. Started 12-of-13 games in '15 and posted 50-6-1 with three tackles for loss and one sack. Was flagged for targeting against Nebraska and was suspended the first half against Cincinnati. Named to AFCA Good Works Team. Did not do shuttles or 3-cone drill at the Combine (left calf strain). During his career was dealing with father having bouts of cancer and uncle needing kidney transplant.

Strengths: Reads and reacts well. Shows

DEFENSIVE BACKS

awareness and recognition in zone coverage. Good range and ball skills. Seeks out high-speed collisions and uses his body like a weapon. Runs the alley and smacks ballcarriers — unafraid to stick his facemask in someone's chest. Mentally strong.

Weaknesses: Short on length and functional strength — struggles taking on and disengaging blocks. Can be mismatched by bigger, stronger tight ends. Average timed speed and flexibility for the position — could be exposed by more explosive receivers in one-on-one. Does not always arrive under control and can miss tackles failing to wrap up. Long-term durability could be an issue given his build and playing style.

Future: Narrow-framed, fairly athletic free safety who roamed all over the field at Miami thanks to his range and aggressiveness. Has eventual starter potential in a predominantly cover-2 and/or cover-3 based scheme, and shares some on-field similarities to Patriots 2007 first-round pick Brandon Meriweather, particularly his nose for big hits.

Draft projection: Third- to fourth-round pick.

Scout's take: "I thought he would run faster. He's tough and athletic and has length. I had him in the third. He plays a lot faster than 4.6. He has burst. Watch him come up and knock people around vs. Clemson. He flies up and knocks the (expletive) out of someone on the first series."

FS KEVIN BYARD, #20 (Sr-5)

MIDDLE TENNESSEE STATE ▶ GRADE: 5.16

Ht: 5-11 3/8 | Wt: 216 | 40: 4.65e | Arm: 33 1/2 | Hand: 9 7/8

History: Last name is pronounced "bye-ERD." Was raised — with six siblings — by a single mother. Played safety, receiver and kick returner as a prep in Georgia, where he also ran track. Intended to commit to Kentucky, but his offer was pulled. Redshirted in 2011. Did not miss a game his first three seasons. Started 12 games at free safety in '12 and produced 74 tackles, two pass breakups and four interceptions (two touchdowns) with two forced fumbles. Started 13 games at FS in '13 and racked up 106-5-5 with one tackle for loss and one forced fumble. Played strong safety in '14 and totaled 66-4-6 (touchdown) with three tackles for loss, two forced fumbles and a blocked point after attempt. In '15, started 10-of-12 games played at FS and logged 66-6-4 with one tackle for loss. Was flagged for targeting against Alabama and suspended the first half against Charlotte. Injured his ankle against Louisiana Tech — sat out against Mar-

shall and did not start against Florida Atlantic. Owns school records for interceptions (19) and interception return yardage (377). Team captain graduated with a health education degree. Participated in the Senior Bowl, but did not receive a Combine invitation.

Strengths: Very good arm length. Experienced four-year starter. Good body control and ball skills. Attacks the ball in the air and makes good adjustments. Very good pattern recognition. Outstanding interception production. Has a passion for the game. Football smart.

Weaknesses: Does not play big or fast and needs to improve as a tackler. Takes some questionable angles. Lacks the range and closing burst desired to be a single-high safety. Does not sacrifice his body around piles.

Future: Instinctive, back-end safety who struggles to get over the top and is more ideally suited to play closer to the box, yet lacks the physicality to mix it up. Shares some similarities to Steelers 2015 seventh-round pick Gerod Holliman out of Louisville, though is more physical.

Draft projection: Fifth- to sixth-round pick.

Scout's take: "I like his instincts. If he makes it in the league, that's why he will make it. He doesn't have the foot speed to play on the back end. If he's in a two-shell, he has to be a short-hole robber."

RCB TAVEZE CALHOUN, #23 (Sr-5)

MISSISSIPPI STATE ▶ GRADE: 5.12

Ht: 6-0 3/8 | Wt: 192 | 40: 4.58 | Arm: 31 7/8 | Hand: 9

History: First name is pronounced "tah-VEZ." Lightly recruited Mississippi native. Redshirted in 2011 after having his right shoulder surgically repaired. Was a reserve/special teams player in '12 when he recorded 24 tackles, zero pass breakups and zero interceptions with one-half tackle for loss and one forced fumble in 13 appearances. Had right shoulder surgery in the spring of '13. Stepped into the lineup in the fall and started all 12 games played, tallying 45-4-3 with 11/2 tackles for loss and one forced fumble. Did not play against Troy (right ankle sprain). Started all 13 games in '14 and produced 53-9-1 with 31/2 tackles for loss and one forced fumble. Had ligaments in his right ankle surgically repaired after the season. Partially tore his left meniscus during '15 fall camp — had arthroscopic surgery, did not play in the season opener against Southern Miss and did not start the following week against LSU. On the season, started 11-of-12 games played and totaled 39-8-2 with 61/2 tackles for loss. Team captain was a fi-

DEFENSIVE BACKS

nalist for the Campbell Trophy ("Academic Heisman") and will obtain a master's degree in workforce leadership. Did not perform the broad jump, shuttles or 3-cone drill at the Combine (left knee).

Strengths: Good dimensions for the position. Three-year starter in the Southeastern Conference — experienced lining up against NFL-caliber receivers. Plays with bounce in his step to plant and drive on plays in the flat. Has length to play the pocket. Intelligent.

Weaknesses: Bean pole. Strength deficient. Gets physically bullied on the outside. Weak, grab-and-drag tackler who is soft on the edge. Leggy mover who gives up separation at the break point. Average speed and leaping ability. Too often out of position.

Future: Very lean, underpowered, finesse, man-cover corner lacking starter-caliber athleticism. Has a chance to latch on as a No. 4 or No. 5, but does not project as a special teams standout.

Draft projection: Fifth- to sixth-round pick.

Scout's take: "He played at 180 pounds when I was through there, and he had no strength. He just bounced off (ballcarriers). He's really weak. Corners that can't tackle don't work for us."

RCB MAURICE CANADY, #26 (Sr-4)

VIRGINIA ▶ GRADE: 5.14
Ht: 6-1 | Wt: 193 | 40: 4.52 | Arm: 31 5/8 | Hand: 9 1/8

History: Richmond, Va. native played cornerback, quarterback and receiver in high school. As a true freshman in 2012, recorded 28 tackles, three pass breakups and two interceptions with one forced fumble in 11 games (two starts). Did not play against North Carolina (concussion). In '13, started 8-of-9 games played and tallied 44-8-0 with two sacks and one forced fumble. Missed three games because of a lacerated kidney. Started all 24 games the next two seasons — totaled 37-12-3 with 11/2 tackles for loss and one forced fumble in '14; and 39-6-0 with three tackles for loss and one forced fumble in '15. Added five punt returns for 126 yards (25.2-yard average), including a 74-yard score against William & Mary.

Strengths: Looks the part with outstanding size. Has less than six percent body fat. Versatile — lined up all over the field. Has a 38-inch vertical jump. Recognizes plays and makes plays when the ball is in front of him. Solid Senior Bowl showing.

Weaknesses: Lacks physicality. Too upright in his pedal. Can be too late out of his pedal and get beat vertically. Gambles too much in coverage, biting on double moves. Gets beat too often. Struggled matching up with Pittsburgh's Tyler Boyd. Average eyes and anticipation. Intermittent physicality — picks and chooses his spots. Marginal tackle production — plays too passively and is not quick to fill against the run. Looks lackadaisical at times.

Future: Big, talented corner who appeared to lose his confidence following a very productive junior season. Was regularly assigned to the opponent's top receiver as a senior and lost as many matchups as he won.

Draft projection: Late draftable pick.

SS-NLB TEVIN CARTER, #9 (Sr-6)

UTAH ▶ GRADE: 4.89
Ht: 6-1 1/4 | Wt: 218 | 40: 4.65e | Arm: 32 | Hand: 9 1/4

History: Grew up in South Central, L.A. Tevin's father, Hilbert, died from cancer when Tevin was nine. Also ran track as a prep (recorded 10.56 100 meters). Signed with California, where he redshirted in 2010. Left the team without asking for a release. In '11, went to L.A. Southwest and recorded 32 tackles, four pass breakups and two interceptions with three tackles for loss, one sack and one forced fumble in eight games. Also returned four kickoffs for 119 yards (29.8-yard average), including one score. In '12, had 62-4-3 with three tackles for loss and one forced fumble in 10 games. Attended El Camino College (Calif.) in '13 while working to gain eligibility. Joined the Utes in '14, but missed spring practice while recovering from surgery to repair torn ligaments in his left ankle. In the fall, managed 16-1-2 (one touchdown) with 31/2 tackles for loss in four starts at free safety. Tore his left meniscus in Week Three against Michigan — had a scope and missed the Washington State contest. Returned for UCLA, but suffered a groin injury — tried to rehab, but ultimately opted for season-ending surgery. After a desperate appeal process, was granted a medical hardship waiver. In '15, started all 12 games played at strong safety and posted 56-3-2 with 51/2 tackles for loss. Did not play against Oregon State (undisclosed injury). Graduated with degrees in sociology and child development. Did not work out at the Combine (right groin injury).

Strengths: Good size. Bench-pressed 225 pounds 19 times, indicating very good strength. Supports the run aggressively. Dependable hands. Hardworking, solid teammate.

Weaknesses: Marginal foot quickness and agility. Tight movement skills. Exposed in space. Liability in man coverage. Has average ball skills due to his limited burst. Durability has been an issue. Tweener traits. Limited upside. Can be slow to trust people. Body fat (16 percent) is more in line with a linebacker than defensive back.

Future: Tightly wound, downhill, box safety lacking the type of athleticism desired on the back end. Will have to stand out on special teams, and could even be considered as a developmental linebacker.

Draft projection: Priority free agent.

Scout's take: "I thought he had a shot to get drafted two years ago before he hurt his knee. He has not been the same player since."

SS-NLB JEREMY CASH, #16 (Sr-5)

DUKE ▶ GRADE: 5.17

Ht: 6-0 3/8 | Wt: 212 | 40: 4.65e | Arm: 32 3/8 | Hand: 10

History: Engaged to a former North Carolina soccer player. Also played basketball and ran track as a Florida prep. Began his college career at Ohio State. As a true freshman in 2011, notched three tackles, zero pass breakups and zero interception in five appearances. Transferred after the departure of Jim Tressel. "I went there because I believed in everything Coach Tressel stood for, and once he was gone, they didn't share those principles outside of football, about life after football," Cash told USA Today. "[Urban Meyer] and I just definitely didn't see eye to eye." Did not play in '12 per NCAA transfer rules. Thrived as the "Strike" (hybrid safety/linebacker) defender in the Blue Devils' 4-2-5 scheme. In '13, started all 14 games and racked up 121-4-4 with 9 1/2 tackles for loss and two forced fumbles. Started all 13 games in '14 and racked up 111-7-2 with 10 1/2 tackles for loss, 5 1/2 sacks and four forced fumbles. Had his broken left pinky finger surgically repaired after the regular season. Sat out '15 spring practice after having his left knee scoped. Was a Thorpe Award finalist in the fall after starting all 12 games played and notching 104-4-0 with 8 1/2 tackles for loss, one sack and two forced fumbles. Played with an injured right wrist all season before having it surgically repaired (did not play in the Pinstripe Bowl). Team captain graduated with a psychology degree. Did not bench press or work out at the Combine because of right wrist and right hamstring injuries.

Strengths: Very good size and arm length for a safety. Was outstanding in run support — highly productive tackler who is exceptionally active near the line of scrimmage. Charges downhill like a bull and chops down

running backs before they get to speed. Secure tackler — gets ballcarriers in his crosshairs and puts them on the ground. Potential to factor as a blitzer. Has plus instincts, smarts and awareness. Showed toughness playing hurt as a senior.

Weaknesses: Production exceeds his athleticism. Exposed in space. Limited suddenness and flexibility. Tight-hipped with marginal transitional quickness, which showed at the Senior Bowl. Can be outflanked by speed. Struggles in coverage. Tackle numbers were inflated by clear-path plays. Has tweener traits.

Future: An oversized safety with straight-line striking ability and limited cover skills. Projects best to a sub-package linebacker in the pros. Has some similarities to Cardinals dime linebacker Deone Bucannon, selected in the first round by the Cardinals in 2014.

Draft projection: Late draftable pick.

Scout's take: "I don't know what you do with him. He has to play linebacker, and he is too small for that. Seriously, I hope someone takes him early, and it knocks down other good players. ... If you watch him against Oregon only, you'd have a free-agent grade on him."

SS-WLB SU'A CRAVENS, #21 (Jr-3)

USC ▶ GRADE: 5.70

Ht: 6-0 3/4 | Wt: 226 | 40: 4.65e | Arm: 32 1/8 | Hand: 9 1/2

History: Comes from a big, athletic family, including his cousin, Jordan Cameron, who plays tight end for the Dolphins. Cravens was a decorated California prep — played all over the field, garnered consensus All-American honors and was named USA Today's Defensive Player of the Year and the state's Gatorade Player of the Year. Graduated early and joined the Trojans for 2013 spring practice, but tore his right meniscus. Still made an immediate impact in the fall when he started 13 games at strong safety in Clancy Pendergast's "52" scheme and recorded 52 tackles, one pass breakup and four interceptions with 11 1/2 tackles for loss and one forced fumble. Strained his groin against Utah and sat out against Oregon State. Transitioned to Justin Wilcox's 3-4 multiple system. Missed time during '14 fall camp because of strep throat and a groin strain. On the season, was deployed as a hybrid outside linebacker/safety — started all 13 games and produced 68 tackles, 17 for loss and five sacks with nine pass breakups and three interceptions (one touchdown). Exited the Washington State contest with an MCL sprain. In '15, started all 14 games as a strong-side hybrid defender, to-

DEFENSIVE BACKS

taling 86-15-51/2 with six pass breakups, two interceptions and two forced fumbles. Will be a 21-year-old rookie. Opted not to run at the Combine.

Strengths: Instinctive and competitive and delivers some big hits with terrific timing and anticipation. Good zone awareness — is capable of matching up with backs and tight ends in man coverage. Good hips and feet to displace outside in the slot and handle matching up with a No. 2 or 3 receiver without losing phase. Surprisingly agile and efficient shadowing and mirroring receivers. Can make spectacular grabs (see interceptions vs. Utah and Stanford). Times up the blitz well. Good versatility.

Weaknesses: Very undersized and strength-deficient for a linebacker. Only bench-pressed 225 pounds 16 times at the Combine, and needs to improve his functional play strength to survive at the point of attack against big-bodied blockers. Recorded a 27-inch vertical jump at the Combine, the shortest of any linebacker or defensive back and indicative of below-average lower-body explosion. Plays a bit recklessly and out of control and could more consistently secure tackles in the open field. Lacks ideal foot speed to match up with quick slot receivers in man coverage as a safety.

Future: Projects as an undersized, run-and-chase "Will" linebacker for a "40" front such as the Cowboys or Panthers where speed and interchangeability is desired at all three LB positions. Was deployed as a hybrid "buck/star" by the Trojans after standing out more as a safety earlier in his career and could still be most optimal in the pros shedding some weight and adjusting back to a box safety role.

Draft projection: Second-round pick.

Scout's take: "(Cravens) is more like Landon Collins as a safety than he is a true linebacker. He is not the big run-support hitter that Landon was. Our scouts are all over the place on him. …I have seen him play live. I don't like him the way a lot of our scouts do. I think he is a hype-buzz guy. …Watch the UCLA game. He was covering on the slot the whole game in man coverage and had a bunch of passes completed on him. I graded him in the back of the second (round)."

RCB KEN CRAWLEY, #2 (Sr-4)

COLORADO   ▶ GRADE: 5.02
Ht: 6-0 3/8 | Wt: 187 | 40: 4.43 | Arm: 30 1/2 | Hand: 9

History: Cornerback-receiver who ran track as a Washington D.C. prep. Factored as a true freshman in 2012 when he started 10-of-11

games played (first eight at left corner, final three at right corner) and totaled 58 tackles, five pass breakups and zero interceptions with three tackles for loss. Also returned 12 punts for 81 yards (6.8-yard average). Sat out against Stanford (flu). Started 10-of-11 games played in '13 and recorded 50-5-2 with two tackles for loss. Did not play against UCLA (ankle). Missed time during '14 practice because of a dislocated finger. In the fall, started 11-of-12 games at RCB and produced 47-13-0 with two tackles for loss and one forced fumble. Started all 13 games at RCB in '15 and posted 46-13-1 with one tackle for loss and one forced fumble. On track to graduate in the spring.

Strengths: Good height for the position. Productive four-year starter with good ball skills. Fluid mover with a smooth, controlled pedal and good transitional quickness out of his turns. Functional re-routing receivers. Supports the run willingly and is a good tackler.

Weaknesses: Has short arms, small hands and a thin bone structure. Allowed too many big plays and was flagged too many times. Lacks functional strength. Will require some time to acclimate to a complex playbook. Tends to catch with his body.

Future: Lean corner whose scheme versatility and run support skill give him a chance to stick if he can impress on special teams.

Draft projection: Priority free agent.

RCB-FS SEAN DAVIS, #21 (Sr-4)

MARYLAND   ▶ GRADE: 5.56
Ht: 6-1 | Wt: 201 | 40: 4.44 | Arm: 31 3/8 | Hand: 9 1/2

History: Also played baseball as a Washington D.C. prep (did not play football until junior year). Suffered a clavicle injury as a junior then broke his right elbow as a senior. As a true freshman in 2012, played all 12 games, drawing starts in the first two, and tallied 13 tackles, zero pass breakups and zero interceptions. Started all 13 games at free safety in '13 and posted 103-3-2 with 11/2 tackles for loss, one-half sack and one forced fumble. In '14, started all 13 games — 11 at FS, two at cornerback — and recorded 115-8-0 with four tackles for loss, one sack and one forced fumble. In '15, the Terps transitioned to a 4-3 scheme and Davis moved to boundary corner — produced 88-3-3 with 51/2 tackles for loss, one sack and five forced fumbles in 12 starts. Davis, whose mother is a nutritionist, speaks three languages.

Strengths: Excellent height for the position. Intriguing size, speed and athleticism. Bench-pressed 225 pounds 21 times at the Combine, indicating excellent strength. Good closing burst. Flashes aggression in the run game (see statement hit on opening play of the Senior Bowl). Hammers receivers in the flat. Clocked a 3.97-second 20-yard shuttle, the second fastest time of any cornerback at the Combine and indicative of outstanding lateral agility. Has played corner and safety and has special teams experience.

Weaknesses: Inconsistent and unpolished. At times plays slower than his stopwatch speed. Instincts are lacking. Needs to speed up his eyes and process information faster. Could stand to improve his route recognition and anticipation. Effectiveness wanes in off-man coverage. Downfield ball reactions leave something to be desired. Could stand to take his mental preparation to another level. Intensity and competitiveness fluctuate.

Future: Talented press corner with desirable body length and speed, though he really stands out for his physicality on the edge. Starter-caliber defensive back that tackles like a safety and offers versatility to be considered at either position. Would fit well with teams such as the Ravens, Seahawks or Patriots.

Draft projection: Third- to fourth-round pick.

Scout's take: "(Davis) had a good workout at the Combine. He just didn't catch the ball very well. He catches your attention in the Senior Bowl right away when he makes that big hit on the first play of the game. Then he didn't do anything the rest of it."

SS KIMLON "K.J." DILLON, #9 (Sr-4)

WEST VIRGINIA ▶ GRADE: 5.24

Ht: 6-0 3/8 | Wt: 210 | 40: 4.51 | Arm: 31 5/8 | Hand: 9 5/8

History: Prepped at Apopka (Fla.) High. Was kicked off the team as a freshman before earning his way back onto the team. As a true freshman in 2012, tallied 20 tackles, zero pass breakups and zero interceptions with one forced fumble in 13 appearances. Played nine games in '13, starting four as a nickel safety, and recorded 28-6-0 with three tackles for loss. Dillon, who has Type 1 diabetes, missed three games because of severe dehydration. Played the "Spur" in the Mountaineers' 3-3-5 scheme. Started 12-of-13 games in '14 and notched 62-7-3 (one touchdown) with 71/2 tackles for loss and one-half sack. Was flagged for "flagrant striking" against Texas and suspended for the first half of the Kansas State contest. Started all 13 games in '15 and posted 55-8-2 with 71/2 tackles for loss and one forced fumble. Also returned eight punts for 50 yards (6.2-yard av-

erage). A left ankle injury prevented him from participating in the vertical jump, shuttles and 3-cone drill at the Combine.

Strengths: Athletic and versatile (allows for disguise). Able to shadow tight ends and slot receivers. Fine zone awareness — reacts well to plays in front of him. Makes impressive plays on the ball. Very good closing speed. Has traits to contribute on special teams. Helped himself at the Senior Bowl.

Weaknesses: Needs to get stronger — bench-pressed 225 pounds just 11 times at the Combine. Gets bounced around in the box. Could stand to iron out his pedal. Average eyes — can be a tick late sorting through what he sees. Gets caught making flat-footed reads. Can let emotion get the best of him.

Future: Loquacious defensive back with starter-caliber athleticism belying his strong safety label. Eyes and instincts could limit his ceiling, but he is suited for a nickel safety role, and his speed and cover skills increase his value.

Draft projection: Fourth- to fifth-round pick.

RCB DeANDRE ELLIOTT, #13 (Sr-5)

COLORADO STATE ▶ GRADE: 5.31

Ht: 6-0 7/8 | Wt: 188 | 40: 4.52 | Arm: 32 | Hand: 9 5/8

History: Played corner, receiver and running back as a prep in Dallas, where he also played basketball and ran track. Redshirted in 2011. Broke his left wrist in the spring of '12. On March 31, was charged with three misdemeanors — one count of unlawful sexual contact and two counts of second degree criminal trespass. According to the police report, Elliott and another player were let into a sorority house during a pizza delivery before he entered a girl's room and groped her. Did not play in the '12 season opener (ankle), but started 7-of-11 games at left cornerback and recorded 33 tackles, seven pass breakups and two interceptions (one touchdown) with two tackles for loss. Changed from jersey No. 19 to No. 13 in '13 when he started 10-of-13 games played and contributed 29-10-1. Did not play against Utah State. Played 12 games in '14, starting five at LCB, and collected 30-6-2 with two tackles for loss. Dealt with a hernia injury that sidelined him against San Jose State and required off-season surgery. In '15, started all 11 games at LCB and logged 32-4-2 with a blocked field goal. Did not play against Colorado (concussion) or Air Force. Graduated with a degree in communication studies.

Strengths: Very good height and arm length. Thin ankles. Well-conditioned athlete with

DEFENSIVE BACKS

157

less than four percent body fat. Showed off impressive leaping ability and lateral agility at the Combine — 41-inch vertical jump and 3.94-second short shuttle both ranked second-best amongst cornerbacks at the Combine.

Weaknesses: Is very lean and needs to get functionally stronger. Rigid movement. Marginal production. Was not challenged by top-notch receivers in the Mountain West. Durability is an issue — has been hampered by repeated soft tissue injuries.

Future: Fragile, finesse, man-cover cornerback who is a better tester than football player. Could be overdrafted based on measurables.

Draft projection: Fourth- to fifth-round pick.

SS CLAYTON FEJEDELM, #20 (Sr-5)

ILLINOIS ▶ GRADE: 5.14

Ht: 5-11 7/8 | Wt: 204 | 40: 4.54 | Arm: 30 3/4 | Hand: 9 3/4

History: Last name is pronounced "FEJ-uh-lem." Also wrestled and played lacrosse as an Illinois prep. Began his college career at NAIA power St. Xavier in Chicago. As a true freshman in 2011, played 13 games, starting three at strong safety for the national champion Cougars — recorded 68 tackles, nine pass breakups and five interceptions (touchdown) with five tackles for loss, one sack, three forced fumbles and one blocked kick. Had a team-high 8 1/2 tackles in the national title game. Sat out two early-season contests (ankle). Started all 13 games at SS in '12 and totaled 87-8-3 with 10 1/2 tackles for loss and one sack. Was deployed in deep coverage approximately 80 percent of the time (also dropped down as part of an eight-man front). Intent on proving himself a Division I player, transferred — as a walk-on — to the U of I in '13 (sat out per NCAA rules). In '14, tallied 51-2-0 with one tackle for loss in 13 games (one start). Was put on scholarship prior to his senior season. In '15, was the Illini's Most Outstanding Defensive Player after finishing fifth nationally in tackles — registered 140-7-2 with 4 1/2 tackles for loss, one forced fumble and a blocked punt return score in 12 starts at free safety in Illinois' predominantly cover-4 scheme. Team captain graduated with a degree in communication.

Strengths: Works hard in the weight room and it shows (muscular physique with six percent body fat). His 40 1/2-inch vertical and 20 bench-press reps would have placed first and second, respectively, amongst safeties at the Combine. Highly productive tackler. Effective in the box — natural coming downhill and fit-ting in the run game. Solid tackler. Made calls and checks. Profiles like a core special teams player. Excellent makeup and character. Smart, confident and motivated.

Weaknesses: Stiff and straight-linish. Was not asked to man up slot receivers. Exposed when isolated in deep coverage. Shows rigidity in his pedal and lacks suddenness to play off the hash. Pedestrian agility and hip flexibility. Is vulnerable to play-action fakes. Takes some false steps and lacks burst to recover. Struggles to redirect and accelerate. Was more productive than impactful.

Future: Walk-on-turned-captain who came out of nowhere to lead the nation's safeties in tackles as a senior then raised eyebrows with his pro day performance. Is the type you root for, but has athletic limitations and will have to carve a niche as a fourth/box safety and core special teams player. Try-hard overachiever who faces an uphill battle to stick, though he's thrived as an overlooked player and has make-it traits. Tackling ability gives him a chance.

Draft projection: Late draftable pick.

SS KAVON FRAZIER, #5 (Sr-4)

CENTRAL MICHIGAN ▶ GRADE: 5.09

Ht: 5-11 7/8 | Wt: 217 | 40: 4.70e | Arm: 32 1/4 | Hand: 9

History: First name is pronounced "KAY-von." Grand Rapids, Mich. native also lettered in basketball and track and field. As a true freshman in 2012 (wore jersey No. 38), recorded 36 tackles, three pass breakups and one interception with one-half tackle for loss in 13 games (two starts). In '13, played the cover safety in the Chippewas' 4-2-5 scheme — started 9-of-12 games and recorded 67-5-3 with one forced fumble. Playing the deep safety in '14, was credited with 58-4-0 in 13 games (three starts). In '15, played a more traditional 4-3 free safety role, and was CMU's Defensive MVP and leading tackler — posted 108-4-1 with 4 1/2 tackles for loss and two forced fumbles in 13 starts. Wore jersey No. 21 against Monmouth and Minnesota, as CMU designated it a legacy number in honor of former teammate Derrick Nash, who died of leukemia. Graduated with a degree in child development. Suffered a hairline foot fracture at the Combine.

Strengths: Looks the part with very good muscularity. Aggressive running the alley and striking ballcarriers. Productive, physical tackler. Plays with urgency and takes good angles. Has a terrific special teams temperament.

Weaknesses: Marginal foot speed and range

DEFENSIVE BACKS

for the back end. Cannot match up with receivers in man coverage. Shows some stiffness in his body and is not smooth or fluid in transition. Faced lesser competition in a non-Power Five conference.

Future: College free safety lacking the foot speed and range to play on the back end in the pros. Big, strong thumper most ideally suited to play near the box and could make a team as a special teams contributor.

Draft projection: Priority free agent.

LCB **KENDALL FULLER**, #11 (Jr-3)

VIRGINIA TECH ▶ GRADE: 5.77

Ht: 5-11½ | Wt: 187 | 40: 4.45e | Arm: 31½ | Hand: 10

History: Younger brother of Vincent (75 games with the Titans, 2005-10), Corey (Lions) and Kyle (Bears). Kendall was a consensus All-American and Maryland's Gatorade Player of the Year as a cornerback-receiver. As a true freshman in 2013, started 12-of-13 games — first six at nickel, four at cornerback — and recorded 58 tackles, 11 pass breakups and six interceptions with 2½ tackles for loss, one-half sack and one forced fumble. Played with a broken left wrist in '14, managing 54-15-2 with 4½ tackles for loss and two sacks in 13 starts at cornerback. Had his wrist repaired after the season. Tore his right meniscus during '15 fall camp — notched 7-1-0 with one sack and one forced fumble before opting for season-ending microfracture surgery (was limited to just the bench press at the Combine). Will be a 21-year-old rookie.

Strengths: Very good instincts and footwork. Has a smooth, balanced pedal and transitions quickly out of breaks. Has NFL bloodlines and comes from a family well-versed in cover concepts. Very willing tackler — will throw his body around. Very good hands and on-the-ball production.

Weaknesses: Lacks ideal bulk and could stand to get stronger. Is overly aggressive jumping routes and taking chances, and gets beat more than he should. Easily lured by double moves. Has some tightness in his hips that affects his transitional quickness. Lacks awareness with his back to the ball.

Future: A wiry, confident and competitive cover corner with the length, ball skills and playmaking ability to earn a starting job. Durability concerns could affect his draft standing.

Draft projection: Top-40 pick.

Scout's take: "He's a first-round talent if he's not hurt. The (medical) re-checks will be important. Microfracture is not a bounce-back surgery."

FS **T.J. GREEN**, #15 (Jr-3)

CLEMSON ▶ GRADE: 5.42

Ht: 6-2¼ | Wt: 209 | 40: 4.34 | Arm: 32 | Hand: 9⅝

History: Safety, receiver and kick returner as an Alabama prep. Was recruited as a receiver (wore jersey No. 82 in 2013) — hyperextended his knee in late August and sat out the season opener before scratching two receptions for zero yards and zero touchdowns, while adding three kickoff returns for 60 yards (20.0-yard average) and eight special teams tackles. Moved to safety in '14 and recorded 24 tackles, zero pass breakups and one interception in 11 games (one start). Returned kickoffs 21-445 (21.2). In '15, started all 15 games at free safety and produced 95-3-0 with 5½ tackles for loss, one sack and two forced fumbles. Was ejected for targeting against North Carolina. Did not do shuttles or 3-cone drill at the Combine (right ankle). Will be a 21-year-old rookie.

Strengths: Looks the part — big, chiseled frame (less than six percent body fat). Exceptional size-speed ratio — blazed sub-4.4 times at the Combine. Explosive athleticism. Flashes playmaking ability. Rangy — covers ground, closes fast and makes plays all over the field. Length is a major asset in pass coverage — can contend and win in the air. Will deliver some big hits. Ascending prospect who is just scratching the surface.

Weaknesses: Raw. Just a one-year starter. Recognition, instincts and awareness are works in progress. Slow to process and late to trigger. Lacks the reactive quickness desired on the frontlines. Takes some untrue angles. Does not have a good feel for coverage to shadow and mirror receivers in his area. Plays out of control and leaves too much production on the field. Inconsistent tackler. Exposed against Alabama in the national championship game — struggled to prevent big plays and got earholed twice. Could stand to get stronger.

Future: Big-framed, athletic, converted receiver who was able to compensate for his inexperience with athleticism during his lone year as a starter. Could have used more collegiate seasoning and will require patience to become a viable, dependable pro, but he can contribute on special teams in the meantime and his best football is ahead of him. Has eventual starter potential given his size, speed, range and striking ability.

Draft projection: Second- to third-round pick.

Scout's take: "There was a buzz about him

DEFENSIVE BACKS

in the fall, but he's got a long ways to go. It comes down to reactive athleticism and the ability to feel (receivers) like a point guard. His ability to mirror is average. He is all over the place. He has a high ceiling."

RCB-FS DEIONDRE' HALL, #1 (Sr-4)

NORTHERN IOWA   ▶ GRADE: 5.34

Ht: 6-15/8 | Wt: 199 | 40: 4.64 | Arm: 34 3/8 | Hand: 9 3/4

History: Safety-receiver also competed in track and field as a Missouri prep. Wore jersey No. 31 as a true freshman in 2012 when he recorded 29 tackles, zero pass breakups and zero interceptions with one-half tackle for loss and one blocked kick in 11 games (three starts at Rover). In '13, started all 12 games — first seven at Rover, final five at cornerback — and had 57-5-2 (one touchdown) with 61/2 tackles for loss, three sacks and one blocked kick. Added 10 kickoff returns for 202 yards (20.2-yard average). A full-time cornerback in '14, started all 14 games and produced 73-6-5 (one touchdown) with 31/2 tackles for loss and one blocked kick. In '15, broke his right hand in Week Two, forcing him to play with a cast for seven weeks. Started all 15 games for the FCS runner-up Panthers — first five at CB, final 10 at free safety — and totaled 82-4-6 (two touchdowns) with 51/2 tackles for loss and three forced fumbles. Also had two career receptions for 45 yards (22.5-yard average) and five career punt returns for 39 yards (7.8-yard average). Did not bench press at the Combine (hand).

Strengths: Outstanding body and arm length. Outstanding hands and interception production. Plays the ball very well in front of him. Good athletic ability. Has a 37-inch vertical jump and explosive 10-foot, 7-inch broad jump, indicating good leaping ability. Efficient in his movement with few wasted steps. Aggressive in run support. Very tough, smart and highly competitive. Good positional workout at the Combine

Weaknesses: Has some tightness in his hips that negates his transitional quickness. Too much of a tweener — lacking the twitch for a corner and the size and strength for a safety. Has not regularly faced top competition at the FCS level. Average recovery speed and closing burst, as evidenced at the top of routes at the Senior Bowl.

Future: Lean, long-levered, competitive corner with safety versatility. Concerns about his top-end speed and ability to shadow NFL receivers could push him to safety.

Draft projection: Third- to fourth-round pick.

Scout's take: "The Raiders drafted this same guy two years ago in the [seventh] round — (Western Kentucky Jonathan) Dowling. He had the same length and the same issues. He was too skinny and too much of a tweener. That is why he slid to the fifth. That's where I have Hall. ... He didn't run well enough to play corner at the Combine. I think more teams will start moving him to safety."

LCB VERNON HARGREAVES III, #1 (Jr-3)

FLORIDA   ▶ GRADE: 6.75

Ht: 5-10 1/2 | Wt: 204 | 40: 4.53 | Arm: 30 5/8 | Hand: 8 3/4

History: Father, Vernon Jr., is the linebackers coach at Arkansas. Vernon III was a decorated player coming out of Tampa, Fla. — Parade All-American, 8A Player of the Year and consensus No. 1 cornerback recruit in America. Dealt with a shoulder sprain during 2013 fall camp. An injury to Marcus Roberson opened the door for Hargreaves to factor as a true freshman — played 12 games, starting the final 10 at left cornerback, and tallied 38 tackles, 11 pass breakups and three interceptions. Started all 12 games in '14 and produced 50-13-3 with two tackles for loss. Sustained a head injury against LSU. Was a Thorpe Award finalist in '15 after starting all 13 games and logging 33-4-4 with one tackle for loss and one forced fumble. Did not play against East Carolina (knee). Was dealing with back pain leading up to the Tennessee contest (reportedly visited a chiropractor) — hurt his back during the game, but returned after he was given topical muscle relaxant. Also had five career kickoff returns for 99 yards (19.8-yard average) and five career punt returns for 41 yards (8.2-yard average). Will be a 21-year-old rookie.

Strengths: Exceptional feet. Terrific eyes and instincts — anticipates routes unfolding, sorts outs route combinations and reacts instantly to what he sees. Advanced football intelligence. Explosive athlete with outstanding reactionary quickness to read the quarterback and break on the ball. Has a 39-inch vertical jump and very good leaping ability to compete for contested balls in the air. Very fluid mover that snaps out of his breaks. Shadows and mirrors and stays in the hip pocket of receivers — can run routes for them. Very technically sound with clean footwork. Extremely competitive and passionate about the game. Willing tackler. Takes a very professional approach to the game.

Weaknesses: Lacks ideal length. Small hands. Has a relatively small bone structure which could be more susceptible to injury in the pros. Short arms factor into production he leaves on the field in terms of plays he posi-

DEFENSIVE BACKS

tions himself to make but doesn't finish. Does not have elite straight-line speed or closing burst to track down defenders. Can be lured by play-action fakes. Got caught with his hand in the cookie jar multiple times as a junior, biting on double-moves and getting burned for big plays (see Michigan). Misses some open-field tackles when he gets overaggressive and does not break down under control. Occasionally lets ballcarriers escape his grasp when he tries for the strip rather than securing the tackle.

Future: The most complete and polished cover corner in the draft capable of playing on or off coverage and locking down his man or defending his zone, Hargreaves has been a playmaker dating back to high school. Could be a turnover machine in the pros given his terrific ball skills. A Day One immediate starter with perennial Pro Bowl potential.

Draft projection: Top-10 pick.

Scout's take: "Hargreaves has the best ball skills of all the corners in the draft. He is better than Joe Haden in my opinion — he has better twitch, feet, hips and ball skills. Everyone was saying he was too small during the fall. He's big enough. He's got everything you want. I actually like Hargreaves better than (Florida State's Jalen) Ramsey."

RCB De'VANTE HARRIS, #1 (Sr-4)
TEXAS A&M ▶ GRADE: 4.87
Ht: 5-10 5/8 | Wt: 176 | 40: 4.56 | Arm: 30 5/8 | Hand: 8 1/8

History: Father, Rod, starred at Texas A&M and played 38 games as a kick returner for the Saints, Cowboys and Eagles (1989-91). De'Vante prepped in Texas. As a true freshman in 2012, started 7-of-12 games and recorded 30 tackles, three pass breakups and one interception with 2 1/2 tackles for loss and one forced fumble. Did not play against LSU. Was suspended for the first two games of the '13 season (violation team rules), but started all 11 games played and tallied 56-8-1 with 2 1/2 tackles for loss. Added 11 punt returns for 74 yards (6.7-yard average). Missed the first three games of the '14 season because of a UTI. On the season, started 7-of-10 games played and managed 53-5-1 with 1 1/2 tackles for loss. Playing left corner for new defensive coordinator John Chavis in '15, started all 13 games and collected 31-8-2 (one touchdown) with one tackle for loss. Did not bench press at the Combine (illness).

Strengths: Experienced four-year starter in the Southeastern Conference. Extremely confident and competitive (and will let you know). Plays with swagger and energy. Good

football intelligence. Has a 38 1/2-inch vertical jump and outstanding shuttle times that correlate to lateral agility. Serves as a jammer on punt return.

Weaknesses: Has a very slight frame. Hands tied for the smallest measured at the Combine. Bounces off too many tackles and will be exposed in run support at the next level. Marginal Combine positional workout — got beat up by the ball, slowing to catch and double-catching. Ankle-biting tackler who misses too many.

Future: Strength-deficient, linear athlete with the football intelligence, competitiveness and playing demeanor to fend for a backup job if he could add some bulk to his narrow frame. Is not built to withstand the rigors of the NFL.

Draft projection: Priority free agent.

FS-RCB DeANDRE HOUSTON-CARSON, #36 (Sr-5)
WILLIAM & MARY ▶ GRADE: 5.45
Ht: 6-0 3/4 | Wt: 201 | 40: 4.54 | Arm: 30 1/8 | Hand: 9 1/8

History: Prepped in Virginia, where he also earned letters in basketball (three) and track (one). Redshirted in 2011. Played cornerback his first three seasons. Started all 11 games in '12 and recorded 55 tackles, six pass breakups and one interception with one blocked field goal. Started all 12 games in '13 and tallied 62-11-2 with 4 1/2 tackles for loss, one sack and two blocked kicks. In '14, totaled 67-4-3 with 2 1/2 tackles for loss and four blocked kicks before suffering a season-ending wrist injury against James Madison. Moved to free safety in '15 and was the Colonial Athletic Association co-Defensive Player of the Year after leading the team in tackles — produced 109-3-4 (94-yard touchdown against Villanova) with 4 1/2 tackles for loss, one sack, one forced fumble and two blocked kicks. Also returned a blocked extra point for two points against Richmond and a blocked field goal 65 yards for a score against Duquesne. Team captain. Earned invitations to the Senior Bowl and Combine.

Strengths: Good pattern recognition and zone awareness (see INT TD vs. Villanova). Comes downhill from depth to support the run. Takes good angles. Versatile and aligned at corner and safety. Stood out on special teams and demonstrated a knack for blocking kicks. Solid personal and football character.

Weaknesses: Has a narrow, lean frame with short arms. Needs to get functionally stronger. Not an intimidating presence or sudden athlete. Has some lower-body stiffness. Lacks power in his body and does not strike with force. Did not produce ideal 20- and 60-yard

DEFENSIVE BACKS

shuttle times at the Combine, indicating below-average lateral agility. Tied for the lowest vertical jump (32 1/2 inches) among free safeties at the Combine, indicating average athletic ability. Has not regularly matched up vs. top competition.

Future: Substance-over-style, FCS defensive back who profiles as a developmental boundary cornerback for a team that deploys predominantly zone coverage. Versatility is a plus, and special teams could be his ticket.

Draft projection: Third- to fourth-round pick.

RCB XAVIEN HOWARD, #4 (Jr-4)

BAYLOR ▶ GRADE: 5.33

Ht: 6-0 1/8 | Wt: 201 | 40: 4.57 | Arm: 31 1/4 | Hand: 9 1/8

History: First name is pronounced "ex-AY-vee-uhn." Quarterback-cornerback also played basketball and ran track as a Texas prep (high school teammate of William Jackson III). Redshirted in 2012. Was a reserve/special teams player in '13 when he notched five tackles, zero pass breakups and one interception with one forced fumble in 13 appearances. Started all 26 games the next two seasons — totaled 51-13-4 with 4 1/2 tackles for loss and 1 1/2 sacks in '14; and 42-10-5 with one tackle for loss in '15.

Strengths: Very well-built. Has raw tools to coach up. Experienced in man coverage. Balanced pedal. Good ball production — flashes hand-eye coordination to break up throws and has good hands to intercept. Was relatively effective suppressing completions in a pass-happy conference. Tough, competitive and durable.

Weaknesses: Doesn't have the juice to stay glued to high-octane receivers. Shows some stiffness in his hips and ankles covering short-to-intermediate routes. Average recovery speed. Press technique needs work. Peeks too much and gets out of phase. Too grabby. Plays into the boundary and is not asked to cover a lot of ground. Inconsistent downfield ball reactions (not a natural ballhawk). Only bench-pressed 225 pounds 11 times at the Combine and recorded a 33-inch vertical jump, both below-average measures of strength and explosion. Does not play big in the run game.

Future: Big boundary cornerback who would have benefited from another year at Baylor, but has size and press ability coveted by teams such as Seattle, Philadelphia or New England where he could maximize his length and ball skills. Is more effective the better he's schemed.

Draft projection: Third- to fourth-round pick.

Scout's take: "What I thought was interesting looking at the numbers was that (Howard) had one of the lowest completion percentages allowed in this draft. He is a big, deceptive athlete. They don't play a lot of coverages — it's a lot of man and cover 2."

LCB WILLIAM JACKSON III, #3 (Sr-4)

HOUSTON ▶ GRADE: 5.63

Ht: 6-0 3/8 | Wt: 189 | 40: 4.36 | Arm: 31 3/4 | Hand: 9 1/4

History: Also ran track as a prep in Houston, where he teamed with Xavien Howard. Was a non-qualifier coming out of high school, and spent 2012 at Trinity Valley Community College (Texas), where he wore jersey No. 1 and compiled 12 tackles, three pass breakups and zero interceptions in nine games. With the Cougars in '13, recorded 35-7-1 (96-yard touchdown against UTSA) and one forced fumble in 13 games (four starts). Started 12-of-13 games in '14 and tallied 37-10-2 with 1 1/2 tackles for loss and one forced fumble. Was ejected for targeting against Temple and suspended the first half of the South Florida contest. In '15, led the nation and set a school single-season school record for pass breakups — produced 43-23-5 (two touchdowns) with 1 1/2 tackles for loss. Injured his MCL against Cincinnati and did not play against Memphis. Did not start against Navy, as the Cougars deployed a bigger lineup to defend the Mids' triple option. Was Defensive MVP of the Peach Bowl against Florida State, but suffered a knee injury that kept him from participating in the Senior Bowl. Cramping at the Combine prevented him from registering a vertical jump, shuttle time or 3-cone drill.

Strengths: Desirable size and speed. Uses his length to jam and disrupt receivers. Shadows off the line. Can flip his hips and run vertically. Outstanding ball production. Is very active and attacks the ball like it's his. Competes with urgency at the catch point — plays the pocket and scraps to prevent completions. Good reactionary quickness.

Weaknesses: Not a workout warrior — did just 10 bench-press reps and recorded an ordinary, 9-foot, 8-inch broad jump at the Combine. Oftentimes shuffled rather than backpedaling. Needs to improve his processing speed. Recognition and anticipation are works in progress. Can be short-circuited by complicated route combos, and will require patience grasping complex NFL concepts. Bites on routes and double-moves too easily. Questionable leaping ability — could lose some battles vs. top above-the-rim receivers. Shows some

DEFENSIVE BACKS

stiffness in space (see Florida State when he was embarrassed by Travis Rudolph). Shoddy tackler. Tends to duck and lead with the crown of his helmet. Low floor.

Future: Lean, smooth-muscled, highly productive, highly competitive cornerback with an enticing combination of speed, man-cover skills and ball skills. However, Jackson is a candidate to get overdrafted, as his production belies unspectacular athleticism.

Draft projection: Second- to third-round pick.

Scout's take: "He was a polarizing conversation in our (draft) room. We were all over the board on him with big discrepancies in grades and a lot of discussion. I've heard it's been like that a few other places too. He's going to be an interesting career to track."

NCB-PR CYRUS JONES, #5 (Sr-4)

ALABAMA ▶ GRADE: 5.36
Ht: 5-9 7/8 | Wt: 197 | 40: 4.46 | Arm: 31 3/8 | Hand: 9 1/8

History: Played cornerback, receiver and running back and ran track as a prep in Baltimore, where he garnered Parade All-American honors and was named Maryland's Gatorade Player of the Year. Was a slot receiver/punt returner as a true freshman in 2012 when he caught four balls for 51 yards (12.8-yard average) and zero touchdowns in 11 games. Returned eight punts for 61 yards (7.6-yard average). Flipped to cornerback in '13 — played 11 games, starting five, and was credited with 25 tackles, five pass breakups and two interceptions with 1 1/2 tackles for loss and one sack. Missed '14 spring practice while recovering from surgery to repair a torn labrum in his hip. Started all 14 games at right cornerback in the fall and produced 46-13-3 with two tackles for loss and two forced fumbles. Added four kickoff returns for 77 yards (19.2-yard average) and 4-82 (20.5) on punts. In '15, started all 15 games at RCB for the national champs — totaled 37-7-2 with four tackles for loss and two forced fumbles. Also was an impact special teams player, returning punts 42-530 (12.6), including four scores to lead the country. Graduated.

Strengths: Quick-footed and agile — 6.71-second 3-cone drill ranked second amongst cornerbacks at the Combine. Good ball skills. Solid tackler. Veteran savvy. Made big plays for an elite, national championship team. Has traits to play inside. Impact punt returner. Smart, tough and competitive. Plays with a chip on his shoulder and does not back down from a challenge. Football is important

to him and he prepares accordingly.

Weaknesses: Lacks ideal height — at a disadvantage when matched against taller receivers who can go up and get it. Ordinary leaping ability. Needs to get stronger. Can be outmuscled and give up separation. Doesn't have elite speed or twitch for his size. Sometimes struggles with his back to the ball. Had six career fumbles.

Future: A compactly built, pesky nickel back, Jones was one of head coach Nick Saban's favorite players on his national championship team, and has punt return skills and professional makeup to win a job as a sub-package and special teams contributor.

Draft projection: Fourth- to fifth-round pick.

NCB JONATHAN JONES, #3 (Sr-4)

AUBURN ▶ GRADE: 5.10
Ht: 5-9 1/8 | Wt: 186 | 40: 4.32 | Arm: 30 1/4 | Hand: 8 3/4

History: Also an elite track athlete as a Georgia prep — 110-meter high hurdles national champion. As a true freshman in 2012, collected 13 tackles, one pass breakup and zero interceptions in 10 games (three starts in nickel package). Was sidelined five of the first six games of the '13 season — missed the first four because of a broken right ankle then sat out against Western Carolina with a left knee injury. On the season, managed 11-1-0 with one tackle for loss in nine appearances. Played the field corner for the Tigers. Stepped in to start all 13 games in '14, contributing 36-11-6 with one tackle for loss and one forced fumble. Pulled his left hamstring in the national championship against Florida State. Had minor foot surgery in the spring of '15. Started all 13 games in the fall and tallied 69-13-1 with 1 1/2 tackle for loss. Played for three defensive coordinators in four years. Graduated with a business administration degree.

Strengths: Can flat-out fly, enabling him to run vertically with wide receivers. Recorded the fastest 10-yard split (1.44 seconds) of any player at the Combine, indicative of outstanding short-area burst and acceleration. Has speed to recover or track down. Good weight-room work ethic and it shows (19 bench-press reps). Solid character.

Weaknesses: Adequate size. Short arms. Straight-linish. Falls out of the hip pocket too easily. Showed stiffness at the Combine and did not look natural catching the football. Can be outmuscled for 50-50 balls. Does not play to his strength in the run game (poor tackler). Eyes, instincts and anticipation are lacking.

DEFENSIVE BACKS

Not equipped to excel in zone coverage.

Future: Developmental, man-cover corner with track speed to be tried as a gunner. Speed is by far his best asset, however, and he will have to develop his positional skills to convince a team he can provide viable depth.

Draft projection: Late draftable pick.

SS KARL JOSEPH, #8 (Sr-4)

WEST VIRGINIA ▶ GRADE: 5.66

Ht: 5-9 5/8 | Wt: 205 | 40: 4.50e | Arm: 32 1/8 | Hand: 9 3/4

History: Also ran track as a Florida prep. Made an immediate impact in 2012 when he started all 13 games at free safety in the Mountaineers' 4-2-5 scheme — had a team-leading 104 tackles, six pass breakups and two interceptions with seven tackles for loss, one sack and three forced fumbles. In February '13, was charged with DUI under 21 — was pulled over at 2:45 in the morning when he was spotted driving without his lights on. Failed two sobriety tests and had a blood-alcohol level more than twice the legal limit for people younger than 21. Started all 12 games at FS in '13 and recorded 68-4-1 with three tackles for loss, two forced fumbles and two fumble recovery touchdowns. Moved to the "Bandit" safety in '14 when he started all 13 games and posted 92-3-1 with 41/2 tackles for loss and three forced fumbles. In '15, managed 20-1-5 with two tackles for loss and one sack in four games before suffering a season-ending torn ACL injury during a non-contact practice drill. Was leading the country in interceptions when he went down. Two-time captain graduated with a degree in multidisciplinary studies. Did not work out at the Combine (knee).

Strengths: Good arm length. High-intensity run defender — runs the alley and is like another linebacker in the box. Arrives with bad intentions. Physical, explosive hitter with knockback power in his body. Delivers some vicious hits. Smooth, balanced pedal. Good range to play off the hash. Tough and competitive. Passionate about the game. Vocal leader.

Weaknesses: Lacks ideal height. Average eyes and instincts. Can be a step late to the perimeter. Misses some tackles when he leaves his feet and launches. Year-One impact has to be considered given his injury. Long-term durability could also be an issue because of how he throws his body around.

Future: Physical, intense, hard-hitting hammer of strong safety with starter potential. At a minimum will be a core special teams player. Has some similarities to Colts 2004 second-round pick Bob Sanders in terms of size, phys-

icality, explosion and durability concerns.

Draft projection: Second-round pick.

Scout's take: "You watch him last year (in 2014) and he's trying to take people's heads off. He is a violent striker."

SS JAYRON KEARSE, #1 (Jr-3)

CLEMSON ▶ GRADE: 5.39

Ht: 6-4 | Wt: 216 | 40: 4.58 | Arm: 34 1/4 | Hand: 9 5/8

History: Has a daughter named Ja'riah. Jayron is nephew of Jevon "The Freak" Kearse, who was an All-Pro defensive end for the Titans, and cousin of cornerback Phillip Buchanon, who was drafted by the Raiders in the first round of the 2002 draft before playing 122 games for five teams over 10 years. In '08, was charged with robbery and residential home invasion after breaking into a house with friends. Kearse played safety and receiver as a Florida prep. Suffered a separated shoulder during '13 fall camp and sat out the season opener before recording 55 tackles, zero pass breakups and four interceptions with one-half tackle for loss and four forced fumbles in 12 games (three starts at free safety). Started 12-of-13 games at FS in '14 and had 54-7-2 with five tackles for loss and three sacks. Yielded the start to Jadar Johnson against South Carolina. Wore jersey No. 20 prior to junior season. Played strong safety in '15 when he produced 62-6-1 with 61/2 tackles for loss one forced fumble and one field goal in 15 starts. Did not do shuttles at the Combine (groin).

Strengths: Big-framed, rangy build with an 82-inch wing span. Has room to pack on muscle. Rare dimensions and surprising athleticism to match with tight ends. Covers ground with long strides. Has NFL bloodlines.

Weaknesses: Borders on too tall, and not many 6-4 safeties have thrived. Straight-linish. Needs to get functionally stronger. See-and-go reactor on the back end. Can be a tick late to key and diagnose. Inconsistent run fits (see Florida State). Is high-cut and struggles to come to balance or redirect. Physicality is just adequate. Absorbs contact. Below-average leaping ability. Could use more glass in his diet.

Future: Tall, sinewy, underdeveloped safety with intriguing size, growth potential and athleticism, though he has not put enough on tape to inspire confidence he'll evolve into a dependable, impactful starter. Has some upside if he can ratchet up his intensity, but leaves you wanting more. Compares favorably to Cowboys 2006 fifth-round pick Pat Watkins, though he is more athletic and intelligent.

Draft projection: Third- to fourth-round pick.

Scout's take: "He is a big, athletic dude. He

has some upside. When it comes to bend, balance, body control and agility, he is surprisingly efficient. You need to see him in person. Trust me on that one. He has some upside. He is just not a big hitter or an explosive striker."

SS-WLB MILES KILLEBREW, #28 (Sr-5)

SOUTHERN UTAH   ▶ GRADE: 5.42

Ht: 6-1 7/8 | Wt: 217 | 40: 4.59 | Arm: 32 1/8 | Hand: 9 1/2

History: Played defensive back, receiver and running back as a Nevada prep. Did not lift weights in high school. Redshirted in 2011 while recovering from a broken clavicle. Played strong safety for the FCS Thunderbirds. Started all 11 games in '12 and produced 69 tackles, five pass breakups and zero interceptions with one-half tackle, a 41-yard blocked punt touchdown and a 49-yard fumble recovery touchdown. Started 12-of-13 games in '13 and was credited with 54-2-0 with 4 1/2 tackles for loss and an 89-yard fumble recovery touchdown. Did not start against Eastern Washington (thigh bruise). Started all 12 games in '14 and produced 101-7-3 (touchdown) with two tackles for loss and four forced fumbles. Was the leading tackler in '15 when he registered 132-7-0 with 2 1/2 tackles for loss and two blocked kicks. Two-year captain graduated with an engineering degree.

Strengths: Has NFL strength right now — led all defensive backs with 22 bench-press reps at the Combine, and it translates to the field. Outstanding tackler with a rare combination of clinic-tape fundamentals and impact striking ability. Punishes ballcarriers by driving through contact — superb knockback body power. Hammer of a run defender — attacks downhill and physically dominates in the box. Violence jumps off the tape. Has traits to be a force on special teams. Surprisingly explosive athlete — posted a 38-inch vertical and 10-foot, 7-inch broad jump. Shows range belying his size. Sparkling intangibles and makeup. Intelligent.

Weaknesses: Has some tightness in his body. Can be overaggressive and miss some tackles. Man-cover limitations. Vulnerable against double-moves. Ball skills are more that of a linebacker than defensive back. Tweener traits. Seemed to tail off late in the season. Did not excel at safety at the Senior Bowl. Was athletically superior to FCS competition. Played at 230 pounds, but weighed 217 at the Combine. Could have a learning curve depending on what position/scheme he plays as a rookie.

Future: Fun to watch, Killebrew was an animal in the best sense of the word at Southern Utah, showcasing eye-opening striking ability supplemented by big-league measurables at the Combine. At a minimum should be a special teams ace, but has the skill set to force his way into a more prominent role, perhaps as a box safety, robber or nickel linebacker. Valuable depth player with make-it qualities.

Draft projection: Third- to fourth-round pick.

Scout's take: "I think he is a better athlete than he is given credit for. He is a good tackler. He's a hammer. If Deone Bucannon can go in the first round, it wouldn't surprise me if this kid did too. ... He fell off late in the season and didn't play as well."

FS DERRICK KINDRED, #26 (Sr-4)

TCU   ▶ GRADE: 5.12

Ht: 5-10 | Wt: 207 | 40: 4.49 | Arm: 31 1/4 | Hand: 9 3/8

History: Texas native played safety and running back in high school. Played two of the safety positions in the Horned Frogs' 4-2-5 scheme. As a true freshman in 2012, tallied 20 tackles (two on special teams), two pass breakups and zero interceptions in 12 appearances (one start). Played all 12 games in '13, starting the final three (two at weak safety, one at free safety), and tallied 48-5-2 with four tackles for loss. Started all 13 games at WS in '14 and produced 80-5-4 (one touchdown) with 4 1/2 tackles for loss and one forced fumble. Played his entire senior season with a broken left collarbone — started all 13 games at FS and totaled 87-3-2 with 3 1/2 tackles for loss and two forced fumbles. Did not bench press at the Combine (left shoulder).

Strengths: Good size, speed and leaping ability (37 1/2-inch vertical). Aggressive in run support — comes downhill and lowers the boom. Has special teams experience. Showed toughness playing through injury as a senior. Solid personal and football character.

Weaknesses: Tight hips. Misses too many tackles and gets exposed in space. Struggles the further he is from the line of scrimmage — liability in man/deep coverage. Limited range and recovery ability. Shoddy ball reactions.

Future: Good-sized, tough, physical safety whose skill set limits him to a reserve box safety and special teams role.

Draft projection: Late draftable pick.

FS JORDAN LOMAX, #27 (Sr-5)

IOWA   ▶ GRADE: 5.03

Ht: 5-9 7/8 | Wt: 202 | 40: 4.72 | Arm: 32 | Hand: 8 3/4

History: Also ran track at DeMatha Catholic (Md.). As a true freshman in 2011, notched seven tackles, zero pass breakups and zero

DEFENSIVE BACKS

interceptions in 11 games. Redshirted in '12 while recovering from a torn labrum. Had an appendectomy in late July '13. On the season, collected 5-2-0 with one tackle for loss in nine appearances. Started the season opener at right cornerback, but suffered a hamstring injury and missed four games. Started 12-of-13 games at free safety in '14 and produced 92-6-1 with one tackle for loss and one forced fumble. Was ejected for targeting against Iowa State and suspended for the first half against Pittsburgh. Started all 14 games at FS in '15 and posted 96-6-1 with one tackle for loss and one forced fumble. Team captain is on track to graduate with an economics degree.

Strengths: Nice arm length. Supports the run aggressively. Likes to hit. Vocal on-field leader communicates calls. Recorded 4.15-second 20-yard shuttle at the Combine, third-best amongst safeties, indicative of short-area quickness. Has special teams experience.

Weaknesses: Has small hands. Lacks ideal height and foot speed. Suspect strength and conditioning — only bench-pressed 225 pounds eight times at the Combine (the lowest of any safety) and body fat was more than 12 percent (relatively high for a defensive back). Must improve his functional strength to survive as a tackler in the NFL. Minimal production on the ball — only had two career interceptions.

Future: Downhill strong safety who can deliver some physical hits, but lacks the overall athletic ability and cover skills to project as more than a No. 4 safety/special teams player.

Draft projection: Priority free agent.

SS JORDAN LUCAS, #9/#5 (Sr-5)

PENN STATE   ▶ GRADE: 5.10
Ht: 5-11 5/8 | Wt: 201 | 40: 4.60e | Arm: 30 1/8 | Hand: 10

History: New York native spent 2011 in prep school at Worcester (Mass.) Academy. Was the first player to commit to PSU and then-head coach Bill O'Brien. With the Nittany Lions in '12 (wore jersey No. 14), was credited with one tackle, zero pass breakups and zero interceptions in 12 appearances. Started all 12 games at cornerback in '13 (changed to jersey No. 9) and produced 65-13-3 with 4 1/2 tackles for loss, one sack and two forced fumbles. Started 12-of-13 games at CB in '14 and logged 58-9-0 with four tackles for loss and two sacks. Was suspended the first quarter of the Pinstripe Bowl against Boston College (curfew violation). Moved to strong safety in '15 — managed 56-3-0 with 2 1/2 tackles for loss, one sack and one forced fumble in nine

starts. Hurt his right shoulder against Buffalo and did not play against San Diego. Injured the same shoulder against Northwestern and missed the final three games as well as the Combine. Team captain.

Strengths: Has very large hands. Good movement skills. Zone aware. Experienced three-year starter. Versatile — has played corner and safety.

Weaknesses: Comes unglued in man coverage. Does not set a hard edge. Struggles to disengage from blocks. Selective hitter. Ankle biter. Marginal ball skills. Regressed as a junior.

Future: Tight-hipped, converted cornerback lacking the size and physicality for the safety position. Ticket will have to come on special teams.

Draft projection: Sixth- to seventh-round pick.

RCB HARLAN MILLER, #1 (Sr-4)

SOUTHEASTERN LOUISIANA   ▶ GRADE: 5.15
Ht: 5-11 7/8 | Wt: 182 | 40: 4.58 | Arm: 31 3/8 | Hand: 9

History: Louisiana native played quarterback in high school. As a true freshman in 2012, tallied seven tackles, zero pass breakups and zero interceptions in 11 appearances. Played left cornerback for the FCS Lions. Started all 14 games in '13 and produced 45-14-4 (one touchdown) with two tackles for loss and one blocked kick. Changed from jersey No. 27 to No. 1. Started 10-of-11 games played in '14 and recorded 21-5-3. Injured his right shoulder against Tulane — did not start against Southeast Missouri and did not play against Incarnate Word or Northwestern State. Started all 11 games in '15 and logged 49-14-4 with six tackles for loss and one blocked kick. Also had 26 career punt returns for 294 yards (11.3-yard average). Team captain graduated with a degree in business management.

Strengths: Three-year starter. Light on his feet. Can flip his hips. Nice range. Good ball production. Active hands at the catch point — fights to break up throws. Gives effort to chase plays away from him. Plays with confidence. Has experience as a gunner and jammer on special teams.

Weaknesses: Lean and underpowered with nearly 12 percent body fat. Bench-pressed 225 pounds just six times at the Combine — fewest of any player — and must get stronger to survive the rigors of the NFL. Weak jam — cannot provide enough resistance to reroute receivers off the line. Average speed and leaping ability. Soft, grab-and-drag tackler. Produced the slowest 3-cone drill time (7.45 seconds) of

DEFENSIVE BACKS

any defensive back at the event, indicative of below-average lateral agility. Carries the ball too loosely as a punt returner.

Future: Smooth-muscled, smooth-moving, off-man corner with nice ball skills, though his deficient strength and leaky tackling will turn off many teams.

Draft projection: Sixth- to seventh-round pick.

SS-NCB JALEN MILLS, #28 (Sr-4)
LSU ▶ GRADE: 5.24
Ht: 6-0 | Wt: 191 | 40: 4.58 | Arm: 31 1/8 | Hand: 9 1/8

History: Prepped in Texas. As a true freshman in 2012, started all 13 games at left cornerback and recorded 57 tackles, five pass breakups and two interceptions. Had surgery in the spring of '13 to repair a torn right labrum. In the fall, started all 13 games — 11 at free safety, one at LCB, one at nickel — and tallied 67-3-3 with four tackles for loss and three sacks. Was arrested in June '14 and charged with second-degree battery, a felony, for allegedly punching a woman — according to the warrant, at about 1 a.m. the victim was looking for her friend at an apartment complex near LSU. She knocked on door of Mills' apartment, where Mills, his girlfriend and some teammates were hanging out. After trying to get in a second time, the victim claims Mills punched her in the mouth from behind, resulting in brief unconsciousness and four stitches. One victim and a witness identified Mills from a police lineup, but the victim's story conflicts with accounts from other witnesses, and Mills' attorney said Mills' girlfriend admitted to punching the victim. The charge was later reduced to misdemeanor simple battery because there was no way to prove the loss of consciousness the victim claimed and insufficient evidence to prove beyond a reasonable doubt the occurrence of "great bodily disfigurement," which is required for second-degree battery. Ultimately Mills pleaded not guilty, and the victim and district attorney agreed to drop the change upon Mills completion of a pretrial diversion program, conditions of which included community service, psychiatric evaluation and drug testing. Mills was suspended from the team from late May until early August. On the '14 season, he started all 13 games at free safety and posted 62-5-1 with three tackles for loss. Fractured his left fibula and damaged ankle ligaments during '15 fall camp, sidelining him the first five games of the season. Played seven games, starting the final six at nickel, and was credited with 30-3-0 with one sack. Sprained his left ankle in the

bowl game against Texas Tech.

Strengths: Quick to read and react. Equipped to align inside with slot receivers. Has a feel for routes and understands leverage. Good awareness and ball skills. His 6.86-second 3-cone drill ranked second amongst safeties at the Combine, indicating nice agility. Has a 37-inch vertical. Physical in run support. Has worked as a gunner and jammer on special teams. Four-down utility. Ultra tough. Has leadership traits. Four-year SEC starter.

Weaknesses: Lacks elite top-end speed. Smoother than sudden. Average playmaking ability. Could stand to improve his ability to jolt and shed blockers. Occasionally takes some poor angles in pursuit. Not an intimidating striker. Ability to play deep coverage is a question mark. Skill set falls somewhere between a true safety and cornerback.

Future: Tough, experienced, fairly athletic safety ideally suited for a role as a nickel safety covering slot receivers. Could prove to be a value selection if off-field incident causes him to slide.

Draft projection: Fourth- to fifth-round pick.

NCB ERIC MURRAY, #31 (Sr-4)
MINNESOTA ▶ GRADE: 5.24
Ht: 5-10 5/8 | Wt: 199 | 40: 4.53 | Arm: 31 3/4 | Hand: 9

History: Also earned letters in baseball, wrestling and track as a Milwaukee prep. Was a reserve/special teams player in 2012 when he notched five tackles, zero pass breakups and zero interceptions in 13 appearances. Stepped into the lineup as a sophomore and started all 38 games the next three seasons — totaled 52-10-0 with one tackle for loss in '13 (13 games); and 69-7-1 with two tackles for loss and two blocked kicks in '14 (13 games); and 64-6-1 with four tackles for loss, one sack and three forced fumbles in '15 (12 games). Team captain.

Strengths: Well-conditioned athlete who maintains four percent body fat. Instinctive defender who reads and reacts alertly. Good route recognition and reactionary quickness. Plants and drives suddenly on plays in front of him. Can play man or zone and has traits to play the slot. Has a 39 1/2-inch vertical leap. Supports the run with urgency — physical taking on blocks and works to disengage. Fluid hips. Good tackler. Short memory. Has special teams experience. Durable three-year starter. The game is important to him, and he takes his craft seriously.

Weaknesses: Lacks elite top-end speed. Not a ballhawk — nabbed just two interceptions

DEFENSIVE BACKS

in the last three years. Inconsistent downfield ball reactions. Tends to clutch and grab when beaten. Can miss some tackles when he gets overaggressive. Will always have physical limitations if matched against bigger, faster, wide receivers.

Future: Tough, aggressive, versatile cornerback who covers, tackles and competes. Is scheme- and position-versatile, including potential to be used as an inside nickel back given his quickness and physicality.

Draft projection: Fourth- to fifth-round pick.

Scout's take: "He has good plant and drive in zone coverage. I worry about him playing off. I wanted to move him to safety at first. If you put him at nickel, I think he holds his value. I worry about him in space."

SS KEANU "KIKI" NEAL, #42 (Jr-3)

FLORIDA ▶ GRADE: 5.68

Ht: 6-0 1/2 | Wt: 211 | 40: 4.64 | Arm: 32 3/4 | Hand: 10 5/8

History: Older brother, Clint Hart, was a safety who played 99 games over seven years for the Eagles, Chargers and Rams (2003-09). Neal is a Florida native who also played basketball and ran track in high school. As a true freshman in 2013, recorded five tackles (special teams), zero pass breakups and zero interceptions in 12 appearances. In '14, started 8-of-10 games played at strong safety and managed 45-4-3 with one tackle for loss, one forced fumble and a 49-yard fumble recovery score. Sustained a high ankle sprain against Georgia — sat out against Vanderbilt and South Carolina and did not start against East Carolina and Florida State. Sat out the first two games of the '15 season (hamstring) before producing 96-1-1 with 31/2 tackles for loss, two sacks and one forced fumble in 12 games (11 starts at SS). Did not start against South Carolina (foot).

Strengths: Good size, with long arms and the biggest hands of any defensive back measured at the Combine. Showed explosion by posting a 38-inch vertical and 11-foot broad jump. Drops downhill like a battering ram. Strong tackler who delivers a blow. Makes receivers think twice about coming over the middle. Tough and intense.

Weaknesses: Has too much stiffness in his body and struggles to break down in the open field and come to balance, resulting in too many missed tackles. Struggles to unlock his hips, redirect and accelerate. Can be mismatched in the passing game. Lacks recovery speed. Average ball skills.

Future: Strong, hard-hitting physical presence lacking ideal hip flexibility and the fluidity in his body desired on the back end. One of the polarizing evaluations in this year's draft, Neal has received grades ranging from the first round to the fifth from NFL evaluators. Lack of reactionary quickness and too many missed tackles will temper big grades. Striking ability and physicality vs. the run do not figure to let him out of the second round. Has drawn some comparisons to Rodney Harrison and has potential to become a solid starter in the pros.

Draft projection: Second- to third-round pick.

Scout's take: "His cover skills are average. He is a big hitter, and that's what is going to excite (scouts), but I don't think he is a great tackler. He has size, but I don't see matching athletic ability. I'm not sure he can run."

NCB KEVIN PETERSON, #1 (Sr-4)

OKLAHOMA STATE ▶ GRADE: 5.21

Ht: 5-10 3/8 | Wt: 181 | 40: 4.59 | Arm: 31 | Hand: 8 5/8

History: Cornerback-running back and Oklahoma native — won state championships in football and track (10.88 100 meters) and played basketball. As a true freshman in 2012, had 20 tackles, two pass breakups and zero interceptions in 13 games (one start). Stepped into the lineup in '13 and started 11-of-12 games played, collecting 24-4-2 with three tackles for loss. Did not play against Texas Tech, and did not start against Texas. Started all 13 games in '14 and produced 59-11-2 with 11/2 tackles for loss. Had a knee scope during '15 fall camp and did not play in the season opener against Central Michigan. Was voted the Cowboys' Most Outstanding Defensive Player after starting all 12 games played and logging 42-6-1 with 41/2 tackles for loss. Sprained his ankle against West Virginia, but had the benefit of two weeks between games and did not miss a start. Team captain.

Strengths: Mirrors receivers off the line and stays in phase downfield. Plays the pocket effectively. Gives effort in run support and uses his hands aggressively to box receivers. Willing tackler. Plays with his head on a swivel and shows good reactionary quickness. Battle-tested — has experience going toe-to-toe with NFL-caliber receivers in a wide-open league. Was instrumental in containing Kevin White (Bears 2015 first-rounder), Baylor's Corey Coleman and TCU's Josh Doctson, among others. Smart and hardworking. Is ultra tough and will play through pain.

Weaknesses: Small-framed and lean. Lacks ideal length (shows on tape when the difference between a completion or a PBU is inches). Average timed speed and ball skills. Could be overmatched by bigger, stronger wide receivers. Needs to get functionally stronger in all areas — press, edge-setting and tackling. Can get caught peeking in the backfield. Was bested by Ole Miss' Laquon Treadwell in the Sugar Bowl.

Future: Tough, confident, fairly athletic cornerback who plays bigger than his size and could make a living as a nickel defender given his smarts, quickness and competitiveness.

Draft projection: Fifth- to sixth-round pick.

Coach's take: "He's got what I call authentic toughness. There aren't a lot of authentic tough guys out there. His toughness came through. He's had some (injury) issues people don't know about. Those young kids, they saw him respond to those injuries. He wasn't tapping out of practice, he wasn't tapping out of drills, he wasn't tapping out of ball games because he was hurt. He has been an unbelievable example." (ESPN) – *Oklahoma State Defensive Coordinator Glenn Spencer*

SS TYVIS POWELL, #23 (Jr-4)

OHIO STATE   ▶ GRADE: 5.36

Ht: 6-2 3/4 | Wt: 211 | 40: 4.46 | Arm: 32 | Hand: 9 1/2

History: Ohio native also earned letters in basketball, baseball and track. Redshirted in 2012. Served as a nickel back in '13 when he recorded 48 tackles, two pass breakups and one interception in 14 games (five starts). Also intercepted a Michigan two-point conversion attempt with less than a minute remaining to preserve a one-point victory. Had surgery in June '14 to repair a sports hernia. In the fall, was a 15-game starter at strong safety for the national champs — produced 76-4-4 with two tackles for loss and one forced fumble. Was named Defensive MVP of the national championship game against Oregon. Started all 13 games at SS in '15 and totaled 71-3-3 with one-half tackle for loss and one blocked field goal. Team captain participated in the Senior Bowl after graduating with degree in sport industry in 3 1/2 years.

Strengths: Excellent size-speed ratio. Good movement skills and range — quietly covers ground. Can carry tight ends and has length to make plays on the ball. Smart and assignment-sound. Low-maintenance team player. Has special teams experience. Durable.

Weaknesses: Misses too many tackles and is not a blow-up striker. Average leaping ability. Too often hesitates before triggering. Plays cautiously and gets caught up in traffic. Did not make many splash plays. Could play with more of an edge.

Future: Has size, athleticism and championship pedigree, but lacks a 'wow' factor, generally leaves you wanting more and is best-suited for a backup role. Is the type you look to replace if he's called upon to start for an extended period of time.

Draft projection: Fourth- to fifth-round pick.

Scout's take: "Powell is just good enough not to get you beat, but he does not make a lot of plays. I didn't see him play with the same speed he ran (at the Combine). He looked like a stiff, 4.6 guy. Then he comes out in shorts and tests through the roof and looks great to the coaches. He checked out on the board when he interviews. He's not a guy that I would jump on the table for, but I think he has something to him."

RCB-FS JIMMY PRUITT, #8 (Sr-4)

SAN JOSE STATE   ▶ GRADE: 5.03

Ht: 5-11 5/8 | Wt: 198 | 40: 4.67 | Arm: 30 3/8 | Hand: 9 3/8

History: San Diego native prepped at Helix High, where he also ran track. As a true freshman in 2012, recorded 41 tackles, 11 pass breakups and one interception with two tackles for loss and three forced fumbles in 12 games (four starts). In '13, started 11-of-12 games — season opener at cornerback, final 10 games at safety — and tallied 52-3-1 with one-half tackle for loss. Sat out the '14 season opener versus North Dakota (right MCL sprain), but returned to CB and started all 11 games played, totaling 37-7-3 with two tackles for loss and two forced fumbles. Played the second half of the season with torn right wrist ligaments (had off-season surgery). Started all 12 games played in '15 and logged 53-7-3 (touchdown) with four tackles for loss and one forced fumble. Did not play against San Diego State (concussion). Team captain. Did not do shuttles or 3-cone drill at the Combine (left hamstring).

Strengths: Good size. Surprisingly strong — pumped 225 pounds 19 times at the Combine. Competes for 50-50 balls and scraps through the whistle, even if beaten. Has played corner and safety. Hardworking and coachable.

Weaknesses: Short arms. Has tweener traits. Undisciplined eyes. Pedestrian timed speed and leaping ability. Loses phase and can be run by. Does not provide enough resistance in run support. Did not distinguish himself when presented with opportunity to step up in class against Auburn.

Future: Good-sized defensive back with

DEFENSIVE BACKS

functional ball skills, though he lacks standout athletic traits. Could battle for a job as a No. 4 or 5, or perhaps be considered as a free safety.

Draft projection: Priority free agent.

Scout's take: "(Pruitt) has adequate athletic ability, feet and hips, but limited speed, burst and acceleration. He doesn't help us."

LCB-FS JALEN RAMSEY, #8 (Jr-3)
FLORIDA STATE ▶ GRADE: 6.97
Ht: 6-1 1/4 | Wt: 209 | 40: 4.38 | Arm: 33 3/8 | Hand: 9 1/2

History: Also starred in track and field as a Tennessee prep, capturing several state titles in multiple events. Was ineligible to play as a sophomore after transferring high schools. Had microfracture surgery on his right knee that year. Five-star recruit originally committed to USC, but flipped his commitment when assistant coach Marvin Sanders was fired. Made an immediate impact as a true freshman in 2013 (wore jersey No. 13) when he started all 14 games — first three at cornerback, final 11 at free safety — and produced 49 tackles, one pass breakup and one interception with two tackles for loss, one sack, one forced fumble and a 23-yard fumble return score. Became the first true freshman to start at CB for the Seminoles since Deion Sanders in 1985. Was kicked out of a '14 fall camp practice session for being insubordinate and overly physical and combative with teammates, knocking teammate Jameis Winston to the ground. Said head coach Jimbo Fisher, per USA Today: "He was told not to do something and he defied me...He'll decide if he wants to play at Florida State...When I tell somebody to do something and they don't do it, it's serious." Was deployed as the 'Noles "Star" defender (hybrid safety/linebacker) in '14 when he notched 79-12-2 with 9 1/2 tackles for loss, three sacks, two forced fumbles and a blocked kick. Was the team's defensive MVP in '15 after moving to the boundary cornerback — recorded 52-10-0 with 3 1/2 tackles for loss, one sack and a 36-yard fumble recovery score in 13 starts. Added two kickoffs for 54 yards (27.0-yard average) — put on Charlie Ward's retired No. 17 for his kickoff returns because primary return man Kermit Whitfield also wore No. 8. Team captain. Tallied 119 solo tackles in three years. Also competed in track and field for FSU, earning All-America recognition as a long jumper.

Strengths: Exceptional size for a corner with very long arms. Rare athlete with exceptional movement skill and lower-body explosion for his size. Very good eyes, anticipation and ball skills. Great zone awareness. Diag-noses quickly and jumps routes. Very good press strength and twitchy plant and drive. Good transitional quickness. Extremely confident and carries a swagger. Recorded a 41 1/2-inch vertical jump, tied for the most explosive jump of any player at the Combine. Aggressive blitzing off the edge. Has a nose for the ball and is always around it as a safety (see Miami in 2014). Unique versatility to line up at any spot in the secondary. Secure wrap, tackler. A gym rat described as an extra coach based on the amount of time he spends at the football facility. Strong leadership traits. Well respected by teammates.

Weaknesses: Is a bit leggy and thin for the safety position. Shows some tightness transitioning in off coverage. Only produced three interceptions the last three years and is not a true ballhawking interceptor. Does not have elite on-the-ball production. Selective hitter.

Future: An elite world-class athlete and difference-making football player with versatility to play multiple positions in the secondary. Has the tools to become a shutdown, press corner capable of taking away half the field and becoming equally impactful at the safety position.

Draft projection: Top-10 pick.

Scout's take: "(Ramsey) is the best corner in the draft. I would not play him at safety. I'd keep him at corner. He's a better press corner than Xavier Rhodes. He is not better than Antonio Cromartie, but Ramsey is more physical. ... You can question why he does not have more production. A big reason why is because he is too physical and locks down his man. He does not have the opportunities to make plays on the ball because his man is covered so well. ...Historically how many guys have had the ability to play corner, safety, nickel and probably be a helluva returner and special teams player. He can do it all. He's a pure athlete with versatility."

NCB WILL REDMOND, #2 (Sr-4)
MISSISSIPPI STATE ▶ GRADE: 5.39
Ht: 5-10 3/4 | Wt: 182 | 40: 4.50e | Arm: 30 3/8 | Hand: 9 1/8

History: Played all over the field as a Tennessee prep. Tore his right MCL in the spring of 2011. Redshirted in 2012. Saw action in the final eight games of the '13 season, recording 23 tackles, two pass breakups and zero interceptions with 2 1/2 tackles for loss. Was the Bulldogs' nickel back in '14 when he tallied 51-5-3 with three tackles for loss in 12 games. Was suspended for the Tennessee-Martin contest (academics). In '15, started the first seven games at cornerback and managed 25-1-2 before suffering a season-ending torn right ACL injury (did not participate at the Combine). Redmond forfeited his eligibility for the '12 season, was suspended the first five games of the '13 season and was required to pay $2,660 in impermissible benefits, as the NCAA punished him and the football program for recruiting violations.

Strengths: Light on his feet. Flips his hips and changes direction efficiently. Good ball skills and hand-eye coordination to get his hands on throws. Gives effort to step up quickly in run support. Has special teams experience as a gunner and jammer.

Weaknesses: Size is just adequate. Short arms. Needs to get stronger — struggles to disengage from bigger, stronger receivers. Too easily opens the gate in press. Can be outmuscled at the top of stems and lose separation on in-breaking routes. Gets in trouble when his eyes get stuck in the backfield. Intermittent physicality. Soft, erratic tackler — see Ole Miss 2014 when a Rebel running back bounced out of Redmond's grasp for a 91-yard TD (also was exploited twice on double-moves, allowing a pair of aerial scores). Dives low and misses tackles.

Future: Fluid, quick-footed, inconsistent, man-cover corner whose ceiling is that of a nickel corner and special teams' contributor. However, Redmond's stock could be affected by his ACL injury which makes him a candidate for a "medical redshirt" as a rookie.

Draft projection: Third- to fourth-round pick.

Scout's take: "I liked him. At worst case, he could be a third nickel type before the injury. Who knows what he is after."

RCB RASHARD ROBINSON, #21 (Jr-3)

EX-LSU ▶ GRADE: 5.17
Ht: 6-1½ | Wt: 171 | 40: 4.44 | Arm: 32¼ | Hand: 9

History: Pompano Beach (Fla.) Blanche Ely product also ran track, blazing a 10.46-second 100 meters. Did not get certification from the NCAA Clearinghouse until three days before the 2013 season opener, but notched 16 tackles, three pass breakups and one interception in 12 games (two starts). Was suspended for the '14 season opener against Wisconsin. Started 6-of-8 games played at left cornerback and collected 17-1-0 with one tackle for loss. Was suspended indefinitely in November and ultimately dismissed from the team. Was arrested in June '15 for unauthorized entry into the apartment of Tigers quarterback Anthony Jennings, who filed a police report claiming items belonging to him were stolen. Robinson admitted to being in the apartment, but police could not link him to the stolen items. Was not apart of the team in '15. Calf cramping prevented him from doing shuttles or 3-cone drill at the Combine. Will be a 21-year-old rookie.

Strengths: Excellent length — tall and long-armed. Has raw tools to coach up. Despite not playing in 2015, showed up at the Combine with less than three percent body fat and ran in the mid 4.4s.

Weaknesses: Has just eight career starts on his résumé. Exceptionally lean — smooth-muscled and underdeveloped physically, lacking body armor to withstand the pro game's physicality. Weighed the lightest of any player at the Combine. Could stand to iron out his pedal and transition. Average leaping ability. Weak tackler. Got physically dominated by Mike Evans (Buccaneers '15 first-rounder) as a sophomore. Character, stability and dependability need to be investigated.

Future: Rail-thin, high-cut, finesse corner whose inexperience and off-the-field issues make it difficult for teams to gauge his projectability and trustworthiness. Has been removed from some teams' draft boards for character concerns.

Draft projection: FIfth- to sixth-round pick.

RCB KeiVARAE RUSSELL, #6 (Jr-4)

NOTRE DAME ▶ GRADE: 5.24
Ht: 5-11⅛ | Wt: 192 | 40: 4.60e | Arm: 31⅝ | Hand: 10

History: First name is pronounced "Kuh-vahr-ee." Was named a U.S. Army All-American after a standout prep career as a running back in Washington. Missed time at the beginning (concussion) and end (high right ankle sprain) of his senior season. As a true freshman in 2012, started all 13 games at cornerback and recorded 58 tackles, two pass breakups and two interceptions with two tackles for loss and one-half tackle for loss. Sustained a head injury against Boston College, but was cleared for the following week. Started all 13 games in '13 and logged 51-8-1 with 11/2 tackles for loss. In '14, served a two-semester suspension for academic fraud. Returned in '15, but played through a stress fracture in his right leg, eventually suffering a more severe break against Boston College (sidelined the final two games). On the season, started all 11 games played and totaled 60-4-2 with 31/2 tackles for loss, one sack and two forced fumbles. Opted to declare for the draft rather than petition the

NCAA for a fifth year of eligibility. Did not work out at the Combine (leg).

Strengths: Good size and big paws. Flashes pop in his hands. Shadows receivers off the line. Nice range. Made a pair of athletic plays on the ball late in the 2015 USC game to preserve a win. Does his part in run support. Plays with vinegar. Aligned outside and inside. Has traits to contribute readily on special teams. Three-year starter. Battle-tested vs. NFL-caliber receivers. Good football character.

Weaknesses: Needs to improve his jam technique. Does not always play with balance. Gets caught flat-footed at times and loses early in downs. Shows hip stiffness in transition. Does not show elite top-end speed or recovery ability. Average instincts and anticipation. Does not thrive in off-man. Inconsistent downfield ball reactions. Missed a year of development.

Future: Well-built, competitive, man-cover corner with size, skills and versatility to contribute readily in sub-packages and on special teams while vying for a more prominent role. Could prove to be a value selection if his injury pushes him down the board.

Draft projection: Fifth- to sixth-round pick.

Scout's take: "Russell is stiff and straight-linish with no ball skills. He looks tight. He is not a smooth or fluid athlete."

RCB ZACK SANCHEZ, #15 (Jr-4)

OKLAHOMA ▶ GRADE: 5.74

Ht: 5-10 7/8 | Wt: 185 | 40: 4.49 | Arm: 31 3/8 | Hand: 9 3/8

History: Two-way standout as a Texas prep. Redshirted in 2012. Started all 13 games in '13 and was credited with 46 tackles, 13 pass breakups and two interceptions with one-half tackle for loss. Also returned a blocked point after attempt for two points against TCU. Started all 13 games in '14 and had 43-8-6 with one tackle for loss. Sprained his right shoulder against Tulsa. Started all 11 games played in '15, totaling 45-7-7 (touchdown) with 3 1/2 tackles for loss and one-half sack. Sprained his right ankle during the first series of the Texas Tech game and did not play against Kansas or Iowa State. Had three career punt returns for 22 yards (7.3-yard average). Did not run or do shuttles or 3-cone drill at the Combine (right ankle).

Strengths: Highly productive on the ball and has finishing ability — nabbed 13 interceptions the last two years. Good plant-and-drive quickness. Jumps routes and snatches throws out of the air. Has a short memory and confidence of a cat burglar. Bench-pressed 225

pounds 19 times at his pro day. Three-year starter with experience matching with top-notch receivers.

Weaknesses: Needs to bulk up. Weight-room strength does not translate to the field. Marginal physicality. Not an explosive athlete. Undisciplined eyes. Gets fixated on interceptions to his detriment. Freelances and finds himself in no man's land. Susceptible to double-moves — too often gambles and gets burned. Gets outmuscled for 50-50 balls. Struggled with the size and physicality of Tulsa's Keyarris Garrett. Barely feigns interest against the run — at times looks like he's playing flag football. Soft, ankle-biting tackler who turns down contact and puts some shameful run-defense "efforts" on tape. Feast-or-famine performer.

Future: Smoother-than-sudden, maddeningly uneven ballhawk whose performance yo-yo'd between flashes of high-caliber playmaking and head-scratching lapses. Is not a finished product and could have benefited from another year in Norman, but his natural ability to intercept passes is a coveted skill. The team that drafts Sanchez will have to be willing to live and die by his riverboat-gambler mentality.

Draft projection: Second- to third-round pick.

Scout's take: "I liked him, but he still gambles way too much. He bites on double moves really bad. When he takes the bait, he really takes it. ... He is uniformly a second-round talent."

RCB KEVON SEYMOUR, #13 (Sr-4)

USC ▶ GRADE: 5.12

Ht: 5-11 1/2 | Wt: 186 | 40: 4.38 | Arm: 30 3/4 | Hand: 9

History: First name is pronounced "KEY-von." Has a twin brother. Grew up in Pasadena's "Snake Pits" housing project. Played all over the field in high school. Was a reserve/special teams player in 2012 when he appeared in eight games and tallied five tackles, zero pass breakups and zero interceptions. Missed five games while dealing with a nerve issue in his right shoulder. Started 11-of-14 games in '13 and produced 48-6-1 with two tackles for loss. Spent a week in the hospital and missed part of '14 fall camp because of a stomach ailment. On the season, played all 13 games, starting the first 11, and totaled 49-13-1 with one tackle for loss. The stomach issue flared up and cost him playing time against Boston College and Arizona. Yielded starts to Josh Shaw in the final two games. Suffered a partial tear of his right labrum in the spring of '15. Was hurt early in the season — sprained his left knee against Idaho, and sat out against Stanford and Arizona State — and fell out of favor, tallying 24-0-1 with one tackle for loss. Also missed the Holiday Bowl against USC (ankle). Graduated with a communications degree.

Strengths: Excellent timed speed. Can keep pace vertically and stay in the hip pocket on crossing routes. Willing run supporter. Has special teams experience as a gunner and jammer.

Weaknesses: Could stand to bulk up and get stronger. Needs technical work. Choppy, unbalanced pedal. Has lower-body stiffness. Comes unglued too easily. Average leaping ability. Was not a playmaker. Regressed as a senior.

Future: Unrefined, developmental cornerback whose speed will give him a chance to carve a niche on special teams. Evaluators had to go back to Seymour's junior tape to see him at his best, as Seymour spent time in the doghouse as a senior.

Draft projection: Late draftable pick.

SS ELIJAH SHUMATE, #22 (Sr-4)
NOTRE DAME ▶ GRADE: 5.07
Ht: 5-11 3/4 | Wt: 216 | 40: 4.59 | Arm: 31 1/8 | Hand: 9 3/4

History: Linebacker-running back won four state championships in New Jersey (two at Paterson Catholic, two at Don Bosco Prep), where he also competed in track. Was primarily a nickel/special teams player as a true freshman in 2012, scratching nine tackles, three pass breakups and zero interceptions. Played nine games in '13, starting four at strong safety, and tallied 23-1-0 with one tackle for loss. Missed three mid-season contests (hamstring) then was suspended against Stanford after he was late to a team meeting. An injury to start Austin Collinsworth opened the door for Shumate in '14 when he started 11-of-13 games at strong safety, contributing 66-4-1 with 2 1/2 tackles for loss and one sack. Started 12-of-13 games at SS in '15 and posted 70-2-1 with 6 1/2 tackles for loss. Was ejected for targeting against Temple and suspended the first half against Pittsburgh.

Strengths: Good bulk, movement and straight-line speed. Zooms downhill. Solid tackler who can generate some pop on contact. Has special teams utility.

Weaknesses: Average eyes and instincts — see-and-go reactor. At times plays too fast, doesn't arrive under control and misses tackles. Tight hips. Struggles in coverage. Recorded the slowest 20-yard shuttle time (4.53 sec-

onds) of any player at the Combine, indicative of below-average short-area quickness.

Future: Good-sized, straight-linish, downhill, box safety with speed and tackling ability to fight for a role as a No. 4 safety and special teams player.

Draft projection: Priority free agent.

FS JUSTIN SIMMONS, #27 (Sr-4)
BOSTON COLLEGE ▶ GRADE: 5.20
Ht: 6-2 3/8 | Wt: 202 | 40: 4.56 | Arm: 32 5/8 | Hand: 9 5/8

History: Engaged to be married in April. Safety-receiver also played basketball and ran track as a Florida prep. Played all 12 games as a true freshman in 2012, starting seven (six at free safety, one at cornerback), and recorded 52 tackles, four pass breakups and one interception with two forced fumbles. Suffered a fractured orbital bone during '13 spring practice. In the fall, tallied 34-3-0 with one tackle for loss in 13 games (two starts — one at nickel, one at FS). In '14, started all 13 games — seven at FS, six at right cornerback — and led Eagles defenders with 76-5-2 with two tackles for loss and one sack. Started all 15 games at FS in '15 and totaled 67-2-5 with one tackle for loss and two forced fumbles.

Strengths: Has desirable length. Well-conditioned athlete (four percent body fat) and it showed at the Combine. Recorded the fastest 20-yard shuttle time (3.85 seconds) of any player at the Combine and quickest 3-cone drill time (6.58) of any defensive back, illustrating outstanding lateral agility and burst. Big-time leaping ability (40-inch vertical). Good range — can play off the hash or run the alley. Good ball skills. Solid wrap tackler.

Weaknesses: High-cut with rigid, leggy movement. Struggles to unlock his hips and redirect. Lacks flexibility and suddenness to stick with slot receivers. Average eyes and instincts. Tepid intensity. Too much body stiffness. Not a violent, blow-up striker. Could stand to add some body armor to his frame.

Future: Lean, narrow-framed, rangy free safety who isn't flashy, but offers length, tackling ability, ball skills and impressive testing numbers. Has a floor as a dependable third safety if he can prove his worth on special teams.

Draft projection: Late draftable pick.

Scout's take: "He doesn't run very well. He has little production on the ball. I question his size and overall fit. There was a buzz on him coming into the season, but I think he was overhyped."

DEFENSIVE BACKS

RCB **LESHAUN SIMS**, #36 (Sr-5)

SOUTHERN UTAH ▶ GRADE: 5.14
Ht: 6-0 1/2 | Wt: 203 | 40: 4.54 | Arm: 31 5/8 | Hand: 8 1/8

History: Las Vegas native played free safety and receiver in high school. Endured a torn right labrum as a senior (had off-season surgery). Redshirted in 2011. Started 7-of-9 games played in '12 and tallied 37 tackles, two pass breakups and three interceptions. Missed two mid-season games (left ankle sprain), and did not start against Montana or Northern Arizona. Started 12-of-13 games in '13 and produced 62-4-3 with 11/2 tackles for loss. Did not start against Fort Lewis. Started 11-of-12 games in '14 and collected 67-9-0. Did not start in the season finale against NAU. Started all 12 games in '15 and posted 54-10-2 with 21/2 tackles for loss and one forced fumble.

Strengths: Has excellent size. Physical press defender to jam and reroute receivers. Mirrors off the line and blankets in short area. Works to leverage and squeeze routes. Shows nice timing to get his hands on balls at the catch point. Has a 37-inch vertical. Willing tackler.

Weaknesses: Hands measured smallest at the Combine (tie). Needs to get stronger. Could struggle vs. longer, faster receivers. Tight hips. Limited suddenness. Ordinary closing burst. Misses too many tackles. Marginal competition.

Future: Tough FCS cornerback who isn't afraid to mix it up, but lacks ideal length and athleticism. Will have to stand out on special teams to compete for a job as a No. 4 or 5.

Draft projection: Late draftable pick.

Scout's take: "Sims is sliding. I thought he would be a mid-rounder early on. He is stiff with small hands and bad ball skills. He falls off too many tackles. He'll get drafted late, especially if he runs fast again at his pro day. He has run in the 4.4's before."

RCB-KR **RYAN SMITH**, #2 (Sr-5)

NORTH CAROLINA CENTRAL ▶ GRADE: 5.05
Ht: 5-11 | Wt: 189 | 40: 4.46 | Arm: 30 1/2 | Hand: 8 7/8

History: Born in Germany, but prepped in Maryland, where he played in a pair of 4A state championship games. Redshirted in 2011 while healing a right ankle injury. Started 8-of-11 games at free safety in '12 and recorded 65 tackles, eight pass breakups and three interceptions. Sustained a concussion during the season, but did not miss a start. Played through a sports hernia in '13 when he started all 12 games at strong safety and carded 88-5-1 with 21/2 tackles for loss. Moved to cornerback in '14 — was hampered by groin pain, but started all 12 games and had 58-7-0 with 11/2 tackles for loss. Started all 10 games played at CB in '15 and posted 52-11-2 with 11/2 tackles for loss. Did not play against Bethune-Cookman (hyperextended knee). Owns the school record with 168 career solo tackles. Also returned 14 career kickoffs for 394 yards (28.1-yard average), including one score. Graduated with a criminal justice degree, and aspires to become a U.S. Marshall.

Strengths: Has good size and posted NFL-caliber measurables at the Combine. Good strength (18 bench-press reps). Nice body control. Can make athletic plays on the ball and pluck interceptions off his frame. Productive tackler. Played cornerback and safety.

Weaknesses: Short arms. Eye discipline is a work in progress. Lacks an extra gear to keep pace with burners. Ordinary transition and closing burst. Was not a ballhawk (just six career interceptions). Bites on double-moves. Could stand to play with more physicality. Marginal competition. Durability has been an issue.

Future: Lean, fairly athletic, small-school cornerback who competes and can make plays on the ball, though you wish he had more juice to inspire confidence he can hang with NFL receivers. Versatility and toughness give him a chance.

Draft projection: Priority free agent.

FS-CB **ALVIN "A.J." STAMPS**, #1 (Sr-4)

KENTUCKY ▶ GRADE: 5.03
Ht: 5-10 7/8 | Wt: 193 | 40: 4.63 | Arm: 31 3/8 | Hand: 9 5/8

History: Uncle, Sylvester, was a running back/kick returner for the Falcons and Buccaneers (1984-89). A.J. was a safety-receiver who played basketball and baseball as a Mississippi prep. Went to East Mississippi Community College, where he played receiver in 2012 (wore jersey No. 15) — had nine grabs for 73 yards (8.1-yard average) and zero touchdowns in nine games. Moved to cornerback in '13 (wore No. 2) and was credited with 51-9-4 with seven tackles for loss, one sack and one forced fumble, as EMCC won the national championship. Picked UK over Ohio State. With the Wildcats in '14, started all 12 games at free safety and produced 56-5-4 with one tackle for loss. Started 10-of-12 games in '15 and recorded 67-8-1 with one-half tackle for loss. Yielded starts against Georgia and Vanderbilt.

Strengths: Former receiver with nice hands to haul in interceptions when opportunities present. Enough range to patrol a third of the

DEFENSIVE BACKS

174

field. Has natural cover skill. Vocal on-field, secondary leader made calls and checks.

Weaknesses: Below-average size and athleticism. Has a lean frame and needs to bulk up and get stronger. Processes slowly and gets manipulated by play-action. Just a 33-inch vertical. Turns down contact. Weak tackler. Doesn't play with intensity, violence or urgency. Lost playing time to underclassmen as a senior.

Future: Lean, smoother-than-sudden safety in cornerback body. Lacks standout traits, does not show instincts to compensate and does not profile like a core special teams player. Just a guy.

Draft projection: Priority free agent.

FS DARIAN THOMPSON, #4 (Sr-5)

BOISE STATE ▶ GRADE: 5.87

Ht: 6-17/8 | Wt: 208 | 40: 4.66 | Arm: 30 3/8 | Hand: 9 1/8

History: Cornerback-receiver also played baseball as a California prep. During 2011 fall camp, sprained his right ankle before redshirting. Manned free safety for the Broncos. Played all 13 games in '12, starting the final six, and collected 43 tackles, three pass breakups and three interceptions. Started all 26 games played the next two seasons — totaled 63-1-4 with 11/2 tackles for loss and one forced fumble in '13; and 71-1-7 with five tackles for loss in '14. Sustained a concussion against Louisiana-Lafayette and sat out against Air Force. In '15, started 11-of-12 games played and posted 65-4-5 with 81/2 tackles for loss, one sack and two forced fumbles. Did not start against Air Force and did not play against San Jose State (concussion). Had a daughter, Novah, with his high school sweetheart in October. Team captain graduated in December with a health science degree. Overtook Eric Weddle for the Mountain West Conference record for career interceptions (19).

Strengths: Good size. Heady defender who plays with controlled aggression. Exhibits starter-caliber recognition, anticipation and instincts. Trusts his eyes — triggers without hesitation and attacks downhill. Field-fast and physical. Delivers some bone-jarring hits. Highly productive ballhawk with good ball skills. Plays with discipline and understands his run fits. Very good football intelligence. Takes good angles. Exceptional work habits — committed to improve. Experienced, three-and-a-half year starter.

Weaknesses: Has short arms. Not a workout warrior. Had nearly 13 percent body fat at the Combine, and managed just 12 bench-press reps of 225 pounds. Posted below-average athletic numbers across the board. Has some stiffness through his hips and lower body. Feasted on mid-major competition. Durability could be an issue given the abandon with which he plays.

Future: A much better football player than athletic tester, Thompson has the smarts, desire and competitiveness to earn a starting job and should contribute on special teams immediately.

Draft projection: Second- to third-round pick.

Scout's take: "I think he will go somewhere early in the second (round). He's not very fast, but he's instinctive and plays fast with good ball skills. That's what separates him. If he would have ran faster, he would have had a shot in the first (round). There are never enough quality safeties. They are getting to be like quarterbacks. Everyone needs them."

RCB CLEVELAND WALLACE III, #6 (Jr-4)

SAN JOSE STATE ▶ GRADE: 5.12

Ht: 5-10 3/4 | Wt: 188 | 40: 4.62 | Arm: 31 3/4 | Hand: 9 1/2

History: San Jose native played cornerback and receiver and competed in track and field in high school. Began his college career at Washington, where he redshirted in 2012 — was named Special Teams Scout Squad MVP. Cleveland's 24-year-old brother Terrence Willis was shot and killed in April '13. Cleveland was a reserve/special teams player that season, producing nine tackles, two pass breakups and one interception in nine appearances. Transferred to SJSU to be closer to home (his mother and grandmother were dealing with health issues in addition to the loss of Cleveland's brother). Was granted a waiver enabling him to play immediately in '14 — started 11-of-12 games and recorded 26-14-1. Was the Spartans' Outstanding Defensive Player in '15 after starting all 13 games and producing 44-7-3 with one-half tackle for loss. Did not bench press (right shoulder) or record shuttles or 3-cone drill (right hamstring) at the Combine.

Strengths: Well-conditioned athlete who maintains less than five percent body fat. Surprisingly quick feet for his build. Can flip his hips while maintaining balance, enabling him to mirror receivers. Good zone awareness and reactions. Shows route recognition and understanding of leverage. Drives on throws and competes at the catch point. Doesn't panic.

Weaknesses: Average size, speed and leaping ability. Needs to get stronger to better equip himself to press and tangle with bigger wide receivers. Inconsistent downfield ball re-actions. Erratic tackler — misses too many and can't yet generate much pop (leaks yards after contact). Gained 10 pounds for the Combine and did not run as well as expected.

Future: Could have used another year in col-lege if for no other reason than to get stronger, but has enough plus traits, including man-cov-er and ball skills, to warrant consideration as a developmental pick. Will have to prove he has enough strength and toughness for the NFL game.

Draft projection: Late draftable pick.

Scout's take: "I expected (Wallace) to run faster than he did. He's a good athlete with adequate hands, ball skills and strength. He needs to get tougher. He could have used an extra year."

NCB DAVID "D.J." WHITE, #28 (Sr-4)

GEORGIA TECH　　　　▶ GRADE: 5.14

Ht: 5-10 7/8 | Wt: 193 | 40: 4.49 | Arm: 31 1/2 | Hand: 9 1/4

History: Full name is David Jamaal White. Georgia native. As a true freshman in 2012, was credited with five tackles, zero pass breakups and zero interceptions with one forced fumble in 10 appearances. Started 9-of-13 games in '13 and totaled 50-5-1 with one tackle for loss and two forced fumbles. Started all 14 games in '14 and produced 66-8-4 (one touchdown) with 2 1/2 tackles for loss and one forced fumble. In '15, started all 11 games played and recorded 41-8-2 with one forced fumble. Did not play against Flor-ida State (ankle). Suffered a hamstring injury on the first day of practice at the East-West Shrine Game. Team captain graduated with a business degree.

Strengths: Has functional strength. Gener-ally does a good job shadowing and staying on top of receivers. Ate up a Keith Marshall slant route near the goal line and made a game-winning, overtime interception against Georgia in 2014. Solid tackler. Posted an 11-foot broad jump at the Combine. Has hus-tle traits (see Pitt 2014 when he sprinted 60 yards to strip a ballcarrier before crossing the goal line). Accountable, hardworking and coachable.

Weaknesses: Lacks ideal size with a small bone structure. Press technique needs work — gets overaggressive and lunges. Allows too much cushion and too many completions in front of him. Just a 33-inch vertical. Lacks elite agility and recovery burst.

Future: Experienced, competitive corner-back who lacks elite traits, but doesn't have overwhelming negative traits, either. Has a chance to carve a role as a nickel back, though he isn't as explosive as you'd like.

Draft projection: Late draftable pick.

RCB-RB BRANDON WILLIAMS, #21 (Sr-4)

TEXAS A&M　　　　▶ GRADE: 5.25

Ht: 5-11 3/8 | Wt: 197 | 40: 4.39 | Arm: 32 1/2 | Hand: 8 5/8

History: Has two daughters, Serenity and Lila. Texas native was one of the top-rated running back recruits in the country. Began his college career at Oklahoma. As a true fresh-man in 2011 (wore jersey No. 23), carried 46 times for 219 yards (4.8-yard average) and zero touchdowns. Transferred to be closer to his daughter, and sat out '12 per NCAA rules. With the Aggies in '13, appeared in 12 games and rushed 44-269-1 (6.1) with five catch-es for 17 yards (3.4-yard average) and one touchdown. Also returned two kickoffs for 16 yards (8.0-yard average). Did not play in the season opener against Rice (ankle) or against Auburn (coach's decision). In '14, started 6-of-13 games — had 87-379-3 (4.4) on the ground and 9-65-0 (7.2) out of the backfield. Converted to cornerback in '15 (changed from jersey No. 1 to 21) and responded by notching 37 tackles, seven pass breakups and zero inter-ceptions with one tackle for loss. Team captain was voted the Aggie Heart Award winner, the highest honor for an A&M player. Graduated with a degree in agricultural leadership and development.

Strengths: Outstanding size with desirable arm length. Maintains less than six percent body fat. Strong upper body. Good speed and agility. Excellent closing burst. Shows willing-ness as a tackler. Has gunner experience. Got thrown into the fire in his lone season at cor-nerback and responded — showed impressive mental toughness, adaptability and natural ath-leticism. Encouraging makeup — has tough-ness and a team-first attitude. Keeps things light among the group. Has upside.

Weaknesses: Managed just a 30 1/2-inch vertical jump at the Combine, indicative of limited leaping ability and athleticism. Very raw and unrefined. Still developing positional instincts and techniques. Could stand to iron out his pedal and transition. Receivers are eas-ily able to separate from him at this stage of his development. Has some underachiever traits. Faces a steep learning curve and will require patience.

Future: A converted running back and spe-cial teams performer following in a similar path as Chicago Bears 1999 fifth-round pick

Jerry Azumah, Williams has the athletic talent to be groomed into an eventual starter if the light bulb keeps getting brighter. Showed remarkable progress in his first year as a cornerback and has ideal length, burst and recovery speed to match up with NFL receivers.

Draft projection: Fourth- to fifth-round pick.

Scout's take: "(Williams) was a running back without instincts or run strength. They moved him to (defensive back) in training camp, and he ended up starting the rest of the year. He's very raw, but very fast. He has a high, high ceiling. He never played DB before and he still held his own against SEC receivers."

RCB DARYL WORLEY, #7 (Jr-3)

WEST VIRGINIA ▶ GRADE: 5.21

Ht: 6-0¾ | Wt: 204 | 40: 4.59 | Arm: 33⅜ | Hand: 10¼

History: Pennsylvania prep played receiver and safety and ran track in high school. Played 11 games as a true freshman in 2013, starting five (three at boundary cornerback, one at field cornerback, one at free safety), and recorded 45 tackles, five pass breakups and one interception with three forced fumbles. Did not play against Kansas State (shin). In '14, started all 11 games played at right cornerback and posted 52-4-3 with 4½ tackles for loss. Was arrested for battery after a nightclub surveillance video showed Worley grabbing a woman by the throat and pushing her to the ground. The incident occurred hours after the Mountaineers' Week-Three win over Maryland. Pleaded no contest to misdemeanor assault and got probation. Was suspended for three weeks (missed two games) before being reinstated. Hurt his ribs against Baylor and hurt his left shoulder against Kansas State. In '15, led the Big 12 in pass breakups and passes defended — started 12-of-13 games and logged 49-12-6 with two tackles for loss and two forced fumbles. Sustained a head injury against Oklahoma State, and was academically ineligible for bowl game against Arizona State. Lone non-start came versus Iowa State when Ricky Rumph started on Senior Day.

Strengths: Looks the part with excellent size and a rangy build — has very long arms (80-inch wing span) and large paws. Equipped to jam and reroute receivers. Has quick, soft hands to pluck or high-point interceptions (see Iowa State). Good ball production.

Weaknesses: Average athletic testing numbers. Tight-hipped with adequate bend, burst and closing speed. Labors to keep pace vertically with burners. Got abused by Baylor's

Corey Coleman. Struggled in man coverage vs. Oklahoma, and had a coverage bust that allowed a big 71-yard touchdown. Up and down performer. Character needs to be looked into.

Future: A big, press corner with ideal length and ball skills for a defense that employs a lot of Cover 2 such as the Panthers, Saints or Cowboys.

Draft projection: Fourth- to fifth-round pick.

NCB TAVON YOUNG, #1 (Sr-4)

TEMPLE ▶ GRADE: 5.03

Ht: 5-9⅛ | Wt: 183 | 40: 4.41 | Arm: 30⅝ | Hand: 9⅛

History: First name is pronounced "Tayvon." Cornerback-receiver also ran track as a Maryland prep — was part of a record-breaking 4X100 team. As a true freshman in 2012, tallied 12 tackles, zero pass breakups and two interceptions with two tackles for loss, 1½ sacks and one forced fumble in 10 games (two starts as a nickel cornerback). Did not play against Army. Started 6-of-12 games played in '13 and recorded 51-5-1 with one tackle for loss and one forced fumble. Did not play against Rutgers. Earned jersey No. 1, signifying his status as one of the toughest players on the team. Started all 12 games at field corner in '14 and collected 23-9-4 (touchdown) with a 63-yard fumble return score. Sustained a concussion against Memphis. Was limited during '15 spring practice after having minor surgery on his left knee. In the fall, started 12-of-13 games played at FCB and totaled 41-7-0 with five tackles for loss and one sack. Did not start against SMU (knee swelling) and did not play against UCONN (knee).

Strengths: Light on his feet. Quick-footed and loose-hipped. Speedy pedal and easy transition. Excellent speed to turn and run deep. Clocked a 3.93-second 20-yard shuttle, the fastest time of any cornerback at the Combine and indicative of outstanding lateral agility. Good ball skills.

Weaknesses: Size is just adequate — is at a physical disadvantage on the outside and does not have unique leaping ability to compensate. Small hands. Too thinly built, and durability could be an issue. Eyes and instincts are lacking. Struggles in zone coverage. Tends to clutch and grab. Does not set a hard edge. Weak tackler. Could struggle grasping complex concepts.

Future: Pesky, athletic, man-cover corner with potential to contribute in sub-packages and on special teams. Has speed and quick twitch to match with slot receivers.

Draft projection: Priority free agent.

DEFENSIVE BACKS

SPECIALISTS

PK ROBERTO AGUAYO, #19 (Jr-4)

FLORIDA STATE ▶ GRADE: 5.37

Ht: 6-0 | Wt: 207 | 40: 4.85e | Arm: 313/4 | Hand: 97/8

History: Florida native grew up playing soccer, but suffered a bone bruise on his right (kicking) knee his freshman year of high school. Redshirted in 2012. Won the Groza Award in '13 after breaking the national record for points by a kicker (157). Kicked off 120 times with a 60.8-yard average and 45 touchbacks (five out of bounds). Nailed 21-of-22 field goal attempts (95.5 percent) with a long of 53 yards, and converted all 94 point after attempts (single-season NCAA record for most made without a miss) for the national champs. Despite dealing with minor hamstring and quad injuries before the season and playing with a lingering hip injury during the season, was a Groza finalist in '14 after kicking off 96-62.8-49 (two out of bounds), kicking field goals 27-30-L49 (90.0) and making all 55 PATs. In '15, kicked off 84-62.8-47 (four out of bounds), drilled field goals 21-26-L51 (80.8) and made all 49 PATs. Did not miss a fourth-quarter kick until the Georgia Tech contest last fall when his potential game-winning kick was blocked and returned for a game-winning touchdown for the Yellow Jackets. Made 267-of-276 career kicks (field goals plus PATs), finishing as the most accurate kicker in NCAA history. Was the 12th kicker in history to never miss a PAT. Special teams captain graduated with his criminology degree and decided to forgo his senior year of eligibility.

Future: One of the most decorated kickers in college football history, Aguayo is a polished, highly confident prospect with rare, deadly accuracy to solidify an NFL team's kicking game right away. With an increased emphasis on longer extra points and Aguayo's automatic range inside 40 yards, he could be the first kicker in a decade drafted in the first three rounds even if his power and kickoff ability don't rate as special.

Draft projection: Third- to fourth-round pick.

PK BRAD CRADDOCK, #15 (Sr-5)

MARYLAND ▶ GRADE: 5.06

Ht: 6-0 | Wt: 186 | 40: 4.90e | Arm: 31 | Hand: 81/4

History: Grew up in Australia playing soccer, tennis, track and Australian Rules football (played one year at Tabor Christian College). With the Terps in 2012, kicked off 52 times for an average of 59.9 yards with five touchbacks (one out of bounds). Made 10-of-16 field goal attempts (62.5 percent) with a long of 52 yards. In '13, kicked off 69-61.4-12 (one out of bounds), kicked field goals 21-25-L50 (84.0) and made 37-of-38 point after attempts. Won the Groza Award in '14 — kicked off 75-62.5-29 (one out of bounds), kicked field goals 18-19-L57 (94.7) and made all 44 PATs. Had his senior season cut short, but made field goals 8-10-L44 (80.0) and hit 22-of-23 PATs. Also punted nine times for a 36.4-yard average with one fair catch, six inside the 20 and one touchback. Sat out the last three games after dislocating his right wrist (required surgery). Special teams captain.

Future: Australian import and Matt Stover protégé who has shown steady improvement transitioning from "footy" to football. Has the leg strength, accuracy and composure to earn a starting job. Low-maintenance specialist who was viewed as a team leader at Maryland.

Draft projection: Priority free agent.

P RILEY DIXON, #92 (Sr-5)

SYRACUSE ▶ GRADE: 5.16

Ht: 6-41/4 | Wt: 221 | 40: 4.95e | Arm: 321/4 | Hand: 95/8

History: Also played baseball as a New York prep. Walked on and redshirted in 2011. Punted three times for a 36.3-yard average with two touchbacks. Earned a scholarship after the '13 season by punting 75-42.1 with 29 fair catches, 21 inside the 20 and six touchbacks. Also kicked off six times for a 56.8-yard average. In '14, punted 75-42.4 with 23 fair catches, 23 inside the 20 and four touchbacks. Also tossed a game-winning touchdown pass on a fake field goal in overtime against Villanova, and had a 42-yard fake-punt rush against Notre Dame. Punted 65-43.7 in '15 with 28 fair catches, 28 inside the 20 and five touchbacks. Had one blocked. Also had three rushes for 29 yards (9.7-yard average), as he gained first downs on two fake punts and one fake field goal (see LSU when he hurdled a tackler). Has held for place kicks. Graduated with an accounting degree, and is on pace to obtain his Master's in accounting.

Future: Big, strong-legged, right-footed punter who looks the part and has raw tools — can launch punts 70 yards downfield — but needs to take his consistency to another level to hold down a pro job. Smart, hard-working, coachable player who should blend into the locker room.

Draft projection: Sixth-round pick.

P LACHLAN EDWARDS, #49 (Sr-4)
SAM HOUSTON STATE ▶ GRADE: 5.08
Ht: 6-4 1/8 | Wt: 209 | 40: 4.85e | Arm: 32 3/8 | Hand: 9 3/8

History: First name is pronounced "Lock-lin." Australian native grew up playing Aussie Rules football, rugby, cricket and track and field. Played Aussie Rules in 2012 at Ballarat University in Victoria, Australia. Attended an Australian punting and kicking academy, earning a scholarship at FCS Sam Houston. Did not have a punt blocked in three years. In '13, had 31 punts for a 42.3-yard average with 10 fair catches, 13 inside the 20 and three touchbacks. Totaled 80-44.1 with 22 fair catches, 28 inside the 20 and five touchbacks in '14; and 74-41.5 with 19 fair catches, 31 inside the 20 and eight touchbacks in '15.

Future: Tall, long-levered, fairly athletic, Australian product with a smooth, natural stroke. Lacks a 'wow' factor, but gets punts off quickly and generates nice hang time. Could stand to improve his directional ability. Has some upside.

Draft projection: Priority free agent.

PK KA'IMI FAIRBAIRN, #15 (Sr-4)
UCLA ▶ GRADE: 5.11
Ht: 5-11 1/2 | Wt: 183 | 40: 4.90e | Arm: 31 1/4 | Hand: 9 1/4

History: Full name is John Christian Ka'i minoeauloameka'ikeokekumupa'a Fairbairn. Goes by Ka'imi ("Kuh-EE-me"). Also played soccer as a Hawaii prep. Stepped right in for the Bruins — made 16-of-22 field goal attempts (72.7 percent) with a long of 48 yards. Added 56-of-59 point after attempts. Kicked 14-21-L48 (66.7) in '13, while kicking off 48 times for a 64.3-yard average with 24 touch-

backs. In '14, had 80-64.3-50 on kickoffs, 18-22-L47 (81.8) on field goals and 47-of-48 on PATs. Won the Groza Award in '15 after booting kickoffs 84-64.5-59, drilling field goals 20-24-L60 (83.3) and making PATs 47-47. Finished his career as the Pac-12's all-time leading scorer (413 points). Graduated.

Future: Prolific, dependable, right-footed kicker with sound, repeatable mechanics and good accuracy. Mentally strong. Brings an intriguing combination of field-goal accuracy and kickoff ability — was 30-for-31 up to 40 yards the last two years while leading the NCAA with a 64.4-yard kickoff average. Despite hitting a 60-yarder as a senior, does not boast elite leg power and might be best suited for a dome or warm-weather location.

Draft projection: Seventh-round pick.

P TOM HACKETT, #33 (Sr-4)
UTAH ▶ GRADE: 5.14
Ht: 5-10 1/2 | Wt: 198 | 40: 4.90e | Arm: 29 3/4 | Hand: 9 1/4

History: Australian native. Played two years of Aussie Rules Football at a Melbourne boarding school before joining the Utes by way of the Pro Kick Australia feeder program. Walked on before earning a scholarship as a sophomore. Played in the last nine games in 2012 when he punted 25 times for a 38.9-yard average with 10 fair catches, 15 inside the 20 and one touchback. Was the Pac-12's leading punter in '13 when he booted 76-43.4 with 19 fair catches, 27 inside the 20 and six touchbacks. Broke out in '14 — punted 80-46.7 with 25 fair catches and 10 touchbacks. Led the nation in punts inside the 20 (36) and inside the 10 (19, including six inside the 5). Took home the Ray Guy Award for the second straight year in '15 — led the nation in net punting (43.7), as he punted 61-48.0 with 21 fair catches, 28 inside the 20 and nine touchbacks. Had 106 yards rushing the last two seasons, including a memorable play against Oregon when he snagged an errant snap one-handed and motored 33 yards for a first down. Tallied 68 career punts of 50+ yards (four of 70+), and did not have a punt blocked at Utah. Also served as the holder for place kicks. Recorded the most career punt yards in school history (10,933), tied the school record for career punts (242) and dropped 43.8 percent of his career punts inside the 20 (51 inside the 10, 21 inside the 5). Was honored as the punter of the Pac-12's

All-Century team. Graduated with a sports management degree.

Future: Built a high profile thanks to his Australian origin, decorated career and YouTube popularity. Has a personality and playing style all his own, and will be a fan favorite and media darling. However, will have to prove that his rugby style can translate or he can adapt to more traditional NFL-style punting — a big "if". Tough and fairly athletic.

Draft projection: Late draftable pick.

P DREW KASER, #38 (Sr-5)

TEXAS A&M ▶ GRADE: 5.12
Ht: 6-17/8 | Wt: 212 | 40: 5.0e | Arm: 31 | Hand: 9

History: Last name is pronounced "Kayser" (like laser). Prepped in Ohio. Joined the Aggies in 2011, but wasn't a factor until '13 — punted 44 times for a 47.4-yard average with 14 fair catches, 17 inside the 20 and seven touchbacks. In '14, punted 62-44.1 with 22 fair catches, 22 inside the 20 and six touchbacks. In '15, punted 60-47.5 (broke his own school record for gross average) with 12 fair catches, 21 inside the 20 and nine touchbacks. Injured his left ankle against Arizona State and sat out against Ball State. Did not have any punts blocked during his career. Also served as the holder for place kicks. Graduated.

Future: Besting some of Shane Lechler's numbers is enough to make you take notice, but Kaser's tape is intriguing, too. Boasts a powerful right leg — capable of booming punts with distance, direction and hang time. Has pro tools which could convince a team to use a draft pick on him.

Draft projection: Late draftable pick.

PK MARSHALL KOEHN, #1 (Sr-5)

IOWA ▶ GRADE: 4.89
Ht: 6-13/8 | Wt: 197 | 40: 4.63 | Arm: 321/4 | Hand: 91/2

History: Last name is pronounced "Kane." Iowa native won four state titles as a kicker, defensive back and receiver (team captain as a senior). Also was an all-state baseball player who earned letters in soccer (four) and wrestling (two). Walked on in 2011, but did not factor until '14 — kicked off 65 times for a 61.8-yard average with 43 touchbacks, made 12-of-16 field goal attempts (75.0 percent) with a long of 52 yards and converted all 38 point after attempts. In '15, kicked off 81-63.4-47, kicked field goals 16-20-L57 (80.0)

and made 47-of-53 PATs. Graduated with a communication studies degree.

Future: Two-and-a-half step, right-footed kicker who put himself on the radar by nailing a 57-yarder as time expired to defeat Pittsburgh then raised eyebrows at the Combine by showing off 4.6 speed. Connected on 12-of-15 attempts beyond 40 yards, but could stand to improve his lift, trajectory and height. Does not project as a kickoff specialist, and needs to find better overall consistency — had some head-scratching misses, including too many botched PATs.

Draft projection: Priority free agent.

LS JIMMY LANDES, #50 (Sr-5)

BAYLOR ▶ GRADE: 5.08
Ht: 6-11/4 | Wt: 240 | 40: 5.15e | Arm: 303/8 | Hand: 95/8

History: Texas native also lettered in baseball in high school. As a true freshman in 2011, an injury to the first-strong long-snapper opened the door for Landes to handle the job for the final 11 games. Was the backup in '13 when he appeared in three games. Was put on scholarship in '14 before handling the long-snapping job in all 26 games 2014-15. Scratched one career tackle and one fumble recovery. Was also on the Baylor baseball team (catcher) for two years. Graduated with a geology degree. Did not bench press at the Combine (left shoulder).

Future: The only long-snapper invited to the Combine, Landes is just adequate athletically, but can fire deep snaps back in the 0.70-second range with precision and consistency. Handled wet conditions well against TCU. Will have the opportunity to win a job in camp.

Draft projection: Priority free agent.

PK JOHN LUNSFORD, #49 (Sr-4)

LIBERTY ▶ GRADE: 5.03
Ht: 6-11/2 | Wt: 214 | 40: 4.95e | Arm: 327/8 | Hand: 101/8

History: Married with a daughter. Has 10 siblings. Also competed in soccer and track and field as a Florida prep. Had left knee surgery before arriving at FCS Liberty. As a true freshman in 2012, kicked off 40 times for a 63.3-yard average with 25 touchbacks (three out of bounds), and made 8-of-12 field goal attempts (66.7 percent) with a long of 50 yards. Missed two games while dealing with right groin/hip flexor injuries. In '13, kicked off 69-61.0-37 (six out of bounds), but struggled on field goals, going 8-19-L52 (42.1). Had three blocked. Served a two-game suspension (academics) to begin the '14 season, but regained his focus and rebounded with 70-62.1-48 (two out of bounds) on kickoffs and 19-24-L60 (79.2) on field goals. In '15, posted 59-64.2-35 (two out of bounds) on kickoffs and 13-24-L57 (54.2) on field goals. Had five blocked. Converted 130-of-134 career point after attempts. Nailed 12 50-plus yard field goals, an NCAA record for FCS kickers.

Future: Lunsford is rough around the edges, but has intriguing raw tools to coach up. Has big-time leg strength and surprising lift — produces a trampoline effect off his foot to get kicks over the line and has proven rare ability to connect from long distance (hits 70-yarders in practice). At a minimum should be considered as a kickoff specialist, but will require patience before his mental and physical consistency is NFL caliber. Will have to earn trust.

Draft projection: Priority free agent.

P WILL MONDAY, #41 (Sr-5)
DUKE   ▶ GRADE: 5.10
Ht: 6-33/4 | Wt: 212 | 40: 5.10e | Arm: 321/2 | Hand: 87/8

History: Also played soccer as a Georgia prep. Redshirted in 2011. Did not miss a game and did not have any punts blocked during his four-year career. Punted 67 times for a 44.6-yard average with 11 fair catches, 19 inside the 20 and six touchbacks in '12; 69-42.7 with 10 fair catches, 21 inside the 20 and six touchbacks in '13; 59-43.0 with 20 fair catches, 17 inside the 20 and six touchbacks in '14; and 65-43.5 with 20 fair catches, 31 inside the 20 and 13 touchbacks in '15. Also served as the holder for place kicks.

Future: Tall, lean, long-levered, right-footed punter who lined up 11 yards deep and got punts off quickly with a two-step delivery. Generates nice hang time and shows potential — his best punts are impressive, and can be a field-position weapon if he can reach another level of refinement and consistency.

Draft projection: Late draftable pick.

PK JADEN OBERKROM, #33 (Sr-4)
TCU   ▶ GRADE: 5.09
Ht: 6-33/8 | Wt: 186 | 40: 5.00e | Arm: 313/4 | Hand: 81/2

History: Last name is pronounced "Ohber-crome." Texas native. Four-year starter who handled kickoffs and place kicks and did not miss a game for the Horned Frogs. As a true freshman in 2012, kicked off 70 times for a 61.5-yard average with 33 touchbacks (one out of bounds), and made 22-of-30 field goal attempts (73.3 percent) with a long of 53 yards. Totaled 60-63.4 with 33 touchbacks (one out of bounds) with 14-18-L56 (77.8) in '13; 78-61.0 with 30 touchbacks (one out of bounds) with 22-27-L47 (81.5) in '14; and 92-62.4 with 56 touchbacks (one out of bounds) with 21-25-L57 (84.0) in '15. For his career converted 214-of-216 point after attempts. Owns the Big 12 record for career field goals made (79). Graduated.

Future: Oberkrom isn't flashy, but is an experienced, steady kicker with good, functional leg strength and nice composure in high-pressure situations. Works hard and is a good teammate. Kickoffs are not special, and will go as far as his accuracy takes him.

Draft projection: Priority free agent.

P NICK O'TOOLE, #91 (Sr-4)
WEST VIRGINIA   ▶ GRADE: 4.97
Ht: 6-33/8 | Wt: 219 | 40: 5.10e | Arm: 321/2 | Hand: 93/4

History: Was born with craniosyostosis, which prevented his skull from expanding with his brain and required surgery when he was four months old. Mater Dei (Calif.) product. Spent 2012 at Fullerton (Calif.) College, where he punted 49 times for a 41.8-yard average with eight fair catches, 15 inside the 20 and three touchbacks. Also tossed a 27-yard touchdown pass and rushed twice for 38 yards. With the Mountaineers in '13, punted 73-44.1 (40.7-yard net) with 23 fair catches, 22 inside the 20 and five touchbacks. Also kicked off six times for a 59.8-yard average with three touchbacks. O'Toole's net dropped to 37.0 in '14, as he punted 57-41.8 with 21 fair catches, 24 inside the 20 and two touchbacks. In '15, punted 71-45.4 with 18 fair catches, 25 inside the 20 and 15 touchbacks, and kicked off 74-61.9 with 18 touchbacks (three out of bounds). Also had a 13-yard rushing first down against Maryland. Was also the holder as a senior. Had just one career punt blocked. Graduated with a psychology degree.

Future: O'Toole is a character with a playful personality so often found in the special teams room. A big, strong-legged punter who shows in flashes, he was plagued by inconsistency, as he did not thrive as a directional punter in Morgantown. Identifies himself as a "banger" and has NFL leg strength, but will have to develop improved command for the finesse game to stick.

Draft projection: Priority free agent.

SPECIALISTS

DRAFT NEEDS

AFC NORTH

BALTIMORE RAVENS	'15 RK		CINCINNATI BENGALS	'15 RK
HC | JOHN HARBAUGH (77-51)	▼		HC | MARVIN LEWIS (111-94)	▼
OC | MARC TRESTMAN (2)	26/8		OC | KEN ZAMPESE (1)	13/15
DC | DEAN PEES (5)	12/10		DC | PAUL GUENTHER (3)	7/20
ST | JERRY ROSBURG (9)	1		ST | DARRIN SIMMONS (14)	8
CLEVELAND BROWNS	**'15 RK**		**PITTSBURGH STEELERS**	**'15 RK**
HC | HUE JACKSON (0-0)	▼		HC | MIKE TOMLIN (92-52)	▼
OC | AL SAUNDERS (1)	22/21		OC | TODD HALEY (5)	16/3
DC | RAY HORTON (1)	30/22		DC | KEITH BUTLER (2)	5/30
ST | CHRIS TABOR (6)	19		ST | DANNY SMITH (4)	6

AFC EAST

BUFFALO BILLS	'15 RK		MIAMI DOLPHINS	'15 RK
HC | REX RYAN (8-8)	▼		HC | ADAM GASE (0-0)	▼
OC | GREG ROMAN (2)	1/28		OC | CLYDE CHRISTENSEN (1)	23/19
DC | DENNIS THURMAN (2)	16/19		DC | VANCE JOSEPH (1)	28/21
ST | DANNY CROSSMAN (4)	16		ST | DARREN RIZZI (7)	15
NEW ENGLAND PATRIOTS	**'15 RK**		**NEW YORK JETS**	**'15 RK**
HC | BILL BELICHICK (187-69)	▼		HC | TODD BOWLES (10-6)	▼
OC | JOSH McDANIELS (5)	30/5		OC | CHAN GAILEY (2)	10/13
DC | MATT PATRICIA (5)	9/17		DC | KACY RODGERS (2)	2/13
ST | JOE JUDGE (2)	11		ST | BRANT BOYER (1)	31

AFC WEST

DENVER BRONCOS	'15 RK		KANSAS CITY CHIEFS	'15 RK
HC | GARY KUBIAK (12-4)	▼		HC | ANDY REID (31-17)	▼
OC | RICK DENNISON (2)	17/14		OC | BRAD CHILDRESS, MATT NAGY (1)	6/30
DC | WADE PHILLIPS (2)	3/1		DC | BOB SUTTON (4)	8/9
ST | JOE DeCAMILLIS (2)	7		ST | DAVE TOUB (4)	9
OAKLAND RAIDERS	**'15 RK**		**SAN DIEGO CHARGERS**	**'15 RK**
HC | JACK DEL RIO (7-9)	▼		HC | MIKE McCOY (22-26)	▼
OC | BILL MUSGRAVE (2)	28/16		OC | KEN WHISENHUNT (1)	31/4
DC | KEN NORTON JR. (2)	13/26		DC | JOHN PAGANO (5)	27/14
ST | BRAD SEELY (2)	25		ST | CRAIG AUKERMAN (1)	32

AFC SOUTH

HOUSTON TEXANS	'15 RK		INDIANAPOLIS COLTS	'15 RK
HC | BILL O'BRIEN (18-14)	▼		HC | CHUCK PAGANO (41-23)	▼
OC | GEORGE GODSEY (2)	15/18		OC | ROB CHUDZINSKI (2)	29/22
DC | ROMEO CRENNEL (3)	10/3		DC | TED MONACHINO (1)	25/24
ST | LARRY IZZO (1)	23		ST | TOM McMAHON (4)	20
JACKSONVILLE JAGUARS	**'15 RK**		**TENNESSEE TITANS**	**'15 RK**
HC | GUS BRADLEY (12-36)	▼		HC | MIKE MULARKEY (2-7)	▼
OC | GREG OLSON (2)	27/10		OC | TERRY ROBISKIE (1)	25/25T
DC | TODD WALSH (1)	15/29		DC | DICK LeBEAU (1)	18/7
ST | MIKE MALLORY (4)	3		ST | BOBBY APRIL (1)	28

Rankings are where the offense, defensive and special teams units finished last year as a measured of average yards per game and Sportsday's rankings based on a calculation of 22 special teams categories.

Rushing yards per game/Passing yards per game and Rushing yards allowed per game/Passing yards allowed per game are listed next to the coordinator.

Coordinator years in position is listed in parentheses.

NFC NORTH

CHICAGO BEARS	'15 RK	DETROIT LIONS	'15 RK
HC	JOHN FOX (6-10)		HC	JIM CALDWELL (18-14)	
OC	DOWELL LOGGAINS (1)	11/23	OC	JIM BOB COOTER (2)	32/9
DC	VIC FANGIO (2)	22/4	DC	TERYL AUSTIN (3)	19/14
ST	JEFF RODGERS (1)	12	ST	JOE MARCIANO (2)	14
GREEN BAY PACKERS	'15 RK	MINNESOTA VIKINGS	'15 RK
HC	MIKE McCARTHY (104-55-1)		HC	MIKE ZIMMER (18-14)	
OC	EDGAR BENNETT (1)	12/25T	OC	NORV TURNER (2)	5/31
DC	DOM CAPERS (8)	21/6	DC	GEORGE EDWARDS (3)	17/12
ST	RON ZOOK (2)	17	ST	MIKE PRIEFER (6)	10

NFC EAST

DALLAS COWBOYS	'15 RK	NEW YORK GIANTS	'15 RK
HC	JASON GARRETT (45-43)	▼	HC	BEN McADOO (0-0)	▼
OC	SCOTT LINEHAN (2)	9/27	OC	MIKE SULLIVAN (1)	18/7
DC	ROD MARINELLI (3)	22/5	DC	STEVE SPAGNUOLO (2)	24/32
ST	RICH BISACCIA (4)	4	ST	TOM QUINN (9)	2
PHILADELPHIA EAGLES	'15 RK	WASHINGTON REDSKINS	'15 RK
HC	DOUG PEDERSON (0-0)		HC	JAY GRUDEN (13-19)	
OC	FRANK REICH (1)	14/12	OC	SEAN McVAY (3)	20/11
DC	JIM SCHWARTZ (1)	32/28	DC	JOE BARRY (2)	26/25
ST	DAVE FIPP (3)	5	ST	BEN KOTWICA (2)	13

NFC WEST

ARIZONA CARDINALS	'15 RK	LOS ANGELES RAMS	'15 RK
HC	BRUCE ARIANS (34-14)	▼	HC	JEFF FISHER (27-36)	▼
OC	HAROLD GOODWIN (4)	8/2	OC	ROB BORAS (2)	7/32
DC	JAMES BETTCHER (2)	6/8	DC	GREGG WILLIAMS (3)	20/23
ST	AMOS JONES (4)	29	ST	JOHN FASSEL (5)	18
SAN FRANCISCO 49ERS	'15 RK	SEATTLE SEAHAWKS	'15 RK
HC	CHIP KELLY (0-0)	▼	HC	PETE CARROLL (60-36)	▼
OC	CURTIS MODKINS (1)	21/29	OC	DARRELL BEVELL (6)	3/20
DC	JIM O'NEIL (1)	29/27	DC	KRIS RICHARD (2)	1/2
ST	DERIUS SWINTON (1)	27	ST	BRIAN SCHNEIDER (7)	24

NFC SOUTH

ATLANTA FALCONS	'15 RK	CAROLINA PANTHERS	'15 RK
HC	DAN QUINN (8-8)	▼	HC	RON RIVERA (47-32-1)	▼
OC	KYLE SHANAHAN (2)	19/6	OC	MIKE SHULA (4)	2/24
DC	RICHARD SMITH (2)	14/18	DC	SEAN McDERMOTT (6)	4/11
ST	KEITH ARMSTRONG (9)	22	ST	BRUCE DEHAVEN (4)	30
NEW ORLEANS SAINTS	'15 RK	TAMPA BAY BUCCANEERS	'15 RK
HC	SEAN PAYTON (87-57)	▼	HC	DIRK KOETTER (0-0)	▼
OC	PETE CARMICHAEL, JR. (8)	24/1	OC	TODD MONKEN (1)	5/17
DC	DENNIS ALLEN (2)	31/31	DC	MIKE SMITH (1)	11/16
ST	GREG McMAHON (11)	21	ST	NATE KAZCOR (1)	26

PLAYER RANKINGS

GRADE SCALE

9.0 — A once-in-a-generation player (e.g. Bo Jackson, Deion Sanders).

8.00-8.99 — Perennial All-Pro (e.g. Anthony Munoz).

7.00-7.99 — Eventual All-Pro.

6.50-6.99 — Sure-fire first-rounder should make immediate impact.

6.00-6.49 — Likely first-rounder capable of starting readily.

5.60-5.99 — Likely second-rounder with immediate starter potential.

5.40-5.59 — Likely third-rounder minimally with sub-starter potential.

5.21-5.39 — Should make a roster and contribute on special teams

5.11-5.20 — Potential late-rounder with fair chance to earn a roster spot.

4.75-5.10 — Late draftable or priority free agent capable of battling for a roster spot.

4.00-4.75 — Solid free agent capable of being invited to an NFL training camp.

ALERT SYMBOLS

Jr. — Player is a junior.

Soph-3 — Player is a third-year sophomore.

QB — Can also play quarterback or the position that is listed, such as RS for return specialist.

Ch. — Character (i.e. history of arrests, team suspensions or off-field problems) can affect draft status.

X — Has a current injury situation that could affect camp status.

XX — Past or present durability concerns could affect draft status.

XXX — Serious injury concern.

About the player rankings: Players are ranked according to their grades, not necessarily in the order they will be drafted. Factors such as a drafting team's needs and the abundance or scarcity of available talent at a given position can cause a player to be drafted higher or lower than his grade would indicate. All grades take into account workouts up to and including the Indianapolis Scouting Combine. Post-Combine workouts were not factored.

QUARTERBACKS

RK. NAME	SCHOOL	GRADE	NOTES
1. Carson Wentz	North Dakota State	6.35	
2. Jared Goff	California	6.24	Jr.
3. Paxton Lynch	Memphis	5.92	Jr.
4. Connor Cook	Michigan State	5.57	
5. Dak Prescott	Mississippi State	5.39	
6. Christian Hackenberg	Penn State	5.37	Jr.
7. Jacoby Brissett	North Carolina State	5.32	
8. Nate Sudfeld	Indiana	5.30	
9. Cardale Jones	Ohio State	5.29	Jr.
10. Kevin Hogan	Stanford	5.27	
11. Joshua Woodrum	Liberty	5.24	
12. Cody Kessler	USC	5.19	
13. Jeff Driskel	Louisiana Tech	5.18	
14. Brandon Allen	Arkansas	5.14	
15. Brandon Doughty	Western Kentucky	5.13	
16. Jake Coker	Alabama	5.09	
17. Vernon Adams	Oregon	5.02	
18. Everett Golson	Florida State	5.01	
19. Joel Stave	Wisconsin	4.98	
20. Trevone Boykin	Texas Christian	4.92	RB, WR, Ch.
21. Jake Rudock	Michigan	4.92	
22. Matt Johnson	Bowling Green	4.80	
23. Raymond Cotton	Mississippi College	4.75	
24. Jason Vander Laan	Ferris State	4.75	
25. Blake Frohnapfel	Massachusetts	4.75	
26. Liam Nadler	Gannon	4.75	
27. Tre Robertson	Illinois State	4.75	
28. Sam Robertson	Iowa State	4.75	
29. Phillip Ely	Toledo	4.75	
30. Jeremy Johnson	Charleston	4.50	
31. Tanner McEvoy	Wisconsin	4.50	
32. Vad Lee	James Madison	4.50	X
33. Jacob Huesman	Tenn.-Chattanooga	4.50	
34. John Robertson	Villanova	4.50	X
35. Marquise Williams	North Carolina	4.50	
36. Travis Wilson	Utah	4.50	
37. Charles Keeton	Utah State	4.50	
38. Kyle Washington	Angelo State	4.50	
39. Gunner Rivers	Northwestern State	4.50	
40. Mike Bercovici	Arizona State	4.50	
41. Robert Brewer	Virginia Tech	4.50	X
42. Moses Skillon	Morgan State	4.50	
43. Sean Goldrich	New Hampshire	4.50	
44. Matthew Soltes	East Stroudsburg	4.50	
45. Morgan Roberts	Yale	4.50	
46. Max Wittek	Hawaii	4.50	
47. Ammon Olsen	Southern Utah	4.50	
48. Cameron Coffman	Wyoming	4.50	

FULLBACKS

RK. NAME	SCHOOL	GRADE	NOTES
1. Dan Vitale	Northwestern	5.19	HB
2. Andy Janovich	Nebraska	5.12	
3. Glenn Gronkowski	Kansas State	5.12	Jr., HB

RK. NAME	SCHOOL	GRADE	NOTES
4. Soma Vainuku	USC	5.10	
5. Quayvon Hicks	Georgia	4.97	
6. Chris Swain	Navy	4.90	RB
7. Trayion Durham	Kent State	4.80	RB
8. Dakota Gordon	San Diego State	4.75	
9. Nick Butier	Northern Arizona	4.75	
10. Jeremy Seaton	Oklahoma State	4.75	

RUNNING BACKS

RK. NAME	SCHOOL	GRADE	NOTES
1. Ezekial Elliott	Ohio State	6.54	Jr.
2. Derrick Henry	Alabama	5.92	Jr.
3. C.J. Prosise	Notre Dame	5.58	Jr., WR
4. Kenneth Dixon	Louisiana Tech	5.52	
5. Devontae Booker	Utah	5.47	X
6. Jordan Howard	Indiana	5.45	Jr.
7. Paul Perkins	UCLA	5.42	Jr., X
8. Kenyan Drake	Alabama	5.38	X, WR, KR
9. Alex Collins	Arkansas	5.31	Jr.
10. Josh Ferguson	Illinois	5.27	KR, X
11. Kelvin Taylor	Florida	5.26	Jr.
12. Jonathan Williams	Arkansas	5.25	X
13. Daniel Lasco	California	5.24	X
14. Keith Marshall	Georgia	5.22	Jr., X, KR
15. Wendell Smallwood	West Virginia	5.20	Jr.
16. Brandon Wilds	South Carolina	5.18	X
17. Tyler Ervin	San Jose State	5.17	RS, WR
18. DeAndre Washington	Texas Tech	5.14	
19. Devon Johnson	Marshall	5.07	X, FB
20. Tra Carson	Texas A&M	5.07	
21. Peyton Barber	Auburn	5.03	Soph-3
22. Curtis Madden	USC	4.91	X
23. Storm Woods	Oregon State	4.90	
24. Marshaun Coprich	Illinois State	4.87	Ch.
25. Shadrach Thornton	North Carolina State	4.84	Ch.
26. Marteze Waller	Fresno State	4.75	
27. Shock Linwood	Baylor	4.75	Jr.
28. Jared Baker	Arizona	4.75	
29. Jaylen Walton	Mississippi	4.75	
30. Dominique Swope	West Alabama	4.75	
31. Don Jackson	Nevada	4.75	
32. Taylor Cox	Kansas	4.75	
33. Paul James	Rutgers	4.75	
34. Jhurell Pressley	New Mexico	4.50	
35. Zac Brooks	Clemson	4.50	Jr.
36. Xavier Roberson	Southeastern Louisiana	4.50	
37. Justin Harris	Murray State	4.50	
38. Russell Hansbrough	Missouri	4.50	
39. Leon Allen	Western Kentucky	4.50	
40. Gary Underwood	Villanova	4.50	
41. Jordan Parker	Middle Tennessee St.	4.50	
42. Johnathan Gray	Texas	4.50	
43. Dyshawn Mobley	Eastern Kentucky	4.50	
44. Jeffrey Seybold	Pittsburg State (Ks.)	4.50	
45. Geremy Alridge-Mitchell	West Texas A&M	4.50	
46. Brandon Ross	Maryland	4.50	
47. Aaron Green	Texas Christian	4.50	
48. Dwayne Washington	Washington	4.50	Jr.
49. Travis Greene	Bowling Green	4.50	
50. Anthony Jordan	Bethune-Cookman	4.50	
51. Brandon Bourbon	Washburn	4.50	
52. Cedric O'Neal	Valdosta State	4.50	
53. Jamaal Williams	Brigham Young	4.50	
54. Brandon Burks	Troy	4.50	
55. Raphael Spencer	Missouri Western St.	4.50	
56. Elijhaa Penny	Idaho	4.50	
57. De'Andre Mann	Kansas	4.50	
58. Khairi Dickson	St Francis (Pa.)	4.50	
59. Shaun Wick	Wyoming	4.50	
60. Anthone Taylor	Buffalo	4.50	

WIDE RECEIVERS

RK. NAME	SCHOOL	GRADE	NOTES
1. Laquon Treadwell	Mississippi	6.24	Jr.
2. Corey Coleman	Baylor	5.97	Jr., RS
3. Will Fuller	Notre Dame	5.92	Jr.
4. Josh Doctson	Texas Christian	5.89	
5. Sterling Shepard	Oklahoma	5.84	
6. Tyler Boyd	Pittsburgh	5.72	Jr.
7. Michael Thomas	Ohio State	5.66	Jr.
8. Paul McRoberts	SE Missouri State	5.42	
9. Braxton Miller	Ohio State	5.38	X, QB
10. Aaron Burbridge	Michigan State	5.36	
11. Jalin Marshall	Ohio State	5.34	Soph-3, PR
12. Tajae Sharpe	Massachusetts	5.32	
13. Malcolm Mitchell	Georgia	5.32	CB
14. Kolby Listenbee	Texas Christian	5.27	
15. Bralon Addison	Oregon	5.27	Jr., PR
16. Chris Moore	Cincinnati	5.24	
17. Charone Peake	Clemson	5.24	
18. Demarcus Robinson	Florida	5.24	Jr., Ch.
19. Pharoh Cooper	South Carolina	5.23	Jr., RS
20. Devon Cajuste	Stanford	5.23	
21. Jordan Payton	UCLA	5.21	
22. Kenny Lawler	California	5.21	Jr.
23. Rashard Higgins	Colorado State	5.19	Jr.
24. Leonte Carroo	Rutgers	5.18	
25. Nelson Spruce	Colorado	5.18	
26. Ricardo Louis	Auburn	5.17	RB
27. Cayleb Jones	Arizona	5.14	Jr.
28. Keyarris Garrett	Tulsa	5.14	
29. Byron Marshall	Oregon	5.12	RB
30. Trevor Davis	California	5.12	Jr., KR
31. Hunter Sharp	Utah State	5.11	
32. Darryll Foster	Arizona State	5.10	
33. Roger Lewis	Bowling Green	5.10	Soph-3, Ch.
34. DeMarcus Ayers	Houston	5.09	Jr., KR
35. De'Runnya Wilson	Mississippi State	5.09	Jr.
36. Cody Core	Mississippi	5.08	
37. Jordan Williams-Lambert	Ball State	5.07	
38. Marquez North	Tennessee	5.07	Jr., X
39. Geronimo Allison	Illinois	5.06	
40. Chris Brown	Notre Dame	5.03	
41. D'haquille Duke Williams	ex-Auburn	5.01	Ch.
42. Alonzo Russell	Toledo	4.94	
43. Johnny Holton	Cincinnati	4.93	
44. Rashawn Scott	Miami (Fla.)	4.86	
45. Lloyd Eagan	Northwestern State	4.80	
46. Darrin Peterson	Liberty	4.80	
47. Daniel Braverman	Western Michigan	4.80	Jr.
48. Quinshad Davis	North Carolina	4.80	
49. Christian Morgan	Southern Utah	4.75	
50. Bryce Treggs	California	4.75	
51. Alton Howard	Tennessee	4.75	
52. Amir Carlisle	Notre Dame	4.75	
53. Mekale McKay	Cincinnati	4.75	
54. Tevaun Smith	Iowa	4.75	
55. Marvin Shinn	South Alabama	4.75	
56. Marcus Leak	Maryland	4.75	
57. Bruce Natson	Utah State	4.50	
58. Donovan Harden	Georgia State	4.50	
59. Thomas Carter	Portland State	4.50	
60. Shaquille Washington	Cincinnati	4.50	
61. Jerel Harrison	Delaware	4.50	
62. Lavon Pearson	Tennessee	4.50	
63. Tres Houston	Arkansas State	4.50	
64. Marcel Caver	Winston-Salem State	4.50	
65. Danny Anthrop	Purdue	4.50	
66. Devonte Robinson	Utah State	4.50	
67. Quenton Bundrage	Iowa State	4.50	
68. Devin Fuller	UCLA	4.50	
69. Marcus Johnson	Texas	4.50	
70. Dominique Williams	Washington State	4.50	
71. Davonte Allen	Marshall	4.50	
72. Alex Erickson	Wisconsin	4.50	
73. John Israel	Coastal Carolina	4.50	
74. Chris King	Duquesne	4.50	
75. Malachi Jones	Appalachian State	4.50	
76. Joseph Morrow	Mississippi State	4.50	
77. Shane Williams-Rhodes	Boise State	4.50	

78. Andre Davis	Kansas State	4.50
79. Joseph Hansley	Colorado State	4.50
80. Max Morrison	Cincinnati	4.50
81. Jamaal Jones	Montana	4.50
82. James Poole	Utah	4.50
83. Tekemian Ceaser	Louisiana-Monroe	4.50
84. Joshua McKissic	Arkansas State	4.50
85. Antwane Grant	Western Kentucky	4.50
86. Mike Thomas	Southern Mississippi	4.50
87. Paul Turner	Louisiana Tech	4.50
88. Keon Hatcher	Arkansas	4.50
89. Quentin Atkinson	North Carolina Central	4.50
90. Andre McCullouch	Rocky Mountain	4.50
91. Durron Neal	Oklahoma	4.50
92. Brandon Swindall	Utah State	4.50
93. Jamal Robinson	Louisiana-Lafayette	4.50
94. Reggie Diggs	Richmond	4.50
95. Kenneth Scott	Utah	4.50
96. Jared Dangerfield	Western Kentucky	4.50
97. Jonathon Lee	Baylor	4.50
98. Andrian Jones	Jacksonville	4.50
99. Melvin Ray	Auburn	4.50
100. Tevin Jones	Memphis	4.50
101. Courtney Whitehead	Central Arkansas	4.50
102. Chris Gallon	Bowling Green	4.50
103. Herb Waters	Miami (Fla.)	4.50
104. Jaydon Mickens	Washington	4.50
105. Dezmon Epps	Idaho	4.50
106. Andrew Flory	Fort Hays State	4.50
107. Timothy Patrick	Utah	4.50
108. Ladarius Brown	Sam Houston State	4.50
109. Gary Chambers	Arizona State	4.50
110. Canaan Severin	Virginia	4.50
111. Nnamdi Agude	Sacramento State	4.50
112. Joshua Mikes	Winona State	4.50
113. Karnorris Benson	Western Carolina	4.50
114. Brandon Sheperd	Oklahoma State	4.50
115. Jenson Stoshak	Florida Atlantic	4.50
116. David Richards	Arizona	4.50
117. Mitchell Mathews	Brigham Young	4.50
118. Seth Devalve	Princeton	4.50
119. Madison Mangum	Idaho State	4.50
120. Marquise Cushon	Pittsburg State (Ks.)	4.50
121. Blair Roberts	Old Dominion	4.50

TIGHT ENDS

RK. NAME	SCHOOL	GRADE	NOTES
1. Hunter Henry	Arkansas	5.92	Jr.
2. Austin Hooper	Stanford	5.64	Soph-3
3. Nick Vannett	Ohio State	5.56	
4. Tyler Higbee	Western Kentucky	5.38	X
5. Jerell Adams	South Carolina	5.36	
6. Thomas Duarte	UCLA	5.28	Jr., WR
7. Temarrick Hemingway	South Carolina State	5.27	
8. Beau Sandland	Montana State	5.24	
9. David Morgan	Texas-San Antonio	5.21	
10. Ben Braunecker	Harvard	5.19	
11. Bryce Williams	East Carolina	5.16	
12. Ryan Malleck	Virginia Tech	5.12	
13. Jake McGee	Florida	5.09	X
14. Stephen Anderson	California	4.92	
15. Henry Krieger-Coble	Iowa	4.90	
16. David Grinnage	North Carolina State	4.89	Jr.
17. Daree Goodwin	West Liberty State	4.80	
18. Caleb Smith	Oregon State	4.80	
19. Braxton Deaver	Duke	4.80	
20. Gabe Hughes	Florida Tech	4.75	
21. Braedon Bowman	South Alabama	4.50	
22. Joshua Perkins	Washington	4.50	
23. Timothy Brown	West Chester	4.50	
24. Kevin Francis	North Carolina A&T St.	4.50	
25. David Reeves	Duke	4.50	
26. Josiah Price	Michigan State	4.50	Jr.
27. Jacob Duzey	Iowa	4.50	
28. Felix Ruiz	Georgia State	4.50	

29. Kyle Carter	Penn State	4.50
30. Steven Scheu	Vanderbilt	4.50
31. John Holtz	Pittsburgh	4.50
32. Kivon Cartwright	Colorado State	4.50
33. Sean Price	South Florida	4.50
34. Steven Walker	Colorado State	4.50
35. Dillon Gordon	LSU	4.50
36. Derek Lee	Bowling Green	4.50
37. Adam Fuehne	Southern Illinois	4.50
38. M.J. McFarland	UTEP	4.50

CENTERS

RK. NAME	SCHOOL	GRADE	NOTES
1. Ryan Kelly	Alabama	5.74	OG, OT
2. Evan Boehm	Missouri	5.54	OG
3. Max Tuerk	USC	5.46	X, OT
4. Nick Martin	Notre Dame	5.37	OG
5. Jack Allen	Michigan State	5.31	
6. Austin Blythe	Iowa	5.21	OG
7. Matt Skura	Duke	5.19	
8. Jacob Brendel	UCLA	5.01	
9. Kyle Friend	Temple	4.80	
10. Robert Kugler	Purdue	4.75	
11. Bruce Johnson	Maine	4.75	
12. Marcus Henry	Boise State	4.75	
13. Joe Hawkins	Weber State	4.50	
14. Tauti Aiono	Utah	4.50	
15. Nick Kelly	Arizona State	4.50	
16. Josh Mitchell	Oregon State	4.50	
17. Mike Matthews	Texas A&M	4.50	
18. Artie Rowell	Pittsburgh	4.50	
19. Quinton Schooley	North Carolina State	4.50	
20. Ross Burbank	Virginia	4.50	
21. Spencer Pulley	Vanderbilt	4.50	
22. Brynjar Gudmundsson	South Florida	4.50	
23. Matt Pierson	Oregon	4.50	
24. Angelo Mangiro	Penn State	4.50	

OFFENSIVE GUARDS

RK. NAME	SCHOOL	GRADE	NOTES
1. Cody Whitehair	Kansas State	5.86	OT
2. Christian Westerman	Arizona State	5.53	C
3. Joshua Garnett	Stanford	5.42	
4. Avery Young	Auburn	5.38	Jr., X, OT
5. Denver Kirkland	Arkansas	5.34	Jr., OT
6. Rees Odhiambo	Boise State	5.31	X, OT
7. Vadal Alexander	LSU	5.30	X, OT
8. Connor McGovern	Missouri	5.29	OT
9. Isaac Seumalo	Oregon State	5.27	Jr.
10. Graham Glasgow	Michigan	5.26	C
11. Joseph Thuney	North Carolina State	5.25	C
12. Caleb Benenoch	UCLA	5.22	Jr., OT
13. Sebastian Tretola	Arkansas	5.20	
14. Joesph Dahl	Washington State	5.14	X, OT
15. Spencer Drango	Baylor	5.12	OT
16. Parker Ehinger	Cincinnati	5.10	OT
17. Landon Turner	North Carolina	5.07	
18. Alex Redmond	UCLA	5.07	Jr.
19. Nila Kasitati	Oklahoma	4.84	
20. Darrell Greene	San Diego State	4.82	C, Ch.
21. Vivii Teofilo	Arizona State	4.75	
22. Jordan Walsh	Iowa	4.75	
23. Mykhael Quave	Louisiana-Lafayette	4.75	
24. Dexter Charles	Washington	4.50	
25. Blake Muir	Baylor	4.50	
26. Frederick Thurman	Florida	4.50	
27. Jay Whitmire	Virginia	4.50	
28. Cayman Bundage	Arizona	4.50	
29. Darius Bladek	Bethune-Cookman	4.50	Jr.
30. Jamelle Naff	Texas Christian	4.50	
31. Jarell Broxton	Baylor	4.50	
32. Garrick Mayweather	Fordham	4.50	
33. Andrew Zeller	Maryland	4.50	
34. Justin Malone	Mississippi State	4.50	
35. Jalen Schlachter	Ball State	4.50	

36. Donavon Clark	Michigan State	4.50
37. Aaron Morris	Mississippi	4.50
38. Marcus Jackson	Tennessee	4.50
39. Terran Vaughn	Stephen F Austin	4.50
40. Josh Campion	Minnesota	4.50
41. Jacob Bernstein	Vanderbilt	4.50
42. Theodore Karras	Illinois	4.50
43. Ryan Doyle	Maryland	4.50
44. Darius Johnson	Middle Tennessee St.	4.50
45. Jamison Lalk	Iowa State	4.50
46. Robert Trudo	Syracuse	4.50
47. Joe Bjorklund	Minnesota	4.50
48. Anthony Fabiano	Harvard	4.50
49. Nick Robinson	Syracuse	4.50
50. Aaron Neary	Eastern Washington	4.50
51. Quincy McKinney	East Carolina	4.50
52. Adam Foltz	Texas Christian	4.50
53. Joseph Cheek	Texas A&M	4.50
54. Boston Stiverson	Kansas State	4.50
55. Alex Huettel	Bowling Green	4.50
56. Luke Hayes	Kansas State	4.50
57. Justin Bell	Mississippi	4.50
58. Robert Blodgett	Buffalo	4.50

OFFENSIVE TACKLES

RK. NAME	SCHOOL	GRADE	NOTES
1. Laremy Tunsil	Mississippi	7.50	Jr., X
2. Ronnie Stanley	Notre Dame	6.74	Jr.
3. Jack Conklin	Michigan State	6.32	Jr.
4. Taylor Decker	Ohio State	6.25	OG
5. Jason Spriggs	Indiana	6.06	
6. Germain Ifedi	Texas A&M	5.72	Jr., OG
7. Le'Raven Clark	Texas Tech	5.52	OG
8. Shon Coleman	Auburn	5.48	Jr., X
9. Brandon Shell	South Carolina	5.32	X
10. Jerald Hawkins	LSU	5.32	Jr.
11. Alexander Lewis	Nebraska	5.27	OG, Ch.
12. Dominique Robertson	West Georgia	5.26	OG, Ch.
13. Stephane Nembot	Colorado	5.23	
14. Joseph Haeg	North Dakota State	5.23	
15. Willie Beavers	Western Michigan	5.19	OG
16. Cole Toner	Harvard	5.16	
17. John Theus	Georgia	5.14	
18. Fahn Cooper	Mississippi	5.12	
19. Kyle Murphy	Stanford	5.10	
20. Pearce Slater	San Diego State	5.09	
21. Tyler Marz	Wisconsin	5.08	OG
22. Halapoulivaati Vaitai	Texas Christian	5.04	
23. Tyler Johnstone	Oregon	5.03	
24. Dominick Jackson	Alabama	4.90	
25. Arturo Uzdavinis	Tulane	4.80	
26. Jordan Swindle	Kentucky	4.80	
27. Zach Martinez	Colorado State-Pueblo	4.80	
28. Lene Maiava	Arizona	4.75	
29. Nicholas Ritcher	Richmond	4.75	
30. Joe Gore	Clemson	4.75	
31. Larsten Hanson	Sacramento State	4.75	
32. Trevor Strickland	Youngstown	4.75	
33. Tyrell Smith	Massachusetts	4.75	Jr.
34. Nathan Theaker	Wayne State (Mich.)	4.50	
35. Dan Buchholz	Duquesne	4.50	
36. Clinton Van Horn	Marshall	4.50	
37. John Weidenaar	Montana State	4.50	
38. Caleb Williams	Rice	4.50	
39. Vernon Anthony	Tennessee State	4.50	
40. Zeth Ramsay	Mesa State	4.50	
41. Taylor Fallin	Memphis	4.50	
42. Ryker Mathews	Brigham Young	4.50	
43. Marquis Lucas	West Virginia	4.50	
44. Keith Lumpkin	Rutgers	4.50	
45. Andrew Oberg	Wagner	4.50	
46. Ryan Mack	Memphis	4.50	
47. Brock Dagel	Iowa State	4.50	
48. Maximilian Sommer	Liberty	4.50	
49. Ramadan Ahmeti	Central Michigan	4.50	

50. Bernard Gauldin	Austin Peay State	4.50
51. Clay Debord	Eastern Washington	4.50
52. Samuel Carlson	Colorado State	4.50
53. Wes Schweitzer	San Jose State	4.50
54. Kolton Houston	Georgia	4.50
55. Chris May	South Alabama	4.50
56. Ben Clarke	Hawaii	4.50
57. Aaron Epps	Louisville	4.50
58. Jacob Spies	Nebraska-Kearney	4.50
59. William Hening	East Central	4.50
60. Alexander Fifita	Fresno State	4.50
61. Dontae Levingston	East Carolina	4.50
62. Jordan Rigsbee	California	4.50
63. Dylan Intemann	Wake Forest	4.50
64. Aleksandar Milanovic	Sacramento State	4.50
65. Givens Price	Nebraska	4.50
66. Geoff Mogus	Northwestern	4.50
67. Matthew Kleinsorge	Kansas State	4.50
68. Torian White	Hampton	4.50
69. Kevin Bowen	East Central	4.50
70. Zach Sterup	Nebraska	4.50
71. Larry Mazyck	Kansas	4.50
72. Amadou Konte'	Benedictine (Ks.)	4.50
73. Jamar Lewter	Virginia-Lynchburg	4.50
74. John Kling	Buffalo	4.50

DEFENSIVE ENDS

RK. NAME	SCHOOL	GRADE	NOTES
1. Joey Bosa	Ohio State	6.94	Jr.
2. DeForest Buckner	Oregon	6.70	DT
3. Kevin Dodd	Clemson	6.12	Jr.
4. Shaq Lawson	Clemson	5.98	Jr.
5. Emmanuel Ogbah	Oklahoma State	5.82	Jr.
6. Jihad Ward	Illinois	5.62	DT
7. Jonathan Bullard	Florida	5.58	DT
8. Shilique Calhoun	Michigan State	5.45	OLB
9. Shawn Oakman	Baylor	5.37	DT
10. Carl Nassib	Penn State	5.28	
11. Bronson Kaufusi	Brigham Young	5.27	OLB
12. Charles Tapper	Oklahoma	5.26	
13. Matt Judon	Grand Valley State	5.24	OLB
14. Jason Fanaika	Utah	5.23	OLB
15. James Cowser	Southern Utah	5.23	OLB
16. Ronald Blair	Appalachian State	5.19	
17. Romeo Okwara	Notre Dame	5.16	OLB
18. Dean Lowry	Northwestern	5.14	DT
19. Alex McAllister	Florida	5.10	Jr., Ch.
20. Ufomba Kamalu	Miami (Fla.)	5.10	
21. Jimmy Bean	Oklahoma State	5.07	OLB, X
22. Sterling Bailey	Georgia	5.07	
23. Giorgio Newberry	Florida State	4.83	
24. Branden Jackson	Texas Tech	4.82	OLB
25. Di'Andre Harrison	Ohio Dominican	4.80	
26. LaMichael Fanning	Jacksonville St. (Ala.)	4.80	E, X
27. Ejuan Price	Pittsburgh	4.75	
28. Sadat Sulleyman	Portland State	4.75	
29. Bryson Albright	Miami (Ohio)	4.75	
30. Eddie Yarbrough	Wyoming	4.75	
31. Ian Seau	Nevada	4.50	
32. Miles Grooms	Hampton	4.50	
33. Sydney Omameh	Ohio Dominican	4.50	
34. Trevor Bates	Maine	4.50	
35. James McFarland	Texas Christian	4.50	X
36. Jamal Palmer	Baylor	4.50	
37. David Perkins	Illinois State	4.50	
38. William Anthony	Navy	4.50	
39. Theiren Cockran	Minnesota	4.50	
40. Roy Robertson-Harris	UTEP	4.50	
41. Amir Bloom	Texas Southern	4.50	
42. Kenton Adeyemi	Connecticut	4.50	
43. Mike Rose	North Carolina State	4.50	
44. Drew Ott	Iowa	4.50	E, X
45. Sonny Sanitoa	UNLV	4.50	
46. Josh Dawson	Georgia	4.50	
47. Pat O'Connor	Eastern Michigan	4.50	

48. Quinton Bradley	Idaho	4.50
49. Silverberry Mouhon	Cincinnati	4.50
50. Eric Lee	South Florida	4.50
51. Alexander Hansen	Air Force	4.50
52. Vontarrius Dora	Louisiana Tech	4.50
53. Michael Bloomfield	Winston-Salem State	4.50
54. Marvin Hunter	Memphis	4.50
55. Terrell Lathan	Texas Christian	4.50
56. Davonte Lambert	Auburn	4.50
57. Jonathan Woodard	Central Arkansas	4.50
58. Nick Mangieri	Indiana	4.50
59. Ryan Brown	Mississippi State	4.50
60. Mike Moore	Virginia	4.50
61. Julien Obioha	Texas A&M	4.50
62. Iosia Iosia	West Texas A&M	4.50
63. Jason Neill	Utsa	4.50
64. Clifton Jones	Nevada	4.50
65. Morgan Fox	Colorado State-Pueblo	4.50
66. Maurice Niles	Central Florida	4.50
67. Ugonna Awuruonye	Campbell	4.50
68. Terrell Stanley	East Carolina	4.50
69. Shaneil Jenkins	Shepherd	4.50
70. Delvon Simmons	USC	4.50
71. Reggie Gilbert	Arizona	4.50
72. Demetrius Cherry	Arizona State	4.50
73. Clayton Callicutt	Angelo State	4.50

DEFENSIVE TACKLES

RK. NAME	SCHOOL	GRADE	NOTES
1. Sheldon Rankins	Louisville	6.42	
2. A'Shawn Robinson	Alabama	6.33	Jr.
3. Robert Nkemdiche	Mississippi	6.26	Jr., Ch.
4. Jarran Reed	Alabama	6.12	DE, Ch.
5. Austin Johnson	Penn State	6.04	Jr.
6. Vernon Butler	Louisiana Tech	5.88	
7. Maliek Collins	Nebraska	5.68	Jr.
8. Chris Jones	Mississippi Stateate	5.56	Jr.
9. Quinton Jefferson	Maryland	5.42	Jr.
10. Adam Gotsis	Georgia Tech	5.37	X
11. Adolphus Washington	Ohio State	5.36	
12. Hassan Ridgeway	Texas	5.33	Jr., X
13. Javon Hargrave	South Carolina State	5.31	
14. Sheldon Day	Notre Dame	5.25	
15. Willie Henry	Michigan	5.20	Jr.
16. Matthew Ioannidis	Temple	5.18	
17. Vincent Valentine	Nebraska	5.13	Jr.
18. Anthony Zettel	Penn State	5.12	
19. Lawrence Thomas	Michigan State	5.12	
20. Connor Wujciak	Boston College	5.10	NT
21. Luther Maddy	Virginia Tech	5.09	
22. Darius Latham	Indiana	5.07	Jr., Ch.
23. Joel Heath	Michigan State	5.02	
24. Mehdi Abdesmad	Boston College	4.92	
25. Devaunte Sigler	Jacksonville St. (Ala.)	4.87	
26. Corey Marshall	Virginia Tech	4.80	
27. Darius Hamilton	Rutgers	4.80	
28. Elijan Daniel	Murray State	4.75	Jr.
29. Anthony McDaniel	Bowie State	4.50	
30. Derrick Mitchell	Florida State	4.50	
31. Brandin Bryant	Florida Atlantic	4.50	
32. Darryl Render	Pittsburgh	4.50	
33. David Dean	Virginia	4.50	
34. Rykeem Yates	Nevada	4.50	
35. Gregory Milhouse	Campbell	4.50	
36. Quentin Thomas	LSU	4.50	
37. Alex Mosley	James Madison	4.50	
38. Pio Vatuvei	Louisville	4.50	
39. Gerald Dixon	South Carolina	4.50	
40. Hershey Walton	Temple	4.50	
41. Tylor Harris	Wake Forest	4.50	
42. Al Page	Wagner	4.50	
43. Julian Campenni	Connecticut	4.50	
44. Michael Rouse	Purdue	4.50	
45. Rodney Coe	Akron	4.50	
46. Andrew Iddings	South Dakota	4.50	

47. Zach Colvin	Bowling Green	4.50
48. Lars Koht	Florida International	4.50
49. Kayembe Matungulu	Western Carolina	4.50
50. Tyler Horn	Boise State	4.50
51. Josh Tupou	Colorado	4.50
52. Khaynin Mosley-Smith	Pittsburgh	4.50
53. Desmond Jackson	Texas	4.50
54. Tutulupeataia Mataele	Boise State	4.50
55. Justin Hansen	Colorado State	4.50
56. Alonzo Williams	Texas A&M	4.50
57. Michael Lovejoy	Florida A&M	4.50
58. Davion Pierson	Texas Christian	4.50
59. Justin Thomason	North Carolina	4.50
60. Jordan Nielsen	Utah State	4.50
61. Trevon Coley	Florida Atlantic	4.50
62. Beau Blackshear	Baylor	4.50
63. Brian Price	UTSA	4.50
64. Demetris Anderson	Central Florida	4.50

NOSE TACKLES

RK. NAME	SCHOOL	GRADE	NOTES
1. Kenny Clark	UCLA	5.62	Jr.
2. Andrew Billings	Baylor	5.56	Jr.
3. Nile Lawrence-Stample	Florida State	5.13	
4. David Reader	Clemson	5.10	OG
5. Chris Mayes	Georgia	4.86	
6. Woodrow Hamilton	Mississippi	4.80	
7. Antwaun Woods	USC	4.77	
8. Melvin Lewis	Kentucky	4.50	
9. Jonathan Desir	Towson	4.50	
10. Calvin Heurtelou	Miami (Fla.)	4.50	
11. Tyler Kuder	Idaho State	4.50	
12. Alex Balducci	Oregon	4.50	
13. Kyle Rose	West Virginia	4.50	

INSIDE LINEBACKERS

RK. NAME	SCHOOL	GRADE	NOTES
1. Reggie Ragland	Alabama	6.30	OLB
2. Joshua Perry	Ohio State	5.47	
3. Nicholas Kwiatkoski	West Virginia	5.40	
4. Blake Martinez	Stanford	5.31	
5. Nick Vigil	Utah State	5.29	Jr.
6. Antonio Morrison	Florida	5.29	X
7. Terrance Smith	Florida State	5.19	
8. Jared Norris	Utah	5.19	
9. Steven Daniels	Boston College	5.08	
10. Cassanova McKinzy	Auburn	5.05	DE
11. Josh Forrest	Kentucky	5.01	
12. Raphael Kirby	Miami (Fla.)	4.97	
13. Gionni Paul	Utah	4.89	
14. Chris Johnson	Mississippi	4.82	
15. Joe Bolden	Michigan	4.80	
16. Luke Rhodes	William & Mary	4.80	
17. Jake Ganus	Georgia	4.80	
18. James Burgess	Louisville	4.80	
19. Reggie Northrup	Florida State	4.80	
20. Ezekiel Bigger	East Carolina	4.80	
21. Jason Whittingham	Utah	4.75	
22. Anthony Sarao	USC	4.75	
23. Antonio Longino	Arizona State	4.75	
24. William Ratelle	North Dakota	4.50	
25. Kyrie Wilson	Fresno State	4.50	
26. Richie Brown	Mississippi State	4.50	Jr.
27. Jarrett Grace	Notre Dame	4.50	X
28. Brandon Chubb	Wake Forest	4.50	
29. Ryan Simmons	Oklahoma State	4.50	
30. Darnell Sankey	Sacramento State	4.50	
31. Joseph Walker	Oregon	4.50	
32. Jalen Jefferson	California	4.50	
33. Joe Schmidt	Notre Dame	4.50	
34. Jeremiah Kose	Montana	4.50	
35. Michael Scherer	Missouri	4.50	Jr.
36. Jovan Santos-Knox	Massachusetts	4.50	
37. Don Cherry	Villanova	4.50	
38. Nicholas Dance	Tennessee-Martin	4.50	

RK. NAME	SCHOOL	GRADE	NOTES
39. Jeffrey Schoettmer	North Carolina	4.50	
40. Franklin Shannon	Oklahoma	4.50	
41. Rodney Hardrick	Oregon	4.50	
42. Jared Barber	West Virginia	4.50	
43. Jeremiah Allison	Washington State	4.50	
44. Manoa Pikula	Brigham Young	4.50	
45. Tyler Gray	Boise State	4.50	
45. Ryan Flannigan	Kentucky	4.50	

OUTSIDE LINEBACKERS

RK. NAME	SCHOOL	GRADE	NOTES
1. Myles Jack	UCLA	6.67	Jr., X
2. Jaylon Smith	Notre Dame	6.20	Jr., X
3. Leonard Floyd	Georgia	6.23	Jr., X
4. Noah Spence	Eastern Kentucky	5.72	Jr., DE
5. Darron Lee	Ohio State	5.72	Soph-3
6. Kamalei Correa	Boise State	5.64	Jr., DE
7. Jordan Jenkins	Georgia	5.57	
8. Kyler Fackrell	Utah State	5.52	
9. Yannick Ngakoue	Maryland	5.52	Jr., DE
10. Ron Thompson	Syracuse	5.44	Jr., DE
11. Deion Jones	LSU	5.42	
12. Dadi Nicolas	Virginia Tech	5.38	DE
13. De'Vondre Campbell	Minnesota	5.34	
14. Tyler Matakevich	Temple	5.31	
15. Travis Feeney	Washington	5.26	
16. Scooby Wright	Arizona	5.25	Jr.
17. Kentrell Brothers	Missouri	5.23	
18. Victor Ochi	Stony Brook	5.21	DE
19. Curt Maggitt	Tennessee	5.18	
20. Stephen Weatherly	Vanderbilt	5.18	Jr.
21. Eric Striker	Oklahoma	5.17	
22. B.J. Goodson	Clemson	5.14	
23. Joe Schobert	Wisconsin	5.14	
24. Devante Bond	Oklahoma	5.12	
25. Cory Littleton	Washington	5.12	
26. Jatavis Brown	Akron	5.10	
27. Darrell Overton	East Carolina	5.08	
28. Steve Longa	Rutgers	5.08	Jr.
29. Dominique Alexander	Oklahoma	5.04	Jr.
30. Kristopher Frost	Auburn	5.03	
31. Dennis Pettway	Alabama	4.97	DE
32. Beniquez Brown	Mississippi State	4.80	Jr.
33. Travis Blanks	Clemson	4.75	Jr.
34. Lamar Louis	LSU	4.75	
35. Terrell Davis	British (Can.) Columbia	4.75	Jr.
36. William Parks	Arizona	4.50	
37. Gabriel Terry	Tennessee State	4.50	
38. Deontae Clarke	Virginia Tech	4.50	
39. James Ross	Michigan	4.50	
40. Ed Davis	Michigan State	4.50	
41. Darien Harris	Michigan State	4.50	
42. Derrick Moncrief	Auburn	4.50	
43. Nicholas Grigsby	Pittsburgh	4.50	
44. Benjamin Kline	Penn State	4.50	
45. Christian French	Oregon	4.50	
46. Leander Williams	Georgia Southern	4.50	
47. Kevin Anderson	Stanford	4.50	
48. Keyen Lage	South Dakota	4.50	
49. Akil Blount	Florida A&M	4.50	
50. Pete Robertson	Texas Tech	4.50	
51. Dominique Tovell	Louisiana-Lafayette	4.50	
52. Desmond Morgan	Michigan	4.50	
53. Quentin Gause	Rutgers	4.50	
54. Tyriq McCord	Miami (Fla.)	4.50	
55. Kache Palacio	Washington State	4.50	
56. Tyson Coleman	Oregon	4.50	
57. Edward Ederaine	Fresno State	4.50	
58. Denzel Devall	Alabama	4.50	
59. Cory James	Colorado State	4.50	
60. Denzel Nkemdiche	Mississippi	4.50	
61. Chukwuemeka Azubike	Vanderbilt	4.50	
62. Deon King	Norfolk State	4.50	
63. Brett McMakin	Northern Iowa	4.50	Jr.

CORNERBACKS

RK. NAME	SCHOOL	GRADE	NOTES
1. Jalen Ramsey	Florida State	6.97	Jr., FS
2. Vernon Hargreaves	Florida	6.75	Jr.
3. Mackensie Alexander	Clemson	5.92	Jr.
4. Kendall Fuller	Virginia Tech	5.77	Jr., X
5. Zack Sanchez	Oklahoma	5.74	Jr.
6. Eli Apple	Ohio State	5.72	Jr.
7. William Jackson	Houston	5.63	
8. Sean Davis	Maryland	5.56	FS
9. Deandre Houston-Carson	William & Mary	5.45	
10. Will Redmond	Mississippi State	5.39	X
11. Artie Burns	Miami (Fla.)	5.37	Jr.
12. Cyrus Jones	Alabama	5.36	RS
13. Deiondre Hall	Northern Iowa	5.34	FS
14. Xavien Howard	Baylor	5.33	Jr., FS
15. Deandre Elliott	Colorado State	5.31	
16. Juston Burris	North Carolina State	5.27	FS
17. James Bradberry	Samford	5.26	
18. Brandon Williams	Texas A&M	5.25	RB
19. Keivarae Russell	Notre Dame	5.24	
20. Kevin Peterson	Oklahoma State	5.21	X
21. Daryl Worley	West Virginia	5.21	Jr., Ch.
22. Briean Boddy-Calhoun	Minnesota	5.18	
23. Rashard Robinson	ex-LSU	5.17	Jr., Ch.
24. Harlan Miller	Southeastern Louisiana	5.15	
25. Leshaun Sims	Southern Utah	5.14	
26. David White	Georgia Tech	5.14	
27. Maurice Canady	Virginia	5.14	
28. Kevon Seymour	USC	5.12	
29. Cleveland Wallace	San Jose State	5.12	Jr.
30. Taveze Calhoun	Mississippi State	5.12	
31. Anthony Brown	Purdue	5.10	
32. Jonathan Jones	Auburn	5.10	
33. Ryan Smith	North Carolina Central	5.05	
34. Tavon Young	Temple	5.03	
35. Jimmy Pruitt	San Jose State	5.03	
36. Kenneth Crawley	Colorado	5.02	
37. De'Vante Harris	Texas A&M	4.87	
38. Richard Leonard	Florida International	4.50	RS
39. Frankie Williams	Purdue	4.80	
40. Brian Poole	Florida	4.80	
41. C.J. Smith	North Dakota State	4.80	
42. Arjen Colquhoun	Michigan State	4.80	
43. Morgan Burns	Kansas State	4.75	
44. Eric Murray	Minnesota	4.75	
45. Clarence Caldwell	Louisiana-Monroe	4.75	
46. Matthew Smalley	Lafayette	4.75	
47. Lafayette Pitts	Pittsburgh	4.75	
48. Jamal Marshall	North Texas	4.75	
49. Cre'Von Leblanc	Florida Atlantic	4.75	
50. Larry Scott	Oregon State	4.75	
51. Blake Countess	Michigan	4.75	
52. Fabian Moreau	UCLA	4.50	
53. Leviticus Payne	Cincinnati	4.50	
54. Adairius Barnes	Louisiana Tech	4.50	
55. Joshua Hawkins	East Carolina	4.50	
55. Demetrious Nicholson	Virginia	4.50	
56. Kenneth Durden	Youngstown	4.50	
57. Ronald Zamort	Western Michigan	4.50	
58. Tyren Quinn	Kentucky	4.50	
59. Tony McRae	North Carolina A&T St.	4.50	
60. Trevor Williams	Penn State	4.50	
61. Kenya Dennis	Missouri	4.50	
62. Ian Wells	Ohio	4.50	
63. Paris Logan	Northern Illinois	4.50	
64. Chris Milton	Georgia Tech	4.50	
65. Robert Porter	Jackson State	4.50	
66. Lloyd Carrington	Arizona State	4.50	
67. Daniel Davie	Nebraska	4.50	
68. Nicholas Vanhoose	Northwestern	4.50	
69. Jeremiah McKinnon	Florida International	4.50	
70. Ahmad Christian	Utah	4.50	
71. Charles Washington	Fresno State	4.50	

RK. NAME	SCHOOL	GRADE	NOTES
72. Darius Hillary	Wisconsin	4.50	
73. Randall Jette	Massachusetts	4.50	
74. Orlando Thomas	Texas	4.50	
75. Adrian Witty	Cincinnati	4.50	
76. Aaron Sibley	Portland State	4.50	
77. Brandon Mobley	Campbell	4.50	
78. Marcus Alford	Northern Arizona	4.50	
79. Antonio Hamilton	South Carolina State	4.50	
80. Anthony Gaffney	Princeton	4.50	
81. Kweishi Brown	Arizona State	4.50	
82. Shakiel Randolph	SMU	4.50	
83. Ayotunde Ogunniyi	Richmond	4.50	
84. Vernon Harris	Dartmouth	4.50	
85. Bernell Brooks	Tennessee State	4.50	
86. Tracy Howard	Miami-Fla.	4.50	
87. Michael Hilton	Mississippi	4.50	
88. Trenier Orr	Sam Houston State	4.50	
89. Winston Rose	New Mexico State	4.50	
90. Samuel Brown	Missouri Western State	4.50	
91. Denzel Thompson	Southeastern Louisiana	4.50	
92. Michael Jordan	Missouri Western State	4.50	
93. Danzel McDaniel	Kansas State	4.50	X
94. Corey Tindal	Marshall	4.50	Jr.
95. Trenton Coles	Duquesne	4.50	Jr.

STRONG SAFETIES

RK. NAME	SCHOOL	GRADE	NOTES
1. Vonn Bell	Ohio State	5.82	Jr.
2. Su'a Cravens	USC	5.70	Jr., OLB
3. Keanu Neal	Florida	5.68	Jr.
4. Karl Joseph	West Virginia	5.66	
5. Miles Killebrew	Southern Utah	5.42	
6. T.J. Green	Clemson	5.42	Jr.
7. Kimlon Dillon	West Virginia	5.24	
8. Jeremy Cash	Duke	5.17	
9. Clayton Fejedelm	Illinois	5.14	
10. Jordan Lucas	Penn State	5.10	
11. Kavon Frazier	Central Michigan	5.09	
12. Elijah Shumate	Notre Dame	5.07	
13. LaMarcus Brutus	Florida State	4.97	
14. Tevin Carter	Utah	4.89	
15. Tony Conner	Mississippi	4.80	Jr.
16. Michael Caputo	Wisconsin	4.80	
17. Marqui Christian	Midwestern State	4.80	
18. Brice Hunter	Florida State	4.50	
19. Demontevious Smith	Georgia Tech	4.50	
20. Stefan McClure	California	4.50	
21. Eric Williams	Indiana (Penn.)	4.50	
22. Jared Roberts	Lafayette	4.50	
23. Andrew Williamson	Vanderbilt	4.50	
24. Jeremiah Hendy	Maryland	4.50	
25. Penisimani Vea	UNLV	4.50	
26. Roger Williamson	Michigan State	4.50	
27. Dwayne Hunter	Marshall	4.50	
28. Matthias Farley	Notre Dame	4.50	
29. Jordan Simone	Arizona State	4.50	
30. Rolan Milligan	Toledo	4.50	
31. Timothy Gurley	South Carolina	4.50	
32. Michael Mudoh	Tulsa	4.50	
33. Joe Powell	Globe	4.50	Jr.
34. Andrew Donahue	Dartmouth	4.50	
35. Hakim Jones	North Carolina State	4.50	
36. Mitchell Lane	Louisiana-Monroe	4.50	
37. Rohan Gaines	Arkansas	4.50	
38. Micah Eugene	Southeastern Louisiana	4.50	
39. Geno Smith	Alabama	4.50	
40. Darion Monroe	Tulane	4.50	

FREE SAFETIES

RK. NAME	SCHOOL	GRADE	NOTES
1. Darian Thompson	Boise State	5.87	
2. Deon Bush	Miami (Fla.)	5.40	
3. Jayron Kearse	Clemson	5.39	Jr.
4. Tyvis Powell	Ohio State	5.36	Jr.

RK. NAME	SCHOOL	GRADE	NOTES
5. Jalen Mills	LSU	5.24	
6. Trenton Matthews	Colorado State	5.24	
7. Justin Simmons	Boston College	5.20	
8. Kevin Byard	Middle Tennessee State	5.16	
9. Derrick Kindred	Texas Christian	5.12	
10. Jordan Lomax	Iowa	5.03	
11. Alvin Stamps	Kentucky	5.03	
12. Jamie Byrd	South Florida	4.80	
13. Demontrae Elston	Mississippi	4.80	
14. Douglas Middleton	Appalachian State	4.75	
15. Quincy Mauger	Georgia	4.75	Jr.
16. Nate Andrews	Florida State	4.75	Jr.
17. Christian Carpenter	Towson	4.50	
18. Damarius Travis	Minnesota	4.50	
19. Devonta Burns	Texas A&M	4.50	
20. Ian Simon	Missouri	4.50	
21. Ekene Iloka	Texas Christian	4.50	
22. Taj Letman	Marshall	4.50	
23. Anthony Nixon	Maryland	4.50	
24. Jamar Allah	Arizona	4.50	
25. Anthony Lennon	East Carolina	4.50	
26. Brian Randolph	Tennessee	4.50	
27. Andrew Adams	Connecticut	4.50	
28. Javonta Golden	Georgia Tech	4.50	
29. Dante Barnett	Kansas State	4.50	
30. Orion Stewart	Baylor	4.50	Jr.

PLACEKICKERS

RK. NAME	SCHOOL	GRADE	NOTES
1. Roberto Aguayo	Florida State	5.37	Jr.
2. Ka'imi Fairbairn	UCLA	5.11	
3. Jaden Oberkrom	Texas Christian	5.09	
4. Bradley Craddock	Maryland	5.06	
5. John Lunsford	Liberty	5.03	
6. Marshall Koehn	Iowa	4.89	
7. John Wallace	Louisville	4.75	
8. Marshall Morgan	Georgia	4.50	
9. Brent Wahle	Ohio Dominican	4.50	
10. Paul Griggs	Purdue	4.50	
11. Michael Schmadeke	Northern Iowa	4.50	
12. Nicholas Hodgson	Oklahoma	4.50	
13. Ross Martin	Duke	4.50	
14. Aldrick Rosas	Southern Oregon	4.50	Jr.
15. Quinn van Gylswyk	British (Can.) Columbia	4.50	Jr.

PUNTERS

RK. NAME	SCHOOL	GRADE	NOTES
1. Riley Dixon	Syracuse	5.16	
2. Thomas Hackett	Utah	5.14	
3. Andrew Kaser	Texas A&M	5.12	
4. William Monday	Duke	5.10	
5. Lachlan Edwards	Sam Houston State	5.08	
6. Nicholas O'Toole	West Virginia	4.97	
7. Eric Anderson	Delaware	4.70	Jr.
8. Timothy Willett	Louisiana College	4.50	
9. Jamie Keehn	LSU	4.50	
10. Peter Mortell	Minnesota	4.50	
11. Alexander Kinal	Wake Forest	4.50	
12. Benjamin Lecompte	North Dakota State	4.50	
13. Anthony Melchiori	Kent State	4.50	
14. A J Hughes	Virginia Tech	4.50	
15. Mattias Ciabatti	South Florida	4.50	
16. Zachary Paul	Akron	4.50	
17. Tyler Williams	Marshall	4.50	
18. Drew Riggleman	Arizona	4.50	
19. Landon Foster	Kentucky	4.50	

LONG SNAPPERS

RK. NAME	SCHOOL	GRADE	NOTES
1. Jimmy Landes	Baylor	5.08	
2. Reed Miller	Stanford	4.90	
3. Taybor Pepper	Michigan State	4.75	
4. Johnathan Depalma	West Virginia	4.75	
5. Chandler Ferguson	LSU	4.50	
6. Todd Phillips	Louisiana-Monroe	4.50	

BEST PLAYER AVAILABLE BY GRADE

RK. POS, NAME	SCHOOL	GRADE	NOTES
1. OT Laremy Tunsil	Mississippi	7.50	Jr., X
2. CB Jalen Ramsey	Florida State	6.97	Jr., FS
3. DE Joey Bosa	Ohio State	6.94	Jr.
4. CB Vernon Hargreaves	Florida	6.75	Jr.
5. OT Ronnie Stanley	Notre Dame	6.74	Jr.
6. DE DeForest Buckner	Oregon	6.70	DT
7. OLB Myles Jack	UCLA	6.67	Jr., X
8. RB Ezekial Elliott	Ohio State	6.54	Jr.
9. DT Sheldon Rankins	Louisville	6.42	
10. QB Carson Wentz	North Dakota State	6.35	
11. DT A'Shawn Robinson	Alabama	6.33	Jr.
12. OT Jack Conklin	Michigan State	6.32	Jr.
13. ILB Reggie Ragland	Alabama	6.30	OLB
14. DT Robert Nkemdiche	Mississippi	6.26	Jr., Ch.
15. OT Taylor Decker	Ohio State	6.25	OG
16. WR Laquon Treadwell	Mississippi	6.24	Jr.
17. QB Jared Goff	California	6.24	Jr.
18. OLB Leonard Floyd	Georgia	6.23	Jr., X
19. OLB Jaylon Smith	Notre Dame	6.20	Jr., X
20. DT Jarran Reed	Alabama	6.12	DE, Ch.
21. DE Kevin Dodd	Clemson	6.12	Jr.
22. OT Jason Spriggs	Indiana	6.06	
23. DT Austin Johnson	Penn State	6.04	Jr.
24. DE Shaq Lawson	Clemson	5.98	Jr.
25. WR Corey Coleman	Baylor	5.97	Jr., RS
26. QB Paxton Lynch	Memphis	5.92	Jr.
27. RB Derrick Henry	Alabama	5.92	Jr.
28. WR Will Fuller	Notre Dame	5.92	Jr.
29. TE Hunter Henry	Arkansas	5.92	Jr.
30. CB Mackensie Alexander	Clemson	5.92	Jr.
31. WR Josh Doctson	Texas Christian	5.89	
32. DT Vernon Butler	Louisiana Tech	5.88	
33. FS Darian Thompson	Boise State	5.87	
34. OG Cody Whitehair	Kansas State	5.86	OT
35. WR Sterling Shepard	Oklahoma	5.84	
36. DE Emmanuel Ogbah	Oklahoma State	5.82	Jr.
37. SS Vonn Bell	Ohio State	5.82	Jr.
38. CB Kendall Fuller	Virginia Tech	5.77	Jr., X
39. C Ryan Kelly	Alabama	5.74	OG, OT
40. CB Zack Sanchez	Oklahoma	5.74	Jr.
41. WR Tyler Boyd	Pittsburgh	5.72	Jr.
42. OT Germain Ifedi	Texas A&M	5.72	Jr., OG
43. OLB Noah Spence	Eastern Kentucky	5.72	Jr., DE
44. OLB Darron Lee	Ohio State	5.72	Soph-3
45. CB Eli Apple	Ohio State	5.72	Jr.
46. SS Su'a Cravens	USC	5.70	Jr., OLB
47. DT Maliek Collins	Nebraska	5.68	Jr.
48. SS Keanu Neal	Florida	5.68	Jr.
49. WR Michael Thomas	Ohio State	5.66	
50. SS Karl Joseph	West Virginia	5.66	
51. OLB Kamalei Correa	Boise State	5.64	Jr., DE
52. TE Austin Hooper	Stanford	5.64	Soph-3
53. CB William Jackson	Houston	5.63	
54. DE Jihad Ward	Illinois	5.62	DT
55. NT Kenny Clark	UCLA	5.62	Jr.
56. DE Jonathan Bullard	Florida	5.58	DT
57. RB C.J. Prosise	Notre Dame	5.58	Jr., WR
58. OLB Jordan Jenkins	Georgia	5.57	
59. QB Connor Cook	Michigan State	5.57	
60. CB Sean Davis	Maryland	5.56	FS
61. TE Nick Vannett	Ohio State	5.56	
62. DT Chris Jones	Mississippi Stateate	5.56	Jr.
63. NT Andrew Billings	Baylor	5.56	Jr.
64. C Evan Boehm	Missouri	5.54	OG
65. OG Christian Westerman	Arizona State	5.53	C
66. RB Kenneth Dixon	Louisiana Tech	5.52	
67. OLB Kyler Fackrell	Utah State	5.52	
68. OT Le'Raven Clark	Texas Tech	5.52	OG
69. OLB Yannick Ngakoue	Maryland	5.52	Jr., DE
70. OT Shon Coleman	Auburn	5.48	Jr., X
71. RB Devontae Booker	Utah	5.47	X
72. ILB Joshua Perry	Ohio State	5.47	
73. C Max Tuerk	USC	5.46	X, OT
74. CB Deandre Houston-Carson	William & Mary	5.45	
75. RB Jordan Howard	Indiana	5.45	Jr.
76. DE Shilique Calhoun	Michigan State	5.45	OLB
77. OLB Ron Thompson	Syracuse	5.44	Jr., DE
78. SS Miles Killebrew	Southern Utah	5.42	
79. OLB Deion Jones	LSU	5.42	
80. WR Paul McRoberts	SE Missouri State	5.42	
81. OG Joshua Garnett	Stanford	5.42	
82. RB Paul Perkins	UCLA	5.42	Jr., X
83. DT Quinton Jefferson	Maryland	5.42	Jr.
84. SS T.J. Green	Clemson	5.42	Jr.
85. FS Deon Bush	Miami (Fla.)	5.40	
86. ILB Nicholas Kwiatkoski	West Virginia	5.40	
87. FS Jayron Kearse	Clemson	5.39	Jr.
88. CB Will Redmond	Mississippi State	5.39	X
89. QB Dak Prescott	Mississippi State	5.39	
90. WR Braxton Miller	Ohio State	5.38	X, QB
91. RB Kenyan Drake	Alabama	5.38	X, WR, KR
92. OLB Dadi Nicolas	Virginia Tech	5.38	DE
93. TE Tyler Higbee	Western Kentucky	5.38	X
94. OG Avery Young	Auburn	5.38	Jr., X, OT
95. DT Adam Gotsis	Georgia Tech	5.37	X
96. DE Shawn Oakman	Baylor	5.37	DT
97. QB Christian Hackenberg	Penn State	5.37	Jr.
98. C Nick Martin	Notre Dame	5.37	OG
99. CB Artie Burns	Miami (Fla.)	5.37	Jr.
100. PK Roberto Aguayo	Florida State	5.37	Jr.
101. CB Cyrus Jones	Alabama	5.36	RS
102. TE Jerell Adams	South Carolina	5.36	
103. DT Adolphus Washington	Ohio State	5.36	
104. FS Tyvis Powell	Ohio State	5.36	Jr.
105. WR Aaron Burbridge	Michigan State	5.36	
106. CB Deiondre Hall	Northern Iowa	5.34	FS
107. OLB De'Vondre Campbell	Minnesota	5.34	
108. WR Jalin Marshall	Ohio State	5.34	Soph-3, PR
109. OG Denver Kirkland	Arkansas	5.34	Jr., OT
110. DT Hassan Ridgeway	Texas	5.33	Jr., X
111. CB Xavien Howard	Baylor	5.33	Jr., FS
112. WR Tajae Sharpe	Massachusetts	5.32	
113. OT Brandon Shell	South Carolina	5.32	X
114. WR Malcolm Mitchell	Georgia	5.32	CB
115. QB Jacoby Brissett	North Carolina State	5.32	
116. OT Jerald Hawkins	LSU	5.32	Jr.
117. RB Alex Collins	Arkansas	5.31	Jr.
118. CB Deandre Elliott	Colorado State	5.31	
119. ILB Blake Martinez	Stanford	5.31	
120. OLB Tyler Matakevich	Temple	5.31	
121. DT Javon Hargrave	South Carolina State	5.31	
122. OG Rees Odhiambo	Boise State	5.31	X, OT
123. C Jack Allen	Michigan State	5.31	
124. QB Nate Sudfeld	Indiana	5.30	
125. OG Vadal Alexander	LSU	5.30	X, OT
126. ILB Nick Vigil	Utah State	5.29	Jr.
127. DE Carl Nassib	Penn State	5.28	
128. ILB Antonio Morrison	Florida	5.29	X
129. OG Connor McGovern	Missouri	5.29	OT
130. QB Cardale Jones	Ohio State	5.29	Jr.
131. TE Thomas Duarte	UCLA	5.28	Jr., WR
132. WR Kolby Listenbee	Texas Christian	5.27	
133. RB Josh Ferguson	Illinois	5.27	KR, X
134. WR Bralon Addison	Oregon	5.27	Jr., PR
135. CB Juston Burris	North Carolina State	5.27	FS
136. TE Temarrick Hemingway	South Carolina State	5.27	
137. QB Kevin Hogan	Stanford	5.27	
138. DE Bronson Kaufusi	Brigham Young	5.27	OLB
139. OT Alexander Lewis	Nebraska	5.27	OG, Ch.
140. OG Isaac Seumalo	Oregon State	5.27	Jr.
141. RB Kelvin Taylor	Florida	5.26	Jr.
142. CB James Bradberry	Samford	5.26	
143. OLB Travis Feeney	Washington	5.26	
144. DE Charles Tapper	Oklahoma	5.26	
145. OG Graham Glasgow	Michigan	5.26	C
146. OT Dominique Robertson	West Georgia	5.26	OG, Ch.
147. CB Brandon Williams	Texas A&M	5.25	RB
148. RB Jonathan Williams	Arkansas	5.25	X
149. OLB Scooby Wright	Arizona	5.25	Jr.
150. DT Sheldon Day	Notre Dame	5.25	

PLAYER INDEX